Real-World Android by Tutorials

By Ricardo Costeira, Subhrajyoti Sen, Kolin Stürt & Antonio Roa-Valverde

Real-World Android by Tutorials

Ricardo Costeira, Subhrajyoti Sen, Kolin Stürt & Antonio Roa-Valverde

Notice of Rights

Notice of Liability

Trademarks

ISBN: 978-1-950325-73-3

Table of Contents

Book License

By purchasing *Real-World Android by Tutorials*, you have the following license:

- You are allowed to use and/or modify the source code in *Real-World Android by Tutorials* in as many apps as you want, with no attribution required.
- You are allowed to use and/or modify all art, images and designs that are included in *Real-World Android by Tutorials* in as many apps as you want, but must include this attribution line somewhere inside your app: "Artwork/images/designs: from *Real-World Android by Tutorials*, available at www.raywenderlich.com".
- The source code included in *Real-World Android by Tutorials* is for your personal use only. You are NOT allowed to distribute or sell the source code in *Real-World Android by Tutorials* without prior authorization.
- This book is for your personal use only. You are NOT allowed to reproduce or transmit any part of this book by any means, electronic or mechanical, including photocopying, recording, etc. without previous authorization. You may not sell digital versions of this book or distribute them to friends, coworkers or students without prior authorization. They need to purchase their own copies.

All materials provided with this book are provided on an "as is" basis, without warranty of any kind, express or implied, including but not limited to the warranties of merchantability, fitness for a particular purpose and noninfringement. In no event shall the authors or copyright holders be liable for any claim, damages or other liability, whether in an action of contract, tort or otherwise, arising from, out of or in connection with the software or the use or other dealings in the software.

All trademarks and registered trademarks appearing in this guide are the properties of their respective owners.

Before You Begin

This section tells you a few things you need to know before you get started, such as what hardware and software you'll need, where to find the project files for this book and more.

What You Need

To follow along with this book, you'll need the following:

- **Android Studio 4.1.x**: Available at https://developer.android.com/studio/. This is the environment in which you'll develop most of the sample code in this book.

Book Source Code & Forums

Where to Download the Materials for This Book

The materials for this book can be cloned or downloaded from the GitHub book materials repository:

- https://github.com/raywenderlich/adva-materials/tree/editions/2.0

Forums

We've also set up an official forum for the book at https://forums.raywenderlich.com/c/books/real-world-android-by-tutorials. This is a great place to ask questions about the book or to submit any errors you may find.

Dedications

To my parents, Céu and Manuel, and sister, Joana, who always gave everything they could and more to ensure my education, happiness and well-being. To my partner, Joana, for all the love, support and unbelievable patience while I was writing the book. To my friend, Carlos, for all the support and understanding every time I told him I didn't have the time to help him with GDG and Kotlin Knights events. And finally, to the amazing Android devs from my team at Mindera - Maja, Rita, Garcês, Belchi and Gui - for all the incredible discussions, for teaching me so much and for making me love what I do even more.

— Ricardo Costeira

I'd like to thank my parents, @StephanieBraganza, Pom-Pom the Pomeranian (IG @PomThePomeranian) and 0xAKBArt, as well as The Wildlife Trade Monitoring Network and The Save Movement for inspiration of the app concepts.

— Kolin Stürt

I'd like to thank my parents, friends, and colleagues, who have always been very supportive and pushed me to achieve more. This book would not have been possible without them.

— Subhrajyoti Sen

To Elisabeth, for your patience and support while the laptop stole part of our time.

—Antonio Roa-Valverde

About the Authors

Ricardo Costeira is an author of this book. He is an Android dev with a crush on clean code and software architecture. Based in Portugal, Ricardo works as a senior Android engineer at Mindera, where he builds and maintains a retailer app with tens of thousands of daily active users. Ricardo loves Android and the community, so it's only natural that he tries to have an active part in it! He's a co-organizer of GDG Coimbra and a co-founder of Kotlin Knights. He occasionally writes (mostly about Android) at his site, ricardocosteira.com, or for raywenderlich.com. He loves cats, food and the gym and he's a specialty coffee hobbyist. You can find him on Twitter at @rcosteira79.

Subhrajyoti Sen is an author of this book. He is an Android Engineer at KeepTruckin, where he develops apps to improve the trucking industry. Before that, he also worked on apps to improve the experience of Indian investors. He believes in the power of open source and communities, and actively tries to give back. When not writing code, you can find him binge-watching anime, reading up on public policy or playing Rocket League.

Antonio Roa-Valverde is an author of this book. Antonio is a software engineer specialized in Android development. He's interested in innovation and shaping new products with potential impact on people. Google Developer Group co-organizer in Innsbruck and Munich. You can find him close to the mountains, either hiking, riding the mountain-bike or catching some curvy roads by motorcycle.

About the Editors

Sandra Grauschopf is the editor of this book. She is a freelance writer, editor and content strategist as well as the Editing Team Lead at raywenderlich.com. She loves to untangle tortured sentences and to travel the world with a trusty book in her hand.

Massimo Carli is the final pass editor of this book. Massimo has been working with Java since 1995, when he co-founded the first Italian magazine about this technology http://www.mokabyte.it. After many years creating Java desktop and enterprise applications, Massimo started to work in the mobile world. In 2001, he wrote his first book about J2ME. After many J2ME and Blackberry apps, he then started to work with Android in 2008. The same year, Massimo wrote the first Italian book about Android, and it became a best seller on Amazon.it; that was the first of a series of 12 books. Massimo is a musical theater lover and a supporter of the soccer team, S.P.A.L.

Acknowledgments

Content Development

We would like to thank **Kolin Stürt** for his work as an author on the previous edition of this book.

Kolin Stürt is a software team lead with a focus on encryption, reverse-engineering, forensics and application hardening. He's worked on many platforms, most notably Android, iOS and Linux. He has an interest in networking and has been hacking and developing apps since 2009. Outside of cybersecurity, he composes and performs music, as well as practicing and holding a black belt in Aikido. You can find him at https://kolinsturt.github.io.

Section I: Developing Real World Apps

In this section, you'll learn how to design and implement PetSave as an example of a professional, real world app. You'll learn how to choose the right architectural pattern and how to structure the code to make the app testable and maintainable.

To make your app easier to change, it's a good practice to define different layers with specific responsibilities. In particular, you'll learn how to design and implement the domain layer for the PerSave app. You'll also see how to access the network efficiently, by implementing the repository pattern in the data layer.

At the end of this section, you'll have a clear idea about how to structure the code of your app.

Chapter 1: Introduction

By Ricardo Costeira

Ever since its inception, Android development has been known for being as frustrating as it is fun. Ironically, both the frustration and the fun come from the same place. Developing an Android app involves not only juggling an ever-changing framework, but also handling interesting and challenging design decisions.

The Android framework keeps growing, and it's not likely to stop anytime soon. Think of the sheer amount of documentation online at the Android Developers site, or even on Kotlin's own documentation pages. On top of this, time and experience have taught us that new architectures and best practices will keep appearing, giving us new and better ways to do the same things.

This isn't necessarily bad, though. Android developers have come a long way since the times when having a god `Activity` was the standard. Over the years, through the effort of an amazing and supporting community, multiple architectures and techniques have surfaced, aiming to improve both app stability and developer quality of life. Even Google has pitched in on this project with their own recommended app architecture.

With such a large, continuously mutating ecosystem, developing even the simplest of features can feel overwhelming for beginners — and, sometimes, even for advanced developers.

For instance, say that you want to get data from a data source and display it. Even if you've implemented this in the past, you know Android. Can you be 100% sure that the way you did it back then is still the *best* way to do it now?

You can't. And that's OK! With an ecosystem that changes so frequently, it's impossible for even the most experienced engineer to be aware of all its quirks and nuances.

Android developers need to know about a wide array of subjects to build apps effectively. That's where this book comes in.

What Is This Book About?

This book covers *a lot* of topics. It shows you how to:

- Build features in a scalable way, covering each architectural layer.
- Modularize your app, if you ever need to, while touching on dynamic features.
- Handle animations, styles, themes and other elements of the UI.
- Make your app more secure.
- Maintain and care for your app.

It does all of this by showing you practical solutions that lead to the desired results. Yet, the idea here is much more than that. Of course, you can study the implementation details if you want, but that's not the main point. Instead of reasoning about *how* to write code, you should instead focus on *why* you write it that way.

The goal is for you to **go beyond the code** and understand *why* you're writing it in the first place. This book doesn't simply cover the basics at the problem's surface or give high-level descriptions of the simplest use cases. Rather, it aims to share with you some of the knowledge that developers acquire over time, while developing real-world apps.

You'll see how to solve real-world problems following real-world best practices and techniques. Sometimes, these best practices and techniques are general rules of thumb regarding software development and design principles. In other cases, they're tightly coupled to the tools used to fix the problem. You can only acquire them by either getting your hands dirty with those tools or by having someone point them out for you.

The book focuses not only on why should you do things a specific way, but also on the corresponding advantages, trade-offs and drawbacks of that solution. It makes it clear when a certain decision is not ideal, explaining the reasoning behind discarding a choice or going through with it anyway.

As you go through the content, you might notice that some of it is opinionated; you might even disagree with some of the statements. That's good! As a developer, it's only natural for you to question other developers' decisions. You might even see some problems that others completely missed.

On the other hand, if you agree with everything and don't see any problems, that's fine too! What's important here is for you to go through the roller coaster ride that is Android, with all its ups and downs, just like developers do in the real world.

Who Is This Book for?

This book is useful for developers of all levels. Some of the content assumes prior knowledge of complex topics, like RxJava and Dagger/Hilt, and is more tailored to intermediate or advanced developers. But there's plenty of content suitable for less-experienced developers as well.

> **Note**: If you need to fill some gaps in your knowledge, www.raywenderlich.com, provides a variety of books to help. If you need to learn Kotlin, Kotlin Apprentice (https://www.raywenderlich.com/books/kotlin-apprentice), is the right book for you. With Reactive Programming with Kotlin (https://www.raywenderlich.com/books/reactive-programming-with-kotlin), you can learn all about RxJava and RxKotlin.

> Dependency injection is a fundamental tool for simplifying the architecture of your app and making it more testable and maintainable. If you need to learn more, Dagger by Tutorials (https://www.raywenderlich.com/books/dagger-by-tutorials), is a must. Finally, good, professional apps must implement different types of tests, from unit tests to end-to-end tests. To learn more about how to do this, Android Test-Driven Development by Tutorials (https://www.raywenderlich.com/books/android-test-driven-development-by-tutorials), is the book for you.

As mentioned already, a large part of the book's focus is around the reasons *why* developers prefer specific solutions. This usually boils down to software design principles, architectural considerations or tidbits of wisdom acquired through experience. In these cases, everyone can benefit from sharing information.

The Sample Project

Throughout this book, you'll work on building and improving a sample project called **PetSave**. PetSave is a pet adoption and fostering app that aggregates and matches animals available to you. It uses the medical history of the pet along with some of your personal information for matching and searching.

Figure 1.1 — PetSave Screen With a List of Animals

When you start, the app will only show a blank screen. Even the screen in the image above doesn't exist yet. It'll be up to you to develop the app from the ground up.

The app connects to an external service, which it uses to fetch the animals. This service, **Petfinder**, is an online, searchable database of animals who need homes. They also have information on shelters and adoption organizations across the United States. Check out their site at https://www.petfinder.com/. Who knows, you might find your new pet. :]

Signing Up for an API Key

Petfinder allows you to access their database, provided that you sign up for one of their API keys. To do so, you first need to go to their site and sign up for an account. After that, head to https://www.petfinder.com/developers/, click the **GET AN API KEY** button and follow the process from there.

After acquiring an API key and its corresponding secret, you'll need to set them for each chapter's starter project. You'll set them in **ApiConstants.kt**, which is in the **common.data.api** package.

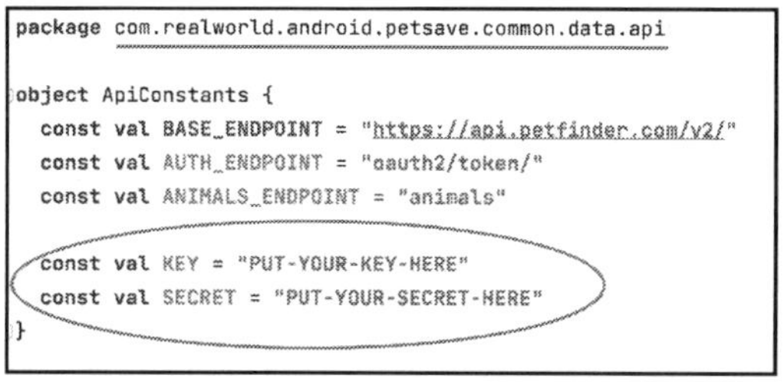

Figure 1.2 — Replace Those Two Strings With Your API Key and Secret

If you're curious about Petfinder's API, check out its documentation at https://www.petfinder.com/developers/v2/docs/.

Where to Go From Here?

Now that you have an idea of what this book is about and how it'll unfold, you're ready to start building PetSave. As you already know, the app is at a very early stage, with very little code written. However, you won't write any code in the next chapter.

Thinking about a problem, getting familiar with it and planning ahead *just enough* that you have a solid starting point is always a better option than starting to write code right away and hoping for the best. So in the next chapter, you'll lay the groundwork to develop a robust and scalable app.

Chapter 2: Starting From the Beginning

By Ricardo Costeira

Android development can be both straightforward and extremely complex. Not only does the framework keep growing at a ridiculously fast pace, but it also repeatedly reinvents itself — think asynchronous programming, lifecycle and state management and even animations. It's common to feel overwhelmed by or even lost amidst all the continuous library releases, shiny new features and multiple ways of achieving the same goals.

One section of this book (or, truth be told, the whole book!) wouldn't be enough to cover everything the Android framework has to offer. However, as you develop real-world apps, you start to notice that apps gravitate around a few common ways to use the framework. Additionally, many design decisions and best practices can be universally applied to produce better software.

In this chapter, you'll read about some of these design decisions and practices that you can follow in the early development stages. They'll allow you to build a solid foundation for your app while avoiding over-engineering.

More specifically, you'll learn:

- How to structure and organize your app so you can tell what it does just by looking at the package names.
- Why it's essential to keep high cohesion and low coupling.
- How to produce better apps by investing in upfront planning.
- Why you should use a layered architecture.

Buckle up!

Package by Feature Approach

First, check out the code you'll work with by opening the **starter project** in the material for this chapter, and examining its contents. Expand the **com.realworld.android.petsave** package. Did you hear that? That was the project **screaming** its purpose at you!

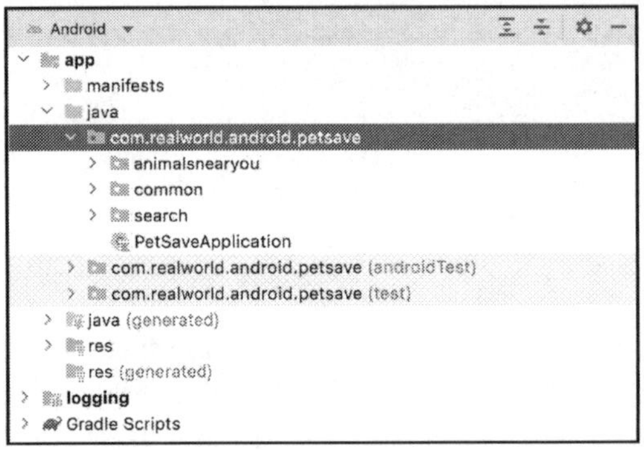

Figure 2.1 — Screaming Architecture

This project is organized in a **package by feature** structure. Everything that's related to a feature, and *only* to that feature, is stored inside the same package. Code shared by two or more features is stored in separate **common** packages. This type of package organization has a few advantages:

1. Just by looking at the package structure, you easily get a feeling for what the app does. Some people also like to call this a **screaming architecture** — hence the awful "screaming" joke attempt earlier.

2. You end up with packages that not only have **high cohesion**, they're also either **loosely coupled** or completely **decoupled** from one another. Cohesion and coupling are two very important metrics in software development that you should always consider.

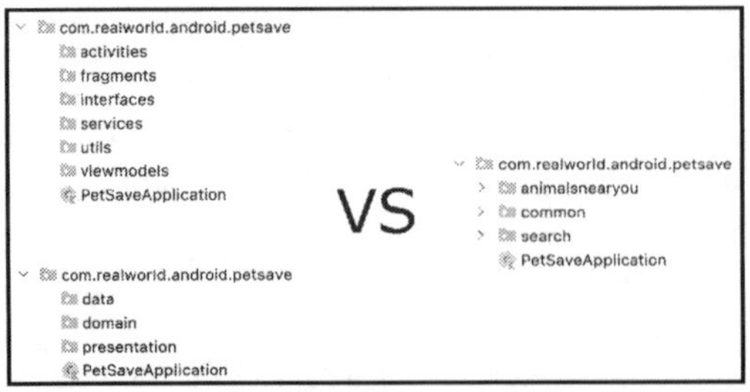

Figure 2.2 — Not Screaming vs. Screaming Architecture

High Cohesion

Cohesion refers to the relationship between different programming elements. The stronger the connection between code inside a component, the more cohesive that component is.

For instance, imagine you have a class that's responsible for applying a cute filter to a cat's picture, called `CatFilter`.

```
class CatFilter(private val picture: Picture) {

  // Properties related to filter and picture state.
  // ...

  private fun parsePixels() {
    // Store individual pixels and the relationships between
them.
  }

  private fun filterPixels() {
    // Apply the filter to each pixel.
  }

  private fun smoothenResult() {
    // Apply picture smoothing techniques.
  }

  fun apply(): Picture {
    // Use methods above.
  }

  // Other methods.
}
```

The methods and properties of this class are all closely related to each other, which means that the class is highly cohesive.

Now, imagine the case where you start adding more responsibilities to the class. Not only does `CatFilter` apply a filter, but now it also saves and loads the result with the help of the file system. You'll start having elements in the class that have nothing to do with each other — `parsePixels()` and `save(picture: Picture)` have completely different purposes.

In other words, your class will now have a lower degree of cohesion.

Low Coupling

Coupling has to do with **dependencies** between programming elements. Continuing from the previous example, say you move the I/O logic to another class called `CatPictureFileSaver`.

```
class CatPictureFileSaver {

  fun save(picture: Picture) {
    // File writing code.
    // Calls compression and encoding methods.
  }

  fun load(picturePath: String): Picture {
    // File reading code.
    // Calls decompression and decoding methods.
  }

  private fun compress(picture: Picture): CompressedPicture {
    // Fancy compression algorithm.
  }

  private fun encode(
    compressedPicture: CompressedPicture
  ): ByteArray {
    // Byte encoding.
  }

  // Other methods.
}
```

This new class also has methods to compress/decompress and encode/decode the image, which are strongly related to its purpose. Nice, now `CatFilter` and `CatPictureFileSaver` are two highly cohesive classes!

After some time, requirements change. You now have to cache the intermediate results of the filtering. To implement this, you call the persistence methods of `CatPictureFileSaver` directly in a few different places in `CatFilter`.

This may seem like the logical way to accomplish your goals but, by doing so, you're forcing `CatFilter` to be **tightly coupled** with `CatPictureFileSaver`. Consider a scenario where a requirement change dictates that you drastically change or even remove `CatPictureFileSaver`. Due to the coupled nature of the classes, you'd have to make significant changes to `CatFilter` as well.

On the other hand, if you have something like a `CatPictureSaver` interface that `CatPictureFileSaver` extends, and have `CatFilter` depend on it, then the classes would be **loosely coupled**. Changes to `CatPictureFileSaver` that don't affect this interface would likely not affect `CatFilter` at all.

```
interface CatPictureSaver {
  fun save(picture: Picture)
  fun load(picturePath: String): Picture
}

class CatPictureFileSaver : CatPictureSaver {
  // Interface overrides and private methods/properties.
}

class CatFilter(
  private val picture: Picture,
  private val pictureSaver: CatPictureSaver
) {

  // Code...

  private fun filterPixels() {
    // ...
    // CatFilter knows nothing about save method's inner
    // workings!
    pictureSaver.save(filteredPicture)
    // ...
  }

  // More code...
}
```

The interface would ideally use generic naming to keep your implementation options open. For example, a `CatPictureSaver` interface with a method named `savePictureToFile()` would be a bad choice. You'd have to change the method name if you stop using the file system to save pictures!

Aiming for Orthogonality

Cohesion and coupling can be observed — and achieved — at different conceptual levels of a project. You just saw a few examples with classes, but the same principles apply to the project's package structure. Generally speaking, these patterns improve software by:

- Making it easier to maintain, less risky to change and more future proof.
- Allowing it to be **orthogonal**. When software is orthogonal, you can change its components freely without affecting the other components' behavior. This is possible because, inside each component, the code is closely related (cohesion) and doesn't depend directly on other components (coupling).

A good way to achieve cohesion is to ensure your code components each have a **single responsibility**. To keep components decoupled, you can use things like interfaces or polymorphism. In other words, by following the **SOLID principles**, you'll automatically follow these two principles as well.

> **Note**: **SOLID** stands for **S**ingle responsibility principle, **O**pen closed principle, **L**iskov substitution principle, **I**nterface segregation principle and **D**ependency inversion principle. These are the priciples that establish practices that lend to development software with consideration for maintainability and extensibility of a project.

You should definitely strive for high cohesion and low coupling, but be warned: Software principles are addictive. As with design patterns, you can easily get carried away and start applying the principles to every corner of your codebase.

If you go down this rabbit hole, you'll end up with an over-engineered app that lost track of its initial purpose. Remember: all things in moderation.

Full Stack Features Through Layers

Back to the project. Locate the **common** package and expand it.

Figure 2.3 — Package by Layer Architecture

You'll see a few other packages inside, but the three main ones are:

- **domain**: Home to all the **use cases**, **entities** and **value objects** that describe the domain of the app.
- **data**: Layer responsible for enabling all the interactions with data sources, both internal, like **shared preferences** or the **database**, and external, like a **remote API**.
- **presentation**: Where the Android framework does most of its heavy lifting, setting up the UI and reacting to user input.

You might have seen Android projects where the outer folder structure is divided into packages named like this. This kind of package organization is called **package by layer** since it separates the code by conceptual layer and responsibility. You'll read why this approach doesn't scale below.

Boundaries Between Layers

Typically, the conceptual layers of an app have well-defined **boundaries** between them so they stay **decoupled** from one another. You create these boundaries using **interfaces**.

It's especially common for projects that follow **clean architecture** to display such boundaries. Clean architecture goes the extra mile, **inverting** the dependencies to ensure that they only flow inwards toward the domain layer at the center. In other words, the domain layer never depends on other layers. This idea borrows from **hexagonal architecture**. As you'll see in the next chapters, **PetSave** borrows it as well.

Why Use Layered Features?

While organizing top-level packages by layer works for simple, small apps, it will become extremely difficult to deal with once the app gets more complicated. Imagine an app with dozens of different screens and features. The **cognitive load** required to be aware of which parts of the enormous presentation package called which specific part of the domain and data package would be astronomical.

This type of organization leads to many problems:

- Features become extremely difficult to implement since it's nearly impossible to understand the entire code structure at scale.
- Developers may duplicate behavior that already exists elsewhere in the codebase without realizing it.
- Routine maintenance turns into something out of a nightmare.

Now, it's not all bad news. If you use it right, packaging by layer can be beneficial. Packaging by feature on the **outside** and by layer on the **inside** enables you to:

- Have highly cohesive, loosely coupled code throughout your app.
- Reduce your cognitive load when dealing with each layer. For instance, you can change the domain layer of a feature while mostly ignoring the presentation and data layers, due to the interface boundaries.
- Test entire layers by replacing other layer dependencies with mocks or fakes.
- Easily refactor a layer's implementation without messing with the other ones. This is somewhat rare, but it *does* happen.

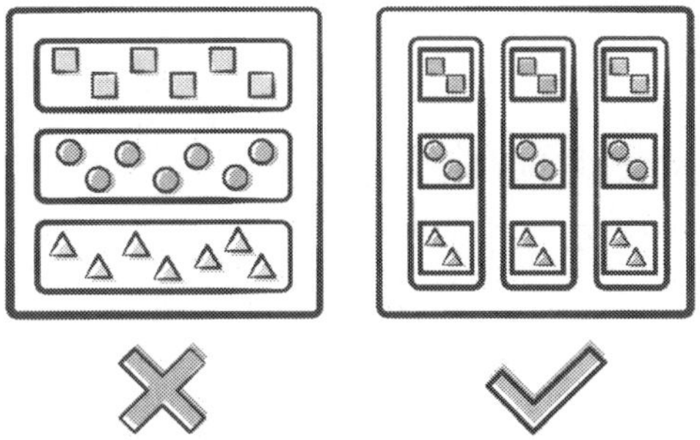

Figure 2.4 — Layer Versus Feature Packages

Each feature will have this structure. Anything that's shared between different features will live in the **common** package. You'll set up the layers in the upcoming chapters. There, you'll also see how defining such a package architecture enables the app to scale more easily.

Having learned how to structure an app in a maintainable and future-proof way, the next step is to go through the process of preparing yourself for the actual development.

Bridging Requirements and Implementation

Before starting any software project, Android or not, you need to understand *what* the system is supposed to do, and *how* it's supposed to do it. You do this by analyzing the requirements that you gathered in the initial stages of the system's development.

These requirements typically come from a joint effort that might involve project owners, senior engineers, architects and stakeholders. In order to achieve the requirements (the *what*), you build features (the *how*).

No, no, don't panic, you're not about to go through the whole software development cycle! The requirements analysis for PetSave is complete. Now, you'll dive directly into the software design and development phase.

Mastering Your Domain

There's no fixed way to start this phase. One reasonable approach is to get acquainted with the **domain** of the problem you're solving. This is valid for both new projects and when *you* are new to an existing project. The domain is the **subject area** the software applies to or provides a solution to. In other words, it's the environment you extract the requirements from, and it's where the app's features act.

Do you have any idea what the domain for PetSave might be? Looking at a few of the feature requirements should give you a hint:

PetSave's Features:

1. A user can see a list of animals near them, possibly from different organizations.
2. A user has the ability to search for animals and get matches according to several different types of filters.
3. A user can report a lost pet.
4. There should be an onboarding process to better match a user with a potential pet.

For this app, you'll work in the domain of pet adoption and fostering. You'll juggle concepts like animals, breeds, species, adoption organizations, animal health and training.

In the next chapter, you'll start reasoning about the domain to define its **entities**. Also, if you're wondering why the name of the app doesn't completely match the domain, it's just that "PetSave" sounds cooler than "PetAdopt" or "PetFoster". At least, that's what the app's stakeholders think, and you know that they're always right — even when they aren't!

Knowing the Problem Space

OK, so why should you know about the app's domain? Here are a few good reasons:

- To properly implement features that cover all the requirements, you need to understand the domain. If you don't establish a clear boundary around the requirements, how can you be sure you're covering all possible use cases? If you don't understand what you're working with and why, you're bound to make mistakes, which usually cost money!
- Your app's users usually have a deep understanding of the domain. This means that you can predict how people will use your app by being aware of the domain's caveats and intricacies. You can anticipate problems and even do a better job testing your app.
- It's an excellent way to communicate with non-technical people about technical stuff. The domain is a language everyone involved in the project shares.
- Requirements might be incomplete or not even make sense. When you understand the domain, you can look at the requirements objectively, contributing to their completeness and checking their sanity.

The list goes on, but you get the point. Domain knowledge is critical! However, it takes time to learn. Some domains are quite complex or can be extremely important to get right. For instance, it might be OK to miss out on some details of PetSave's domain, but the domain of a water treatment and supply station is different.

On an important note, don't expect to master every little detail instantly. Doing so can be challenging, especially before you get your hands dirty with the code. Until you see the app's rules and logic flow through the code, the domain is just a set of abstract ideas about a subject that you might have never even heard about before.

So *do* take some time to get familiar with the domain initially, but don't worry about going much deeper than that. You'll inevitably learn significantly more while you're implementing the code.

Software Is Liquid

Now that you're aware of the app's domain, you're probably eager to start the actual implementation. However, there are still a few things to consider before that. They'll be quick, promise!

One of the most important tenets to consider is that requirements change. Your stakeholders' needs are not set in stone, and your software shouldn't be, either.

You should build your app in a way that makes it relatively easy or, in some unfortunate cases, just possible, to both add and remove behavior. This need for extensibility is one of the reasons why you use development patterns and architectures.

Nevertheless, you do have to be careful to avoid over-engineering things: Consider the future possibilities, but always focus more on what's happening in the present.

Another important thing is to be aware of is that building software is an iterative process, sometimes due to changing requirements. You analyze what you need to implement, implement it and possibly return to the analysis stage in the future.

Don't be bummed if this happens. It's natural, and good! It usually means your software is gaining traction.

Devising a Plan of Attack

It's time for you to look at the features you'll develop in this section. You'll reason about what you need to do for each one and try and predict any difficulties that might arise. Here's a quick recap of the features:

- **Animals near you**: Displays a list of animals near you, according to your postal code and a specific distance threshold.
- **Search**: Searches for an animal by name, type and age.

Animals Near You

For simplicity, you'll use hard-coded postal code and distance values for now because you won't implement the mechanism to get the real values until later.

Designing the UI

The list part seems fairly easy: It screams `RecyclerView` all over the place. And where there's a `RecyclerView`, there's also an `Adapter`. Your requirement is to show a fairly simple item with the animal picture and name, so one `ViewHolder` should be sufficient. The UI code seems fairly straightforward.

Adding Data Sources

For the data source, you'll use a remote API called **Petfinder**. Petfinder matches almost all the data needs of the entire app, and everything you need for these specific features.

This one's also easy: **Retrofit** is the standard for Android networking nowadays. You might need to adjust the data so it matches the domain, and a few interceptors might also come in handy. The API returns chunks of paginated data, so you'll have to handle that pagination. Otherwise, it should be a fairly standard implementation.

The app needs to work offline, so you'll need to store the data in some format. This complicates things a little, as having both a **cache data source** and a **network data source** can become tricky to manage.

The safest approach is to follow a **single source of truth** implementation. Keep the cache in sync with the network, but ensure that the UI accesses only the cache. This way, the app displays the latest data both on and offline. Still, keeping everything in sync can be tricky, so you should expect some complexity.

Relational databases perform well for reading large amounts of data. You'll use **Room** to implement the cache.

Modeling the Domain

You'll define the **core domain entities** in the next chapter. However, you'll leave the use cases until you're ready to connect all the layers. Use cases are feature specific so by implementing them later, development will flow much more naturally. Implementing them now would require a lot of abstract thinking, which would just waste your time.

Making a Dry Run

Your goals for this feature are: Fetch data from the API, store it in the database, feed the UI with data from the database, display the data with the `RecyclerView` and handle possible errors. When considering what you'll implement ahead of time, it always helps to try and put yourself in the user's shoes… while also not forgetting that you're the developer. Try to understand how the user will feel while using your app. At the same time, keep an eye out for potential technical issues.

Picture for a moment that you're a user opening your app for the first time:

- You open the app and see a blank screen. This happens because the cache is still empty. Whoops! That's not good **UX** (user experience). You should at least show a **progress bar** while the adapter has no data.
- As soon as the data arrives, your app stores it. Since the UI feeds itself from the cache, the progress bar should disappear while the `RecyclerView` displays the data.
- You scroll down the list of animals. Whoops! Another issue: Nothing's triggering a request for more data, so you're stuck with just the first chunk of cached data. To fix this, you need to add a **callback** for the `RecyclerView`'s scrolling that triggers a new network request when the scroll reaches a specific position.

This is a simple feature with a simple use case. Still, as you can see, there were some details missing. *That's OK.* There are probably even more missing, but you'll only find them at development time. Still, dry runs like this help you find the most noticeable issues before touching the code.

This sums up the "animals near you" feature. On to the next one!

Search

The goal here is to type a search query, possibly filter it and show either results or a warning saying that there are no results. This feature will be harder to implement, given the added complexity of the mutating state.

Designing the UI

OK, so you'll need a **search bar**, a few **drop-down menus** with options for filtering, and a `RecyclerView` to display the results. You'll display animals as well, so you'll be able to reuse the `RecyclerView` from the other feature.

Adding Data Sources

The search should go through the cache and, if it doesn't find anything, try to find results via a network call. If there aren't any results there, either, then you show the "no results" warning.

It seems like you can reuse the data handling code from "animals near you". Nice! You might need to add new queries and change requests, but that shouldn't be a problem.

Modeling the Domain

It shouldn't come as a surprise that you'll reuse the domain entities. You'll probably need to create new ones specific to this feature to better handle the search state, but that's something you can only be sure about when you dig into the code.

As for use cases, you'll follow the same approach as with the previous feature.

Making a Dry Run

Here are your goals: Write a query, maybe filter it, search for results, show them in the `RecyclerView`, show a warning if no results exist and handle possible errors.

Now, thinking like a user:

- You get to the screen, and there's nothing there other than the search interface. Maybe adding a **placeholder** for the items is a good idea.
- You start searching, and items from the cache might appear. If not, the app makes a network request, but no items will appear until the response arrives. Again, a progress bar can save the day.
- If the app finds no results, a warning shows up. Otherwise, a list of cute little animals, ready to be loved, appears.

Again, the trick here will be to manage the constantly mutating state. You'll have to juggle the constant changes due to:

- Result list values that can be empty.
- The search query.
- The search filters.

There will be *a lot* of **intermediate states**, so you'll have to be careful to avoid inconsistencies. But there's no use in rambling about it now. You know it'll be tricky, so wait until you're working on the code to figure out the best way to do it. The important thing is that you're already aware of the increased difficulty.

So, What's the Plan?

At this point, you know the features and their main pain points. You're ready to begin development, but where should you start?

You can't build a house starting from the roof, and the same is valid in software. There's no use in starting to develop features without a **solid foundation** to build them on. If you try, be ready for future refactoring.

A great way to build a solid base is by starting with **feature-independent** code. This is why, in the next chapter, you'll start with the most central part: the domain layer.

Key Points

- Packaging by feature enables you to work out what an app does just by looking at the packages.
- You should strive for high cohesion and low coupling on every level of your apps.
- Separating the code of each feature by internal layers is an excellent way to have maintainable and flexible code, while also achieving high cohesion and low coupling.
- Being familiar with your app's domain enables you to better understand what it does and what its users expect.
- When you're planning your work, thinking about the implementation ahead of time is a helpful way of mitigating surprises in the future.
- Putting yourself in your users' shoes helps you identify potential problems with your app.

Chapter 3: Domain Layer

By Ricardo Costeira

Having your **business logic** smeared throughout your app is a recipe for disaster. In time, things will get messy:

- Code will become hard to find.
- You'll start reimplementing logic by accident.
- Logic will get more and more coupled to the code that calls for it.
- Your code will have **mixed responsibilities**. As the project grows, it'll become harder to change.

That's why it's a good practice to decouple your business logic. A nice way to do that is to implement a **domain layer**.

In this chapter, you'll learn:

- What a **domain layer** is, why you need it — and when you don't.
- The difference between **domain entities** and **value objects**.
- How to determine which entities and/or value objects to model.
- Common issues in domain modeling.
- The role of a **repository** in the domain layer.
- What you should test.

Although use cases are also part of this layer, you won't implement any for now because they're tailored for features.

What Is a Domain Layer?

The domain layer is the central layer of your app. It includes the code that describes your **domain space** along with the logic that manipulates it. You'll probably find *at least* the following objects in every domain layer you work with:

- **entities**: Objects that model your domain space.
- **value objects**: Another kind of object that models your domain space.
- **interactors/use cases**: Logic to handle entities and/or value objects and produce a result.
- **repository interfaces**: Define contracts for data source access.

This layer encompasses the **business logic** of the app. Your business logic is one of the most important parts of your app, as it defines how the app works. The less you mess with it, the better! That's why the domain layer shouldn't depend on other layers.

For example, imagine you change your data layer by migrating from **REST** to **GraphQL**. Or you change your presentation layer by migrating the UI to **Jetpack Compose**. None of those changes have anything to do with the business logic. As such, they shouldn't affect the domain layer at all.

Do You Really Need a Domain Layer?

Whether a domain layer is necessary is a source of debate in the Android community. Some people argue that it doesn't make sense to have one in Android apps. Google, in their architecture guide, also mark the domain layer as optional.

At a high level, a lot of Android apps follow the same simple pattern. They:

1. Get data from a data source.
2. Show the data in the UI.
3. Update the data source with new data.

From a layered architecture point of view, it seems like a data and a presentation layer would be enough!

And they are — for the app to work, at least. You just need to pass data between the layers, maybe add some logic in your `ViewModels` to handle the data, and off to the Play Store it goes.

You have a working app, but you forgot about something — or someone — really important. You forgot about **you**.

Having a domain layer is a way of protecting yourself as a developer. Sure, it can seem like unnecessary, redundant work, but it pays off in the long run by:

- Keeping your **code clean and easy to maintain** by focusing the business logic in one layer only, and decoupled from data source code. **Single responsibility** code is easier to manage.
- Defining **boundaries** between code that implements app logic and code that has nothing to do with that logic, like UI or framework code. Given how fast the Android framework changes, this separation is critical.
- Easing the onboarding of future developers, who can study the layer to understand how the app works.

If you're working with a small codebase, it's true that having a domain layer might be over-engineering. If all your app does is transform API data to show it to the user, then you can just use the repository for those transformations and your code will work, nice and simple. Yet, small apps are becoming increasingly rare. Even for apps that are small feature-wise, code gets really complex, really fast. It might seem like over-engineering at first, but sooner rather than later, it'll turn out to be a life- and sanity-saving design decision.

In the end, it's something you should consider, or discuss with your team. It might even make sense to start without a domain layer, and then add one in the future if needed.

At this point, **PetSave** has a relatively small codebase. As you go through the book and add more code, however, you'll start to see how the domain layer really shines. You'll see how nice it is to have a clear **separation of concerns**, which in turn allows for easily tested logic.

But that's in the future. For now, it's time to add your first domain entities.

Creating Your Domain Model

Use Android Studio and open the **PetSave** project you find in the **starter** folder in the material for this chapter, and expand the **common.domain** package. You'll see two other packages inside:

- **model**: Where all entities and value objects live.
- **repositories**: Where you'll find any repository interfaces.

You'll come back to the repositories later. For now, focus on the **model** package. As you start exploring it, you'll notice that it already has quite a few files inside.

Figure 3.1 — Domain Package Structure

Entities and Value Objects

Now's a good time to establish the difference between **entities** and **value objects**. Expand the **common.domain.model.organization** package and open **Organization.kt**. Focus on the first data class:

```
data class Organization(
    val id: String,
    val contact: Contact,
    val distance: Float
)
```

This class represents the **organization entity**. It has an `id` that identifies it and a few properties that describe it. Look at that `Contact`, and you'll notice that it doesn't have an ID.

```
data class Contact(
    val email: String,
    val phone: String,
    val address: Address
)
```

This is what distinguishes entities from value objects:

- Entities **have an ID** that allows you to tell them apart. Their properties can change, but the ID always remains the same.
- Value objects describe some aspect of an entity. They don't have IDs, and if you change one of their properties, you create a new value object. For this reason, they should always be immutable.

> **Note**: The concept of entities and value objects comes from **Domain Driven Design**. Although the distinction between them goes deeper, the key thing to remember is this: Identity is important for entities.

As long as the ID remains the same, entities' properties can change. However, the `Organization` entity only has immutable properties.

That's because it's good practice to favor immutable objects until you need to make them mutable. This does wonders for avoiding bugs that stem from mutable objects. A very common example is mutable object handling with asynchronous code.

What Should You Model?

In a real-world situation, you wouldn't have to think about what to model at this point. You would have info from stakeholders and project owners and decisions from meetings that would guide you on what to implement.

Frequently, apps are built to support a pre-existing business. In these cases, the domain model already exists somewhere — typically in the **back end**. Therefore, reproducing the back end's domain model is usually enough.

This last option is actually the case for PetSave. Most of the domain is based on the **petfinder API**. And why not? They already have a working back end with a matching front end. Plus, it's the only API PetSave will use in the foreseeable future.

More often than not, the domain model entities end up being manifestations of the domain's **names**. For PetSave, you know the domain has to do with animal adoption and care. You adopt animals from organizations that care for them. **Animals** and **organizations** seem like a starting point!

Adding the Animal Entities

As you've seen, `Organization` already exists. Next, you'll add the `Animal` entities.

Expand the **animal** package, then expand the **details** package inside it. Every file you see inside the animal package is a value object. Each data class represents a collection of related attributes, while each `enum` represents a **closed attribute set**. They are simple objects, but a few are worth checking out. You'll get to them in a few minutes.

For now, you need to add the `Animal` entity.

Create a new **Animal.kt** file in the **animal** package. In it, add the `Animal` class:

```
data class Animal(
    val id: Long,
    val name: String,
    val type: String,
    val media: Media,
    val tags: List<String>,
    val adoptionStatus: AdoptionStatus,
    val publishedAt: LocalDateTime
)
```

Don't forget to import `LocalDateTime` from the **java.time** library. Gradle will handle the desugaring for you.

This entity is fairly simple. It has a few primitive properties, a `LocalDateTime` for the publishing date and two value objects:

- **media**: A `Media` value object instance that handles photos and videos of the animal.
- **adoptionStatus**: An `enum` value from `AdoptionStatus`.

`adoptionStatus` can be one of four values:

```
enum class AdoptionStatus {
  UNKNOWN,
  ADOPTABLE,
  ADOPTED,
  FOUND
}
```

There's not much to see here, just a simple enum. Open `Media` and take a look at how it's implemented. You can see that it has two properties:

- **photos**: A list of `Photo` objects.
- **videos**: A list of `Video` objects.

Both `Photo` and `Video` classes are nested in `Media` for ease of access.

Now, take a closer look at `Photo`:

```
data class Photo(
    val medium: String,
    val full: String
) {

  companion object {
    const val NO_SIZE_AVAILABLE = ""
  }

  fun getSmallestAvailablePhoto(): String {  // 1
    return when {
      isValidPhoto(medium) -> medium
      isValidPhoto(full) -> full
      else -> NO_SIZE_AVAILABLE
    }
  }

  private fun isValidPhoto(photo: String): Boolean { // 2
    return photo.isNotEmpty()
  }
}
```

It's a value object with two properties:

- **medium**: A link for the medium-sized photo.
- **full**: A link for the full-sized photo.

There's also some logic in it:

1. Returns the smallest-sized photo available, which will be useful to display the animal images in the animal list. You don't need high-resolution images for a list and the smaller the image, the fewer bytes to request from the API.
2. Checks if the photo link is valid. For simplicity, it just checks if the link is not an empty string.

This is good! When you have a piece of logic related to a domain model object, it's a good practice to keep that logic contained within the object.

Remember the concept of **high cohesion**? This is a good example of it. The logic has a close relationship with the object, to a point where it ends up using all the object's properties. This means that you're not **tightly coupling** `Photo` to something else.

Another important thing to mention in `Photo` is its **companion object** — more specifically, `NO_SIZE_AVAILABLE`. This property represents the empty state of a `Photo`. It's a simplified version of the **Null Object Pattern**, and it's a nice way to avoid **null values**.

Yes, you could simply just return an empty string in `getSmallestAvailablePhoto()`, like so:

```
fun getSmallestAvailablePhoto(): String {
    return when {
      isValidPhoto(medium) -> medium
      isValidPhoto(full) -> full
      else -> ""
    }
  }
```

But that's not the point. Since it's such a simple example, `NO_SIZE_AVAILABLE` just happens to be an empty string. Don't look at the **values** the code is handling; instead, look at its **intent**. You shouldn't care about `NO_SIZE_AVAILABLE` being an empty string — the important thing here is that `NO_SIZE_AVAILABLE` tells you that a `Photo` has no sizes available.

Zoom out to `Media` and you'll see that it follows the same approach. It has:

- Highly cohesive logic.
- A simplified **Null Object Pattern** with `NO_MEDIA`.

> **Note**: For simplicity, this code ignores `Video`. In a more complex example, it would follow the same approach as `Photo`, but with logic for video handling.

AnimalWithDetails Entity

The `Animal` entity is enough for this section's features. However, there will be a **details screen** later that will need more details than `Animal` provides. So you might as well add that functionality now.

In the **details** package, create a new file, **AnimalWithDetails.kt**. In it, add `AnimalWithDetails`:

```
data class AnimalWithDetails(
    val id: Long,
    val name: String,
    val type: String,
    val details: Details,
    val media: Media,
    val tags: List<String>,
    val adoptionStatus: AdoptionStatus,
    val publishedAt: LocalDateTime
)
```

This entity is exactly the same as `Animal`, but it has an extra `details` property. You might wonder why you don't just add a nullable `details` property to the `Animal` entity. Well, you could. This is just a design choice for the sake of avoiding nullable values. It would be totally OK to go with the nullable property option.

The `Details` value object uses the remaining value objects in the packages, along with the `Organization` entity.

```
data class Details(
    val description: String,
    val age: Age,
    val species: String,
    val breed: Breed,
    val colors: Colors,
    val gender: Gender,
    val size: Size,
```

```
    val coat: Coat,
    val healthDetails: HealthDetails,
    val habitatAdaptation: HabitatAdaptation,
    val organization: Organization
)
```

Nothing's new here except the `Breed` data class. Open it, there's an interesting detail here that you should be aware of. This is the data class:

```
data class Breed(val primary: String, val secondary: String) {
  val mixed: Boolean
    get() = primary.isNotEmpty() && secondary.isNotEmpty()

  val unknown: Boolean
    get() = primary.isEmpty() && secondary.isEmpty()
}
```

And this is an example of what the API returns regarding breeds:

```
"breeds": {
  "primary": "Golden Retriever",
  "secondary": null,
  "mixed": false,
  "unknown": false
}
```

The first obvious change is that `secondary` goes from a nullable `String` to a non-nullable one. You'll explore this kind of mapping in the next chapter, so don't bother with it for now. Apart from this, notice any differences in how information is being passed?

Take a closer look at the properties to understand what they are:

- **primary**: The primary breed.
- **secondary**: The secondary breed.
- **mixed**: Tells you if the animal has mixed breeds — it has both a primary and a secondary breed.
- **unknown**: Tells you if the animal's breed is unknown — it has neither a primary nor a secondary breed.

Only the first two properties — `primary` and `secondary` — are a part of `Breed`'s constructor. The other properties, `mixed` and `unknown`, are deduced from the first two.

> **Note**: Since `Breed` is a data class, it has a few auto-generated methods. Be aware that, in this case, both `mixed` and `unknown` are **not accounted for** by those methods, as they're outside the constructor.

In all fairness, it's quite possible that the API also deduces `mixed` and `unknown` from the other two. It returns them all as independent properties because it has no other option. While it's true that `mixed` and `unknown` only add noise, it's a totally valid way of building a back end: When in doubt, return everything you have. :]

By having some properties depend on others, you increase the cohesion of the class. This increases the amount of **information** conveyed when you read the class. Also, if you create a copy of the class but change one of the constructor values, both `mixed` and `unknown` will update. Talk about a good deal!

Adding the PaginatedAnimals Value Object

The previous chapter talks about the API returning **chunks of paginated data**. The pagination information is also relevant to the UI, letting `RecyclerView` request the correct data chunk. It's a data layer **implementation detail**, but it ends up **leaking** to the presentation layer.

So, why not model this information as well? Yes, it doesn't exactly fit the domain. Still, it's better to have it modeled and maintain the boundaries between layers than to break the dependency rule *even once*.

Try not to cut corners on this kind of decision. Otherwise, you'll start to notice broken windows in your app.

> **Note**: The **broken window theory** is a theory that describes *software decay*. It states that visible signs of *crime* create an environment that fosters more crime. In other words, as soon as you start cutting corners in your app, you'll do it more and more often.

Expand the **pagination** package next to the **animal** and **organization** packages. Inside, you'll find there's already a `Pagination` value object. This is the generic representation of the API's pagination. You'll now add the specific **animal pagination**.

Inside the **pagination** package, create a new file called **PaginatedAnimals.kt**. Add the following class to the file:

```
data class PaginatedAnimals(
    val animals: List<AnimalWithDetails>,
    val pagination: Pagination
)
```

This value object associates a list of animals with a specific page. It's exactly what the UI needs to know which page to request next.

You added two entities, a value object, and learned some of the intricacies of domain modeling. Well done! Before diving into repositories, there are still a few domain modeling topics worth addressing.

To Type or Not to Type

Look at `Animal` again:

```
data class Animal(
    val id: Long,
    val name: String,
    val type: String,
    val media: Media,
    val tags: List<String>,
    val adoptionStatus: AdoptionStatus,
    val publishedAt: LocalDateTime
)
```

If you exclude the value objects and the `publishedAt` property, you're left with:

```
data class Animal(
    val id: Long,
    val name: String,
    val type: String,
    val tags: List<String>
)
```

These properties all have one thing in common: None of them have **specific domain types**. In fact, they're just a mix of standard types from the language.

When modeling your domain, you need to make some choices, and those choices have trade-offs. One of the hardest choices to make is how many new **domain-specific types** you should create.

Types provide safety and robustness in exchange for complexity and development time. For instance, what's keeping you from creating `Animal` with the `id` of `-1L`? It's just a `Long` type. It doesn't care about the value you set it to, as long as it's of type `Long`.

However, adding a new type called `Id` changes things:

```
@JvmInline
value class Id(val value: Long) { // 1
  init { // 2
    validate(value)
  }

  private fun validate(id: Long) {
    if (id.hasInvalidValue()) { // 3
      throw InvalidIdException(id)
    }
  }
}
```

Here are some things to note in this code:

1. Kotlin's **value classes** are a neat way to wrap your primitives into custom types, since they (mostly) spare you from the overhead of handling a normal class.
2. `init` blocks run immediately after the primary constructor, so this calls `validate` as soon as you create an instance of `Id`.
3. `hasInvalidValue` is an extension function on `Long` that verifies whether the ID value is `-1L` or `0`. If so, `validate` will throw an `InvalidIdException`.

Now, imagine that `Id` has a specific format. Then, you need to add a new validation:

```
private fun validate(id: Long) {
  if (id.hasInvalidValue()) {
    throw InvalidIdException(id)
  }

  if (id.hasInvalidFormat()) {
    throw InvalidIdFormatException(id)
  }
}
```

Suppose that the formatting spec determines the size limit of the ID. It's a specific case of format validation that deserves its own validation for clarity. By updating the code:

```
private fun validate(id: Long) {
  when {
    id.hasInvalidValue() -> throw InvalidIdException(id)
    id.hasInvalidFormat() -> throw InvalidIdFormatException(id)
    id.exceedsLength() -> throw InvalidIdLengthException(id)
  }
}
```

You also change from a chain of `if` conditions to a `when`.

It looks clean, but it now throws a bunch of exceptions. You start worrying that it might be hard to maintain the code in the future, especially if you add new validation rule. So, you refactor the whole thing:

```
@JvmInline
value class Id private constructor(val value: Long) { // 1
  companion object {
    fun of(id: Long): Either<IdException, Id> { // 2
      return when {
        id.hasInvalidValue() ->
Either.Left(IdException.InvalidIdException(id))
        id.hasInvalidFormat() ->
Either.Left(IdException.InvalidIdFormatException(id))
        id.exceedsLength() ->
Either.Left(IdException.InvalidIdLengthException(id))
        else -> Either.Right(Id(value = id))
      }
    }
  }

  sealed class IdException(message: String): Exception(message)
{ // 3
    data class InvalidIdException(val id: Long):
IdException("$id")
    data class InvalidIdFormatException(val id: Long):
IdException("$id")
    data class InvalidIdLengthException(val id: Long):
IdException("$id")
  }
}

sealed class Either<out A, out B> { // 4
    class Left<A>(val value: A): Either<A, Nothing>()
    class Right<B>(val value: B): Either<Nothing, B>()
}
```

Here's what's happening, step by step:

1. You make the constructor private so that you can fully control new `Id` instance creation.
2. The old `validate` function is now called `of`, and works as a **factory function** of `Id`'s companion object. With the constructor being private, you're now forced to do `Id.of(123L)` if you want to create an instance of `Id`. You also change the functions's signature to be explicit about what's happening inside.
3. You encapsulate all the exceptions in the `IdException` sealed class.
4. You create the `Either` sealed class, a **disjoint union** to represent success and failure values.

As you can see, it's pretty easy to get carried away.

Dealing with `Booleans` is also fun. For instance, consider this class:

```
class User(name: String, email: String, isAdmin: Boolean)
```

You can see where this is going, can't you? That `isAdmin` is a disaster waiting for the worst moment possible to explode in your face. A simple mistake or a bug that makes the property `true` when it should be `false` can completely wreck your app.

A common way to avoid stuff like this is to use inheritance:

```
open class User(name: String, email: String)

class Admin(name: String, email: String) : User(name, email)
```

Congratulations! You now have one extra class to maintain, and possible inheritance issues that might come from it. You have to agree though, that the code is *a lot* safer this way.

There's usually some uncertainty over whether all the extra work will pay off in the future or not. For instance, in the `Id` example: Is all of that needed? Maybe some of those cases that you took measures against would never happen anyway. You'd be maintaining all that complexity for nothing!

It's up to you and your team to decide. Do you want to follow a straightforward, "we'll refactor when we get there", **YAGNI** (You Aren't Gonna Need It) approach? Or a more time-consuming, type-safe, "model all the things!" way of working?

In general, a solution somewhere in the middle, with just enough design upfront, will fit your needs the best.

Anemic Model

Managing types is not the only common problem in domain models. Sometimes, domain models can become **anemic**, which means that they mainly consist of data without behavior.

On Android, it's common for the domain layer to work mainly as a bridge between the other layers. In fact, this is one of the most common arguments **against** having a domain layer on Android.

PetSave is an example: Other than `Breed`, `Media` and `Photo`, no other domain class has any kind of logic in it. PetSave has what seems like a few **anemic models**.

However, note that your domain is only starting to take shape. The app is at an early stage, so it's normal that you don't have enough **domain knowledge** to add logic to the models.

It's possible for the app to grow and its domain to remain anemic. But even so, it's good to weigh the advantages of having a domain layer on an ever-changing ecosystem like Android before deciding to completely remove it.

This wraps up the domain modeling topics. When you implement use cases later, you'll need them to access data sources. You'll have to do it without forcing a dependency on the data layer, to preserve the **dependency rule**. This is where repositories come in handy.

Inverting Dependencies With Repositories

A repository is a very common **pattern** for **data source abstraction**. You use it to abstract away all the data sources you want. Anything that calls the repository can access data from those sources, but will never know which sources even exist.

In the domain layer, you won't actually implement a repository. Instead, you'll only have a repository **interface**. This allows you to **invert the dependency** on the layers, making the data layer depend on the domain layer, instead of the other way around!

How? it's simple, and you can start putting it into place right away. In the **repositories** package, create **AnimalRepository.kt**. In it, add your interface:

```
interface AnimalRepository
```

Later, you'll implement an actual repository class in the data layer. That class will implement this interface and any of its methods. Then, any time a use case needs data access, you'll pass it that repository class as a dependency, but the **dependency's type** will match the interface's.

This way, use cases can access all the methods in the interface's **contract**, without ever knowing the class that fulfills it. The use case does its job *and* preserves the dependency rule. Win-win!

For now, you'll leave the interface just like this. It might be anticlimactic, but it's much easier to add methods later, when you're developing the features and know exactly what data you need.

That's it for the app code for this chapter. For your work as a developer to be complete, though, you're still one thing missing: tests!

Testing Your Domain Logic

When you build the project, there won't be any UI changes to let you know that your code works. Still, at least you can rely on tests to tell you that your code does what you expect.

You'll definitely do some heavy testing later, when you implement use cases. For now, though, there's not *that much* to test. Regardless, you want to make sure you start testing **as soon as possible**.

Your next step is to add tests to verify the domain logic you saw earlier. Adding tests to every class would be redundant for your purposes, so you'll focus on **unit tests** for `Photo`.

Collapse the **petsave** package, the root of the project. You'll see three main packages.

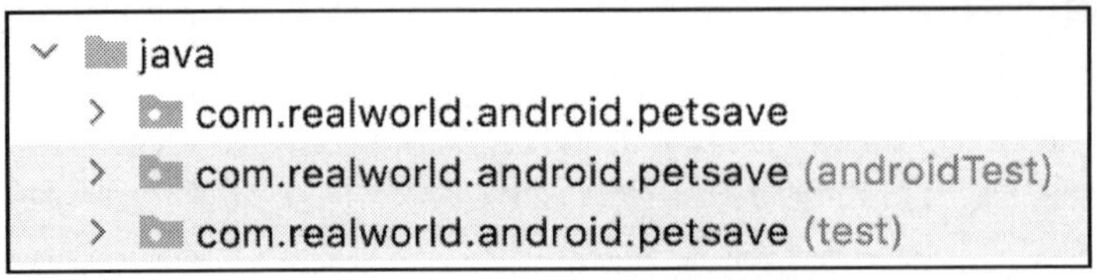

Figure 3.2 — Android Project Build Types

Expand the package that has the **(test)** label in front of it. This is where you'll add your tests, since it's the place where tests that don't rely on the Android framework should live.

A good way to organize your tests is to mimic the package structure of the app code. This makes it possible for tests to access any internal properties of the code, since anything with the **internal** visibility modifier is only accessible to code in the same package.

At the root of the package, create the following structure: **common/domain/model/animal**. Inside **animal**, create **PhotoTests.kt**. You'll end up with something like this:

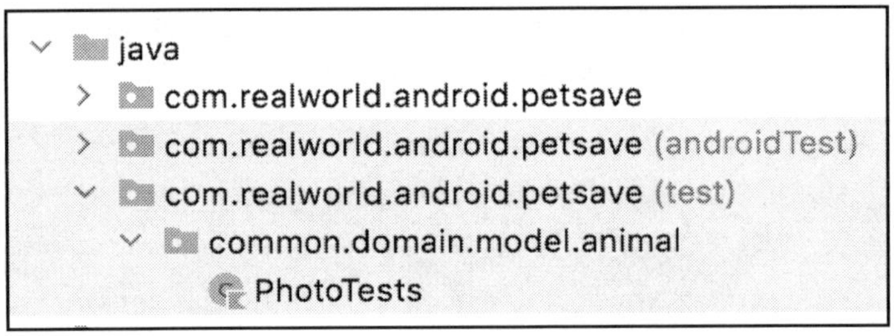

Figure 3.3 — Testing Source Structure

Test dependencies are already taken care of. Open the file you just created and add the class along with a test:

```
class PhotoTests {

  private val mediumPhoto = "mediumPhoto"
  private val fullPhoto = "fullPhoto"
  private val invalidPhoto = "" // what's tested in
Photo.isValidPhoto()

  @Test
  fun photo_getSmallestAvailablePhoto_hasMediumPhoto() {
      // Given
```

```
        val photo = Media.Photo(mediumPhoto, fullPhoto)
        val expectedValue = mediumPhoto

        // When
        val smallestPhoto = photo.getSmallestAvailablePhoto()

        // Then
        assertEquals(smallestPhoto, expectedValue)
    }
}
```

This test verifies the **happy path**, with the photo at its smallest available resolution. This **Given – When – Then** structure is a nice way of organizing your test code. If you maintain these comments, it gets easier to maintain the actual code in the future.

It's true: The words "maintenance" and "comments" don't mix. Still, you should keep your tests small and focus on one thing at a time. If you do, it won't be too hard to keep the comments in place.

Go ahead and add more tests below this one:

```
@Test
fun photo_getSmallestAvailablePhoto_noMediumPhoto_hasFullPhoto()
{
    // Given
    val photo = Media.Photo(invalidPhoto, fullPhoto)
    val expectedValue = fullPhoto

    // When
    val smallestPhoto = photo.getSmallestAvailablePhoto()

    // Then
    assertEquals(smallestPhoto, expectedValue)
}

@Test
fun photo_getSmallestAvailablePhoto_noPhotos() {
    // Given
    val photo = Media.Photo(invalidPhoto, invalidPhoto)
    val expectedValue = Media.Photo.NO_SIZE_AVAILABLE

    // When
    val smallestPhoto = photo.getSmallestAvailablePhoto()

    // Then
    assertEquals(smallestPhoto, expectedValue)
}
```

The first test checks if you're returning the larger photo, in case the medium one is invalid. The second test checks if you're returning `NO_SIZE_AVAILABLE` when both photo sizes are invalid. The only missing test now is for the case when you have a medium photo, but not a full photo. No point in adding it though, as it would be similar to the first test you just added.

These tests are simple. And they should be! They're unit tests, after all. The important thing here is that they're actually testing behavior.

Take the last test, for example. You're initializing `Photo` with `invalidPhoto`, and the `expectedValue` is `NO_SIZE_AVAILABLE`. You *know* that both are empty strings, so why not use the same property everywhere?

As discussed earlier, that's not the behavior the code wants to achieve. They just happened to both be empty strings — their meanings are vastly different. This is what you have to test: You should **test behavior, not code or data**.

Key Points

- Domain layers protect you, the developer, and the app's logic from external changes.
- Entities have an identity that allows you to distinguish between them.
- Value objects enrich your domain and can either contain entities or be contained by them.
- Defining how many custom types to have in your domain is something you should consider carefully. Try to find a balance between under typing and over typing, as both are troublesome.
- Be careful when adding logic to your app that relates to your domain model: That logic might belong inside the actual model classes.
- Repository interfaces allow for dependency inversion, which is essential to keep the domain layer isolated.
- Test behavior, not code or data.

You've reached the end of the chapter. Awesome! Next, you'll learn about the data layer.

Chapter 4: Data Layer — Network

By Ricardo Costeira

Every software application needs data, and Android is no different. In fact, Android apps are almost always heavily dependent on data. That's why it's important to organize your data-centric code in its own layer, where you implement both data access and caching.

Creating this layer is a lot of work, so you'll build yours across two chapters, starting with network access. In this chapter, you'll learn why you need a data layer and how to:

- Map data to the domain layer.
- Connect to a network API.
- Handle dependencies with Hilt.
- Create and test network interceptors.

Now, it's time to jump in.

What Is a Data Layer?

The data layer is where you put the code responsible for interacting with your data sources.

An app can have multiple data sources, and they can change over time. For instance, you can migrate from a REST server to a GraphQL server, or from a **Room** database to a **Realm** database, https://www.mongodb.com/realm/mobile/database. These changes only matter to the data handling logic, and should not affect the code that needs the data.

A data layer has two responsibilities. It:

- Keeps your data I/O code organized in one place.
- Creates a boundary between the data sources and their consumers.

The Repository Pattern

One way to create this boundary is by following the **repository pattern**. This is a popular pattern to use in Android because Google recommends it.

The repository is just an **abstraction** over the way you access data. It creates a thin layer over data sources — a class that wraps up calls to the objects that do the heavy lifting. While this sounds a bit redundant, it has its purposes. It lets you:

- Swap data sources without affecting the rest of the app. Swapping sources is rare, but trust me, it happens. :]
- Create the boundary between the data layer and the other layers that need to operate on data.
- Orchestrate the different data sources to produce a result the domain expects, while keeping that orchestration logic hidden away.

You already took the first step in creating this boundary by creating the **repository contract** in the domain layer. You'll now implement a repository that fulfills that contract. This makes the data layer depend on the domain layer, as the dependency rule demands.

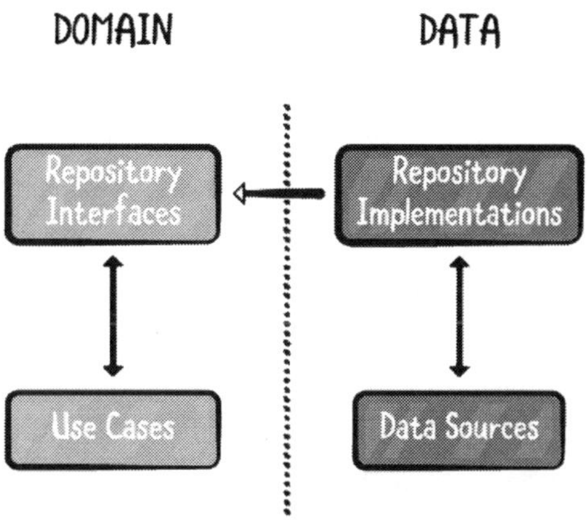

Figure 4.1 — Closed Arrows Represent Data Flow. The Open Arrow Means "Implements".

You can have as many repositories as you want. A popular choice is to have **one repository per domain entity type**. This is a nice rule of thumb, but in the end, it's up to you to decide what works best.

For instance, in this app, you'll use only one repository to deal with both `animal` and `organization` entities. The latter just completes the former's information, for now, so giving it its own repository isn't worth it.

Before implementing your repository, you need data sources. You'll start by working with the API. If you haven't done so already, now's a good time to look at PetFinder's documentation at https://www.petfinder.com/developers/v2/docs/, which will help you understand some of the decisions you'll make in this chapter.

Network Data Models

No, no, calm down, you're not implementing any more data models! The models are already in the project, but they're worth taking a look at.

Open the **ApiAnimal.kt** file in the **common.data.api.model** package.

You'll see a bunch of different data classes. The first one is `ApiAnimal`. It corresponds to `Animal` in your domain, but is modeled exactly after the information the back end sends. The rest of the classes compose `ApiAnimal`, so they're in the same file for convenience.

All classes follow the same building logic, so look at any of them to understand that logic. For instance, take `ApiBreeds`:

```
@JsonClass(generateAdapter = true) // 1
data class ApiBreeds(
    @field:Json(name = "primary") val primary: String?, // 2
    @field:Json(name = "secondary") val secondary: String?,
    @field:Json(name = "mixed") val mixed: Boolean?,
    @field:Json(name = "unknown") val unknown: Boolean?
)
```

Here you can see that:

1. This annotation decorates every class. The app uses **Moshi** to parse the JSON from API responses. This annotation lets Moshi know it can create an object of this type from JSON data. Moshi will also automagically create an adapter if you set `generateAdapter` to `true`. It'll then use it to create an instance of the class. Without this parameter, you'll get a runtime error from Moshi, unless you create the adapter yourself.

2. There are two different things to notice here. First, the Moshi annotation maps the **JSON variable** called `primary` to the **code variable** called `primary`. In this case, you didn't need the annotation because the names are the same. Still, it's there for consistency's sake. Second, you used a nullable type. Long story short, never trust your backend. :] Using nullable types ensures that even if something goes wrong and you get unexpected nullable values in the response, the app won't crash.

Next, you'll see how to map these **DTOs** (data transfer objects) into your domain.

Mapping Data to the Domain

There are two typical ways of mapping data to the domain layer. One uses interfaces and independent classes, while the other uses static and/or member functions of the model. Here, you'll use the former. You'll try the other option later. :]

In the **model** package, expand **mappers**. You'll see a lot of mappers there already, along with an `ApiMapper` interface:

```
interface ApiMapper<E, D> {

  fun mapToDomain(apiEntity: E): D
}
```

Having all the mappers follow this interface gives you the advantage of **decoupling** the mapping. This is useful if you have a lot of mappers and want to make sure they all follow the same contract.

Now, open **ApiAnimalMapper.kt** and remove the block comment. The class already has a few delegate methods for value objects and entities, using the appropriate mappers. The only thing missing is to fulfill the interface's contract, which you'll do by adding the following code below the `add code here` comment:

```
override fun mapToDomain(apiEntity: ApiAnimal):
AnimalWithDetails {
  return AnimalWithDetails(
      id = apiEntity.id
        ?: throw MappingException("Animal ID cannot be
null"),  // 1
      name = apiEntity.name.orEmpty(), // 2
      type = apiEntity.type.orEmpty(),
      details = parseAnimalDetails(apiEntity), // 3
      media = mapMedia(apiEntity),
      tags = apiEntity.tags.orEmpty().map { it.orEmpty() },
      adoptionStatus = parseAdoptionStatus(apiEntity.status),
      publishedAt =
        DateTimeUtils.parse(apiEntity.publishedAt.orEmpty()) //
4
  )
}
```

A few things worth noting here:

1. If the API entity doesn't have an ID, the code throws a `MappingException`. You need IDs to distinguish between entities, so you want the code to fail if they don't exist.
2. If `name` in the API entity is `null`, the code sets the `name` in the domain entity to empty. Should it, though? Can`AnimalWithDetails` entities have empty names? That **depends on the domain**. In fact, mappers are a good place to search for **domain constraints**. Anyway, for simplicity, assume an empty name is possible.
3. `details` is a value object, so the code delegates its creation to an appropriate method. Clean code keeps responsibilities well separated.
4. `DateTimeUtils` is a custom `object` that wraps **java.time** library calls. `parse` will throw an exception if it gets an empty string. This is also a domain constraint. There are future plans to order the animal list so the oldest ones in the system appear first, so the date can't be empty.

Now that the mapping is done, you'll start implementing the API requests.

Connecting to the API With Retrofit

Retrofit is the go-to **HTTP client** for Android. It allows you to build an HTTP API in record time, even with almost no knowledge about HTTP. It's especially powerful when coupled with **OkHttp**, which gives you more control over your requests.

In the **api** package, open **PetFinderApi.kt**. Retrofit lets you define your API as an interface. `PetFinderApi` is empty right now. Which methods should you add?

For now, you'll focus only on the data needs for the **Animals near you** feature, leaving **Search** for later. That way, you'll see how to develop a feature one layer at a time versus jumping around through the layers.

Animals near you needs to retrieve animal data from the API according to your postal code and the distance you specify. Knowing that, you'll add the following method to the interface:

```
@GET(ApiConstants.ANIMALS_ENDPOINT) // 1
suspend fun getNearbyAnimals( // 2
    @Query(ApiParameters.PAGE) pageToLoad: Int, // 3
    @Query(ApiParameters.LIMIT) pageSize: Int,
    @Query(ApiParameters.LOCATION) postcode: String,
    @Query(ApiParameters.DISTANCE) maxDistance: Int
): ApiPaginatedAnimals // 4
```

Be sure to import Retrofit dependencies. Gradle already knows about them.

In this code:

1. You tell Retrofit you want to perform a **GET request** through the `@GET` annotation, passing in the endpoint for the request.
2. You add the `suspend` modifier to the method. A network request is a **one-shot operation**, so running it in a coroutine fits perfectly.
3. You specify the request's parameters through the `@Query` annotation. For instance, if you're loading the first page of 20 items, the request will have parameters like `page=1&limit=20`.
4. You return `ApiPaginatedAnimals`, which will map to the domain's `PaginatedAnimals`.

The **PetFinder** server uses **OAuth** for authentication. OAuth works with **access tokens**. To get an access token, you have to send an authentication request with your **API key** and **API secret**. You then use the token you receive to authenticate your request, sending it as an **authorization header**.

You need a token for every request, except the authentication request itself. If the token expires, you have to request a new one.

In other words, for each request, you have to:

1. Store the original request.
2. Request a token if you don't have one, or a new token if the current one has expired.
3. Send a valid token in the header of the original request.

That's a lot of work! Fortunately, OkHttp has a neat feature that can help: **interceptors**.

Interceptors

OKHttp lets you manipulate your requests and/or responses through interceptors, which let you monitor, change or even retry API calls.

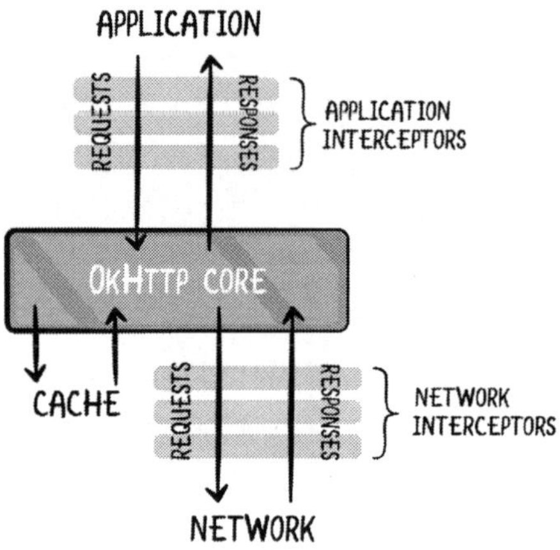

Figure 4.2 — OKHttp interceptors

OkHttp allows two types of interceptors:

- **Application interceptors**: Act between your code and OkHttp. You'll probably use these most of the time. They have access to the full request along with the already-processed response, and let you act on that data.
- **Network interceptors**: Act between OkHttp and the server. Useful in cases where you have to worry about intermediate responses, like redirects. They give you access to the data in the raw format it's sent to the server, and to the actual `Connection` object.

Expand the **interceptors** package inside **api**. You'll see three different interceptors already:

- **LoggingInterceptor**: Logs request details to Android Studio's **Logcat**.
- **NetworkStatusInterceptor**: Uses `ConnectionManager` to check the internet connection, then either throws a custom `NetworkUnavailableException` or lets the request proceed.
- **AuthenticationInterceptor**: Checks for token expiry, then requests a new one, if needed, and stores it. If a valid token already exists, it adds it to the request's headers.

Before you continue, here are two things to consider about `NetworkUnavailableException`:

1. The presentation layer needs to know about it in order to inform the user. However, the dependency rule states that dependencies flow inwards, not sideways. Since the data and presentation layers are at the same level, you want to keep them decoupled. So, the exception is modeled as a **domain exception**. This might seem awkward, but it's conceivable for network unavailability to be part of an Android app's domain. Plus, this keeps your dependencies clean with minimum effort.
2. It extends `IOException`. This is where the boundary between the layers starts to blur. It extends `IOException` because Retrofit **only** handles `IOExceptions`. So, if `NetworkUnavailableException` extends from any other type, the app is likely to crash. This implicitly couples the domain layer to the data layer. If, someday, the app stops using Retrofit in favor of a library that handles exceptions differently, the domain layer will change as well.

You could invert the dependency by creating a domain interface for the exception and implementing it in the data layer, but is the extra code and work really worth it for such a simple case? This kind of situation is common when you're trying to follow an architectural pattern — you'll eventually break it for simplicity. :]

You'll have to weigh in the pros and cons of every outcome, then decide on one. The important thing is to not get stuck in **analysis paralysis**. You can always change things in the future. **Refactoring** is part of your job as a developer.

In this case, the decision is simple: It's unlikely that the project will ever use an HTTP client other than Retrofit, so it should be safe to keep the exception in the domain layer. Even if you do change it, the only domain layer change will be the type your custom exception extends.

AuthenticationInterceptor

Open **AuthenticationInterceptor.kt** and take a closer look at intercept's signature:

```
override fun intercept(chain: Interceptor.Chain): Response
```

The method takes in a Chain and returns a Response. Chain is the active chain of interceptors running when the request is ongoing, while Response is the output of the request.

There's some code missing here that you'll add to help understand how interceptors work. It's a fairly complex piece of code, so you'll add it in parts.

Checking the Token

Delete all the code in the method, then add the following in its place:

```
val token = preferences.getToken() // 1
val tokenExpirationTime =
  Instant.ofEpochSecond(preferences.getTokenExpirationTime()) //
2
val request = chain.request() // 3

// if (chain.request().headers[NO_AUTH_HEADER] != null) return
chain.proceed(request) // 4
```

Here's what's happening in this code:

1. You get your current token from **shared preferences**.
2. You get the token's expiration time.
3. You get your current request from the interceptor chain.
4. This is a special case for requests that don't need authentication. Say you have a login request, for instance. You can add a custom header to it in the API interface — like NO_AUTH_HEADER — then check if the header exists here. If so, you let the request proceed. You won't need this logic in this case, but it's good to be aware of it.

You might find the access to preferences weird. Typically, a repository mediates between the different data sources, while they remain unaware of each other. One of its purposes in this layered architecture is not only to pass the other layers the data they need, but also to keep data sources unaware of each other.

In this case, though, all the action happens inside the data layer itself. You'd be introducing **accidental complexity** by creating a **circular dependency** between the API and the repository code. Also, `Preferences` is an interface, so the implementation details are still decoupled. You must resist "convention triggered" over-engineering. :]

Handling Valid Tokens

With that out of the way, add the next block of code below the one you just added:

```
val interceptedRequest: Request // 1

if (tokenExpirationTime.isAfter(Instant.now())) {
  interceptedRequest =
    chain.createAuthenticatedRequest(token) // 2
} else {

}

return chain
    .proceedDeletingTokenIfUnauthorized(interceptedRequest) // 3
```

In this code:

1. You declare a new request value. You'll assign the authenticated version of the original request to it.
2. If the token is valid, you create an authenticated request through `createAuthenticatedRequest`. This function creates a request from the original one and adds an authorization header with the token.
3. You tell the chain to proceed with your new request. `proceedDeletingTokenIfUnauthorized` calls `proceed` on the chain, which does all the HTTP magic and returns a response. If the response has a `401` code, `proceedDeletingTokenIfUnauthorized` deletes the token.

Good, you have the happy path implemented! As long as you have a valid token, your requests will go through. Now it's time to cover the cases where the token is invalid or doesn't exist yet.

Handling Invalid Tokens

Add the following block of code inside the empty `else`:

```
val tokenRefreshResponse = chain.refreshToken() // 1

interceptedRequest = if (tokenRefreshResponse.isSuccessful) { //
2
  val newToken = mapToken(tokenRefreshResponse) // 3

  if (newToken.isValid()) { // 4
    storeNewToken(newToken)
    chain.createAuthenticatedRequest(newToken.accessToken!!)
  } else {
    request
  }
} else {
  request
}
```

This is the most complex part. Here:

1. You call `refreshToken`. This function does all the magic of fetching you a new token. It creates a whole new request pointing to the authentication endpoint and adds the necessary API key and secret to its body. It executes the request by calling `proceedDeletingTokenIfUnauthorized`, returning its response, then stores the response in `tokenRefreshResponse`.

2. You set `interceptedRequest` with the result of the `if-else` condition. Remember that in Kotlin, `if-else` is an expression. You check if `refreshToken` was successful. If not, you return the original request.

3. If `refreshToken` is successful, you have a new token to work with. But since the Moshi converter hasn't run yet, you're stuck with the JSON version of the response instead of an actual DTO. As such, you call `mapToken` to get the token DTO, `ApiToken`. Take a quick peek inside `mapToken`. This is what you'd have to do for each DTO if Moshi didn't provide that handy `generateAdapter` parameter with the `@JsonClass` annotation. Plus, notice how it returns an invalid token when it can't parse what comes from the network. This is the **null object pattern**.

4. Finally, you check if the new token is valid — in other words, if the DTO values aren't either `NULL` or empty. If so, you store the token in shared preferences and call `createAuthenticatedRequest` with it. If the token is invalid, you set `interceptedRequest` to the original request, since you still need one.

Build and run to make sure everything works. Whew! You now have a way of checking your token validity for every request and refreshing it if necessary. The only thing missing now is to pass the interceptor to the OkHttp instance for Retrofit to use.

You now need to add your interceptor to the dependency graph for the app.

Wiring Up the Interceptor

Expand the **data.di** package and locate and open the **ApiModule.kt** file. Focus on the `provideOkHttpClient` method, for now. This creates the OkHttp instance that Retrofit uses:

```
fun provideOkHttpClient(httpLoggingInterceptor:
HttpLoggingInterceptor): OkHttpClient {
  return OkHttpClient.Builder()
      .addInterceptor(httpLoggingInterceptor)
      .build()
}
```

As you see, the code already adds an interceptor. The parameter, `HttpLoggingInterceptor`, is an OkHttp class. This instance is provided by the method below, `provideHttpLoggingInterceptor`. It uses the `LoggingInterceptor` in the **interceptors** package. It logs the headers and body of both requests and responses.

Look at the code inside `provideOkHttpClient`. You use `addInterceptor` to add **application interceptors**. For network interceptors, you'd have to use `addNetworkInterceptor`.

Ordering the Interceptors

There's an important detail you must consider before adding the other interceptors. Like Retrofit's type converters, interceptors are **called in order**. So, if you do something like:

```
OkHttpClient.Builder()
    .addInterceptor(A)
    .addInterceptor(C)
    .addInterceptor(B)
```

The interceptors will run in that order: A → C → B.

With this in mind, replace the method with:

```
fun provideOkHttpClient(
    httpLoggingInterceptor: HttpLoggingInterceptor, // 1
    networkStatusInterceptor: NetworkStatusInterceptor,
    authenticationInterceptor: AuthenticationInterceptor
): OkHttpClient {
  return OkHttpClient.Builder()
      .addInterceptor(networkStatusInterceptor) // 2
      .addInterceptor(authenticationInterceptor) // 3
      .addInterceptor(httpLoggingInterceptor) // 4
      .build()
}
```

In this code, you add:

1. The needed dependencies as parameters.
2. `networkStatusInterceptor` first. If the device doesn't have an internet connection, there's no need to allow the request to go further.
3. `authenticationInterceptor` after the network interceptor so the token refresh logic only executes if there's a connection.
4. `httpLoggingInterceptor`, which wraps `LoggingInterceptor`.

Is it weird to put `httpLoggingInterceptor` last? Should it be the first one to run, so it can log even `authenticationInterceptor`'s requests?

Nope! If you add it first, it'll run while there's still **nothing** to log. Interceptors work on the chain they receive, so you want the logging interceptor to get the **final** chain.

This concludes your work with the interceptors. Well done! The last thing missing before you proceed to tests is dependency management.

Managing API Dependencies With Hilt

Dependency injection is a great way to maintain a decoupled and testable architecture as your project grows in complexity — but it's hard to do by hand. Using a **DI framework** like **Dagger** helps, but then you have to deal with Dagger's own quirks.

> **Note**: If you want to learn everything about Dagger, Hilt and dependency injection, Dagger By Tutorials, https://www.raywenderlich.com/books/dagger-by-tutorials, is the right place for you.

PetFinder uses **Hilt**, Google's Android DI solution. Although it's built on top of Dagger, it's *a lot* easier to use.

Open **ApiModule.kt** again. Although `ApiModule` has the word **Module** in its name and is located in a **di** package, it's not a Hilt module... Yet.

You'll change that next.

Turning ApiModule Into a Hilt Module

Annotate `ApiModule` with `@Module`:

```
@Module
object ApiModule
```

Build the app and you'll get a Hilt error. Unlike common Dagger errors, you can actually read and understand it!

The error states that `ApiModule` is missing an `@InstallIn` annotation. This relates to one of the best Hilt features. When you use Hilt, you don't need to create **Dagger components**.

Hilt generates a hierarchy of predefined components with corresponding **scope annotations**. These components are **tied** to Android **lifecycles**. This makes it a lot easier for you to define the lifetime of your dependencies.

Define the component where you'll install `ApiModule` by adding:

```
@Module
@InstallIn(SingletonComponent::class)
object ApiModule
```

You're installing the module in `SingletonComponent`. This component is the **highest** in the component hierarchy — all other components descend from it. By installing `ApiModule` here, you're saying that any dependency it provides should **live as long as the app itself**. Also, since each child component can access the dependencies of its parent, you're ensuring that all other components can access `ApiModule`.

Defining Dependencies

With the module installed, you now need to define the dependencies it provides. Just like with Dagger, Hilt allows you to inject dependencies with a few annotations:

- **@Inject**: Use in class constructors to inject code you own, such as the data mappers.
- **@Provides**: Use in modules to inject code you don't own, like any library instance.
- **@Binds**: Use in modules to inject interface implementations when you don't need initialization code. You'll see an example later.

In this case, annotate **every method** with `@Provides`. For `provideApi`, add the `@Singleton` annotation as well:

```
@Provides
@Singleton
fun provideApi(okHttpClient: OkHttpClient): PetFinderApi
```

`@Provides` works as it does in traditional Dagger. `@Singleton`, on the other hand, is the **scope annotation** for `SingletonComponent`. You can only add annotations to a module that **match the scope** of the component. If you try to use other scope annotations, you'll get a compile-time error. You won't get any errors if you try that now though, because your code doesn't request `PetFinderApi` yet.

`@Singleton` ensures that **only one instance** of `PetFinderApi` exists during the app's lifetime. For a stateless class whose job is to make requests and return responses, that makes sense, especially if it's supposed to work as long as the app lives. Having the `@Singleton` annotation **reveals the intent** of the class. Plus, there are also two important details about OKHttp that you have to consider:

- Each OkHttp instance has its own **thread pool**, which is expensive to create.
- OkHttp has a **request cache** on disk. Different OkHttp instances will have different caches.

Of course, in some cases, it makes sense to have more than one instance of OkHttp. For example, if you need to connect with two APIs, you might have two Retrofit interfaces. If the APIs are different to the point where it doesn't even make sense for them to have a common cache, you might choose to have more than one OKHttp instance. In that case, however, you'd also have to distinguish the bindings with **qualifiers**. In the end, as always, it depends.

As a final note, you might wonder why `ApiModule` is an `object`. Well, it could be a class, or even an abstract class. The thing is, if a module only has `@Provides` and is stateless — as every module should be! — making it an `object` allows Hilt or, more specifically, Dagger, to provide the dependencies without incurring the costs of creating object instances. All this becomes irrelevant if you're using **R8**, because that can turn providers that come from stateless module instances into static ones. Regardless, it's a good practice.

Build and run to make sure everything works. You're done with dependency management... For now. :] In fact, you're almost done with the chapter. There's only one thing missing: tests!

Testing the Network Code

There are a few things you can test at this point:

- The data mappers
- The interceptors

There's no point in testing the API requests, since you'd be testing Retrofit itself, not your app.

You also won't test the data mappers here, as testing an interceptor covers the same testing details and more. That doesn't mean you don't need to test them in a real app, however! Though most of them start as simple builders, some can evolve to have some logic. In fact, the `Enum` mappers already have logic to test if the input can be translated into an `Enum` type.

Anyway, you'll only test `AuthenticationInterceptor`. The package structure in **test** doesn't exist yet. You'll use a nifty Android Studio trick to create the whole thing automatically.

Expand **api.interceptors**, then open **AuthenticationInterceptor.kt**. Place the cursor on the class name and press **Option-Enter** on MacOS or **Alt-Enter** on Windows. On the small context menu that appears, click **Create test**. On the window that opens, choose **JUnit4** as the testing library. Finally, in the second window, choose the **src/test** directory under the **unitTest** package.

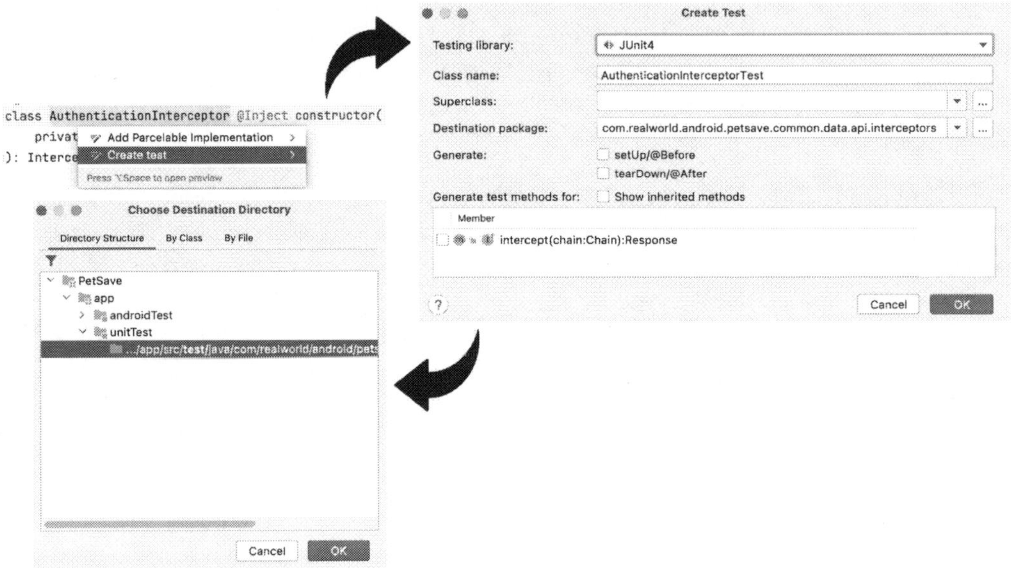

Figure 4.3 — Creating Tests With Android Studio's Help.

Preparing Your Test

You need to create an instance of `AuthenticationInterceptor` for testing. Remember, the constructor requires an instance of `Preferences`. You have three options. You can provide either:

1. A real `Preferences` instance using `PetSavePreferences`.
2. A fake `Preferences` instance.
3. A mock `Preferences` instance.

Providing a real one is out of the question, since you'd mess with the real shared preferences data. So you need to either fake it or mock it.

Fakes are useful whenever you need the dependency to have some sort of complex **state**. If that state varies a lot in your tests, it's much easier to have a fake with a mutating state that you verify as the tests run.

With a mock, you have to define the behavior for each individual test, along with verifying all the calls you expect to happen. For this case, although `Preferences` is stateful — that is, it reads and writes API token info — you'll go with a mock just to see how much work it takes, even for simple states.

To test the interceptor, you'll need to add it to an OKHttp instance. You need a real instance to enqueue a request and use the interceptor on it. Connecting to a real API would make the test slow and flaky, so you'll use **MockWebServer** to mock out the API.

Using MockWebServer

MockWebServer lets you test your network code *without* connecting to a real server. It creates a local web server that goes through the whole HTTP stack. You can use it like any other mocking framework and actually mock server responses.

There's a mock response in **src/debug/assets/networkresponses** that mocks a server response for when you request a new token. It's in the **debug** folder so instrumented tests can also access it in the future.

To access the file, you have to do some configuration work. Open the **app** module's **build.gradle**. Add the following **inside** the `Android` block, just below `buildFeatures`:

```
testOptions {
  unitTests {
    includeAndroidResources = true
  }
}
```

Sync Gradle. Now, your unit tests can access all the resources, assets and manifests. Next, go to the **utils** package inside the **api** test package and open **JsonReader.kt**. You'll use `getJson` in the object to read the mocked response in your test.

As you can see, it needs a `Context`:

```
val context =
InstrumentationRegistry.getInstrumentation().context
```

In other words, your tests will need access to the Android framework. To avoid having to run them on the emulator, you'll use **Robolectric**.

The way to do it is simple. Back in your test class, add the following annotations to the class:

```
@RunWith(RobolectricTestRunner::class)
class AuthenticationInterceptorTest
```

Testing

With that out of the way, you can start testing. In `AuthenticationInterceptorTest`, add the properties you'll need in yout tests.

```
private lateinit var preferences: Preferences
private lateinit var mockWebServer: MockWebServer
private lateinit var authenticationInterceptor:
AuthenticationInterceptor
private lateinit var okHttpClient: OkHttpClient

private val endpointSeparator = "/"
private val animalsEndpointPath =
  endpointSeparator + ApiConstants.ANIMALS_ENDPOINT
private val authEndpointPath =
  endpointSeparator + ApiConstants.AUTH_ENDPOINT
private val validToken = "validToken"
private val expiredToken = "expiredToken"
```

You'll test the **valid token** and **expired token** use cases. For both tests, you need to: Start MockWebServer, mock `Preferences` and create the interceptor and the OkHttp instances. To do so before every test, add the following below the properties:

```
@Before
fun setup() {
  preferences = mock(Preferences::class.java)

  mockWebServer = MockWebServer()
  mockWebServer.start(8080)

  authenticationInterceptor =
    AuthenticationInterceptor(preferences)
  okHttpClient = OkHttpClient().newBuilder()
      .addInterceptor(authenticationInterceptor)
      .build()
}
```

Pretty straightforward. `@Before` ensures that this runs before every test. The method creates the `Preferences` mock, starts MockWebServer on port 8080 and creates the interceptor and OkHttp instances. You also need to close the server at the end of each test, so add the following method as well:

```
@After
fun teardown() {
  mockWebServer.shutdown()
}
```

`@After` is the reverse of `@Before`, making this method run after every test.

Writing Your First Test

For the first test, you'll check the **valid token** use case. Below `teardown`, add:

```
@Test
fun authenticationInterceptor_validToken() {
  // Given

  // When

  // Then
}
```

Having those comments is a neat way of keeping the code inside tests organized.

Replacing // Given

Next, below `// Given`, add:

```
`when`(preferences.getToken()).thenReturn(validToken)
`when`(preferences.getTokenExpirationTime()).thenReturn(
    Instant.now().plusSeconds(3600).epochSecond
)

mockWebServer.dispatcher = getDispatcherForValidToken()
```

The two `when` calls set what the mock should return for this test: A valid token and a time in the future when the token will expire. The last line is more interesting. MockWebServer can take a `Dispatcher` that specifies what to return for each request.

Below your test method, define `getDispatcherForValidToken()`:

```
private fun getDispatcherForValidToken() = object : Dispatcher()
{ // 1
  override fun dispatch(request: RecordedRequest): MockResponse
{
    return when (request.path) {  // 2
      animalsEndpointPath ->
{ MockResponse().setResponseCode(200) } // 3
      else -> { MockResponse().setResponseCode(404) } // 4
    }
  }
}
```

This method:

1. Returns an anonymous MockWebServer `Dispatcher`.
2. Checks for the path the request points to in the `dispatch` method override.
3. If the path is the `/animals` endpoint, the method returns a `200` response code. That's all you need for this test.
4. For any other endpoint, it returns a `404` code which means that the resource is not available.

Replacing // When

Back to the test method, below `// When`, add the OKHttp call:

```
okHttpClient.newCall(
  Request.Builder()
      .url(mockWebServer.url(ApiConstants.ANIMALS_ENDPOINT))
      .build()
).execute()
```

Here, you're telling OkHttp to make a new request. You use MockWebServer to create the URL for it, passing in the `/animals` endpoint.

Replacing // Then

Finally, add the verifications below `// Then`:

```
val request = mockWebServer.takeRequest() // 1

with(request) { // 2
  assertThat(method).isEqualTo("GET")
  assertThat(path).isEqualTo(animalsEndpointPath)
  assertThat(getHeader(ApiParameters.AUTH_HEADER))
      .isEqualTo(ApiParameters.TOKEN_TYPE + validToken)
}
```

If the `assertThat` calls do not automatically resolve, add `import com.google.common.truth.Truth.*` at the top of the file.

This code:

1. Awaits the next HTTP request. For this case, there should only be one request to begin with. This is a **blocking method**, so if anything goes wrong and the request never executes, the code will hang here until it times out.
2. Scopes the `request` and checks a few of the request's parameters. If it's a `GET` request, the path points to the `/animals` endpoint and it has the authorization header, the test passes.

Build and run your test. Everything should work!

Writing Your Second Test

Now, you're ready to write the second test, following the previous format:

```
@Test
fun authenticatorInterceptor_expiredToken() {
  // Given

  // When

  // Then
}
```

Replacing // Given

The `// Given` part is similar:

```
`when`(preferences.getToken()).thenReturn(expiredToken)
`when`(preferences.getTokenExpirationTime()).thenReturn(
    Instant.now().minusSeconds(3600).epochSecond
)

mockWebServer.dispatcher = getDispatcherForExpiredToken()
```

The difference is that `preferences` now returns `expiredToken` and an expired token time. This forces the interceptor to make an authentication request. Also, you're setting `MockWebServer` to a different dispatcher.

Below the other dispatcher method, define `getDispatcherForExpiredToken()` as:

```
private fun getDispatcherForExpiredToken() = object :
Dispatcher() {
  override fun dispatch(request: RecordedRequest): MockResponse
{
    return when (request.path) {
      authEndpointPath -> {

MockResponse().setResponseCode(200).setBody(JsonReader.getJson("
networkresponses/validToken.json"))
      }
      animalsEndpointPath ->
{ MockResponse().setResponseCode(200) }
      else -> { MockResponse().setResponseCode(404) }
    }
  }
}
```

The difference from the other method is this one returns a specific response for the authentication endpoint. Not only does it set the response code to `200`, it also sets the body to the mocked token response. This allows the interceptor to proceed with making a call to the `/animals` endpoint.

Replacing // When

The `// When` part is exactly the same:

```
okHttpClient.newCall(
  Request.Builder()
      .url(mockWebServer.url(ApiConstants.ANIMALS_ENDPOINT))
      .build()
).execute()
```

This is where you're actually sending the request to the `mockWebServer`.

Replacing // Then

The largest change is to the `// Then` part:

```
val tokenRequest = mockWebServer.takeRequest() // 1
val animalsRequest = mockWebServer.takeRequest() // 2

with(tokenRequest) { // 3
  assertThat(method).isEqualTo("POST")
  assertThat(path).isEqualTo(authEndpointPath)
}

val inOrder = inOrder(preferences) // 4

inOrder.verify(preferences).getToken()
inOrder.verify(preferences).putToken(validToken)

verify(preferences, times(1)).getToken() // 5
verify(preferences, times(1)).putToken(validToken)
verify(preferences, times(1)).getTokenExpirationTime()
verify(preferences, times(1)).putTokenExpirationTime(anyLong())
verify(preferences,
times(1)).putTokenType(ApiParameters.TOKEN_TYPE.trim())
verifyNoMoreInteractions(preferences)

with(animalsRequest) { // 6
  assertThat(method).isEqualTo("GET")
  assertThat(path).isEqualTo(animalsEndpointPath)
  assertThat(getHeader(ApiParameters.AUTH_HEADER))
      .isEqualTo(ApiParameters.TOKEN_TYPE + validToken)
}
```

In this code, you:

1. Await the next request. Since `preferences` returns an expired token, the first request coming in should be for a new token.
2. Wait for the next request. If the code works, after the new token request, there should be a request on the `/animals` endpoint.
3. Verify the token request by checking whether it's a `POST` request and if it points to the authentication endpoint.
4. Use Mockito to verify the actions on `preferences`. You check that `getToken` is called **before** `putToken(validToken)`. That should be the normal workflow to invalidate the old token and get a new one.
5. You use `times(1)` to check that each of the `Preferences` you expect to be called is only called **once**. Also, `verifyNoMoreInteractions(preferences)` ensures that **no** methods other than these are called. Note that `putTokenExpirationTime` can be called with **any long** value. The code creates a timestamp at the moment it's called, so trying to get that exact time here could cause the test to fail randomly.
6. Verify the animal request, just as you did in the other test.

If you were to use a fake `Preferences` instance instead of a mock, you'd only need to verify its final state. In the end, all you care about is that your code has the correct **behavior** to produce the correct state.

With Mockito, however, it's easy to get carried away, as in the test above. In no time, you'll be **encoding implementation details** in your tests through Mockito. Imagine that, in the future, the way the interceptor interacts with preferences changes but the end result remains the same. Your tests will fail!

Strive to test behavior and state instead of the implementation itself.

Again, mocks can be useful to mock boundary dependencies or objects you don't own. They just require some discipline to use. In a case like this, a fake would be better. It's more work at the beginning, but it pays off in the long run.

Build and run your tests to make sure everything works. And that's it! You're done with the network code at this point. Now that you can connect to an external data source, you need a way of saving the data you retrieve from it. In the next chapter, you'll dive into caching.

Key Points

- A data layer keeps your data I/O organized and in one place.
- The repository pattern is great for abstracting data sources and providing a clear boundary around the data layer.
- OkHttp's interceptors are useful to fine tune requests.
- When properly configured, dependency injection frameworks do a lot of the heavy lifting of managing dependencies for you.
- MockWebServer allows you to create a test environment that's close to the real thing.

Chapter 5: Data Layer — Caching

By Ricardo Costeira

In this chapter, you'll complete the data layer you started in the previous chapter by adding caching capabilities to it. At the end of the chapter, you'll pull everything together by assembling the repository.

In the process, you'll learn:

- How to cache data.
- Another way of mapping data to the domain layer.
- More about dependency management.
- How to bundle everything in the repository.
- How to test the repository.

You'll do this by working on the **PetSave** app.

Cache Data Models

The models are in the materials for this chapter, but they still need some work. You'll use **Room** to create the caching system. Since Room is an abstraction over **SQLite**, you have to establish the **relationships** between database entities. SQLite is a **relational database** engine, after all.

Start by expanding **common.data.cache.model**. Inside, you'll find two other packages, one for each **domain** entity. This kind of structure didn't exist in the network code because you had to adapt to whatever the server sends. With caching, you have full control over the data.

Look at this entity relationship diagram:

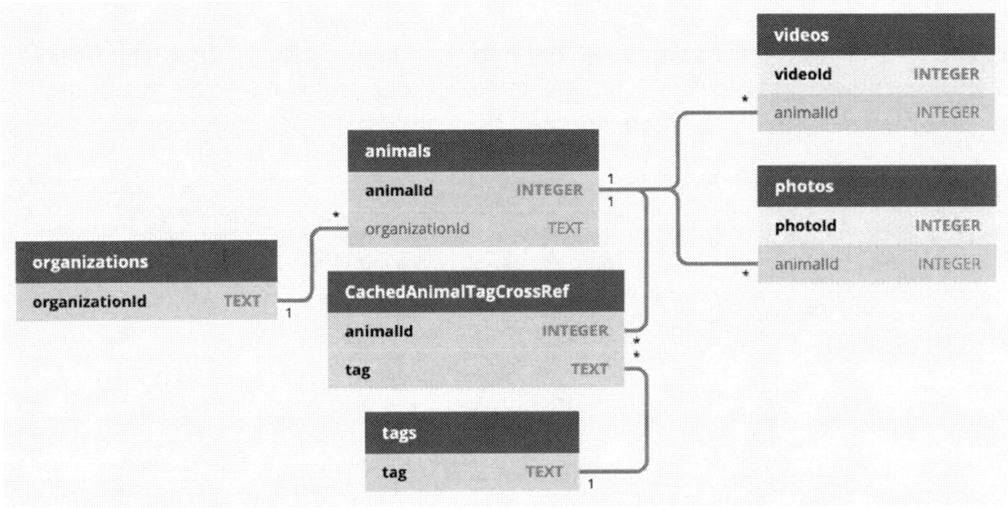

Figure 5.1 — PetSave entity relationship diagram. Made with dbdiagram.io.

Using database jargon:

- **One** organization has **many** animals.
- **One** animal has **many** photos.
- **One** animal has **many** videos.
- **Many** animals have **many** tags.

The **organization to animals** relationship is there for completeness only; you won't implement it.

If you're wondering about the last relationship, it's easy to understand. Tags are attributes of the animal. They include descriptions like "cute", "playful" and "intelligent". So, an animal can have many tags, and a tag can be associated with many animals. Hopefully, more than one animal has the "cute" tag. :]

Expand the **cachedanimal** package. In it, you'll find a few different files that correspond to most of the tables in the diagram above.

Now, open **CachedPhoto.kt**. The `@Entity` annotation specifies the table name, while `@PrimaryKey` defines the **primary key** — which is `photoId`, in this case. Having `autoGenerate = true` as a `@PrimaryKey` parameter tells Room that it might need to generate a new ID for new entries. It checks `photoId`'s value to determine if it needs to do so. If the value is zero, Room treats it as **not set**, creates a new ID and inserts it with the new entry. That's why `photoId` has the default value of zero.

Adding Foreign Keys

Before creating relationships, you need to add the **foreign keys** that allow you to establish them. Complete the `@Entity` above the class with:

```
@Entity(
    tableName = "photos",
    foreignKeys = [
      ForeignKey(
          entity = CachedAnimalWithDetails::class, // 1
          parentColumns = ["animalId"], // 2
          childColumns = ["animalId"], // 3
          onDelete = ForeignKey.CASCADE // 4
      )
    ],
    indices = [Index("animalId")] // 5
)
```

This annotation defines a lot of stuff for you. It:

1. Specifies the entity that the foreign key belongs to: `CachedAnimalWithDetails`, in this case. Although you have `Animal` and `AnimalWithDetails` as domain entities, there's no `CachedAnimal` in the database. Having two sources of truth for the same thing goes against **database normalization**, so you should avoid it.
2. Defines the column that matches the foreign key in the parent table, `CachedAnimalWithDetails`.
3. Defines the column in this table where you find the foreign key.
4. Instructs Room to delete the entity if the parent entity gets deleted.
5. Sets the foreign key as an **indexed** column.

Setting columns as indices is a way for Room to locate data more quickly. Here, you set `animalId` as an index because it's a foreign key. If you don't set a foreign key as an index, changing the parent table might trigger an unneeded **full table scan** on the child table, which slows your app down. Fortunately, Room throws a compile-time warning if you don't index the key.

Having indices speeds up `SELECT` queries. On the other hand, it slows down `INSERT`s and `UPDATE`s. This is nothing to worry about with PetSave, as the app will mostly read from the database.

Setting Up Relationships With Room

Starting on version **2.4**, Room gives you two possible approaches for establishing relationships between entities:

- Using intermediate data classes (already available before 2.4).
- Using **multimap** return types.

Intermediate data classes allow you to be explicit about the relationships between entities through annotations at the expense of, well, having more classes to maintain. What you gain in return is that you avoid having to write complex SQL queries by making your query methods return these intermediate classes.Multimap return types allows your query methods to simply return a mapping of your entities instead of having to create an intermediate data class type for it. The catch here is that the SQL associated with said method will do most of the work.

You can go with whichever option you prefer. Google recommends multimap... so we're going with data classes, not only due to (way) simpler SQL, but also to follow the screaming architecture workflow. It's a lot easier to spot what kind of entities your database can return when you've named your classes properly. Besides, are you even an Android developer if you don't ignore half of Google's recommendations? :]

Setting Up Your One-to-Many Relationships

The `@Entity` annotations in `CachedVideo` and `CachedAnimalWithDetails` already adhere to the diagram in Figure 5.1, which means that everything's ready to set up your one-to-many relationships. To model these with Room, you have to:

1. Create one class for the parent and another for the child entity. You already have these.
2. Create a data class representing the relationship.
3. Have an instance of the parent entity in this data class, annotated with `@Embedded`.
4. Use the `@Relation` annotation to define the list of child entity instances.

The data class that models the relationship already exists. It's called `CachedAnimalAggregate`. You'll use this class later to map cached data into domain data since it holds all the relevant information.

Open **CachedAnimalAggregate.kt** and annotate `photos` and `videos` in the constructor like this:

```
data class CachedAnimalAggregate(
    @Embedded // 1
    val animal: CachedAnimalWithDetails,
    @Relation( // 2
        parentColumn = "animalId",
        entityColumn = "animalId"
    )
    val photos: List<CachedPhoto>,
    @Relation(
        parentColumn = "animalId",
        entityColumn = "animalId"
    )
    val videos: List<CachedVideo>,
    // ...
) {
  // ...
}
```

In this code you used:

1. `@Embedded` for the `animal` property of type `CachedAnimalWithDetails`.
2. `@Relation` for the `photos` and `videos` properties of types `List<CachedPhoto>` and `List<CachedVideo>`, respectively. By specifying the keys of both the parent (CachedAnimalAggregate through the embedded animal property) and the children (photos and videos), Room can use this annotation to handle the relationships for you.

You've now prepared all your one-to-many relationships. But before proceeding, let's talk about multimaps for a second.

So, multimaps allow Room to return a mapping of entities, rather than a custom class that defines the relationship between said entities, at the expense of a more complex SQL query. For instance, imagine that you want all animals that have photos, along with the corresponding photos. You'd have something like:

```
@Query(
  "SELECT * FROM animals " +
  "JOIN photos ON animals.animalId = photos.animalId"
)
abstract fun loadUserAndBookNames():
Map<CachedAnimalWithDetails, List<CachedPhoto>>
```

That's all fine and dandy, but now try to get the same result that `CachedAnimalAggregate` gives you — an animal with (or without) photos, videos and tags — through a multimap. Go ahead, I'll wait. Not that easy, huh?

Multimaps work fine for the simpler cases, but if you find yourself in despair over a multimap with an extremely complex SQL statement, just go with an extra class. Be kind to yourself!

With that out of the way, on to the next relationship you need to handle.

Setting Up the Many-to-Many Relationship

Now, you'll handle the many-to-many relationship, which you need to model a little differently from the one-to-many case. Here, you need to create a:

1. Class for each entity (already done).
2. Third class to **cross-reference** the two entities by their primary keys.
3. Class that models the way you want to query the entities. So, either an animal class with a list of tags, or a tag class with a list of animals.

In this case, you want an animal class with a list of tags. You already have that with `CachedAnimalAggregate`, so add the following above `tags` in the constructor, like this:

```
data class CachedAnimalAggregate(
    // ...
    @Relation( // 1
        parentColumn = "animalId", // 2
        entityColumn = "tag", // 2
        associateBy =
Junction(CachedAnimalTagCrossRef::class) // 3
    )
    val tags: List<CachedTag>
) {
  // ...
}
```

In this code, you:

1. Define a many-to-many relation with `@Relation`.
2. Define the parent and child entities, although they're *not exactly* parent and child. Again, this just defines the way you want to query the entities.
3. Use `associateBy` to create the many-to-many relationship with Room. You set it to a `Junction` that takes the cross-reference class as a parameter. As you can see from the entity relationship diagram, the cross-reference class is `CachedAnimalTagCrossRef`.

You now need to define the cross reference through the `CachedAnimalTagCrossRef` class.

Implementing the Cross-Reference Table

All that's missing now is to deal with the cross-reference table. Open **CachedAnimalTagCrossRef.kt**. You need to annotate the class as a Room entity:

```
@Entity(
    primaryKeys = ["animalId", "tag"], // 1
    indices = [Index("tag")] // 2
)
data class CachedAnimalTagCrossRef(
    val animalId: Long,
    val tag: String
)
```

Two things to note here:

1. You're defining a **composite primary key** with `animalId` and `tag`. So, the primary key of this table is always a combination of the two columns.
2. While primary keys are indexed by default, you're explicitly indexing `tag`, and `tag` only. You need to index both, because you use both to resolve the relationship. Otherwise, Room will complain.

What's happening here?

It has to do with how SQLite works. A query can use a composite index or a subset of that index, as long as the subset matches the original index from the beginning. So in this case, since the index is `(animalId, tag)`, both `(animalId)` and `(animalId, tag)` are valid. If you change the primary key above to `["tag", "animalId"]`, then you'd have to index `animalId` instead of `tag`:

```
@Entity(
    primaryKeys = ["tag", "animalId"], // HERE
    indices = [Index("animalId")]
)
data class CachedAnimalTagCrossRef(
    val animalId: Long,
    val tag: String
)
```

Anyway, you're adding a new Room entity, so you need to inform Room about it. Open **PetSaveDatabase.kt** in the **cache** package. Add `CachedAnimalTagCrossRef` to the list of entities already there:

```
@Database(
    entities = [
      CachedVideo::class,
      CachedTag::class,
      CachedAnimalWithDetails::class,
      CachedOrganization::class,
      CachedAnimalTagCrossRef::class // HERE
    ],
    version = 1
)
abstract class PetSaveDatabase : RoomDatabase()
```

Rebuild your project and run the app. Everything works as expected!

This concludes the work on the models. However, you still need to map them to the domain.

Another Way of Data Mapping

When you worked with the API, you created specialized classes for data mapping. Remember reading about using static or member functions to achieve the same goal? Well, open **CachedPhoto.kt** and look at the companion object:

```
@Entity(tableName = "photos")
data class CachedPhoto(
  // ...
) {
  companion object {
    fun fromDomain( // HERE
        animalId: Long,
        photo: Media.Photo
    ): CachedPhoto {
      val (medium, full) = photo
      return CachedPhoto(
          animalId = animalId,
          medium = medium,
          full = full
      )
    }
  }
  // ...
}
```

In this code, `fromDomain` returns a `CachedPhoto` instance, which it builds from a domain `Photo` and the corresponding `animalId`. It has to be a **companion object function** due to dependencies. To make it a class member function, you'd have to add it to `Photo`, which would make the domain aware of the data layer.

You could also achieve the same result with an **extension function**, as long as it extends `CachedPhoto`. In the end, both options boil down to static functions. The extension function does have the advantage of extending `CachedPhoto`'s behavior without changing the class. However, people like to keep the extension in the same file for convenience.

Picking one or the other in this simple case is mostly a matter of preference. Choosing the companion object means keeping the mapping behavior close to the class. It's a simple class, and its job is to be a DTO, so there's no particular reason to hide the mapping.

Anyway, look below the companion and you'll find `CachedPhoto`'s only function:

```
@Entity(tableName = "photos")
data class CachedPhoto(
  // ...
```

```
) {
  // ...
  fun toDomain(): Media.Photo = Media.Photo(medium, full) //
HERE
}
```

This does the reverse of the other function, creating a domain model out of the cache DTO. Simple. :]

Cache models have `toDomain` and `fromDomain` functions, while API models only have `toDomain`. That's because you won't send anything to the API, so there's no need to translate domain models into API DTOs.

OK, this wraps up model mapping. Time to get yourself some of those sweet SQL statements that everyone loves! The **DAOs** (data access objects) are waiting.

Caching Data With Room

Think back to when you implemented the API interface. You added the API method to meet the data needs for the **Animals near you** feature. Now, it's just a matter of accessing the data. :]

Room uses DAOs to manage data access. Typically, you'll want **one DAO per domain entity** since they're the objects whose identity matters. You already have `OrganizationsDao` but you need to add one for animals.

Create a new file with name **AnimalsDao.kt** in **common.data.cache.daos** and add the following code:

```
@Dao // 1
abstract class AnimalsDao { // 2
  @Transaction // 3
  @Query("SELECT * FROM animals") // 4
  abstract fun getAllAnimals():
Flowable<List<CachedAnimalAggregate>> // 5
}
```

In this code, you:

1. Use `@Dao` to tell Room that this abstraction will define the operations you want to use to access the data in its database.
2. Create `AnimalsDao` as an abstract class because you'll need to add some concrete methods. Room also supports interfaces in case you just need operations that you can specify solely through annotations.

3. Use `@Transaction` to tell Room to run the specific operation in a single transaction. Room uses a buffer for table row data, `CursorWindow`. If a query result is too large, this buffer can overflow, resulting in corrupted data. Using `@Transaction` avoids this. It also ensures you get consistent results when you query different tables for a single result.
4. Define the SQL query to retrieve all the animals with `@Query`.
5. Declare `getAllAnimals()` as the function to invoke to fetch all the animals and their corresponding photos, videos and tags. This operation returns **RxJava**'s `Flowable`. This creates a **stream** that will **infinitely** emit new updates. That way, the UI always has live access to the latest cached data. It returns a list of `CachedAnimalAggregate`, which is the class with all the information you need to produce a domain `AnimalWithDetails`.

When you build the app, Room will create all the code you need to fetch all the animals from the database. Of course, you also need a way to insert the data.

Inserting New Animals

You've now gotten all the animals. To insert new ones, add the following code in **AnimalsDao.kt**:

```
@Dao
abstract class AnimalsDao {
  // ...
  @Insert(onConflict = OnConflictStrategy.REPLACE) // 1
  abstract suspend fun insertAnimalAggregate( // 2
      // 3
      animal: CachedAnimalWithDetails,
      photos: List<CachedPhoto>,
      videos: List<CachedVideo>,
      tags: List<CachedTag>
  )
}
```

In this code:

1. You annotate the method declaration with `@Insert`. This tells Room that it's a database insertion. Setting `onConflict` to `OnConflictStrategy.REPLACE` makes Room replace any rows that match the new ones. There's no `@Transaction` annotation because Room already runs inserts within a transaction.

2. By default, Room won't let you perform I/O operations on the UI thread. If you did, you'd most likely block the thread, which means freezing your app! A great way to avoid this is by using `suspend` functions. Since an insert is a one-shot operation, you don't need anything fancy like **reactive streams**. Plus, using the `suspend` modifier here makes Room run the insert on a background thread.

3. You can't insert `CachedAnimalAggregate` because it's not a Room entity. However, you can decompose it into its `@Entity`-annotated components and pass them into this method. Since they're all Room entities, Room will know how to insert them.

The previous operation allows you to insert a single entity. In practice you usually need to insert many of them. In the next paragraph you'll see how.

Mapping the API Results to the Cache

After parsing the results from the API, you need to map them to the cache. Since you'll get a list of animals from the API, you'll end up with a list of `CachedAnimalAggregate` after the mapping. The last method will handle the decomposing mentioned above.

In the same **AnimalsDao.kt** file, add the following code:

```
@Dao
abstract class AnimalsDao {
  // ...
  suspend fun insertAnimalsWithDetails(animalAggregates:
List<CachedAnimalAggregate>) {
    for (animalAggregate in animalAggregates) {
      insertAnimalAggregate(
          animalAggregate.animal,
          animalAggregate.photos,
          animalAggregate.videos,
          animalAggregate.tags
      )
    }
  }
}
```

Here, the method goes through the list and calls `insertAnimalAggregate` for each one. This is why you're using an abstract class. Although interfaces can also have method implementations, they can be extended. This way, since the method doesn't have the `open` modifier, it's clear that it should not be extended in any way. It's just a matter of better conveying the code's intent.

Each iteration of this method's `for` loop will trigger the `Flowable` from `getAllAnimals`. Worst case, this can cause some **backpressure** in the stream. This isn't a problem — Room's backpressure strategy keeps only the **latest** event, which is what you want in the end. Still, it's something important to be aware of.

You don't need to declare any more methods for now. Open the **PetSaveDatabase.kt** file in the **common.data.cache** package and add the following code:

```
@Database(
  // ...
)
abstract class PetSaveDatabase : RoomDatabase() {
  // ...
  abstract fun animalsDao(): AnimalsDao // HERE
}
```

By adding `animalsDao()`, you tell Room that `AnimalsDao` is also available so it'll provide a way to access it.

Build the app. Go back to `AnimalsDao` now and you'll see that the IDE displays a little green icon on the left, meaning that something implemented the abstract methods.

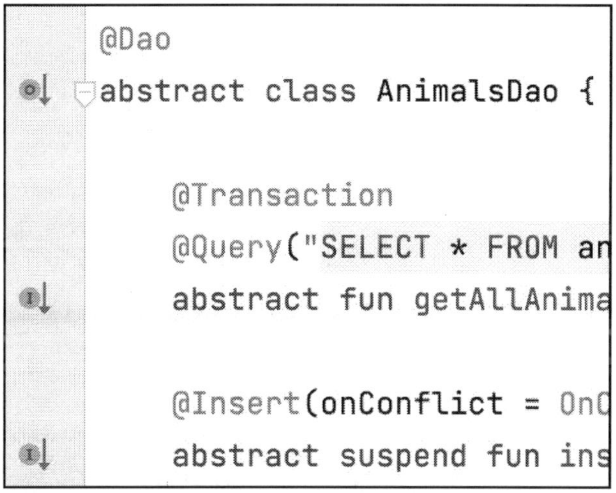

Figure 5.2 — Room Dao implementation

Room automagically did all the hard work for you!

Updating the Cache to Handle the Data

You now need to update the cache implementation to handle animal data. Open **Cache.kt** under **common.data.cache**. This is the interface that exposes the caching methods for the repository to use. In terms of abstraction level, it's on par with `PetFinderApi`. The difference is that you have to implement it manually because Room only creates the lower-level stuff for you.

`Cache` already has code for organizations. The code for animals is the DAO equivalent of the methods you just created.

Add the following code:

```
interface Cache {
  // ...
  fun getNearbyAnimals(): Flowable<List<CachedAnimalAggregate>>
  suspend fun storeNearbyAnimals(animals:
List<CachedAnimalAggregate>)
}
```

Now, open **RoomCache.kt** in the **common.data.cache** package that contains the class that implements `Cache`. Notice how the name is the interface's name prefixed with the mechanism you'll use to handle caching. Always try to name interface implementations based on their purpose and/or functionality. Suffixing interface implementations with `Impl` doesn't give you any information about them.

Next, update its code, like this:

```
class RoomCache @Inject constructor(
    private val animalsDao: AnimalsDao, // 1
    private val organizationsDao: OrganizationsDao
) : Cache {
  // ...
  override fun getNearbyAnimals():
Flowable<List<CachedAnimalAggregate>> { // 2
    return animalsDao.getAllAnimals()
  }

  override suspend fun storeNearbyAnimals(animals:
List<CachedAnimalAggregate>) { // 3
    animalsDao.insertAnimalsWithDetails(animals)
  }
}
```

In this code, you:

1. Add the primary constructor parameter of type `AnimalsDao`.
2. Implement `getNearbyAnimals()`, which delegates the operation to `animalsDao` by invoking `getAllAnimals()` on it.
3. Do the same for `storeNearbyAnimals()`, delegating again to `animalsDao`, but this time invoking `insertAnimalsWithDetails`.

These simply wrap the DAO calls with more domain-friendly names.

And... you're done! Build and run to ensure everything still works.

You just injected an `AnimalsDao` instance. However, you can't annotate abstract classes with `@Inject`. Even if you could, you'd still want Room's implementation of it, and not Hilt's. That said, you don't have a way to provide an instance yet. But not for long!

Managing Cache Dependencies With Hilt

Open **CacheModule.kt** in **common.data.di**. It's already a Dagger module, but it's missing some provider methods:

1. `PetSaveDatabase`
2. `AnimalsDao`
3. `Cache`

You'll work on the methods in that order. Update the code like this:

```
@Module
@InstallIn(SingletonComponent::class)
abstract class CacheModule {

  companion object {

    @Provides
    @Singleton // 1
    fun provideDatabase(
        @ApplicationContext context: Context // 2
    ): PetSaveDatabase {
      return Room.databaseBuilder( // 3
          context,
          PetSaveDatabase::class.java,
          "petsave.db"
      )
```

```
            .build()
    }

    @Provides
    fun provideAnimalsDao(
        petSaveDatabase: PetSaveDatabase
    ): AnimalsDao = petSaveDatabase.animalsDao() // 4
    // ...
  }
}
```

A few different things are happening here:

1. Due to all the SQLite setup, creating a Room database is expensive. Ideally, you create a reference and reuse it, instead. For that reason, you annotate the method with `@Singleton`.
2. This `@ApplicationContext` is another one of Hilt's useful features. You don't need to use Dagger's `@BindsInstance` to provide a `Context` anymore. Instead, you annotate a `Context` with `@ApplicationContext` and Hilt automatically injects it for you. You could also use `@ActivityContext`, but here you want the context for the application because you want the database to have the lifetime of the app itself.
3. You return a Room database instance specifying `PetSaveDatabase`, which is the class type that extends `RoomDatabase`. You then give the database a name which, for consistency, is the same name the app uses.
4. You inject the `PetSaveDatabase` parameter you provide in the previous method, then you use it to call `animalsDao()`. This returns Room's own implementation of the class.

The bindings for the DAOs and the database are in the dependency graph. You need now to add the `Cache`.

Adding the Cache

You'll handle `Cache` a little differently. You want to provide the `Cache` interface type, but you also have to provide the class that implements it, `RoomCache`. This is where Dagger's `@Binds` comes in. In the same **CacheModule.kt** in **common.data.di**, add the following code **outside** the companion object:

```
@Module
@InstallIn(SingletonComponent::class)
abstract class CacheModule {
```

```
    @Binds
    abstract fun bindCache(cache: RoomCache): Cache // HERE

    companion object {
      // ...
    }
  }
```

This allows you to provide the return type, but under the hood, along with whatever you pass in as a parameter. The parameter has to be **assignable** to the return type.

This is why `CacheModule` is an abstract class instead of an `object` like `ApiModule`. You can only apply the `@Binds` annotation to abstract methods, which an `object` can't have. Regardless, by having the `@Provides`-annotated bindings inside the companion, you get the same benefits as if you were using an `object` module.

That's it for cache dependency injection. Following the same pattern you've used so far, the next step would usually be to test the code. In this case, however, you'll skip that and leave it as a challenge you can do to get some extra practice. Now, you'll move on to assembling the repository.

Putting It All Together

At this point, you already have a sense of the data your app needs. You now have to update the repository interface in the **domain layer** accordingly.

It's funny that the data layer actually helps you to figure out the domain layer — but, hey, that's Android for you. It might seem that the domain layer has an implicit dependency on the data layer. This also makes it clearer why some people just prefer to skip the domain layer altogether. In all fairness, you need the data for the features that the domain defines. It can become tricky to understand what depends on what. :]

Anyway, climbing back out of the "Android doesn't need a domain layer" rabbit hole, go to **domain.repositories** and open **AnimalRepository.kt**. Unless I've done a horrible job up to now, you should already expect the repository to provide ways to:

- Get cached data.
- Store cached data.
- Get remote data.

Turning that into code, change `AnimalRepository`, like this:

```
interface AnimalRepository {
  fun getAnimals(): Flowable<List<Animal>> // 1
  suspend fun requestMoreAnimals(pageToLoad: Int, numberOfItems:
Int): PaginatedAnimals // 2
  suspend fun storeAnimals(animals: List<AnimalWithDetails>) //
3
}
```

These should be self-explanatory. The declaration:

1. Returns the `Flowable` that emits when the database updates.
2. Calls the API to get more animals, passing in the page number and how many animals you want. Like the API call, it's a `suspend` function.
3. Stores a list of animals in the database.

Now, the implementation. In **common.data**, create a new file called **PetFinderAnimalRepository.kt**. In it, create `PetFinderAnimalRepository`, like this:

```
class PetFinderAnimalRepository @Inject constructor( // 1
    private val api: PetFinderApi, // 2
    private val cache: Cache,
    private val apiAnimalMapper: ApiAnimalMapper,
    private val apiPaginationMapper: ApiPaginationMapper
) : AnimalRepository
```

Here, you:

1. Annotate the constructor with `@Inject`, both to inject `PetFinderAnimalRepository` when needed and to inject other dependencies into it.
2. Add the dependencies you need to fulfill the interface contract. Since it implements a domain interface, this class defines a boundary between layers. That's why you need those two mappers.

Since you haven't implemented the interface yet, there's a red squiggly line under the class's name. To fix that, place the cursor on the class name and press **Option-Enter** on MacOS or **Alt-Enter** on Windows.

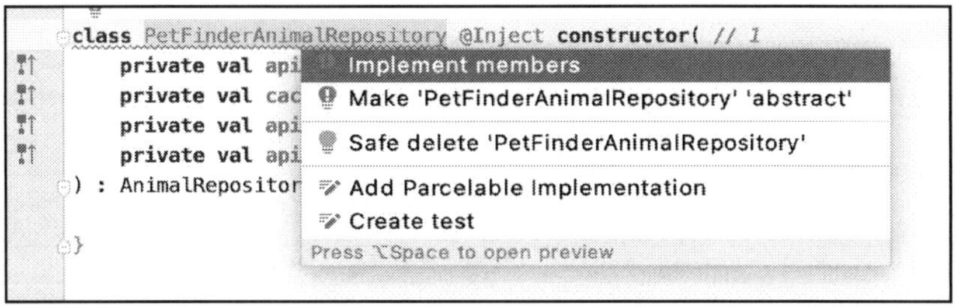

Figure 5.3 — Implement missing members

Choose the **Implement members** option, then select all three in the dialog that opens.

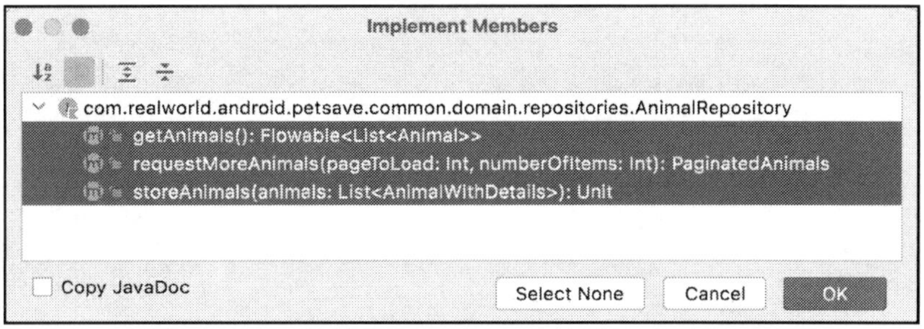

Figure 5.4 — Select all operations

This creates the stubs for the missing classes. They contain some TODOs, but you'll come back to work on them soon.

Returning the Flowable

Going one by one, delete the `TODO` comments in `getAnimals` and add the following in their place:

```
class PetFinderAnimalRepository @Inject constructor(
    private val api: PetFinderApi,
    private val cache: Cache,
    private val apiAnimalMapper: ApiAnimalMapper,
    private val apiPaginationMapper: ApiPaginationMapper
) : AnimalRepository {
  override fun getAnimals(): Flowable<List<Animal>> {
    return cache.getNearbyAnimals() // 1
        .distinctUntilChanged() // 2
        .map { animalList -> // 3
          animalList.map {
            it.animal.toAnimalDomain(
                it.photos,
                it.videos,
                it.tags
            )
          }
        }
  }
  // ...
}
```

This code:

1. Calls the corresponding cache method, which returns a `Flowable`.
2. Calls `distinctUntilChanged` on the stream. This is important because it ensures only events with new information get to the subscriber. For instance, since the insertion abstract method has the `REPLACE` conflict strategy, the same items can get inserted. In general, it's a good practice to use this operator with Room because Room knows *when* a table is modified, but doesn't know *what* was modified. That means, if you're observing only one item, you'll get false updates when *any* table involved in the corresponding SQLite query changes.
3. Maps the `CachedAnimalAggregate` list to the `Animal` list by calling the `toAnimalDomain` mapper for each `CachedAnimalAggregate` instance.

The previous operation returns all the `Animals` in the repository. You need now to implement the other operations.

Calling the API for More Animals

Next, you'll modify `requestMoreAnimals`. Replace the `TODO` with the following code:

```
class PetFinderAnimalRepository @Inject constructor(
    private val api: PetFinderApi,
    private val cache: Cache,
    private val apiAnimalMapper: ApiAnimalMapper,
    private val apiPaginationMapper: ApiPaginationMapper
) : AnimalRepository {
  // ...
  override suspend fun requestMoreAnimals(pageToLoad: Int,
numberOfItems: Int): PaginatedAnimals {
    val (apiAnimals, apiPagination) = api.getNearbyAnimals( // 1
        pageToLoad,
        numberOfItems,
        postcode,
        maxDistanceMiles
    )

    return PaginatedAnimals( // 2
        apiAnimals?.map {
          apiAnimalMapper.mapToDomain(it)
        }.orEmpty(),
        apiPaginationMapper.mapToDomain(apiPagination)
    )
  }

  private val postcode = "07097" // 3
  private val maxDistanceMiles = 100 // 3
  // ...
}
```

Here, you:

1. Call the corresponding API method and **destructure** the resulting `ApiPaginatedAnimals` instance.
2. Build a `PaginatedAnimals` instance with the destructured components, using the mappers in the process.
3. `postcode` and `maxDistanceMiles` don't exist yet. You'll get these later, by using another feature. Right now, you just use temporary values so you can add them as properties.

You're still missing one final operation.

Storing the Animal List in the Database

Finally, you'll handle `storeAnimals`. Add the following code:

```
class PetFinderAnimalRepository @Inject constructor(
    private val api: PetFinderApi,
    private val cache: Cache,
    private val apiAnimalMapper: ApiAnimalMapper,
    private val apiPaginationMapper: ApiPaginationMapper
) : AnimalRepository {
  // ...
  override suspend fun storeAnimals(animals:
List<AnimalWithDetails>) {
    val organizations = animals.map
{ CachedOrganization.fromDomain(it.details.organization) } // 1

    cache.storeOrganizations(organizations)
    cache.storeNearbyAnimals(animals.map
{ CachedAnimalAggregate.fromDomain(it) }) // 2
  }
}
```

Here's what's going on in this code:

1. You map each `Organization` to a `CachedOrganization`, creating a list. Don't forget that organizations have a one-to-many relationship with animals, so you have to insert them **before** inserting animals. Otherwise, Room will complain about not being able to satisfy the foreign key's constraint in `CachedAnimalWithDetails`.
2. After inserting all the organizations, you insert the animals, mapping them to the appropriate type.

That's it! Build and run, and everything should go smoothly. Well, really, it has to. You implemented this data layer code, but so far, no other code is using it — and won't until the next chapter. If only you could *assert* the correctness of your code somehow… You know where this is going. :]

Testing Your Repository

The repository is a great opportunity to venture into **integration tests**. In fact, unit testing wouldn't add anything new to what you've seen so far, so you'll only do integration tests. This means that instead of using fake or mock dependencies, you'll use the real thing! Most of it, at least. :]

Start by creating the test file for `PetFinderAnimalRepository` with Android Studio's aid, just as you did for the interceptor. Only this time, instead of choosing the **test** directory, choose **androidTest**. You'll see why later.

You'll start by testing the integration with the network code. This involves:

- The API itself
- The interceptors
- Preferences

You need to build an instance of the API, using an instance of OkHttpClient that has the interceptors. It, in turn, needs a fake/mock `Preferences`. Plus, you also need a `Cache` instance to create the repository, along with mapper instances.

Ugh. No wonder so many people just skip testing completely! The thing is, those people probably aren't aware of the power a DI framework leverages to make testing a breeze.

Integration Tests With Hilt

Hilt has some built-in features specifically for testing. It requires some configuration in the beginning, but that work pays off later. Your steps are to:

1. Implement a custom `AndroidJUnitRunner` implementation for testing with Hilt.
2. Configure the custom runner for Instrumentation tests.
3. Set up an instrumented test for `PetFinderAnimalRepository`.
4. Prepare the dependency graph for the instrumentation test.
5. Implement `@Before` with code that all the tests have in common.
6. Write your tests.

It's time to have some more fun. :]

Implementing HiltTestRunner

You'll run instrumented tests here, so the first thing to do is tell your **test runner** to run them with an `Application` object that supports Hilt. For this, Hilt provides its own instance, `HiltTestApplication`.

In the **petsave** package of **androidTest**, create a file called **HiltTestRunner.kt**. In it, add:

```
class HiltTestRunner : AndroidJUnitRunner() {

  override fun newApplication(cl: ClassLoader?, name: String?,
context: Context?): Application {
    return super.newApplication(cl,
HiltTestApplication::class.java.name, context)
  }
}
```

Here, you create a test runner that forces the tests to run in `HiltTestApplication`. Now, you need to set your test configuration to use this test runner.

Configuring the HiltTestRunner

You need to tell Gradle to use `HiltTestRunner` when running an instrumentation test. Open **build.gradle** in the **app** module and apply the following changes:

```
// ...
android {
  compileSdkVersion rootProject.ext.compileSdkVersion

  defaultConfig {
    // ...
    testInstrumentationRunner
"com.realworld.android.petsave.HiltTestRunner" // 1
    // ...
  }
  // ...
  sourceSets { // 2
    androidTest {
      assets.srcDirs = ["src/debug/assets"]
    }
  }
}
// ...
```

In this definition, you:

1. Tell Gradle to use `HiltTestRunner` as the `AndroidJUnitRunner` for instrumentation tests.

2. Configure Gradle to reach the assets in the **debug** package, like you did for the unit tests earlier. You'll use MockWebServer for these tests, so you need this code to access the mocked API responses.

Sync Gradle to make sure it accepts the settings. Now, it has all it needs to run the instrumentation test with Hilt. It's time to write the test for `PetFinderAnimalRepository`.

Preparing Your Instrumentation Test

Now, for the fun stuff! Back in **PetFinderAnimalRepositoryTest.kt**, add:

```
@HiltAndroidTest // 1
@UninstallModules(PreferencesModule::class) // 2
class PetFinderAnimalRepositoryTest
```

This code:

1. Marks the test class for injection. This way, Hilt will know it has to inject some dependencies here.
2. Tells Hilt to not load the original `PreferencesModule`, so you can replace it with a test module.

You need to add a few properties to the class now. Inside the same **PetFinderAnimalRepositoryTest.kt**, add:

```
@HiltAndroidTest
@UninstallModules(PreferencesModule::class)
class PetFinderAnimalRepositoryTest {
  private val fakeServer = FakeServer() // 1
  private lateinit var repository: AnimalRepository
  private lateinit var api: PetFinderApi

  @get:Rule // 2
  val hiltRule = HiltAndroidRule(this)

  @Inject // 3
  lateinit var cache: Cache

  @Inject
  lateinit var retrofitBuilder: Retrofit.Builder

  @Inject
  lateinit var apiAnimalMapper: ApiAnimalMapper

  @Inject
  lateinit var apiPaginationMapper: ApiPaginationMapper
}
```

Here, you:

1. Add `AnimalRepository` and `PetFinderApi` properties, which you'll initialize later. You also create something called `FakeServer`. This is a helper class that will handle MockWebServer for you, including reading from the assets.
2. Add a **Hilt rule** that you'll use later to tell Hilt *when* to inject the dependencies. This is important because it gives you leeway to handle any configuration you might need before the injection.
3. Mark every dependency you want to inject with `@Inject` so Hilt knows what you need.

At this point, you're injecting all the dependencies you need to build a `PetFinderAnimalRepository` instance, except for the API. That's because you need to configure the API manually, using the `Retrofit.Builder` you're injecting here.

You'll get to that in a second; there's still one dependency missing. Remember that you told Hilt to ignore `PreferencesModule` through `@UninstallModules`? You need to provide a replacement, or the test won't even build.

Providing the Dependency Graph for Testing

When you implement an instrumentation test with Hilt and want to inject test dependencies, you need to provide a different dependency graph than the one you use in the production app. In your case, you need to replace `PreferencesModule`.

Hilt gives you two options here:

1. Build an entirely new module to replace the original binding.
2. Use a special set of annotations that both replace the original binding and bind anything else in its place.

For now, you'll go with the second option. In the same **PetFinderAnimalRepositoryTest.kt** file add the following code:

Below the other dependencies you just added, add:

```
@HiltAndroidTest
@UninstallModules(PreferencesModule::class)
class PetFinderAnimalRepositoryTest {
  // ...
  @BindValue // 1
  val preferences: Preferences = FakePreferences() // 2
}
```

Going line-by-line:

1. This annotation handles the replacement and injection for you. If you need to need to work with **multibindings**, there are other variants to use, like `@BindValueIntoSet` and `@BindValueIntoMap`.
2. This is what you replace the original binding with. You're providing a fake implementation of `Preferences` that simply has a private map to read and write the properties.

Now, it's time to implement your tests. They'll have some initalization in common. You can handle this in `@Before`.

Implementing the @Before Function

With this done, you can now implement the typical "before and after" test configuration methods. Add `setup` and `teardown` below what you just added:

```
@HiltAndroidTest
@UninstallModules(PreferencesModule::class)
class PetFinderAnimalRepositoryTest {
  // ...
  @Before
  fun setup() {
    fakeServer.start() // 1

    // 2
    preferences.deleteTokenInfo()
    preferences.putToken("validToken")
    preferences.putTokenExpirationTime(
        Instant.now().plusSeconds(3600).epochSecond
    )
    preferences.putTokenType("Bearer")

    hiltRule.inject() // 3

    // 4
    api = retrofitBuilder
        .baseUrl(fakeServer.baseEndpoint)
        .build()
        .create(PetFinderApi::class.java)

    // 5
    repository = PetFinderAnimalRepository(
        api,
        cache,
        apiAnimalMapper,
        apiPaginationMapper
    )
  }
```

```
  @After // 6
  fun teardown() {
    fakeServer.shutdown()
  }
}
```

In this code:

1. You tell the fake server to start itself. This will start the MockWebServer instance.
2. This is a cool thing that Hilt lets you do. Since you already created the instance that will replace the original `Preferences` binding, you can change it. So here, you delete any previous information and add the information you need for the "happy path". You'll only test happy paths. Note that you could also mark the property as a `lateinit var` and initialize it here.
3. You've configured all the dependencies, so you're ready for Hilt to inject them. To do so, you call `inject` on the rule instance.
4. Before creating the repository instance, you still need to configure the API. You need to redirect the calls to MockWebServer instead of the real endpoint, so you take the `Retrofit.Builder` you injected earlier, change its base URL and, finally, create a `PetFinderApi` instance.
5. Lastly, you create the repository instance.
6. This just shuts off the server, like you did in the unit tests.

Finally, you can start writing your tests.

Writing Your Tests

Whew! That took some work, but you're finally able to write your tests. In the same **PetFinderAnimalRepositoryTest.kt** file add the following code:

```
@HiltAndroidTest
@UninstallModules(PreferencesModule::class, CacheModule::class)
class PetFinderAnimalRepositoryTest {
  // ...
  @Test
  fun requestMoreAnimals_success() = runBlocking { // 1
    // Given
    val expectedAnimalId = 124L
    fakeServer.setHappyPathDispatcher() // 2

    // When
    val paginatedAnimals = repository.requestMoreAnimals(1, 100)
// 3
```

```
      // Then
      val animal = paginatedAnimals.animals.first() // 4
      assertThat(animal.id).isEqualTo(expectedAnimalId)
    }
    // ...
}
```

In this code, you use:

1. `runBlocking`, which makes the test run inside a coroutine. You need it because the network request is a `suspend` function.
2. Set MockWebServer to choose the happy path: Return a successful response on the `animals` endpoint.
3. Make the request. MockWebServer doesn't check the request parameters in this case, but in theory, it could.
4. Get the first — and only, since the mocked response only has one in the list — animal, and check if its ID matches the expected value.

> **Note**: Never use `runBlocking` in production code! It completely blocks the thread the coroutine runs on, defeating the purpose of having coroutines in the first place.

This test starts at the repository, goes to the API, works through the interceptors and goes back up again. With Hilt's help, not only can you test the way all the bits and pieces fit together, but you can also make little tweaks here and there to test a wide variety of scenarios.

Now that you've covered the API integration, you'll test how the cache fits into all this. There's one small problem though: You don't want to mess with the real database in your tests!

Using Room's In-Memory Database

Fortunately, Room provides a neat way to work around this: an **in-memory database**. You'll inject that instead of the production database, then use it to test the repository. That's why you're running the tests in **androidTest**: Room needs to run on a device.

First, tell Hilt to remove `CacheModule` by updating `@UninstallModules`:

```
@UninstallModules(PreferencesModule::class, CacheModule::class)
```

Then, remove the `@Inject` annotation from `cache`:

```
private lateinit var cache: Cache
```

Below it, inject `PetSaveDatabase`:

```
@Inject
lateinit var database: PetSaveDatabase
```

Now, to replace `CacheModule`, you'll try the other option. Add a new module below `Preferences`:

```
@Module
@InstallIn(SingletonComponent::class) // 1
object TestCacheModule {

  @Provides
  fun provideRoomDatabase(): PetSaveDatabase { // 2
    return Room.inMemoryDatabaseBuilder(
        InstrumentationRegistry.getInstrumentation().context,
        PetSaveDatabase::class.java
    )
        .allowMainThreadQueries() // 3
        .build()
  }
}
```

In this code, you:

1. Install `TestCacheModule` in the same component as `CacheModule`.
2. Provide a single `PetSaveDatabase` instance, as you don't need any of the other dependencies.
3. Call `allowMainThreadQueries` when building the in-memory database, which lets you ignore the thread where you run the queries in your tests. Please, never do this in production code!

Building the Cache

With the module ready, you can now build your own `Cache` with the test database. In `setup`, between `api` and `repository`, add the line:

```
cache = RoomCache(database.animalsDao(),
database.organizationsDao())
```

And that's it! It's time for an actual test now. You'll test the insertion into the database. To assert the result, you'll use `getAllAnimals` and check if the `Flowable` stream returns anything. Technically, it's almost like doing two tests in one!

Speaking of streams, you want it to emit the new event right away, so you need to ensure that Room executes all its operations instantly. To do this, you have to use a **JUnit rule** that swaps the background executor used by Architecture Components with one that's synchronous. This rule is called **InstantTaskExecutorRule**. Add it below the Hilt rule:

```
@get:Rule
val instantTaskExecutorRule = InstantTaskExecutorRule()
```

With that out of the way, you'll create your test. At the bottom of the class, add:

```
@Test
fun insertAnimals_success() {
  // Given
  val expectedAnimalId = 124L

  runBlocking {
    fakeServer.setHappyPathDispatcher()

    val paginatedAnimals = repository.requestMoreAnimals(1, 100)
// 1
    val animal = paginatedAnimals.animals.first()

    // When
    repository.storeAnimals(listOf(animal)) // 2
  }

  // Then
  val testObserver = repository.getAnimals().test() // 3

  testObserver.assertNoErrors() // 4
  testObserver.assertNotComplete()
  testObserver.assertValue { it.first().id == expectedAnimalId }
}
```

Here's a breakdown of this code:

1. To save you from creating an `Animal` instance, the code uses the mocked data that MockWebServer returns.
2. You store the animal...
3. ... And then subscribe to the `getAnimals` stream. Calling `test()` on it returns a special `TestObserver` that allows you to assess both its state and the stream's.
4. Using the test observer, you assert that there were no errors on the stream and it didn't complete. It's an infinite stream after all. Finally, you call `assertValue` on the observer, which asserts that the stream emitted **one event only**. It also gives you access to event data for you to make sure that it's what you expect.

This test is not completely contained in `runBlocking`, like the previous one. JUnit tests are expected to return `Unit` and that last `testObserver` line returns a type. Having it inside `runBlocking`'s scope would return that type.

Build and run your tests. Congratulations on making sure your different components are well integrated!

This concludes this chapter. In the next chapters, you'll include the presentation layer in your work and, finally, wrap up a basic version of the **Animals near you** and **Search** features.

Key Points

- Room relationships allow you easily manipulate data... after you go through the effort of creating them.
- Dependency injection is helpful, not only with dependency management, but with testing as well.
- Just like MockWebServer, Room's in-memory database allows you to build more robust and realistic tests.

Chapter 6: Building Features — Animals Near You

By Ricardo Costeira

Until now, you focused your efforts on building a solid foundation for **PetSave**. You created the main entities and value objects in your domain layer, and you have a data layer ready to handle and shape data.Now that you've laid that foundation, you'll start building features that people can use. You'll look at the **presentation layer** and set up the app's **user interface**. You'll also visit the domain layer again to create **use cases**.

In this chapter, you'll learn:

- What a presentation layer is.
- How to create a deterministic data flow.
- How to leverage UI Android framework components like `ViewModel`, `Fragment` and `ViewBinding`.
- What defines the state of your app and how to manage state.
- How to build use cases.

By the end of the chapter, you'll have your first feature!

What Is a Presentation Layer?

To create this feature, you'll start by adding a presentation layer. But what, exactly, is that and why do you need it?

The **presentation layer** encapsulates all the code related to the UI, holding all the UI-related components. In other words, this layer deals with framework code.

App UI and UX are typically more prone to change than business logic. That means you'll find yourself changing UI code more often than any other code.

At the same time, UI toolkits are well known for being **hard to test**. In fact, the whole Android framework makes it hard to write tests. That's why you should avoid using it in your business logic code as much as possible.

You can test Android UI with **instrumented tests** and **Espresso**. These tests need to run on a device, which makes them slow compared to unit tests. Plus, they're also flakier, because the code changes more often. In some cases, the framework actually prevents you from being able to test at all!

For those reasons, it's a good idea to make the UI **as dumb as possible**. You should strive to keep any logic unrelated to the UI decoupled from it. It's a good thing you have a domain layer. :]

By keeping all the UI code in the same place, you protect both your business logic and yourself. It lets you test your logic, regardless of the UI. You'll have less of a headache when you try to introduce that new shiny Android UI library in your codebase, because you can do so without messing with the logic — and knowing Android, that's bound to happen!

Working with the presentation layer offers some challenges, however. You'll learn about some of them next.

Lifecycles of UI Components

The presentation layer is both the easiest layer to understand and the hardest to work with.

Android UI components have their own individual **lifecycles**. Picture an `Activity` hosting a `Fragment`. The system can destroy and recreate that `Fragment` multiple times throughout the `Activity`'s lifetime. At the same time, that `Fragment`'s `View` can be destroyed and recreated multiple times while the `Fragment` lives on.

Juggling different lifecycles can be daunting. For instance, imagine that you have a `Fragment` that calls `postDelayed` on a local `Handler`, and you forget to remove the callbacks from the `Handler` in the `Fragment`'s `onDestroy()`. This might cause a **memory leak**, as the garbage collector can't clean up the `Fragment` because something still references it.

In this case, the problem is simple to solve. Other cases, however, can become so complex that it's difficult to even understand what's going on.

State Management

There's also the problem of **state management**, which is the information your app is holding at any given time. Your UI has a given state, which mutates according to user input and other events.

Different parts of that state may or may not affect one other. Depending on your implementation and needs, changes can even happen concurrently, meaning that even simple states can be hard to implement correctly. With time, bad state management leads to maintenance nightmares. Bugs start creeping in from one part of the code when you change something in another part.

Your app's state not only includes the data regarding the business logic but also the **framework component state**. This includes things like the color of a `Button` or the visibility of a `TextView`. These types of intrinsic properties also represent the state.

Making Your Life Easier With Architecture

App development can be challenging. You have the typical software problems to deal with, like state management and increasing complexity. On top of that, you have to worry about the framework. As a developer, you must do everything you can to make development easier and, more importantly, fun! Choosing the right architecture is a great start.

Android has seen a few different architectural patterns throughout the years. The most common patterns are **MVP** (Model-View-Presenter) and **MVVM** (Model-View-ViewModel). The reason for their popularity is simple: They do an excellent job of decoupling the UI from the business logic. Keep the UI dumb, remember?

These patterns help keep your concerns separated and well defined. Still, things can get messy when you start considering state. For instance, presenters in MVP are usually **stateless**. Even if you make them **stateful**, the way the architecture works can make it hard to sync it with the `View`'s state.

MVVM Architecture

MVVM makes this a lot easier, as state management is built into the architecture. The `View` communicates with the `ViewModel` by **subscribing to changes** on its state. This lets you use the `ViewModel` to represent the View's state.

Even so, it can get tricky if the `View` subscribes to a lot of different state properties — especially if those properties depend on each other. It's not hard to imagine an Android `ViewModel` with a few different `StateFlow` instances emitting tightly coupled properties. For instance:

```
class MyViewModel() {

  val isLoading: StateFlow<Boolean>
  val items: StateFlow<List<Item>>
}
```

Handling the properties incorrectly can lead to **impossible states**, like showing a loading `ProgressBar` when you have already have the item list. Plus, as the number of properties increases, so does the complexity.

> **Note**: Keep in mind that using the `ViewModel` Android component doesn't necessarily mean that you're following the MVVM pattern. You can use a `ViewModel` in many other ways. It's not the best component name. :]

MVI Architecture

So, what should you use? You might have heard about the new kid on the block: **MVI** (Model-View-Intent). This pattern enforces a few interesting rules:

- **Immutable state**: You create updated copies of the state, rather than mutating it. This avoids bugs stemming from mutability.
- **One single view state per screen**: A view state can be a data class with all the state's properties, or even a set of sealed classes representing the different possible states. Using sealed classes solves the problem of impossible states.
- **Unidirectional data flow**: Makes your state **deterministic** — which makes testing actually enjoyable!

You won't exactly follow an MVI pattern in this chapter, as you don't need to create reducers and/or intents. Instead, you'll do something simpler, somewhere between MVVM and MVI. The Android community likes to call it a **unidirectional data flow** architecture. In fact, even Google's architecture guide reccomends it now. Here's a high-level view, where the black arrows represent data flow and the open arrow represents inheritance:

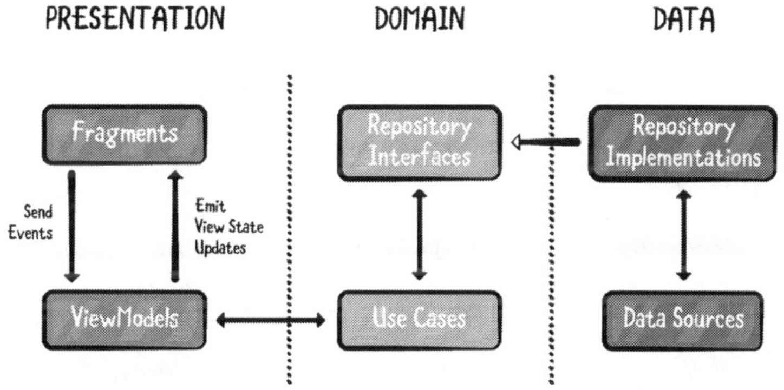

Figure 6.1 — High-Level View of the Architecture

Now, it's time to start coding your new feature!

Building Animals Near You

Make sure you're running the **starter** project, then build and run the app. The bottom navigation bar is there to let you navigate between the screens of the two features.

Figure 6.2 — Petsave Starter App

The bottom navigation bar uses the **Navigation component**, from Android Jetpack Components. Clicking on the bar's icons lets you navigate between screens, although they don't show anything but an infinite spinner at this point.

> **Note**: If you're interested in using the Navigation component with the bottom navigation bar, you can check out **Navigation Component for Android Part 3: Transition and Navigation** here: https://www.raywenderlich.com/8279305-navigation-component-for-android-part-3-transition-and-navigation.

Open **AnimalsNearYouFragment.kt** in the **animalsnearyou.presentation** package. The app uses **view binding** to access view elements. If you don't need two-way data binding or layout variables, view binding is the best choice. It provides the null and type safety that `findViewById` doesn't. It's also easier to use than **data binding** and compiles faster.

As with data binding, there's one thing to remember when using view binding in a `Fragment`: `Fragments` can outlive their `Views`. So you need to **clear up the binding** in the `Fragment`'s `onDestroyView`:

```
override fun onDestroyView() {
  super.onDestroyView()
  _binding = null
}
```

This is why there are two different binding variables. The nullable one sets and destroys the binding, and the non-nullable binding accesses the view elements without the safe call operator, **?.**. Accessing the latter from outside the `View`'s lifecycle will crash the app. If that happens, you're doing something wrong. :]

To set up the UI, you need:

1. A `RecyclerView` for the list.
2. An `Adapter` for the `RecyclerView`.
3. View state and events for state management.
4. Use cases.
5. A `ViewModel` to handle events and update the view state.
6. To observe the view state.

You'll start with the UI components. The XML layouts are ready, so you'll just work on the code.

Creating the UI Components

For your first step, you'll create the UI for your feature in the existing `AnimalsNearYouFragment`.

In **AnimalsNearYouFragment.kt**, add the following code:

```
// 1
override fun onViewCreated(
  view: View,
  savedInstanceState: Bundle?
  ) {
  super.onViewCreated(view, savedInstanceState)

  setupUI()
}

// 2
private fun setupUI() {
  val adapter = createAdapter() // 3
  setupRecyclerView(adapter)
}

private fun createAdapter(): AnimalsAdapter {
  return AnimalsAdapter()
}

// 4
private fun setupRecyclerView(animalsNearYouAdapter:
AnimalsAdapter) {
  binding.animalsRecyclerView.apply {
    adapter = animalsNearYouAdapter
    layoutManager = GridLayoutManager(requireContext(),
ITEMS_PER_ROW)
    setHasFixedSize(true)
  }
}
```

Here's what's happening above:

1. `onViewCreated()` executes immediately after `onCreateView()`. The framework makes sure that you've correctly initialized all `Views` at this point, so you should do all your `View` setup here. For instance, if you use `LiveDatas`, observing them here ensures they're unsubscribed in `onDestroyView()`. By creating the view in `onCreateView()`, then initializing it in `onViewCreated()`, you maintain a good **separation of concerns** (SoC). Plus, you don't need to worry about **null pointer exceptions** (NPEs) on `View` access.

2. Create a method to glue together all the UI setup code. Inside it, you delegate each component's setup to other methods.

3. Create an `adapter` value and initialize it.

4. Run some standard `RecyclerView` code. You set the `Adapter`, a `GridLayoutManager` with two items per row, and tell the `RecyclerView` that all elements have the same size. This way, the `RecyclerView` can skip some measuring steps and perform some optimizations.

There's a good reason why the adapter value only exists in `setupUI()`'s scope. Having an `Adapter` as a property of a `Fragment` is a known way of **leaking** the `RecyclerView`.

That's because, when the `View` is destroyed, the `RecyclerView` is destroyed along with it. But if the `Fragment` references the `Adapter`, the garbage collector won't be able to collect the `RecyclerView` instance because `Adapter` s and `RecyclerViews` have a **circular dependency**. In other words, they reference each other.

Making an Adapter a Property of a Fragment

If you need the `Adapter` as a property of a `Fragment`, don't forget to either:

1. Null out the `Adapter` property in `onDestroyView`.

2. Null out the `Adapter` reference in the `RecyclerView` itself, before doing the same for the binding.

So, if you needed the `Adapter` as a property of the `Fragment` in this code, you'd have something like:

```
override fun onDestroyView() {
  super.onDestroyView()

  // either
  adapter = null

  // or
  binding.recyclerView.adapter = null

  _binding = null
}
```

By the way, `AnimalsAdapter` already exists. It's in the **common.presentation** package because the search screen also uses it.

Open **AnimalsAdapter.kt** and have a look at the code inside. You'll notice that this file contains the definition of a simple adapter, with a single view type. Since the code is so simple, `ViewHolder` is also here as an inner class. If you had more view types and more complex `ViewHolders`, it would be best to decouple them from the adapter for proper SoC.

Defining the UI Model

As you know, `Adapter` is the abstraction Android uses for the object responsible for providing the `View` for each item in a `RecyclerView`. Each `View` is then encapsulated in a `ViewHolder` that's responsible for:

1. Creation of the `View` to recycle for other items of the same type.
2. Binding the data of each item you want to display to the `View` created for that specific time.

To see how this works, examine `AnimalsViewHolder`'s `bind`:

```
fun bind(item: UIAnimal) {
  binding.name.text = item.name
  binding.photo.setImage(item.photo)
}
```

`setImage` is an `ImageView` extension function that internally calls **Glide** to load the picture.

This binding requires a name and a photo, which come from a `UIAnimal`. Like the domain and data layers, the presentation layer also has its own **model**. `UIAnimal` is a simple data class:

```
data class UIAnimal(
    val id: Long,
    val name: String,
    val photo: String
)
```

Remember that you want to keep the UI dumb. Ideally, a UI model will consist of simple primitive types like this one. The model should have only the *minimum necessary* information to do its job — in other words, only enough to satisfy the UI's needs.

Using DiffUtil for AnimalsAdapter

Items in the model can change over time, and so can the RecyclerView that displays them. To minimize the work and make the transition smooth, Android provides a special Adapter: the ListAdapter.

AnimalsAdapter extends ListAdapter, which requires a DiffUtil.ItemCallback. There's an ITEM_COMPARATOR property at the bottom of the file with an anonymous class extending DiffUtil.ItemCallback. It already overrides the areItemsTheSame and areContentsTheSame abstract methods.

For your next step, complete them by replacing their contents with:

```
private val ITEM_COMPARATOR = object :
DiffUtil.ItemCallback<UIAnimal>() {
  override fun areItemsTheSame(oldItem: UIAnimal, newItem:
UIAnimal): Boolean {
    return oldItem.id == newItem.id // 1
  }

  override fun areContentsTheSame(oldItem: UIAnimal, newItem:
UIAnimal): Boolean {
    return oldItem == newItem // 2
  }
}
```

1. This method has the job of checking if oldItem and newItem are the same. That means you have to compare their **identities** and nothing else. If the contents of an item change and you compare them here, the method will return false instead of true — which will cause the item to flicker in the RecyclerView!
2. This method is called only if areItemsTheSame returns true. Here's where you should compare the contents. Since UIAnimal is a data class, using == will compare all of its properties.

Build and run. You'll see the same screen as before because there's no view state yet.

Figure 6.3 — Petsave Starter App

Creating the View State

Now, you need to create a class that stores the current state of your `View`.

To do this, open **AnimalsNearYouViewState.kt** in the **animalsnearyou.presentation** package and add the following code:

```
data class AnimalsNearYouViewState(
    val loading: Boolean = true, // 1
    val animals: List<UIAnimal> = emptyList(), // 2
    val noMoreAnimalsNearby: Boolean = false, // 3
    val failure: Event<Throwable>? = null // 4
)
```

This state is as simple as it gets. It contains:

1. A Boolean representing the **loading state**.
2. A list of items to display.
3. A Boolean representing the **no more animals nearby** state.
4. A value for possible errors. It defaults to `null`, representing the absence of errors.

The default values represent the **initial state**. When you launch the app for the first time, you won't have any items and will need to show a loading screen while you get them.

You want your UI to always have the latest view state. To do so, you use either something like `LiveData` or a reactive stream like `StateFlow` to emit the state for an observer in the UI.

You want this object to survive configuration changes, so you put it in the `ViewModel`. This way, if the configuration changes, you can display the state immediately. Even if you need to update it, at least you're showing something already.

However, there's something to note here: If you're modeling errors as part of the state, you'll display those errors as well! Imagine showing a `Snackbar` at the bottom saying **Something went wrong** every time you flip the phone. I've uninstalled apps for less!

Using `Event` prevents your app from handling the error more than once. You might've seen examples using `SingleLiveEvent` to work around this issue, but it doesn't solve the problem.

Errors are results, or **effects**, that are consequences of specific actions. Therefore, some developers — like me! — prefer to **treat them differently** from the rest of the state. They can happen for a variety of reasons; they might not even relate to the state at all.

Just as you have a stream for your state, you can have a separate stream for your effects. That stream should hold things like errors, navigation, dialogs... anything you want to **consume once**.

A nice way to model this is with a **hot reactive stream**, like a `PublishSubject` or a `SharedFlow`. You emit on it, properly react to it and don't look back.

Now that you understand the theory, you're ready to work on your view state. You need to wire everything up so that the view can observe it.

Creating the Data Flow

You need to make some changes so that your view state works properly. Here's how it should work when you're done:

1. The UI sends **events** to the `ViewModel`.
2. `ViewModel` reacts to those events by triggering the use cases.
3. The use cases return state information.
4. `ViewModel` updates the view state, which the UI observes.

You'll work through these, step-by-step.

Handling Events

Events are **actions** that the UI triggers. What does the UI need when you open the app? A list of animals! That's what you'll work on next.

In **animalsnearyou.presentation**, create a new **AnimalsNearYouEvent.kt** and write a sealed class to represent both the UI events and the event that requests the animals list:

```
sealed class AnimalsNearYouEvent {
  object RequestInitialAnimalsList: AnimalsNearYouEvent()
}
```

Now, create **AnimalsNearYouFragmentViewModel.kt** in the same package. Start by defining the class:

```
class AnimalsNearYouFragmentViewModel constructor(
    private val uiAnimalMapper: UiAnimalMapper, // 1
    private val compositeDisposable: CompositeDisposable // 2
): ViewModel() {

  override fun onCleared() {
    super.onCleared()
    compositeDisposable.clear() // 3
  }
}
```

In this code, you have:

1. A mapper that translates the domain model to the UI model.
2. A `CompositeDisposable` for RxJava. You don't need to inject schedulers because RxJava provides a way to override them all while testing.
3. Something to clear the disposable, which you never want to forget. You don't need to worry about coroutines here; instead, you'll use `viewModelScope`. `ViewModel` will clear them internally.

Exposing the State

Every time you get a new state, you need to update the UI. `StateFlow` is a good choice to do this.

In the same **AnimalsNearYouFragmentViewModel.kt**, add the following code:

```
private val _state = MutableStateFlow(AnimalsNearYouViewState())
// 1
private var currentPage = 0 // 2

val state: StateFlow<AnimalsNearYouViewState> =
_state.asStateFlow() // 3

// 4
fun onEvent(event: AnimalsNearYouEvent) {
  when(event) {
    is AnimalsNearYouEvent.RequestInitialAnimalsList ->
loadAnimals()
  }
}
```

Here's what's going on:

1. You create a private `MutableStateFlow` with the initial state of `AnimalsNearYouViewState`. You'll use this property to update the state, which will be exposed to `AnimalsNearYouFragment` through an immutable `StateFlow`. Unlike `LiveData`, `StateFlow` doesn't benefit from lifecycle-aware behavior, so you'll have to take some extra steps when subscribing to the stream.
2. You need to track the page you're on to request the right data. Knowing the exact page isn't relevant for the UI state — unless it's the last one, but that's why you have `noMoreAnimalsNearby`. This lets you keep this property out of the exposed state.
3. You set `_state` to the immutable `StateFlow` that actually exposes the state.
4. You create the only public method in the `ViewModel`. `AnimalsNearYouFragment` calls this method whenever it has an event to trigger.

Triggering the Initial API Request

Next, you'll use `loadAnimals` to trigger the initial API request for animals. To do this, add this code below `onEvent()`:

```
private fun loadAnimals() {
  if (state.value.animals.isEmpty()) { // 1
    loadNextAnimalPage()
  }
}

private fun loadNextAnimalPage() {
  val errorMessage = "Failed to fetch nearby animals"
  val exceptionHandler =
viewModelScope.createExceptionHandler(errorMessage)
{ onFailure(it) } // 2

  viewModelScope.launch(exceptionHandler) { // 3
    // request more animals!
  }
}
```

Here's what you're doing:

1. The `if` condition checks if the state already has animals. `Fragment` will send the `RequestInitialAnimalsList` event every time it's created. Without this condition, you'd make a request every time the configuration changes. This way, you avoid making unnecessary API requests. If there are no animals, though, you call `loadNextAnimalPage()`.

2. You create a `CoroutineExceptionHandler` through a custom `createExceptionHandler` extension function on `viewModelScope`. It takes in a lambda, which in turn takes a `Throwable`. You call `onFailure()` in the lambda, then pass it that same `Throwable`.

3. You launch a coroutine on `viewModelScope`, passing in the `CoroutineExceptionHandler` to the `launch` extension function.

`CoroutineExceptionHandler` is a global solution for exception handling that will catch exceptions even from child coroutines. It only works if you set it on the **parent** coroutine. It'll ignore exceptions if you set it on a child coroutine.

You only call `CoroutineExceptionHandler` when the parent coroutine has already finished. As such, there's no coroutine to recover from the exception it catches. If you need the coroutine to recover or you need more control over exceptions, go with `try-catch`, which also works with child coroutines.

You can call `CoroutineExceptionHandler` **from any thread**. If you need to access the UI thread in the lambda that you pass to a `CoroutineExceptionHandler`, you have to force it. That's why `createExceptionHandler` is an extension function on `viewModelScope`. This scope runs on the UI thread, so calling `launch` inside the function will run on the UI thread as well.

Handling Errors

Getting back to the code, create `onFailure` below the method above:

```
private fun onFailure(failure: Throwable) {
  when (failure) {
    is NetworkException, // 1
    is NetworkUnavailableException -> {
      _state.update { oldState -> // 2
        oldState.copy(
            loading = false,
            failure = Event(failure) // 3
        )
      }
    }
  }
}
```

Here's what's happening:

1. For now, you're only handling `NetworkException` and `NetworkUnavailableException`. The former is a new exception that avoids having Retrofit code in the presentation layer. Check `requestMoreAnimals` in `PetFinderAnimalRepository` and you'll see that it throws a `NetworkException` — a domain exception — when Retrofit's `HttpException` occurs.

2. You update the state by calling `update` on the `MutableStateFlow`. This method is **thread-safe**, meaning that it's OK if multiple events come in at the same time and try to change the state. The `update` method has a lambda as a parameter, which in turn reveives an object of type `AnimalsNearYouViewState` as a parameter, only to return another instance of the same type. You can see where this is going, right? The lambda receives the old state as a parameter, and whatever it returns will become the new state. Notice that you're not mutating the old state, but rather replacing it with an updated copy of itself. Data classes implement this `copy` method, which really comes in handy here.

3. Again, you use `Event` to wrap `Throwable` so the UI reacts to it only once.

You'll add more code here later. But first, you need to implement the logic to fetch the animals.

Your First Use Case

Use cases keep your app's logic well-separated and testable. Each use case will be a class. The use case you're about to create belongs in the app's domain, but only **animals near you** uses it. For that reason, create **RequestNextPageOfAnimals.kt** in **animalsnearyou.domain.usecases** and add the following code:

```
// 1
class RequestNextPageOfAnimals @Inject constructor(
    private val animalRepository: AnimalRepository, // 2
    private val dispatchersProvider: DispatchersProvider // 3
) {

}
```

Here's what's happening:

1. Use case names should be specific, but at the domain level. You can't tell where the data comes from by the name, for instance.
2. You inject an `AnimalRepository`, allowing the use case to access the data sources.
3. You inject a coroutine dispatchers provider. Rule of thumb: Always inject coroutine dispatchers. They help with testing! Injecting it in the use case also helps keep the `ViewModel` simple since it doesn't have to worry about which dispatcher it should run the use case on.

A use case has a purpose, so it makes sense for the class to have only one method. However, using it as `requestNextPageOfAnimals.run()` when your use case already has a good name is just adding noise. It would be a lot cooler to do `requestNextPageOfAnimals()`.

You can do that by overloading the `invoke` operator of the class. Add the following operator to the class:

```
suspend operator fun invoke( // 1
    pageToLoad: Int,
    pageSize: Int = Pagination.DEFAULT_PAGE_SIZE
): Pagination {
  // 2
  return withContext(dispatchersProvider.io()) {
    // 3
    val (animals, pagination) =
        animalRepository.requestMoreAnimals(pageToLoad,
pageSize)
```

```
      // 4
      if (animals.isEmpty()) {
        throw NoMoreAnimalsException("No animals nearby :(")
      }

      animalRepository.storeAnimals(animals) // 5

      return@withContext pagination // 6
    }
  }
```

This code implements pagination. Note that:

1. It's a `suspend` function. Neat!
2. It uses calls `withContext`, which shifts code execution to a background thread — in this case, a thread on the IO dispatcher pool. Note that you don't need this for Room or Retrofit. Room calls an IO dispatcher internally, and Retrofit's `suspend` functions already delegate to a background executor. Still, the code performs some operations before reaching Room and Retrofit, and coroutine context switching is cheap, so you might as well use an IO dispatcher, anyway. Apart from this, `withContext` returns the scope's result, so by calling `return` here you have to make the scope return something of type `Pagination`.
3. You're calling `requestMoreAnimals` on the repository and destructuring its result.
4. If there are no animals, you throw the `NoMoreAnimalsException` exception, which you'll handle in `onFailure`.
5. You call `storeAnimals` to store the animals you got from the API in the database.
6. You return the pagination information that handles paging on the view.

That's it. Plain and simple!

Now that you've created the use case, it's time to use it.

Connecting the Layers

Go back to `AnimalsNearYouFragmentViewModel`. You have to inject the use case before you can use it.

Start by updating the constructor by adding this line above `uiAnimalMapper`:

```
private val requestNextPageOfAnimals: RequestNextPageOfAnimals,
```

Now, you can update `loadNextAnimalPage()`. In `launch`'s scope, add:

```
Logger.d("Requesting more animals.")
val pagination = requestNextPageOfAnimals(++currentPage) // 1

onPaginationInfoObtained(pagination) // 2
```

In this code, you:

1. Call the use case, passing in the current page after incrementing the value.
2. Pass the `pagination` result to `onPaginationInfoObtained`.

That last method doesn't exist yet, so create it below `loadNextAnimalPage`:

```
private fun onPaginationInfoObtained(pagination: Pagination) {
  currentPage = pagination.currentPage
}
```

Although the page should be the same one you asked for, you still update it for good hygiene. Also, don't forget to update `onFailure` by adding this to the `when`:

```
is NoMoreAnimalsException -> {
  _state.update { oldState ->
    oldState.copy(
        noMoreAnimalsNearby = true,
        failure = Event(failure)
    )
  }
}
```

This updates the state to the **no more animals nearby** state.

Triggering the Event

You now need to trigger the event in `AnimalsNearYouFragment`. In `onViewCreated`, below `setupUI`, add:

```
requestInitialAnimalsList()
```

Create the method below `setupRecyclerView`, to keep the code organized:

```
private fun requestInitialAnimalsList() {

viewModel.onEvent(AnimalsNearYouEvent.RequestInitialAnimalsList)
}
```

You don't have a `viewModel` property yet, so add it at the top of `Fragment`, above `binding`:

```
private val viewModel: AnimalsNearYouFragmentViewModel by
viewModels()
```

The `viewModels()` delegate will create the `ViewModel` for you.

Build and run. It crashes! Check Logcat and you'll find an error stating that `AnimalsNearYouFragmentViewModel` doesn't have a zero-argument constructor.

If you were to do things manually, you'd have to create a `ViewModelFactory` which, in turn, would create your `ViewModel`. You'd then pass it as a lambda to the `viewModels` property delegate.

But you don't have to do this manually — instead, you'll use Hilt, which you'll implement next.

Hilt on Android Components

Although you've already done some work with Hilt, you can't inject dependencies yet.

With vanilla Dagger, you'd include the main modules in a main `Component`, then use that `Component` to create the dependency graph.

With Hilt, it's simpler. A *lot* simpler. At the root of the project, locate and open **PetSaveApplication.kt**. Annotate the class:

```
@HiltAndroidApp
```

```
class PetSaveApplication: Application()
```

Done. :]

No main Dagger `Component`, no `AndroidInjector`, `AndroidInjectionModule`, `@ContributesAndroidInjector`, nothing. Just a single annotation!

Build and run — and you'll still get the same runtime exception regarding `AnimalsNearYouFragmentViewModel`. To fix it, go to the class and annotate the constructor:

```
@HiltViewModel
class AnimalsNearYouFragmentViewModel @Inject constructor
```

This `@HiltViewModel` is a Hilt annotation specific to `ViewModel` injection. Using it together with the already known `@Inject` ensures your `ViewModel` instances get injected — you don't need anything else. Yes, no more multibinding for `ViewModel` instances!

Binding the Repository

Build the app again. You'll get a compile-time Hilt error stating that it doesn't know how to inject `AnimalRepository` — which makes sense, since you didn't `@Bind` the interface yet.

Open **ActivityRetainedModule.kt** in **common.di** and replace the comment with:

```
@Binds
@ActivityRetainedScoped
abstract fun bindAnimalRepository(repository:
PetFinderAnimalRepository): AnimalRepository
```

The app follows a **single Activity, multiple Fragments** architecture. You want to retain the repository when you swap `Fragments`. You also want it to survive configuration changes. To enable this, you add the `@ActivityRetainedScoped` annotation to the binding method. It makes `PetFinderAnimalRepository` live as long as the `Activity` and also survive configuration changes. You could also add this annotation to the class itself — the effect would be the same.

I bet you're starting to get the same feeling I had when I first used Hilt: "This seems too easy. When will it blow up in my face?"

Well... It kinda will as soon as you build and run the app. You'll get the `ViewModel` runtime exception again!

While you marked the `ViewModel` for injection, Hilt can't reach it yet. As far as Hilt knows, you're not injecting it into any other component. That's because it doesn't know that `AnimalsNearYouFragment` is a target for injection.

As you might already expect, you can solve the problem with a simple annotation:

```
@AndroidEntryPoint
class AnimalsNearYouFragment : Fragment()
```

This annotation marks Android components for injection. Comparing this to what you had to do with vanilla Dagger, it's pretty cool that you only need a simple annotation now.

Build and run. Yes, it crashes again. But this time, the error is different: **Hilt Fragments must be attached to an @AndroidEntryPoint Activity**.

Easy. Open **MainActivity.kt** in the **common** package and annotate it:

```
@AndroidEntryPoint
class MainActivity : AppCompatActivity()
```

Build and run. No crashes! Check Logcat and you'll see that network requests are happening.

Your next step is to connect to your single source of truth — the database — and display its contents.

Displaying Cute Animals

Before you can make the view observe the data updates, you have to get the stream of data itself. For that purpose, create **GetAnimals.kt** in **animalsnearyou.domain.usecases**. In it, create the following use case:

```
class GetAnimals @Inject constructor(
    private val animalRepository: AnimalRepository
) {

  operator fun invoke() = animalRepository.getAnimals()
      .filter { it.isNotEmpty() }
}
```

You might wonder whether it's worthwhile to have a use case this small. Why not just call the repository in `ViewModel`? Well, while it seems like unneeded complexity, you can look at it as a case of "avoiding broken windows" — that is, inviting more bad behavior.

Say you add the repository to `ViewModel`. It's just a matter of time until other developers use it for other things, instead of creating use cases for whatever they need. With this little bit of overhead, you gain a lot in terms of consistency and code management. In the end, as always, it's a matter of coming to an agreement with your team about how to handle these cases.

Injecting the Use Case

Head back to `AnimalsNearYouFragmentViewModel` and inject the use case in the constructor, just above the other one:

```
private val getAnimals: GetAnimals,
```

You'll use it in a new method, `subscribeToAnimalUpdates`. Create it just below `onEvent()`:

```
private fun subscribeToAnimalUpdates() {
  getAnimals()
      .map { animals -> animals.map
{ uiAnimalMapper.mapToView(it) } } // 1
      .subscribeOn(Schedulers.io()) // 2
      .observeOn(AndroidSchedulers.mainThread()) // 3
      .subscribe(
          { onNewAnimalList(it) }, // 4
          { onFailure(it) }
      )
      .addTo(compositeDisposable) // 5
}
```

Here's what you've done above:

1. You go through the animal list and map each element to its UI counterpart.
2. Room handles the `Flowable` in a background thread for you, but you still have some code (like mapping above and in the repository) between this code and Room. As such, you call `subscribeOn(Schedulers.computation())` to move that work off the main thread.
3. Calling `observeOn(AndroidSchedulers.mainThread())` ensures you access the items on the UI thread. You need to do that to update the UI.

4. You pass each new list to `onNewAnimalList`, which you'll create in a minute. If an error occurs, you pass `Throwable` to the already familiar `onFailure`.
5. Never, ever forget to add the subscription to `CompositeDisposable`. Otherwise, you might leak it.

`onNewAnimalList` will finally update the view state with the list of animals. Create it below `subscribeToAnimalUpdates`:

```
private fun onNewAnimalList(animals: List<UIAnimal>) {
  Logger.d("Got more animals!")

  // 1
  val updatedAnimalSet = (state.value.animals + animals).toSet()

  // 2
  _state.update { oldState ->
    oldState.copy(
        loading = false,
        animals = updatedAnimalSet.toList()
    )
  }
}
```

Step by step:

1. The API returns unordered pages. The item with ID 79 can appear on page 12, while the item with ID 1000 can show up on the first page. Room returns the elements ordered by their IDs. This means that on each update, you can have new elements appearing amid old ones. This will cause some weird UI animations, with items appearing out of nowhere. To work around it, you concatenate the new list to the end of the current one, and convert the whole thing to a `Set`. By definition, sets can't have repeated elements. This way, you'll get a nice animation where new items appear below the old ones. Another possible fix is to locally add something like an `updatedAt` field for each item, and use it to order the list.
2. Update the state with the new item list.

To invoke `subscribeToAnimalUpdates()`, create an `init` block in **AnimalsNearYouFragmentViewModel.kt**, like this:

```
@HiltViewModel
class AnimalsNearYouFragmentViewModel @Inject constructor(
    private val getAnimals: GetAnimals,
    private val requestNextPageOfAnimals:
RequestNextPageOfAnimals,
    private val uiAnimalMapper: UiAnimalMapper,
    private val dispatchersProvider: DispatchersProvider,
    private val compositeDisposable: CompositeDisposable
): ViewModel() {

  init { // HERE
    subscribeToAnimalUpdates()
  }
  // ...
}
```

Build and run to make sure everything's OK.

Observing the State

The last step is to observe the state in the `Fragment`. In `AnimalsNearYouFragment`, add this method below `setupRecyclerView()`:

```
private fun subscribeToViewStateUpdates(adapter: AnimalsAdapter)
{
  viewLifecycleOwner.lifecycleScope.launch { // 1

viewLifecycleOwner.repeatOnLifecycle(Lifecycle.State.STARTED)
{ // 2
      viewModel.state.collect { // 3
        updateScreenState(it, adapter)
      }
    }
  }
}
```

Going step by step:

1. You only care about observing the state while the `Fragment`'s `View` is alive. As such, you call `launch` on `viewLifecycleOwner` so the coroutine gets scoped to the `View`.
2. Since Kotlin Flows don't come with native support to Android component lifecycles, you have to be explicit about how you want to handle it. By using `repeatOnLifecycle`, you can force the coroutine to run when the `View`'s lifecycle is **at least** at the state you pass in as parameter (in this case, `STARTED`), and to get cancelled when the opposite lifecycle event happens (in this case, `ON_STOP`). Not only that, but it'll restart again whenever the `ON_START` event occurs. On a different note, you're telling the coroutine to run when the lifecycle reaches the `STARTED` state because at that point, while the `View` is already laid out and ready, it's still not visible to the user — which makes this a great moment for an update.
3. You call `collect` on the `StateFlow` to receive any state events that it might emit.

Rendering the State

`updateScreenState()` is responsible for rendering the view state. Add it below, along with the related methods:

```
private fun updateScreenState(
  state: AnimalsNearYouViewState,
  adapter: AnimalsAdapter
) {
  // 1
  binding.progressBar.isVisible = state.loading
  adapter.submitList(state.animals)
  handleNoMoreAnimalsNearby(state.noMoreAnimalsNearby)
  handleFailures(state.failure)
}

// 2
private fun handleNoMoreAnimalsNearby(noMoreAnimalsNearby:
Boolean) {

}

// 3
private fun handleFailures(failure: Event<Throwable>?) {
  val unhandledFailure = failure?.getContentIfNotHandled() ?:
return

  val fallbackMessage = getString(R.string.an_error_occurred)
```

```
    val snackbarMessage = if
  (unhandledFailure.message.isNullOrEmpty()) {
      fallbackMessage
    }
    else {
      unhandledFailure.message!! // 4
    }

    if (snackbarMessage.isNotEmpty()) {
      Snackbar.make(requireView(), snackbarMessage,
  Snackbar.LENGTH_SHORT).show()
    }
  }
```

In the code above:

1. You update **every** property of the state. If you don't need to update something, it has no place in the view state.
2. This is a placeholder method. It'll prompt the user to try a different distance or postal code if there aren't any more animals nearby. For the purposes of this chapter, this method isn't worth implementing. Plus, you haven't created the code for distance and postal code selection yet.
3. Handling failures can be complex, involving things like retrying requests or screen navigation. In this case, you're handling every failure the same way: by using a `Snackbar` to display a simple message on the screen. You can also see how `Event` lets you handle each error just once, through its `getContentIfNotHandled()`.
4. Yes, those double bangs are on purpose. Don't be afraid of using them when you want to make sure that nullable values exist. The sooner your app crashes, the sooner you can fix the problem. Of course, don't use them without weighing the consequences. If, for some reason, you can't use tests or don't have a QA team testing the app, be more careful. My late uncle always said: "With great power, comes great responsibility." Just kidding, I never really liked *web* development. :]

Calling the Subscriber

Last, but not least, you need to call `subscribeToViewStateUpdates()`. Add it at the end of `setupUI()`, below the `setupRecyclerView()` call, and pass in the adapter:

```
observeViewStateUpdates(adapter)
```

Build and run. You did it! Look at all those cute animals! Hopefully, you got lucky with the request and got real images instead of the placeholder Glide's using. :]

Figure 6.4 — These Pictures Make Everything Worthwhile!

Great job! You can finally visualize the work you did over the last few chapters. You built the basis for a scalable and maintainable app — you should be proud of yourself.

There's a lot still missing here — and it will continue to be missing, because there isn't enough time to fix everything. For instance, if an animal disappears from the API, you don't have a way of syncing the cache. There also is no refresh mechanism.

You will add one last thing for this feature, though, because it exposes some interesting topics. In the app, scroll to the bottom of the list and you'll notice it doesn't add any more items. You'll fix that next.

Allowing an Infinite Scroll

Paging is a hard problem to solve, but you won't use the Paging library here. It adds a *lot* of complexity, and it's not that compatible with this architecture because you'd need it in every layer. What matters here is the state management aspect of paging, not what you use to implement it.

Instead, you'll use a simple infinite scrolling class, which you'll attach to the `RecyclerView`. You've probably seen **InfiniteScrollListener.kt** in **animalsnearyou.presentation** already. Take a peek if you want; it just checks if `RecyclerView` scrolled close to the last item. Until now, you requested only the first page of animals. With infinite scrolling, you'll start requesting more pages.

Start by adding a new event in `AnimalsNearYouEvent`, right below `RequestInitialAnimalsList`:

```
object RequestMoreAnimals: AnimalsNearYouEvent()
```

Now, switch to `AnimalsNearYouFragment`. Add this method just below `setupRecyclerView()`:

```
private fun createInfiniteScrollListener(
    layoutManager: GridLayoutManager
): RecyclerView.OnScrollListener {
  return object : InfiniteScrollListener(
      layoutManager,
      AnimalsNearYouFragmentViewModel.UI_PAGE_SIZE
  ) {
    override fun loadMoreItems() { requestMoreAnimals() }
    override fun isLoading(): Boolean =
viewModel.isLoadingMoreAnimals
    override fun isLastPage(): Boolean = viewModel.isLastPage
  }
}
```

`isLoading()` and `isLastPage()` both use properties that come from `ViewModel`. These properties don't exist yet. The `loadMoreItems` override calls `requestMoreAnimals()`. This method also doesn't exist yet, but it should be obvious what it does. Add it below:

```
private fun requestMoreAnimals() {
  viewModel.onEvent(AnimalsNearYouEvent.RequestMoreAnimals)
}
```

Then, call `createInfiniteScrollListener()` in `setupRecyclerView()`, below `setHasFixedSize(true)`, like so:

```
addOnScrollListener(createInfiniteScrollListener(layoutManager
as GridLayoutManager))
```

Modifying ViewModel

Now, continue to `ViewModel`. First, you'll create all the properties to get rid of the errors. At the beginning of the class, add:

```
companion object {
  const val UI_PAGE_SIZE = Pagination.DEFAULT_PAGE_SIZE
}
```

This gets the page size limit defined in the domain. Then, just below `state`, add:

```
val isLastPage: Boolean
  get() = state.value.noMoreAnimalsNearby

var isLoadingMoreAnimals: Boolean = false
  private set
```

Finally, react to the event in `onEvent()` by adding this line to `when`:

```
is AnimalsNearYouEvent.RequestMoreAnimals ->
loadNextAnimalPage()
```

You can build, and even run, the app now. In fact, the scrolling already works, although a few details are still missing.

Before dealing with those missing details, however, it's important to talk about why although `isLastPage` derives its value from the domain, the same is not true for `isLoadingMoreAnimals`. In fact, this one has nothing to do with the view state.

That's because `isLoadingMoreAnimals` is an **implementation detail**, since the view doesn't need to know that the loading is ongoing — at least for now. Things would be different if the UI had something like a **Loading more** view type.

Another relevant point here is the use of `isLastPage`, instead of using `viewModel.state.value.noMoreAnimalsNearby` directly. There are two reasons for this:

- You want the `Fragment` to access `viewState` only when collecting it. Try to avoid accessing it in other places or the code might get harder to maintain.
- Notice the different **meaning** that each name conveys. While `noMoreAnimalsNearby` alludes to the domain of the app, `isLastPage` is actually an **implementation detail** of the infinite scroll. It just happens to have the view state as its source.

In the end, it's a trade-off: What you lose by exposing properties other than the view state, you win in code simplicity, intent expression and SoC.

Using the Properties

You don't need to do anything else for `isLastPage` — its custom getter will make sure you always get the most up-to-date value from the view state. However, for `isLoadingMoreAnimals`, you want it to be `true` when you're waiting for the API request to finish and `false` when you have its result. You'll make this happen in `loadNextAnimalPage()`.

Right on top of the method, above `errorMessage`, add:

```
isLoadingMoreAnimals = true
```

And at the end, right after the `onPaginationInfoObtained()` call and still inside the coroutine's scope, add:

```
isLoadingMoreAnimals = false
```

This avoids triggering more requests while another request is running. The infinite scrolling methods run on the UI thread, so there's no risk of concurrency here.

Build and run. Look at the logs and you'll see that the infinite scroll works one request at a time. If you're patient enough, you'll see that it stops loading more items when it reaches the end.

And that's it — you're done with the **Animals near you** feature. Great work! By implementing this feature, you learned the basics of state management.

You won't add any tests in this chapter. In fact, if you try to run the tests in the **androidTest** package now, Hilt will complain about dependencies. That's expected due to the current configuration, as you're not providing every dependency needed. This will be fixed in the next chapter, where you'll also take the development up a notch by implementing a constantly changing state.

Key Points

- Keep the UI as dumb as possible.
- View states represent the state that the user sees.
- UI models should contain the minimum information necessary for display, in the simplest format possible.
- You can handle exception handling in coroutines with a `CoroutineExceptionHandler` or, for more control, with `try-catch` blocks.
- Encapsulate your logic in use cases.
- Inject your dependencies with Hilt, using the Android-specific features it provides.

Chapter 7: Building Features — Search

By Ricardo Costeira

In the previous chapters, you developed the **Animals near you** feature. You built it one layer at a time, with the small exception of the use cases. For the **Search** feature, you'll follow a more dynamic approach, adding code to the layers as you need it.

In this chapter, you'll learn about:

- Handling user-triggered events.
- Reacting to different events and reducing them to the same view state.
- Handling pending requests.
- Testing, and the advantages that this architecture brings to it.

There's a lot of fun ahead!

Building a Search Feature

Your goal now is to create a search function to help potential owners find their perfect pet. Here's a breakdown of how the feature works:

1. The user types the animal's name in the search query.
2. The user can filter the queries by the age and type of animal.
3. The app searches the cache for matching animals.
4. If no animals exist locally, the app sends a request to the **PetFinder** API.
5. The app stores the API result, if it finds one, and shows the search results to the user.

Now, it's time to jump in and start finding pets!

Getting Started

To start, go to the `fragment_search` layout and look around. The whole UI is ready to go: You have a search widget and `Views` to display the **remote search** and **no results** cases.

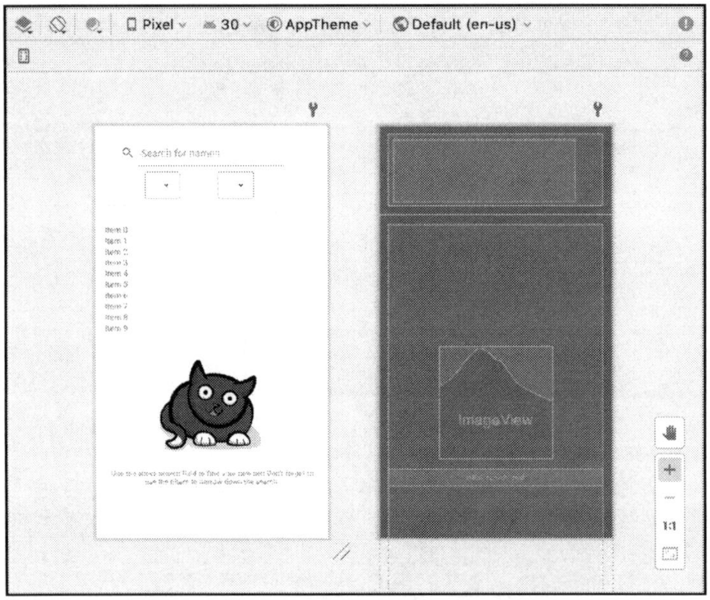

Figure 7.1 — SearchFragment Layout

In the code, notice how every `View` has an ID. As a best practice, you should have IDs for all your `Views`. `Views` can be stateful and the Android system needs those IDs to restore their state when necessary. For instance, if a `ScrollView` doesn't have an ID, the system won't restore its scroll position after a configuration change.

Another thing to keep in mind is that you should strive for unique IDs whenever possible. This applies not only to the layout you're working on, but throughout the whole app. This helps the system search for the correct `View` in the hierarchy tree. Having the same IDs can lead to subtle bugs in cases where you include different layouts under the same `View` hierarchy.

Searching Locally

According to your plan, the app should search for pet names locally before calling on the remote API.

The classes you need to do this already exist. Open **SearchFragment.kt** in the **search.presentation** package. You'll notice that it has a similar basic UI code as **AnimalsNearYouFragment.kt**, in the **animalsnearyou.presentation** package, does.

The app only has these two `Fragments`, so it's not a big deal. With more `Fragments`, it might make sense to extract the common code into a common class or set of functions. Just don't create a `BaseFragment` class. Over time, base classes get polluted with code that only specific child classes use. This creates an implicit coupling between that code and classes that don't use it. It also turns the base class into a spaghetti mess, making maintenance and refactoring harder.

Ideally, you'd delegate the intended behavior through well-defined, single-responsibility classes that `Fragments` can then use through composition.

You need to set up a few things before the user can start interacting with the UI:

- **Search field**: The search field is a `SearchView`. You need to set it up with an `OnQueryTextListener` to react to text changes.

- **Filters**: Both filters are `AutoCompleteTextView` instances. You need to add an `OnItemClickListener` to both, so you can retrieve the selected option.

Every interaction will trigger an event, and each event is sent to the `ViewModel`. You can find the pre-created events in **SearchEvent.kt**:

```
sealed class SearchEvent {
  object PrepareForSearch : SearchEvent()
  data class QueryInput(val input: String): SearchEvent()
  data class AgeValueSelected(val age: String): SearchEvent()
  data class TypeValueSelected(val type: String): SearchEvent()
}
```

Recognizing Text in the Search Field

Your first step is to change the search field so it recognizes when the user types a query. Start by adding the following method in the **SearchFragment.kt**:

```
@AndroidEntryPoint
class SearchFragment : Fragment() {
  // ...
  private fun setupSearchViewListener() {
    val searchView = binding.searchWidget.search

    searchView.setOnQueryTextListener(
        object : SearchView.OnQueryTextListener {
          override fun onQueryTextSubmit(
              query: String?
          ): Boolean {
            viewModel.onEvent(
              SearchEvent.QueryInput(query.orEmpty())  // 1
            )
            searchView.clearFocus()
            return true
          }

          override fun onQueryTextChange(
              newText: String?
          ): Boolean {
            viewModel.onEvent(
              SearchEvent.QueryInput(newText.orEmpty()) // 2
            )
            return true
          }
        }
    )
  }
  // ...
}
```

Be sure to import the **AndroidX** dependency. This method creates and sets `OnQueryTextListener` on `SearchView`. It sends a `SearchEvent.QueryInput` event:

1. With the text you receive as a parameter of the `onQueryTextSubmit()` callback that's invoked when you submit the text in input.
2. With the `String` you get every time the text in input changes and `onQueryTextChange()` is invoked.

Both of the overrides trigger events on the `ViewModel`, updating the search query. The difference between them is that `onQueryTextSubmit` also calls `clearFocus` on the `SearchView`. This hides the soft keyboard when the user taps its **Search** button.

Handling the Search Filters

Next, you need to add the functionality that lets the user filter their results by age and type of animal. To handle the filters, add these methods to the same **SearchFragment.kt**:

```
@AndroidEntryPoint
class SearchFragment : Fragment() {
  // ...
  // 1
  private fun setupFilterListeners() {
    with (binding.searchWidget) {
      setupFilterListenerFor(age) { item ->
        viewModel
          .onEvent(SearchEvent.AgeValueSelected(item)) // 2
      }

      setupFilterListenerFor(type) { item ->
        viewModel
          .onEvent(SearchEvent.TypeValueSelected(item)) // 3
      }
    }
  }

  // 4
  private fun setupFilterListenerFor(
      filter: AutoCompleteTextView,
      block: (item: String) -> Unit
  ) {

    filter.onItemClickListener =
        AdapterView.OnItemClickListener { parent, _, position, _
->
          parent?.let {
            block(it.adapter.getItem(position) as String)
          }
```

```
            }
        }
        // ...
    }
```

This code defines:

1. `setupFilterListeners()` as a utility method that allows you to set up the filter logic for the age and type of animal, passing in a lambda that triggers the `ViewModel` event that updates each filter.
2. The event to trigger when the user selects a new age.
3. The event to trigger when the user selects a new type.
4. `setupFilterListenerFor` as a method that sets the listener on the filters. The listener gets the filter at a given position and passes it into the lambda. The behavior is the same for both filters, so you reuse it.

To call all these methods, update `SearchFragment` like this:

```
@AndroidEntryPoint
class SearchFragment : Fragment() {
  // ...
  private fun prepareForSearch() { // 1
    setupFilterListeners()
    setupSearchViewListener()
    viewModel.onEvent(SearchEvent.PrepareForSearch) // 2
  }

  override fun onViewCreated(view: View, savedInstanceState:
Bundle?) {
    super.onViewCreated(view, savedInstanceState)
    setupUI()
    prepareForSearch() // 3
  }
  // ...
}
```

In this code you:

1. Add `prepareForSearch()` as a convenience method that invokes both `setupFilterListeners()` and `setupSearchViewListener()`.
2. Send the `SearchEvent.PrepareForSearch` event to the `ViewModel`, so it knows when the UI is ready to start searching.
3. Call `prepareForSearch()` when you initialize the UI for `SearchFragment`.

Build and run to make sure you didn't break anything. You haven't handled the events on the `ViewModel` side yet, so you'll see the same incomplete UI as Figure 7.2:

Figure 7.2 — SearchFragment in Action

Dealing With a More Complex State

Before going to the `ViewModel`, open **SearchViewState.kt**. It might not look like it, but this view state is *a lot* more complex than the other one:

```
data class SearchViewState(
    val noSearchQuery: Boolean = true,
    val searchResults: List<UIAnimal> = emptyList(),
    val ageFilterValues: Event<List<String>> =
Event(emptyList()),
    val typeFilterValues: Event<List<String>> =
Event(emptyList()),
    val searchingRemotely: Boolean = false,
    val noRemoteResults: Boolean = false,
    val failure: Event<Throwable>? = null
)
```

The filters are modeled as `Event`'s for performance reasons.

`AutoCompleteTextView` uses an `Adapter` — not the same `Adapter` you used with `RecyclerView` — to display items. The simplest way to update that `Adapter` is to create a new one with the updated data. Once you set the filters, the data they display doesn't change. However, creating a new `Adapter` on each state update is a waste of resources. Using the `Event` wrapper class, you ensure you only create one `Adapter` for each filter.

This feature has a lot of different states. It would get too complex to manage them without losing track of what they mean. That's why `SearchViewState` has a few methods to manage that for you. Each method copies the original state into a new one associated with the method's name.

You could also use sealed classes here, keeping a class for each state. Sealed classes have no `copy` method, though. So in that case, you'd either have to handle the state update itself or apply a **State pattern**.

The methods help give you an idea of the current state, but you can still have impossible state updates like going to a **no remote results** state immediately after a **no search query** state. At this point, the code is still simple enough to catch bugs like this quickly, but you might have to update to sealed classes if the state gets more complicated.

Populating the Filters

Open **SearchFragmentViewModel.kt**. You can see that `onEvent()` already reacts to events, but the methods it calls don't do anything yet. You'll change that now adding `loadFilterValues()` like this:

```
@HiltViewModel
class SearchFragmentViewModel @Inject constructor(
    private val uiAnimalMapper: UiAnimalMapper,
    private val compositeDisposable: CompositeDisposable
) : ViewModel() {
  // ...
  private fun loadFilterValues() {
    // 1
    val exceptionHandler =
        createExceptionHandler(
            message = "Failed to get filter values!"
        )
    viewModelScope.launch(exceptionHandler) {
      val (ages, types) = getSearchFilters() // 2
      updateStateWithFilterValues(ages, types) // 3
    }
```

```
  }
}
```

This code:

1. Creates `CoroutineExceptionHandler` through `createExceptionHandler()`, which you defined in the `ViewModel`.
2. Launches a coroutine in `viewModelScope`. The coroutine calls `getSearchFilters()` in the background. The return value is destructured into `ages` and `types`. `getSearchFilters()` is a use case.
3. Calls `updateStateWithFilterValues()` and passes in the filter values.

Before creating the use case, create `updateStateWithFilterValues()` like this:

```
@HiltViewModel
class SearchFragmentViewModel @Inject constructor(
    private val uiAnimalMapper: UiAnimalMapper,
    private val compositeDisposable: CompositeDisposable
) : ViewModel() {
  // ...
  private fun updateStateWithFilterValues(
      ages: List<String>,
      types: List<String>
  ) {
    _state.update { oldState ->
      oldState.updateToReadyToSearch(ages, types)
    }
  }
}
```

Now that it has the filter data, the UI is ready for the user, so you update the state to **ready to search**.

Updating the Domain With Search

You need to create `getSearchFilters()`, the use case that gets the data to populate the filters.

First, think about what the use case should return. Strings? Animals? According to the use case's name, it should return **search filters**. But the domain layer doesn't know what a search filter is, nor does it have any knowledge about the search.

To change this, go to the **search.domain.model** package and create the **SearchFilters.kt** file with the following code:

```
data class SearchFilters(
    val ages: List<String>,
    val types: List<String>
)
```

Now, create **GetSearchFilters.kt** in the **search.domain.usecases** package and write the use case class, like this:

```
class GetSearchFilters @Inject constructor(
    private val animalRepository: AnimalRepository,
    private val dispatchersProvider: DispatchersProvider
) {

  companion object {
    const val NO_FILTER_SELECTED = "Any"
  }

  suspend operator fun invoke(): SearchFilters {

  }
}
```

The `companion object` property is the default value for both filters. The use case will get both ages and types from the repository. The methods for this already exist. Don't worry, you'll create the whole method chain for the next use case. :]

Getting Data From the Repository

Now, you're going to add the functionality to get the search results from the repository.

Complete `invoke()` with the following code:

```
suspend operator fun invoke(): SearchFilters {
  return withContext(dispatchersProvider.io()) {
    val unknown = Age.UNKNOWN.name

    //1
    val types =
        listOf(NO_FILTER_SELECTED) +
animalRepository.getAnimalTypes()

    // 2
    val ages = animalRepository.getAnimalAges()
        .map { age ->
```

```
        if (age.name == unknown) {
          NO_FILTER_SELECTED
        } else {
          age.name
              .uppercase()
              .replaceFirstChar { firstChar ->
                if (firstChar.isLowerCase()) {
                  firstChar.titlecase(Locale.ROOT)
                } else {
                  firstChar.toString()
                }
              }
        }
      }

    return@withContext SearchFilters(ages, types)
  }
}
```

Here, you:

1. Request the animal types from the repository and add a default value, `Any`, to the head of the type list.
2. Get the ages from the repository, then map the `Enums` to their names, replacing `UNKNOWN` with `Any` and capitalizing the words. After that, you return `SearchFilters` with the ages and types.

The default value will be at the head of the ages list as well. This is due to the order you set the `Enum` values.

> **Note**: It's not advisable to rely on `Enum`'s value order, which can change over time. By doing so, you create a tight coupling between this code and the `Enum`'s implementation.

Head to `SearchFragmentViewModel`. Inject the use case in the constructor:

```
@HiltViewModel
class SearchFragmentViewModel @Inject constructor(
    private val uiAnimalMapper: UiAnimalMapper,
    private val getSearchFilters: GetSearchFilters, // HERE
    private val compositeDisposable: CompositeDisposable
): ViewModel()
```

Finally, in the empty `prepareForSearch()` method of the `VIewModel`, call `loadFilterValues()`:

```
private fun prepareForSearch() {
  loadFilterValues()
}
```

Build and run to make sure everything works. You won't see any differences yet because the `Fragment` isn't observing these changes.

Updating the UI

To update the UI with the filter information, you need to implement two methods. Go to `SearchFragment` and add:

```
@AndroidEntryPoint
class SearchFragment : Fragment() {
  // ...
  // 1
  private fun setupFilterValues(
      filter: AutoCompleteTextView,
      filterValues: List<String>?
  ) {
    if (filterValues == null || filterValues.isEmpty()) return

    filter.setAdapter(createFilterAdapter(filterValues))
    filter.setText(GetSearchFilters.NO_FILTER_SELECTED, false)
  }

  // 2
  private fun createFilterAdapter(
      adapterValues: List<String>
  ): ArrayAdapter<String> {
    return ArrayAdapter(
        requireContext(),
        R.layout.dropdown_menu_popup_item,
        adapterValues
    )
  }
  // ...
}
```

Here's what's going on in this code:

1. You'll use this method for both filters. It returns early if the list is either null or empty — for instance, on the initial state or when the filter content was already handled. It creates the adapter for a given filter and sets the filter to show the default value from the use case. Both filters will have the default value as the first one on the list. However, to avoid relying on the age `Enum`'s value order, it's best to use the default value from the use case instead. Having the `Fragment` access the use case isn't great either, but it's better. A workaround here would be to have the `ViewModel` declare a property for the default value, which it would get from the use case, and have the `Fragment` access that instead.
2. Creates an `ArrayAdapter` that displays a `TextView` for each element, as per the `dropdown_menu_popup_item` layout.

Finally, locate `updateScreenState()`, the method responsible for rendering the state. Update it to call `setupFilterValues()` for both filters, like this:

```
private fun updateScreenState(
    newState: SearchViewState,
    searchAdapter: AnimalsAdapter
) {
  val (
      inInitialState,
      searchResults,
      ageFilterValues,
      typeFilterValues,
      searchingRemotely,
      noResultsState,
      failure
  ) = newState

  updateInitialStateViews(inInitialState)

  with (binding.searchWidget) {
    setupFilterValues(
        age,
        ageFilterValues.getContentIfNotHandled()
    )
    setupFilterValues(
        type,
        typeFilterValues.getContentIfNotHandled()
    )
  }

  handleFailures(failure)
}
```

The view state subscriber already calls `updateScreenState()`, so view state updates will already trigger it.

Build and run. The app now displays the filters with data!

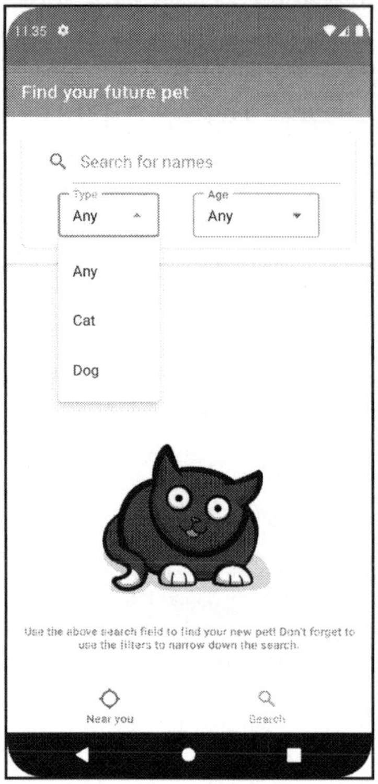

Figure 7.3 — Working Search Filters

Cool. Now you can use this data, along with a search query, to search for animals.

Triggering the Search

Earlier, you set up the search parameters' change events, but the code doesn't react to them yet. You'll change that next.

Open **SearchFragmentViewModel.kt**. At the top of the class is one `BehaviorSubject` for the search query and two others for the age and type filters. You'll use all three of them, merge them into one single `Flowable` and operate on it so it searches the cache. This same `Flowable` will then update the view state.

Locate `onSearchParametersUpdate()` in `SearchFragmentViewModel` and update it to:

```
private fun onSearchParametersUpdate(event: SearchEvent) {
  when (event) {
    is SearchEvent.QueryInput -> updateQuery(event.input)
    is SearchEvent.AgeValueSelected -> updateAgeValue(event.age)
    is SearchEvent.TypeValueSelected ->
updateTypeValue(event.type)
  }
}
```

This method is already called in `onEvent()` and, in turn, calls a different method for each event.

You're probably getting an orange squiggly line under the `when`. You could solve this by having these cases join `PrepareForSearch` in `onEvent`, instead of having them in a separate method. However, bear with it for now — this separation will make sense later.

None of the methods exist, so add them in ´SearchFragmentViewModel`:

```
@HiltViewModel
class SearchFragmentViewModel @Inject constructor(
    private val uiAnimalMapper: UiAnimalMapper,
    private val getSearchFilters: GetSearchFilters,
    private val compositeDisposable: CompositeDisposable
): ViewModel() {
  // ...
  private fun updateQuery(input: String) {
    resetPagination() // 1

    querySubject.onNext(input) // 2

    // 3
    if (input.isEmpty()) {
      setNoSearchQueryState()
    } else {
      setSearchingState()
    }
  }

  // 4
  private fun updateAgeValue(age: String) {
    ageSubject.onNext(age)
  }

  private fun updateTypeValue(type: String) {
    typeSubject.onNext(type)
  }
```

```
    // ...
  }
```

In this code, you:

1. Reset the pagination with each query. The search screen needs infinite scrolling for the cases where the remote results return more than one page. For simplicity, though, some parts of that code were omitted.
2. Send the input to the input's `BehaviorSubject`.
3. Want to show different things on the screen, depending on whether the input is empty or not. The **no search query** state is visually identical to the **ready to search** state. For instance, if you write something on the `SearchView` and then delete it, you want to revert to **no search query**.
4. Send the selected filter values to the corresponding `BehaviorSubjects`.

Build and run. Now, when you type something into the search, the background cat will disappear as you update to the **searching** state.

Tying Everything Together

You now have all the ingredients for the local search. You just need to tie everything together to make the search work.

You'll now create a `SearchAnimals` use case. Just like before, this use case returns a specific domain model: `SearchResults`.

Start by creating the model. In the **search.domain.model** package, create **SearchResults.kt** with the code:

```
data class SearchResults(
    val animals: List<Animal>,
    val searchParameters: SearchParameters
)
```

It's composed of a list of animals and `SearchParameters`, a value object that models the search parameters. You'll use it to search the cache and to propagate the search parameters to a remote search, in case nothing in the cache matches.

Create **SearchParameters.kt** in the same package, with the value object code:

```
data class SearchParameters(
    val name: String,
    val age: String,
```

```
    val type: String
)
```

Finally, in the **search.domain.usecases** package, create **SearchAnimals.kt**. In it, add the code:

```
class SearchAnimals @Inject constructor(
    private val animalRepository: AnimalRepository
) {
  operator fun invoke(
      querySubject: BehaviorSubject<String>,
      ageSubject: BehaviorSubject<String>,
      typeSubject: BehaviorSubject<String>
  ): Flowable<SearchResults> {

  }
}
```

This use case takes in all the `BehaviorSubjects` and outputs a `Flowable` of `SearchResults`. This `Flowable` emits new values every time one of the `BehaviorSubjects` emits something new.

You need to do some work on the streams before you're able to use them. You'll start with the query stream first.

Handling Search Queries

There are a few steps to follow to handle the search queries properly. Update the `invoke` operator method of the use case:

```
operator fun invoke(
    querySubject: BehaviorSubject<String>,
    ageSubject: BehaviorSubject<String>,
    typeSubject: BehaviorSubject<String>
): Flowable<SearchResults> {
  val query = querySubject
      .debounce(500L, TimeUnit.MILLISECONDS) // 1
      .map { it.trim() } // 2
      .filter { it.length >= 2 } // 3
}
```

Here's what's going on above:

1. `debounce` is important because it helps you avoid reacting to every little change in the query. There's no need to react instantly to what a user types when waiting half a second longer might allow you to provide more information. The user won't notice, you'll provide a better service and you'll lighten the load on the device, performance-wise.
2. The user might add unnecessary spaces before or after the query, and the app considers these to be characters. It's best to remove them.
3. This avoids events with a single character or less. Hopefully, there are no animals called Z or something. :]

Removing the Any Value

For the filters, you need to replace the `Any` value with an empty string because you don't want ages or types that match `Any`. The reason for this will become clearer when you implement the cache search method. For now, add these two lines to `invoke`:

```
operator fun invoke(
    querySubject: BehaviorSubject<String>,
    ageSubject: BehaviorSubject<String>,
    typeSubject: BehaviorSubject<String>
): Flowable<SearchResults> {
  val query = querySubject
      .debounce(500L, TimeUnit.MILLISECONDS)
      .map { it.trim() }
      .filter { it.length >= 2 }

  val age = ageSubject.replaceUIEmptyValue() // This
  val type = typeSubject.replaceUIEmptyValue() // And this
}
```

And create the `replaceUIEmptyValue()` private extension function in the use case's scope:

```
class SearchAnimals @Inject constructor(
    private val animalRepository: AnimalRepository
) {
  // ...
  private fun BehaviorSubject<String>.replaceUIEmptyValue() =
map {
    if (it == GetSearchFilters.NO_FILTER_SELECTED) "" else it
  }
  // ...
}
```

This extension function handles the required string replacement. You can now merge the `BehaviorSubjects` and use their joint result to output a `Flowable`.

To do so, you need to add the following property, called `combiningFunction`, to the class. You'll see why in a second:

```
class SearchAnimals @Inject constructor(
    private val animalRepository: AnimalRepository
) {
  // ...
  private val combiningFunction: Function3<String, String,
String, SearchParameters>
    get() = Function3 { query, age, type ->
      SearchParameters(query, age, type)
    }
  //...
}
```

To avoid trouble with `Function3`, add this import at the top:

```
import io.reactivex.functions.Function3
```

Make the final update to `invoke` by adding the return statement:

```
operator fun invoke(
    querySubject: BehaviorSubject<String>,
    ageSubject: BehaviorSubject<String>,
    typeSubject: BehaviorSubject<String>
): Flowable<SearchResults> {
  val query = querySubject
      .debounce(500L, TimeUnit.MILLISECONDS)
      .map { it.trim() }
      .filter { it.length >= 2 }

  val age = ageSubject.replaceUIEmptyValue()
  val type = typeSubject.replaceUIEmptyValue()

  return Observable.combineLatest(query, age, type,
combiningFunction) // 1
    .toFlowable(BackpressureStrategy.LATEST) // 2
    .switchMap { parameters: SearchParameters -> // 3
      animalRepository.searchCachedAnimalsBy(parameters)
    }
}
```

Here's what this does:

1. `combineLatest` joins the **latest** results of each stream, using the combining function. In this case, your combining function is the property you just created. It outputs a `SearchParameters` instance with the values from all the streams. Every time a stream emits something new, `combineLatest` creates an updated `SearchParameters` instance.

2. The `toFlowable` operator transforms the stream into a `Flowable`. You need to do this to wire the stream up to the `Flowable` you'll get from the repository. When you create a `Flowable` with this operator, you need to specify a backpressure strategy. Only the most recently emitted event matters. As such, you create the `Flowable` with `BackpressureStrategy.LATEST`, which discards any previous event it's holding in favor of the new one.

3. `switchMap` discards any old events in favor of new ones. This is exactly what you want for a search. Also, using `switchMap` makes the backpressure definition above unnecessary. Regardless, since you have to specify one anyway, you might as well use the one that fits better. Inside `switchMap`, you call the repository's `searchCachedAnimalsBy()`, passing in the search parameters.

The repository method doesn't exist yet. In fact, none of the needed methods exist, so buckle up: You need to go through the layers and create all the necessary methods.

Adding Search to the Repository

Since you're already calling the repository's method in the use case, it makes sense to start from there. Go to `AnimalRepository` and add the method declaration:

```
interface AnimalRepository {
  // ...
  fun searchCachedAnimalsBy(searchParameters: SearchParameters):
Flowable<SearchResults>
  // ...
}
```

Then, implement it in `PetFinderAnimalRepository`:

```
class PetFinderAnimalRepository @Inject constructor(
    private val api: PetFinderApi,
    private val cache: Cache,
    private val apiAnimalMapper: ApiAnimalMapper,
```

```
    private val apiPaginationMapper: ApiPaginationMapper
) : AnimalRepository {
  // ...
  override fun searchCachedAnimalsBy(
      searchParameters: SearchParameters
  ): Flowable<SearchResults> {
    val (name, age, type) = searchParameters

    return cache.searchAnimalsBy(name, age, type)
        .distinctUntilChanged()
        .map { animalList ->
          animalList.map {
            it.animal.toAnimalDomain(
                it.photos,
                it.videos,
                it.tags
            )
          }
        }
        .map { SearchResults(it, searchParameters) }
  }
  // ...
}
```

This is similar to `getAnimals`, which also returns a `Flowable`. The difference is that there's an extra `map` at the end.

Of course, `searchAnimalsBy()` also doesn't exist yet. Add it to the `Cache` interface:

```
interface Cache {
  // ...
  fun searchAnimalsBy(
      name: String,
      age: String,
      type: String
  ): Flowable<List<CachedAnimalAggregate>>
  // ...
}
```

And implement it in `RoomCache`:

```
class RoomCache @Inject constructor(
    private val animalsDao: AnimalsDao,
    private val organizationsDao: OrganizationsDao
) : Cache {
  // ...
  override fun searchAnimalsBy(
      name: String,
      age: String,
      type: String
  ): Flowable<List<CachedAnimalAggregate>> {
```

```
    return animalsDao.searchAnimalsBy(name, age, type)
  }
  // ...
}
```

Finally, add the most interesting method of them all, in `AnimalsDao`:

```
@Dao
abstract class AnimalsDao {
  // ...
  @Transaction
  @Query("""
      SELECT * FROM animals
        WHERE name LIKE '%' || :name || '%' AND
        AGE LIKE '%' || :age || '%'
        AND type LIKE '%' || :type || '%'
  """)
  abstract fun searchAnimalsBy(
      name: String,
      age: String,
      type: String
  ): Flowable<List<CachedAnimalAggregate>>
  // ...
}
```

This query uses the search parameters to filter the table elements. Using `"""` lets you write multiline statements. SQLite's `LIKE` operator is **case-insensitive**, so you don't need to worry about capitalization. `'%' ||` and `|| '%'` search for the parameters, even if they're prefixed or suffixed with other characters. So for instance, searching by **rce** will return an animal named "Marcel".

Here, you can see why you replaced `Any` with empty strings. Using `LIKE` with an empty string matches every item, so it works as if you're not using any filter at all.

Whew! That's the price you pay for organized layers. The only thing missing now to call the search use case and observe its `Flowable` to see the search results.

Adding Search to the ViewModel

Head back to **SearchFragmentViewModel.kt** and inject the `SearchAnimals` use case in the constructor:

```
@HiltViewModel
class SearchFragmentViewModel @Inject constructor(
    private val uiAnimalMapper: UiAnimalMapper,
    private val searchAnimals: SearchAnimals, // HERE
```

```
    private val getSearchFilters: GetSearchFilters,
    private val compositeDisposable: CompositeDisposable
): ViewModel()
```

Then, update prepareForSearch():

```
private fun prepareForSearch() {
  loadFilterValues()
  setupSearchSubscription() // WITH THIS
}
```

This method is where you'll call the use case. Add it to SearchFragmentViewModel:

```
@HiltViewModel
class SearchFragmentViewModel @Inject constructor(
    private val uiAnimalMapper: UiAnimalMapper,
    private val searchAnimals: SearchAnimals,
    private val getSearchFilters: GetSearchFilters,
    private val compositeDisposable: CompositeDisposable
): ViewModel() {
  // ...
  private fun setupSearchSubscription() {
    searchAnimals(querySubject, ageSubject, typeSubject)
        .observeOn(AndroidSchedulers.mainThread())
        .subscribe(
            { onSearchResults(it) },
            { onFailure(it) }
        )
        .addTo(compositeDisposable)
  }
  // ...
}
```

Nothing new here, but you still need to create onSearchResults(). Add it to SearchFragmentViewModel as well:

```
@HiltViewModel
class SearchFragmentViewModel @Inject constructor(
    private val uiAnimalMapper: UiAnimalMapper,
    private val searchAnimals: SearchAnimals,
    private val getSearchFilters: GetSearchFilters,
    private val compositeDisposable: CompositeDisposable
): ViewModel() {
  // ...
  private fun onSearchResults(searchResults: SearchResults) {
    val (animals, searchParameters) = searchResults

    if (animals.isEmpty()) {
      // search remotely
    } else {
```

```
        onAnimalList(animals)
      }
    }
    // ...
  }
```

This is where you'll decide whether you need to search remotely. You'll do that later. `onAnimalList()` already updates the state with the search results. You now have to update `updateScreenState()` in `SearchFragment` to react to those changes.

To do this, go to **SearchFragment.kt**. Add this line in `updateScreenState()`:

```
@AndroidEntryPoint
class SearchFragment : Fragment() {
  // ...
  private fun updateScreenState(
      newState: SearchViewState,
      searchAdapter: AnimalsAdapter
  ) {
    val (
        inInitialState,
        searchResults,
        ageFilterValues,
        typeFilterValues,
        searchingRemotely,
        noResultsState,
        failure
    ) = newState

    updateInitialStateViews(inInitialState)
    searchAdapter.submitList(searchResults) // HERE

    // ...
  }
  // ...
}
```

Build, run, and try out the search! You'll see some results now, provided you have some animals cached. Check out **Figure 7.4** — no filter on the left, while the results on the right are filtered.

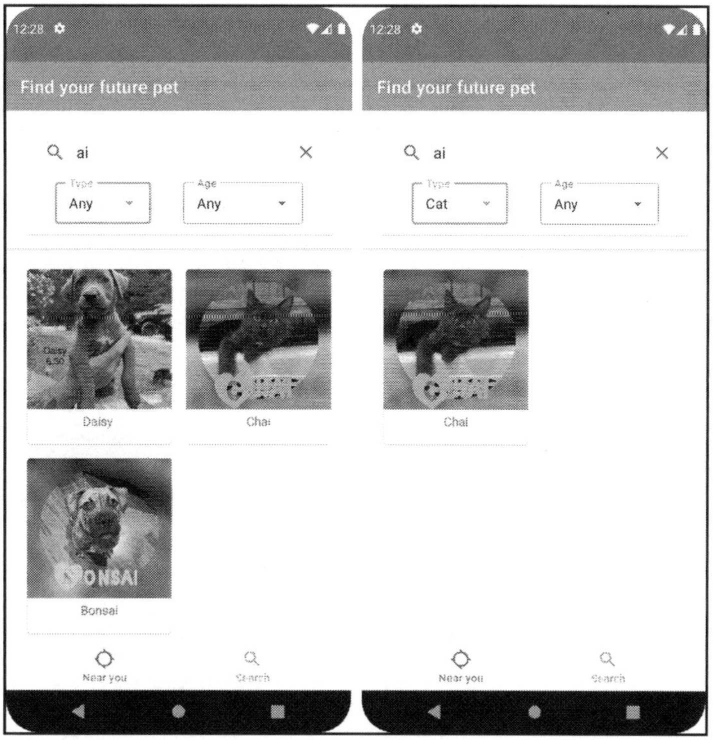

Figure 7.4 — Search Results!

If there aren't any results, the screen will just stay empty. Also, the state doesn't update properly when you display results, change the search parameters and don't get any results for that change.

To fix that, you'll implement remote searching next.

Searching Remotely

Go back to `onSearchResults()` in `SearchFragmentViewModel`. There's an empty `if` inside, reserved to act upon an empty animal list. That's where the remote search will start.

Delete the comment inside the `if` (if any) and add this line in its place:

```
private fun onSearchResults(searchResults: SearchResults) {
  val (animals, searchParameters) = searchResults

  if (animals.isEmpty()) {
    onEmptyCacheResults(searchParameters) // THIS ONE
  } else {
    onAnimalList(animals)
  }
}
```

Then create the method:

```
@HiltViewModel
class SearchFragmentViewModel @Inject constructor(
    private val uiAnimalMapper: UiAnimalMapper,
    private val searchAnimals: SearchAnimals,
    private val getSearchFilters: GetSearchFilters,
    private val compositeDisposable: CompositeDisposable
): ViewModel() {
  // ...
  private fun onEmptyCacheResults(searchParameters:
SearchParameters) {
    _state.update { oldState ->
      oldState.updateToSearchingRemotely()
    }
    searchRemotely(searchParameters)
  }
  // ...
}
```

This method updates the state to **searching remotely**, which shows a `ProgressBar` and a warning message. You still have to update the `Fragment` to see these changes, but you'll leave that for later.

Most of what you need to do now just copies what you've done so far. To reduce repetition, most of the code already exists, you just have to uncomment it.

Locate **SearchAnimalsRemotely.kt** in the **search.domain.usecases** package and uncomment `invoke`.

Then, go to `AnimalRepository` and uncomment the `searchAnimalsRemotely()` declaration.

Finally, go to `PetFinderAnimalRepository` and uncomment the implementation.

The API method already exists, so you don't need to worry about it. It's similar to the **animals near you** method, but with added fields for the search.

Before building and running the app to make sure everything works, you need to wrap up the work on the `ViewModel`.

Triggering the Search API Call

Go back to `SearchFragmentViewModel`. Just like before, inject a `SearchAnimalsRemotely` instance in the constructor:

```
@HiltViewModel
class SearchFragmentViewModel @Inject constructor(
    private val uiAnimalMapper: UiAnimalMapper,
    private val searchAnimalsRemotely: SearchAnimalsRemotely, //
HERE
    private val searchAnimals: SearchAnimals,
    private val getSearchFilters: GetSearchFilters,
    private val compositeDisposable: CompositeDisposable
): ViewModel()
```

Next, create `searchRemotely()`:

```
@HiltViewModel
class SearchFragmentViewModel @Inject constructor(
    private val uiAnimalMapper: UiAnimalMapper,
    private val searchAnimalsRemotely: SearchAnimalsRemotely,
    private val searchAnimals: SearchAnimals,
    private val getSearchFilters: GetSearchFilters,
    private val compositeDisposable: CompositeDisposable
): ViewModel() {
  // ...
  private fun searchRemotely(searchParameters: SearchParameters)
{
    val exceptionHandler = createExceptionHandler(message =
"Failed to search remotely.")

    viewModelScope.launch(exceptionHandler) {
      Logger.d("Searching remotely...")
      val pagination = searchAnimalsRemotely(
          ++currentPage,
          searchParameters
      )
```

```
      onPaginationInfoObtained(pagination)
    }
  }
  // ...
}
```

This is a one-shot operation, as any network operation should be. You have the search results `Flowable` up and running. This operation will store any results in the database, triggering the `Flowable` to display them.

Finally, go to `SearchFragment` and update `updateScreenState()`:

```
  private fun updateScreenState(
      newState: SearchViewState,
      searchAdapter: AnimalsAdapter
  ) {
    val (
        inInitialState,
        searchResults,
        ageFilterValues,
        typeFilterValues,
        searchingRemotely,
        noResultsState,
        failure
    ) = newState

    // ...

    updateRemoteSearchViews(searchingRemotely) // WITH THIS LINE

    handleFailures(failure)
  }
```

You also have to create the method in `SearchFragment`:

```
@AndroidEntryPoint
class SearchFragment : Fragment() {
  // ...
  private fun updateRemoteSearchViews(searchingRemotely:
Boolean) {
    binding.searchRemotelyProgressBar.isVisible =
searchingRemotely
    binding.searchRemotelyText.isVisible = searchingRemotely
  }
  // ...
}
```

Build and run, then try searching for random names. Your remote search now works. :]

Figure 7.5 — Searching Remotely

There's something important to consider regarding remote search: What happens when the user starts a new remote search before the old one is complete? The previous one keeps going!

You won't see this in the UI. Even if you store items that come from an old request, they probably won't pass the search parameters' filtering. However, behind the curtain, you can have the bad luck of a previous request taking longer to finish than a new one. This can mess up the pagination data, for instance. For safety and good hygiene, you should cancel old requests.

Canceling Old Search Requests

When you call `launch` on a `CoroutineScope`, you create a coroutine. `launch` returns a `Job` that represents that coroutine. You'll use this `Job` to control the remote requests.

In `SearchFragmentViewModel`, add:

```
@HiltViewModel
class SearchFragmentViewModel @Inject constructor(
    private val uiAnimalMapper: UiAnimalMapper,
    private val searchAnimalsRemotely: SearchAnimalsRemotely,
    private val searchAnimals: SearchAnimals,
    private val getSearchFilters: GetSearchFilters,
    private val compositeDisposable: CompositeDisposable
): ViewModel() {
  // ...
  private var remoteSearchJob: Job = Job()
  // ...
}
```

You'll set this property to any new job you create for remote search. That said, go to `searchRemotely()` and update the `launch` call to:

```
private fun searchRemotely(searchParameters: SearchParameters) {
  // ...

  remoteSearchJob = viewModelScope.launch(exceptionHandler) { //
THIS
    // ...
  }
}
```

Here, you're getting the job for each coroutine and storing it. But when should you cancel it?

When you change any of the search parameters, you search for a different parameter set. Therefore, `onSearchParametersUpdate()` seems like the best place to cancel the old coroutine.

To implement this, update the method, like so`:

```
private fun onSearchParametersUpdate(event: SearchEvent) {
  remoteSearchJob.cancel( // cancels the job
      CancellationException("New search parameters incoming!")
  )

  when (event) {
```

```
    is SearchEvent.QueryInput -> updateQuery(event.input)
    is SearchEvent.AgeValueSelected -> updateAgeValue(event.age)
    is SearchEvent.TypeValueSelected ->
updateTypeValue(event.type)
  }
}
```

That's why these `SearchEvents` are handled separately by this method, instead of being together with `SearchEvent.PrepareForSearch` in `onEvent`.

Be that as it may, the orange squiggly still persists, as Kotlin will interpret non-exhaustive `whens` as errors in future versions. To fix it without having `PrepareForSearch` here, add an `else` at the end of the `when`:

```
when (event) {
  is SearchEvent.QueryInput -> updateQuery(event.input)
  is SearchEvent.AgeValueSelected -> updateAgeValue(event.age)
  is SearchEvent.TypeValueSelected ->
updateTypeValue(event.type)
  else -> Logger.d("Wrong SearchEvent in
onSearchParametersUpdate!") // HERER
}
```

Build and run. Everything works as before, but how do you know you're canceling the coroutine? An easy way to verify that is to check when the job completes, and why.

Checking That the Coroutine Canceled

Back in `searchRemotely()`, at the bottom of the method and **outside** `launch`'s scope, add:

```
private fun searchRemotely(searchParameters: SearchParameters) {
  // ...

  remoteSearchJob = viewModelScope.launch(exceptionHandler) {
    // ...
  }

  remoteSearchJob.invokeOnCompletion
{ it?.printStackTrace() } // THIS LINE
}
```

Now, build and run. Try changing search parameters while a remote search is running. You'll now see the `CancellationException` above printed in Logcat with that same message!

Another way of knowing if the coroutine was canceled is by checking Logcat for interceptor logs. Retrofit supports coroutine cancellation, so the request gets canceled and logged.

If `SearchAnimalsRemotely` wasn't using Retrofit, nothing in it would check for coroutine cancellation. In this case, since **coroutine cancellation is cooperative**, you'd have to do the check yourself.

For instance, imagine that Retrofit didn't care about coroutine cancellation. In that case, right after a Retrofit call, you'd need something like:

```
if (!coroutineContext.isActive) {
  throw CancellationException(
      "Cancelled - New data was requested"
  )
}
```

Fortunately, Retrofit is a great library and it handles all of this for you!

Finishing Touches

You're almost done. Your search is just missing a state update in the `Fragment`.

`SearchAnimalsRemotely` throws a `NoMoreAnimalsException` when the search has no results. `onFailure()` in `SearchFragmentViewModel` already handles this, updating the state to **no results**.

So go to `SearchFragment` and update it by adding this line to `updateScreenState()`:

```
private fun updateScreenState(
    newState: SearchViewState,
    searchAdapter: AnimalsAdapter
) {
  val (
      inInitialState,
      searchResults,
      ageFilterValues,
      typeFilterValues,
      searchingRemotely,
      noResultsState,
      failure
  ) = newState

  // ...
  updateNoResultsViews(noResultsState)
```

```
}
```

Then, create this method:

```
@AndroidEntryPoint
class SearchFragment : Fragment() {
  // ...
  private fun updateNoResultsViews(noResultsState: Boolean) {
    binding.noSearchResultsImageView.isVisible = noResultsState
    binding.noSearchResultsText.isVisible = noResultsState
  }
  // ...
}
```

Build, run, and search for **qwe**. Hopefully, no one has terrible taste in pet naming. The remote search won't have any results, and you'll see a sad little pug in the background.

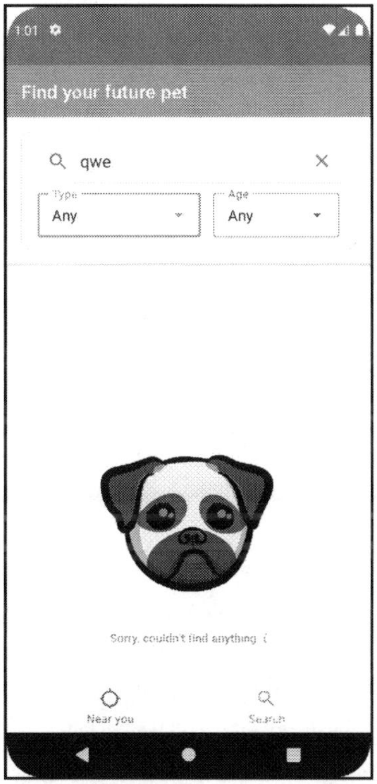

Figure 7.6 — No Results Pug

You're done! To sum up the chapter so far:

- You implemented two new features with cache and network data sources.
- You separated your logic into well-defined and easily testable layers.
- You did all that while following a unidirectional data flow approach.

Of course, even though you did a lot, there are still things missing: Cache invalidation, better error handling, request retries, possibly one or two bugs to solve... Regardless, these changes only require their **essential complexity**, as the overall architecture of the app makes it easier to apply changes and extend behavior.

Now, I don't want to be that guy, but you know that there's still one thing to do before proceeding to the next chapter. Trust me, as you do it more and more in this kind of architecture, you actually start to enjoy it. :]

Testing

To test the presentation layer, you'll use two different kinds of tests. You'll test:

1. The `ViewModel`
2. The UI

You won't test the use cases directly because there's nothing new to learn from that — that would be a simple unit test of a class. You *will* test how the use cases integrate with the `ViewModel`, however.

ViewModel Tests

Thanks to this architecture, testing the `ViewModel` is only a matter of sending events in and getting view states out. It's so clean and straightforward that it's actually enjoyable. Also, since `ViewModel` doesn't require a device to run, you can run the tests on the JVM.

> **Note**: If you want to do full integration tests, like testing the `ViewModel` and use cases along with the real repository using Retrofit and Room, you need to put the tests in the `androidTest` package because Room needs the framework to run.

You'll find **SearchFragmentViewModelTest.kt** in the **test** package, in a directory matching the original `ViewModel`. It has an empty class for now. Before writing any tests, there's something you need to do.

Setting up Your Tests

In the **debug** package, locate **common.data.FakeRepository.kt**. Open it and uncomment everything. As the name suggests, it's a fake `AnimalRepository` implementation to use with tests.

Go back to `SearchFragmentViewModelTest`. Start by adding these rules to the class:

```
class SearchFragmentViewModelTest {
  @get:Rule
  val testCoroutineRule = TestCoroutineRule() // 1

  @get:Rule
  val rxImmediateSchedulerRule = RxImmediateSchedulerRule() // 2
}
```

This code overrides:

1. Coroutine dispatchers, replacing the main dispatcher with a test dispatcher. You need them because the Android UI thread isn't available in JVM tests. This is also one of the reasons why the class needs the `@ExperimentalCoroutinesApi` annotation.
2. RxJava schedulers, setting them all to execute immediately.

`TestCoroutineRule` and `RxImmediateSchedulerRule` are custom rules. Both are defined in the **debug** package, which means tests in both **test** and **androidTest** can use them.

Below the rules, inside `SearchFragmentViewModelTest`, add these properties:

```
private lateinit var viewModel: SearchFragmentViewModel
private lateinit var repository: FakeRepository
private lateinit var getSearchFilters: GetSearchFilters

private val uiAnimalsMapper = UiAnimalMapper()
```

And below them, `setup()`:

```
@Before
fun setup() {
  // 1
  val dispatchersProvider = object : DispatchersProvider {
```

```
      override fun io() = testCoroutineRule.testDispatcher
    }

    // 2
    repository = FakeRepository()
    getSearchFilters = GetSearchFilters(repository)

    viewModel = SearchFragmentViewModel(
        SearchAnimalsRemotely(repository),
        SearchAnimals(repository),
        getSearchFilters,
        uiAnimalsMapper,
        dispatchersProvider,
        CompositeDisposable()
    )
  }
```

Here's what's happening above:

1. This anonymous class implements `DispatchersProvider` by replacing the `IO` dispatcher with the test dispatcher from the coroutine rule.
2. You instantiate the `lateinit` properties.

Now, to the actual test.

Building Your Test

You'll start by testing the case where you do a remote search and get results. Add the method signature:

```
@Test
fun `SearchFragmentViewModel remote search with success`() =
runTest {
  // Given

  // When

  // Then
}
```

You could use `runBlocking` here like you did in other tests, but `runTest` is a coroutine builder designed for tests. It gives you more control over coroutines, like **advancing** the test clock or defining **when to run the coroutines**. It's also the other reason why you need the `@ExperimentalCoroutinesApi` annotation.

Adding the Initial Conditions

Below `// Given`, add the initial conditions:

```
// 1
val (name, age, type) = repository.remotelySearchableAnimal
val (ages, types) = getSearchFilters()

val expectedRemoteAnimals = repository.remoteAnimals.map {
  uiAnimalsMapper.mapToView(it)
}

// 2
val expectedViewState = SearchViewState(
    noSearchQuery = false,
    searchResults = expectedRemoteAnimals,
    ageFilterValues = Event(ages),
    typeFilterValues = Event(types),
    searchingRemotely = false,
    noRemoteResults = false
)
```

1. The fake repository has a few helper properties for testing. Here, you get the name, age and type to use for searching, along with the list of remote animals you expect.
2. At the end of the test, you expect a certain state. Since you're testing for the remote search case, you expect that the view state corresponds to that case.

Triggering the Events to Test

Now, for the `// When`:

```
viewModel.onEvent(SearchEvent.PrepareForSearch)
viewModel.onEvent(SearchEvent.TypeValueSelected(type))
viewModel.onEvent(SearchEvent.AgeValueSelected(age))
viewModel.onEvent(SearchEvent.QueryInput(name))
```

The view state can only reach the **remote search** state after a specific sequence of view state updates. As such, you need to trigger the events on the `ViewModel` that lead to that state.

Checking the Results

Finally, the `// Then`:

```
val viewState = viewModel.state.value

assertThat(viewState).isEqualTo(expectedViewState)
```

So simple, yet so effective. You get the state and compare it to what you expect it to be. You're effectively testing **the whole state of your screen** by doing so.

On a side note, you had to convert `Event` to a data class so it implements `equals()`.

Tests like this make you think about what each state should represent. They'll fail if you mess those states up. Build and run the test to make sure it works.

That's it for the `ViewModel` tests, as every test will follow this same recipe. It's time to test the UI.

UI Tests

Animations affect UI tests, so you need to disable them before testing. Go to your device's developer options. If you don't have developer options, go to the **About** section of the settings and click **Build number** until you unlock them.

Change the animation settings so:

- Window animation scale is off.
- Transition animation scale is off.
- Animation duration scale is off.

See the image below:

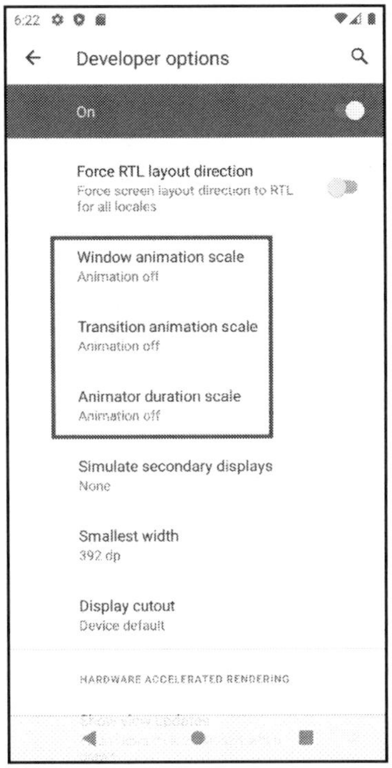

Figure 7.7 — Changing the animation settings.

To create a UI test, the **androidTest** code needs to implement the full DI graph. You might recall that when you finished the previous chapter, you couldn't run tests in this package. This was because Hilt needed the dependencies to inject in `AnimalsNearYouFragmentViewModel`, and you weren't providing them all in tests.

Most of that is now fixed. To wrap it up, go to **common.di.TestActivityRetainedModule.kt** in **androidTest**. This module uses **TestInstallIn** to replace the production bindings in `ActivityRetainedModule`.Inside the abstract class, uncomment `bindAnimalRepository()` and its annotations. This injects the `FakeRepository` instead of the real one.

With that out of the way, go to **search.presentation.SearchFragmentTest.kt**. You'll test a case that's similar to the one before, but from the UI perspective. It'll test the integration of the `Fragment`, `ViewModel` and use cases. It stops testing real code at the `FakeRepository`, but you could easily make it an **end to end** test by uninstalling **TestActivityRetainedModule.kt** instead of **ActivityRetainedModule**, and setting up a fake server with mockWebServer.

Building Your Test

Locate `searchFragment_testSearch_success()`. Below `// Given`, add:

```
val nameToSearch =
    FakeRepository().remotelySearchableAnimal.name
launchFragmentInHiltContainer<SearchFragment>()
```

As in the `ViewModel` test, you get the name of the animal to search. The second line is a lot more interesting though.

When you run tests on `Fragments`, you'd typically use a **FragmentScenario**, which lets you launch your `Fragment` and control its lifecycle state. However, Hilt doesn't support that, at least for now.

Instead, you'll do what the Hilt team recommends and use `launchFragmentInHiltContainer()`.

You declare this function in the **debug** package. Along with it, you declare a `HiltTestActivity` annotated with `@AndroidEntryPoint`. The function creates an `Intent` to launch the `HiltTestActivity`, then creates an **ActivityScenario** with it and uses it to host your `Fragment`. Just like any `Activity`, you'll find the `HiltTestActivity` definition in the (debug) manifest.

Triggering What to Test

At this point, your `Fragment` is running. You want to test the search, so you need to write `nameToSearch` in the `Fragment`'s `SearchView`. Below `// When`, add:

```
with(onView(withId(R.id.search))) {
  perform(click())
  perform(typeSearchViewText(nameToSearch))
}
```

Using Espresso, you access the `SearchView` through its ID. You click it for focus, then run `typeSearchViewText()`. Typing in `SearchView` programmatically is a little more complex than typing in a simple `TextView`. Therefore, using Espresso's `typeText()` won't work.

You can see `typeSearchViewText()` below the test method. It creates an anonymous `ViewAction` class, where the two main methods are:

```
// 1
override fun getConstraints(): Matcher<View> {
  return allOf(
      isDisplayed(),
      isAssignableFrom(SearchView::class.java)
  )
}

// 2
override fun perform(uiController: UiController?, view: View?) {
  (view as SearchView).setQuery(text, false)
}
```

The previous code defines:

1. Every `View` the `ViewAction` can operate on.
2. The action you want to perform.

Checking the Results

Go back to the test and add the final code below `// Then`:

```
with(onView(withId(R.id.searchRecyclerView))) {
  check(matches(childCountIs(1)))
  check(matches(hasDescendant(withText(nameToSearch))))
}
```

This code checks if `RecyclerView` has only one item and if the text in that item matches what you expect. `childCountIs()` is also custom. It's defined below `typeSearchViewText()`, and it compares the value you pass to `Adapter`'s item count.

Build and run the test. Look at your device while the test runs and you'll see the changes in the UI.

There you have it. By adding these two tests, you are now testing every layer of your app. Well done!

This concludes your work on the **Search** feature. In the next chapter, you'll work on a new feature while learning how to create a multi-module app.

Key Points

- Avoid using base classes for Android components.
- View state management can get complex when you use data classes. Consider using functions to transition states, a state pattern or sealed classes.
- Avoid relying on `Enum`'s value order.
- A great way to handle user input is to treat it as a reactive stream, especially when input from one source can influence another.
- I can't stress this enough: Network requests are one-shot operations. So don't handle them like they're event streams!
- Always consider the network requests you make. If you have requests that don't matter anymore, find a way to cancel them. Coroutines allow you to do this organically, thanks to structured concurrency and cooperative cancellation.
- Following a unidirectional data flow makes unit testing the `ViewModel` a breeze.
- Hilt makes it easy to include test dependencies, but it has some limitations.

Section II: Modularizing Your App

As you add new features to your app, the code becomes more complex and difficult to maintain. For this reason, it's important to separate your app into different libraries to make your code both maintainable and reusable. This also improves the app's build time, which is a very important metric for your CI.

In this section, you'll learn how to split your app into different modules. In particular, you'll learn how to use the **dynamic feature** option, which optimizes the size of the code your users have to download to use your app.

Chapter 8: Multi-Module Apps

By Ricardo Costeira

Imagine you have a working app. You release it and it's a success! Business is blooming, your app keeps growing and new people join the team. However, as time goes by, all the extra code and extra developers start to take a toll on the development process itself. Pull requests become more complex, build times increase, technical debt starts to accumulate… It's time you sit down with your team and figure out a way to mitigate these problems and make your life easier.

One of the possibilities, in this case, is **modularization**. In this chapter, you'll focus on multi-module architecture. You'll learn:

- The benefits and drawbacks of modularization.
- The different kinds of modules and how they relate to one another.
- How to create a feature module.
- Some of the many things to consider when modularizing your app.
- Ways to navigate between features.

You'll start with the basics.

What is Modularization?

Modularization is the process of refactoring your app into separate modules. For **PetSave**, this implies transforming some — or all — of the packages into their own modules.

Open the **starter** project and look at the project's structure. It now represents a full-blown multi-module architecture.

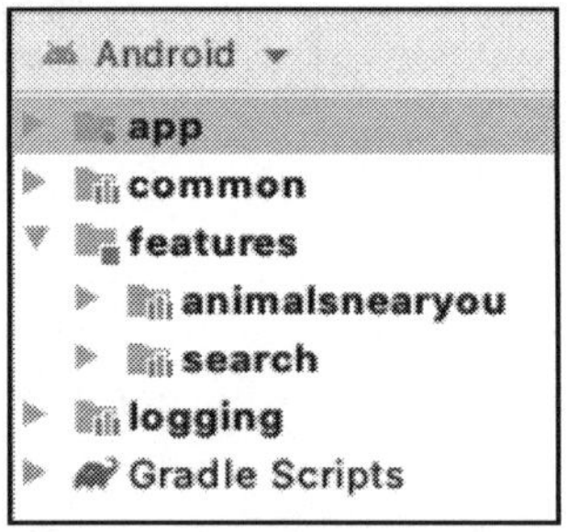

Figure 8.1 — Multi-Modular PetSave!

Modules represent either shared behavior or features. Here, `common` and `logging` represent shared behavior. The app won't work without the shared behavior modules, so they're known as **core** modules.

`logging` works as an **abstraction** module because it abstracts away a specific kind of behavior. This is a clean way of encapsulating third-party libraries. At this point, it only encapsulates the **Timber** library but you could extend it to handle more complex tools, like **Crashlytics** or **Bugfender**.

The `animalsnearyou` and `search` modules are inside the **features** folder. They represent the features you already know. Feature modules should depend only on core modules, and **never** on other feature modules.

Before you go any further, take a moment to see which types of modules are available.

Types of Modules

You define the kind of module you create through its **build.gradle**. There are a few different types, but you'll only look at three in this chapter. You'll explore others in the next chapter.

Application Modules

When you create a new Android project, you get a default app module automatically. This module is called an **application** module. You define it through this line at the top of its **build.gradle**:

```
apply plugin: 'com.android.application'
```

This is the main module of your app. It's responsible for:

1. Defining the app's base configuration.

2. Orchestrating the feature modules.

This module will behave differently depending on the kind of feature modules you're working with. You'll learn more about this in the next chapters.

Library Modules

Unless you want to create different APKs, you only need one application module in your app. Any other modules you create will be **library** modules. You define these with the following plugin at the top of their **build.gradle** files:

```
apply plugin: 'com.android.library'
```

These modules implement the logic that adds a behavior to your app, whether user-facing logic or not. This is the case for all modules in PetSave other than app. The naming is a bit confusing, but even the current feature modules are, in fact, library modules.

Kotlin/Java Modules

You define both application and library modules with plugins in the com.android namespace. This makes them Android modules, meaning you should use Android code with them.

What if you want a module composed only of pure logic, free from the shackles of the Android framework? In that case, you can create a **Java** or, even better, a **Kotlin** module. You can do this using the following plugin in the module's **build.gradle**:

```
apply plugin: 'kotlin'
```

These are the same as library modules, but without all the Android gunk. Don't get too excited, these are rare. :]

Why Modularization Is Good

Refactoring features into independent modules allows you to focus on each feature individually. This offers a few advantages:

1. Changing one feature won't affect the others, simplifying development.
2. It opens the path to things like **instant apps** and **dynamic feature modules**, which you'll learn about in the next chapter.
3. When your codebase is large enough for it to make sense, modules allow you to have dedicated teams for each feature.
4. You can reuse features in other apps. For instance, you might need to launch an app similar to the one you have, but with slightly different requirements. Just import the matching feature modules to that new app and half your work is done. You don't want to develop the same feature three times. Take it from someone who's done that in the past. :]
5. You can try out new tech on one module without affecting the others. If you like it, you can then refactor the other modules. If you don't, you can just refactor the module you changed to use the old tech again, and all is well.
6. Refactoring becomes easier because each feature has clear boundaries. Even if you decide that refactoring is not worthwhile and build the whole thing over from scratch, modules make it easier.
7. You can use conditions and/or feature toggles to try out new code and make sure it works before deleting old code.
8. It offers a great way of doing A/B testing without making a mess of the code.

These are just a few of the positive things about multi-module architecture. The last ones are true not only for feature modules, but for other modules in general.

One specific improvement that's usually mentioned, but wasn't here, is build speed — for a good reason.

In large projects, build times can become long, to the point of disrupting your workflow. Many developers modularize their apps in an attempt to reduce those build times.

However, just because you refactor everything into a module, it doesn't mean that the project's build time will decrease. Sometimes, it even increases! Like (too) many things on software development, *it depends™*.

Using Gradle With Modules

A modularized project's build time depends on many things: how your modules depend on each other, how you set up your Gradle dependencies, if you use incremental annotation processing or not...

You can tackle almost everything related to build performance by using Gradle. The deeper you go, though, the more you need to know about Gradle. Gradle is complex to the point where focusing on it would require a chapter on its own. That said, there are a few simple things to consider when working with Gradle in a multi-module app:

Gradle Properties

Properties like **parallel project execution** and **configure on demand** are very helpful. You'll learn more about these later.

Incremental Annotation Processing

Libraries like Hilt and Room use annotation processing. Without incremental processing, any small change that triggers the `kapt` compiler forces it to process the whole module.

Incremental processing has been active by default since Kotlin 1.3.50 — but it only works if **all** the annotation processors you're using are incremental. Lucklily for PetSave, all libraries that use annotation processing already make use of incremental annotation processing by default.

Kotlin Symbol Processing

Kotlin Symbol Processing API, or **KSP** for short, aims to eventually replace `kapt` as the standard tool for annotation processors. It's still under development at the time of this writting, but some libraries — like Room — already offer some experimental support. Since it's not fully supported yet (Hilt doesn't support it, for instance), you won't use it here. However, it still deserves an honorable mention as it has shown to be much faster than `kapt` in testing. Something to keep an eye out for!

Leaking Dependencies

If you change a module internally, Gradle recompiles only that module. If you change that module's external interface, you'll trigger an update to the application binary interface, or **ABI**. This makes Gradle recompile that module as well as all modules that depend on it, and all modules that depend on those and so on.

You add a Gradle dependency to a module by using either `implementation` or `api`. If you include it through `api`, you'll leak its interface through the interface of the module itself. In other words, whenever you change a dependency included through `api`, you'll cause every module that depends on your module to be recompiled.

Long story short, try to use `implementation` in modularized projects whenever possible.

Setting Gradle Properties

Going back to the Gradle properties, you'll set a few of them for PetSave.

In the project's root, or under **Gradle Scripts**, if you're using the Android project structure, open **gradle.properties**. In it, uncomment `org.gradle.parallel=true` at the end of the file. This allows Gradle to compile independent modules in parallel.

While you're at it, add these lines below:

```
org.gradle.caching=true
org.gradle.configureondemand=true
```

`caching` tells Gradle to store and reuse any files it can from previous builds.

`configureondemand` is worthwhile for projects with many modules. Gradle builds have three phases: Initialization, configuration and execution. Setting `configureondemand` to `true` tells Gradle to not reconfigure modules that aren't involved in the tasks it's running.

Sync your Gradle configuration and run the app. Don't expect any major difference in build time. This is a small project after all, so the build time was already small. In fact, is it worth it to modularize a project like PetSave?

The short answer is: No. Probably.

Looking Back Over Your Decisions so Far

Now, for the long answer. Modularization brings a whole new set of complexity to module configuration and dependency management. You should be aware of this before you start modularizing your app. The complexity involved can become difficult to handle.

From a high-level perspective, the process you followed for PetSave so far was to:

1. Create new modules for each feature and for `common`. This involved creating the new folder structure, adding a **build.gradle** for each module and moving code to the correct module.
2. Extract the common dependencies between the modules into a common Gradle file named **android-library.gradle**.
3. Make sure dependency injection still works.
4. Extract the resources — strings, layouts and everything else — to their corresponding modules. This also includes creating two new navigation graphs, one for each feature. These are included in the main graph.
5. Fix the tests.

Now, look at each one in more detail.

Creating the Modules

The module creation was straightforward; even the package names are the same. `common` could be further divided into more modules, but it doesn't seem worthwhile here.

In Figure 8.2 below, you can see a before (a) and after (b) view of the folder structure. You can also see that the search domain models are now in the common module, since the repository contract (c), which is in the common module as well, depends on them.

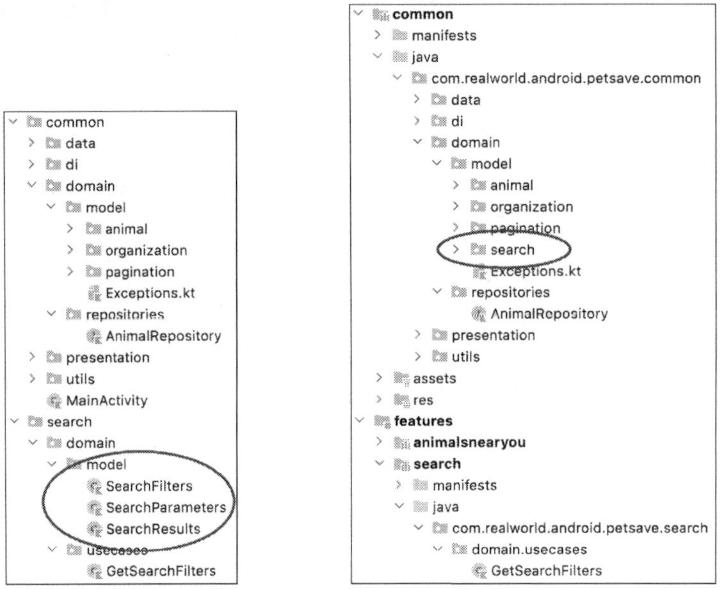

(a) (b)

```
interface AnimalRepository {
  fun getAnimals(): Flowable<List<Animal>>
  suspend fun requestMoreAnimals(pageToLoad: Int, numberOfItems: Int): PaginatedAnimals
  suspend fun storeAnimals(animals: List<AnimalWithDetails>)
  suspend fun getAnimalTypes(): List<String>
  fun getAnimalAges(): List<Age>
  fun searchCachedAnimalsBy(searchParameters: SearchParameters): Flowable<SearchResults>
  suspend fun searchAnimalsRemotely(
      pageToLoad: Int,
      searchParameters: SearchParameters,
      numberOfItems: Int
  ): PaginatedAnimals
```

(c)

Figure 8.2 — Folder Structure Before and After

Sometimes, for instance, it makes sense to have a module for the domain layer only — or a module for the data layer, so you can use it in another app.

All the domain models now live in the `common` module. This includes the few models that **search** had in its package because, otherwise, `common` would depend on `search`, and core modules should not depend on feature modules.

Extracting Common Dependencies

Things got a little more complicated with dependencies. You had to decide how to deal with them. Should you add the required dependencies to each module, or gather the common ones into a single Gradle file and share it?

The three newly created modules share most of the dependencies. In this case, you aggregated the common ones in **android-library.gradle**. Open the file — it's next to all the other **build.gradle** files.

The `com.android.library` is at the top, followed by an `android` block and a `dependencies` block. There are no `api` dependencies. You do this to avoid unneeded recompilation of modules that don't use this configuration but depend on modules that do.

Although there are some slight differences, the `android` block is similar to the one in `app`'s Gradle file. You *could* extract it, but would you really gain something here? Probably just more complexity. If you don't see a clear advantage, let future you worry about it. :]

Besides, if you need to override some configuration or add something new, you can still do it for the modules that need it. For instance, open `common`'s **build.gradle**. It includes the **android-library.gradle** configuration through the `apply from` at the top. It also adds some extra Room-related configuration to the `android` block and its own dependencies.

Handling Resources and Themes

After completing the Gradle configuration, it was time to compile the app and make sure everything still worked. The main concern was Hilt, due to past Dagger experiences.

Fortunately, Hilt has seen some development in multi-module support over the last few versions. In other words, Hilt raised no problems at all.

However, the app wouldn't run yet. The code was still trying to import resources from the app module. It was just a matter of moving the resources to the correct modules and updating the imports.

An important thing to note regarding the app's theme: Remember that core modules shouldn't depend on any other modules except other core modules. By default, the app theme is declared in the app module's **styles.xml**. So, since all modules that have anything UI-related in them can depend on `common`, you moved the app theme to `common`.

It's a simple app, with a single simple theme, so this will do. Just know that sometimes, if an app follows a more complex **design system**, with different themes and/or styles for different cases or a lot of custom UI components, you should consider encapsulating those things into a module of its own.

Extracting the Navigation Graphs

At this point, the app was running but all the navigation logic was still in the app module. It's a good practice to have nested graphs for bottom navigation destinations, as they tend to include a few different screens. With nested graphs, you can isolate the navigation behavior in the module of the feature it belongs to.

This was a little more complex to deal with. With each feature module having its own graph, you had to make the appropriate changes done. You needed to:

1. Include the graphs in the main graph.
2. Update the bottom navigation menu to match the IDs of the graphs instead of the `Fragments`.

Fixing the Tests

After all this, it was time to check the impact on the tests — which was significant. All tests were still in the app module, so the first step was to move them to their corresponding modules. The second step was to fix all the damage that doing so caused.

The main problem was that tests in a module can't access test files from other modules. So, the UI test in the `search` module stopped working, mainly due to Hilt test files being declared in `common`. This is where you start to consider having independent test files for each module, even if you repeat behavior, or a module just for test files.

The solution was twofold. You decided to:

1. Rework the test bindings and provide them all through test modules, via `@testInstallIn`.

2. Grant the module access to the missing files through Gradle.

Open `search`'s **build.gradle** and you'll see some test configuration details in the `android` block. These give the module access to the specified package. The shortcoming here is that the `search` module can now see the files in the package, which means that it needs to know how to handle any dependencies. The `androidTestImplementation` declarations below, in the `dependencies` block, work around this.

It's now time for you to create your own library module. It will be an easier ride than what you've done so far. :]

Creating the Onboarding Feature Module

You might have noticed that the app has a new feature now. If not, do a clean install and run the app. You'll see a new screen: **onboarding**.

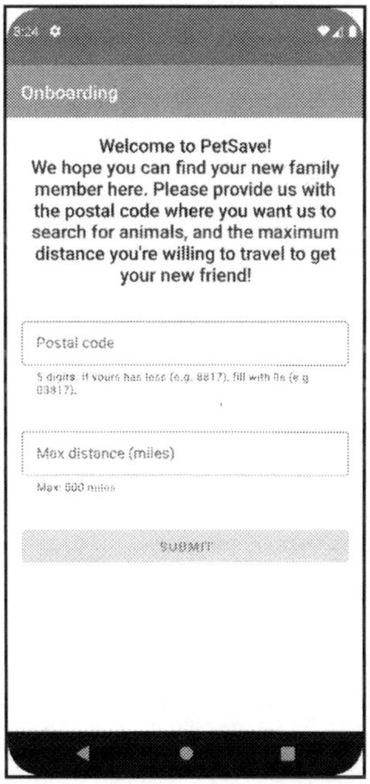

Figure 8.3 — The Onboarding Feature

It's a simple screen that asks the user for a postal code and a distance. It stores that information, then uses it to search for animals. The idea for this screen is for it to evolve into a questionnaire about the user's choices and preferences for pets. For now, though, making the search work is enough. :]

Currently, the feature is a part of the `app` module, but you'll refactor it to be its own module.

Locate the code in the **petsave.onboarding** package in the **app** module. The implementation is similar to the other features. However, there's one difference: The view state doesn't handle errors. Instead, `ViewModel` has a `viewEffects` property that handles one-time effects like errors or navigation.

After the user enters the postal code and distance, the app stores them in the shared preferences. This translates into a dependency on the `common` module. The tricky part comes from a business rule that states that this screen should appear at startup if the user hasn't filled in the details yet. The app has to decide which screen to show at the beginning, or to which screen it should **navigate**.

`Activity` is responsible for triggering this decision. `MainActivity` now also has a `ViewModel`, along with a use case. The use case tells the `ViewModel` whether the onboarding process is complete. If so, `ViewModel` tells `Activity` to show **animals near you**. Otherwise, it shows **onboarding**.

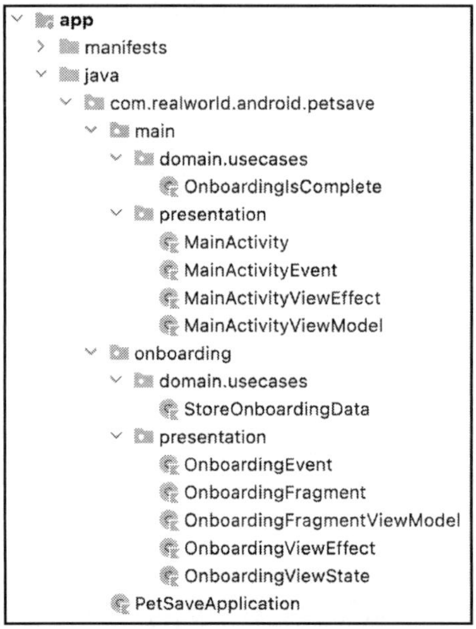

Figure 8.4 — Current App Module Structure

Tapping **Submit** causes the app to store the data and navigate to **animals near you**. This gives the **onboarding** feature a direct dependency on **animals near you**. You'll need to change this when **onboarding** becomes a module because feature modules shouldn't depend on each other.

Now that you know what you need to do, it's time to get to work.

Adding a New Module

In the project structure, right-click **features**. Select **New ▸ Module** from the context menu.

In the window that appears, select **Android Library**. Also, change **Module name** to **:features:onboarding**, which places the new module inside the **features** folder. Change the **Package name** to **com.realworld.android.petsave.onboarding** to preserve the package structure. Click **Finish** at the bottom of the window.

Wait while Android Studio does its magic. When it's done, you'll have your new module!

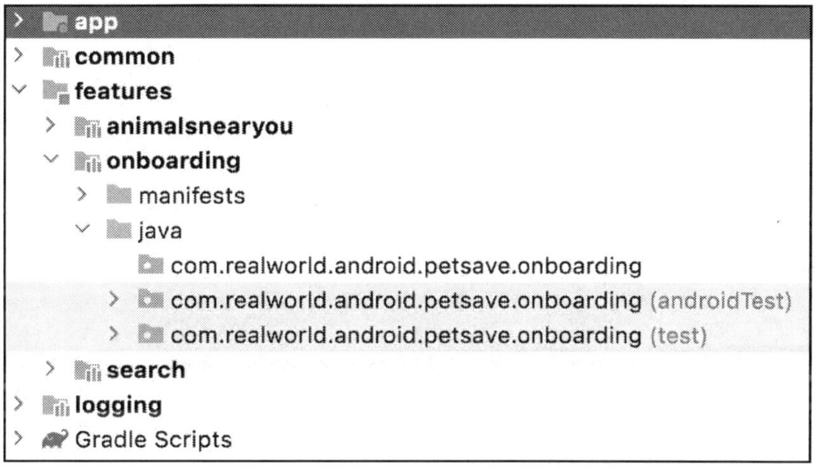

Figure 8.5 — The Onboarding Module

Adding Code to Your Module

Now, you have to move the **onboarding** code from the app module to your new module. Moving packages between modules is tricky in Android Studio. To make things easier, disable **Compact Middle Packages** in the project structure:

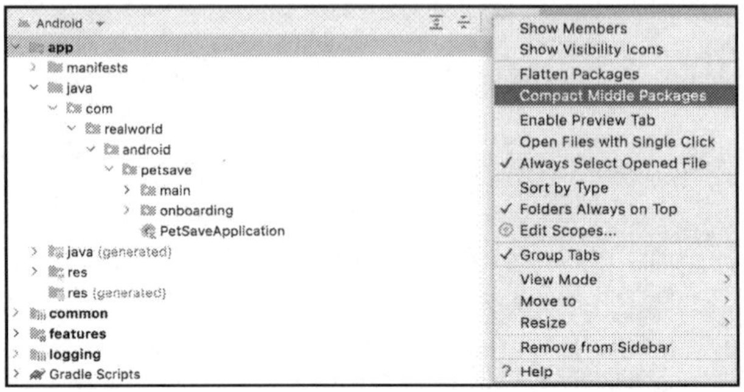

Figure 8.6 — Disabling The Compact Middle Packages Option

As you can see in the image, this separates the packages instead of showing them in the compact format.

Now, drag the **onboarding** package in the app module to the **petsave** package in the `onboarding` module. This will replace the empty **onboarding** package inside and make the **Select Refactoring** dialog appear. Pick the **second** option: **Move everything from <app module onboarding** directory> to another directory. Click **OK** and let Android Studio work on it.

Eventually, a **Problems Detected** window will appear. It's complaining about inaccessible dependencies.

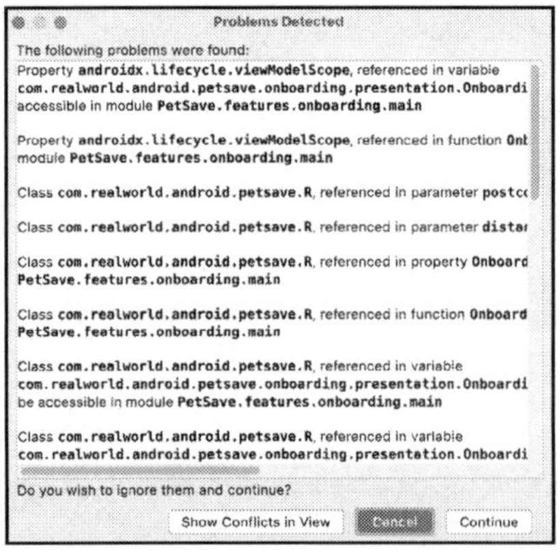

Figure 8.7 — Problems Detected Window

You'll fix that later. For now, just click **Continue**. When Android Studio finishes, the code will be in the `onboarding` module.

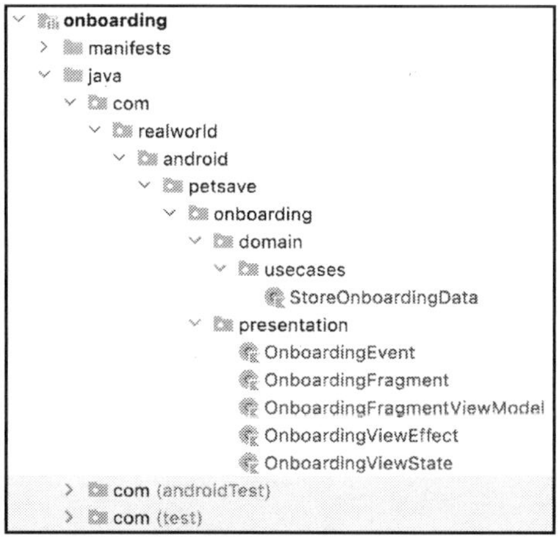

Figure 8.8 — Final Onboarding Module Structure

You can enable **Compact Middle Packages** again, if you want. Clean the project, then build and run it. The app will run... but it'll crash into flames. If you look at the error in Logcat, it says that it can't instantiate `OnboardingFragment`. This instantiation occurs in the app module. As it turns out, you created a new module but didn't tell the app module to depend on it.

Fixing the App Module's Dependency

Open the app module's **build.gradle**. Add the project import line in the `dependencies` block, along with the ones already there:

```
dependencies {
  implementation fileTree(dir: 'libs', include: ['*.jar'])

  // Modules
  implementation project(":features:animalsnearyou")
  implementation project(":features:search")
  implementation project(":features:onboarding") // HERE
  implementation project(":common")
  implementation project(":logging")

  // ...
}
```

Clean the project and build it again. The build will immediately fail due to missing dependencies — as you'd expect.

Organizing Your Dependencies

When Android Studio creates a module, it also creates a corresponding **build.gradle**. Go to the Gradle scripts and locate the one that refers to `onboarding`. Open it and delete everything inside.

This is a library module, so you'll apply the **android-library.gradle** configuration. Add this as the first line:

```
apply from: "$rootProject.projectDir/android-library.gradle"
```

This already does a lot of the work for you, adding the main plugins and dependencies you'll need in the project, but you still need to add something more. Create a `dependencies` block:

```
dependencies {
  implementation project(":common")

  // Navigation
  implementation "androidx.navigation:navigation-fragment-ktx:
$nav_version"
  implementation "androidx.navigation:navigation-ui-ktx:
$nav_version"
}
```

Like the other features, this one depends on the `common` module. You'll need the screen to navigate to **animals near you**, so you add in the navigation dependencies as well. You don't put this in the **android-library.gradle** configuration because `common` doesn't handle navigation.

Sync Gradle, clean the project and build again. You'd think that it would work, but there's one final change you need to make.

You got an error in `OnboardingFragment`. It's complaining that it can't find `R`. That's because it's still using the old import from when it was in the app module.

Update the import by adding the **onboarding** package. While you're at it, do the same to the view binding dependency. So, remove this:

```
import com.realworld.android.petsave.R
import
com.realworld.android.petsave.databinding.FragmentOnboardingBind
ing
```

And add this instead:

```
import com.realworld.android.petsave.onboarding.R
import
com.realworld.android.petsave.onboarding.databinding.FragmentOnb
oardingBinding
```

The view binding dependency still has a squiggly red line under it. That's because the resources are still in the `app` module!

Handling Module Resources

For some reason, Android Studio doesn't create a **res** directory when you create a module, so you have to do it yourself. Right-click the `onboarding` module and select **New ▸ Android Resource Directory**. In the next window, choose **layout** from the drop-down menu in **Resource type**, then click **OK** at the bottom. This will create the **res.layout** package structure.

Next, go to the `app` module's **res** directory. Expand **layout** and find **fragment_onboarding.xml**. All you have to do now is drag it down to the **layout** package in `onboarding`.

In the **Move** window that appears, click **Refactor**, then open **fragment_onboarding.xml**, if it doesn't open automatically. It's in the `onboarding` module now, but it can't find the string resources.

Fortunately, there's a simple fix. First, right-click **res** in `onboarding`, and select **New ▸ Android Resource File**. In the window, enter **strings** as the **File name**. Make sure **Resource type** is **Values**, then click **OK**. This creates the **res.values.strings.xml** file.

Next, inside the `app` module, open **res/values/strings.xml**. With a simple cut and paste, move every string resource — *except* for `app_name` — over to `onboarding`'s **strings.xml**. Be sure to paste them inside the `resources` tag in the `onboarding` module's **strings.xml**.

Build and run. You'll get a new error, but this one's related to the navigation action to **animals near you**. You'll fix that in a second.

For now, comment out the line that causes the error and build again. You'll get the familiar `R` error, but in `OnboardingFragmentViewModel` this time. Fix it like you did before, and build again. And now, you get the same error in `OnboardingViewState`. Fix it and build again! Everything will work now.

One thing to keep in mind: Although you're using resources in different modules, resource merging rules still apply. So, for instance, say you have two string resources in different modules. If they have the same name, one will override the other.

With that, you're done with the resources. Now, to fix the navigation issue.

Navigating Between Feature Modules

Navigation between modules is a complex problem in modularized architectures. If you need to navigate between different screens of the same feature, it's business as usual. But what about navigation between different features? Features can't depend on each other, so how do you navigate between them?

First, you'll refactor the navigation logic, moving it to `onboarding` and including it in `app`. The **onboarding** feature is just a screen for now, and probably will be in the future. You'll refactor it for consistency and decoupling, but it's a judgment call, in this case.

Right-click `onboarding`'s **res** directory and select **New ▸ Android Resource File**. Enter **nav_onboarding** in **File name** and choose **Navigation** in **Resource type**. Click **OK**.

Now, go to the `app` module's **nav_graph.xml**, under **res.navigation**. Cut the whole `<fragment>` tag and paste it in **nav_onboarding.xml**, inside the `<navigation>` tag.

Still in **nav_onboarding.xml**, add the import for `tools`. Set the `startDestination` of the graph by adding this property to the `<navigation>` tag:

```
app:startDestination="@id/onboardingFragment"
```

Go back to the `app` module's **nav_graph.xml**. Add the include for `nav_onboarding`. Change the start destination accordingly, because you have to depend on the whole nested graph now.

When you're done, it should look like this:

```
<?xml version="1.0" encoding="utf-8"?>
<navigation android:id="@+id/nav_graph"
  xmlns:android="http://schemas.android.com/apk/res/android"
  xmlns:app="http://schemas.android.com/apk/res-auto"
  app:startDestination="@id/nav_onboarding">

  <include app:graph="@navigation/nav_onboarding" />
  <include app:graph="@navigation/nav_animalsnearyou" />
  <include app:graph="@navigation/nav_search" />
</navigation>
```

Finally, you have to update `MainActivityViewModel`, located in **main.presentation** of the app module. Go to `defineStartDestination()` and replace `R.id.onboardingFragment` with `R.id.nav_onboarding`. If you don't depend on the whole graph, the app will crash with an error stating that the destination is not a part of the navigation graph.

Adding the Navigation Ability

Next, you'll deal with navigating between features. Up until now, the `app` module used a normal Navigation component action to navigate from **onboarding** to **animals near you**. But now, you've defined that action in `onboarding`'s **nav_onboarding.xml**:

```
<action
  android:id="@+id/action_onboardingFragment_to_animalsNearYou"
  app:destination="@id/nav_animalsnearyou"
  app:popUpTo="@id/onboardingFragment"
  app:popUpToInclusive="true"
  app:enterAnim="@anim/nav_default_enter_anim"
  app:exitAnim="@anim/nav_default_exit_anim" />
```

`app:destination="@id/nav_animalsnearyou"` has a red squiggly below it because `onboarding` doesn't depend on `animalsnearyou`.

You have a few options to solve this, and it's not rare to find solutions with a mix of different options. The most common options are:

1. Having a `navigation` module that's aware of every module and can navigate everywhere.
2. Using **deep links**.

You'll go with the second option here. Navigation component has native support for deep links. This makes your life because you don't need to manually create any **intent filters**.

Using Deep Links

First, go to `animalsnearyou`. Open **res.navigation.nav_animalsnearyou.xml**. Delete the comment inside the `<fragment>` tag and add this line in its place:

```
<deepLink app:uri="petsave://animalsnearyou" />
```

This allows the app to deep-link into this `Fragment` through that `Uri`.

Next, go to the app module and open its **AndroidManifest.xml**. With deep links, you need to add an **intent filter** to the `Activity` you want to deep link into. Since you're using a "single `Activity`, multiple `Fragments`" architecture, you'll add it to `MainActivity`.

The Navigation component makes your life easier here. It builds the intent filter for you through a tag called `nav-graph`.

In the `<activity>` tag, replace the comment with the line:

```
<nav-graph android:value="@navigation/nav_graph" />
```

`<nav-graph>` requires you to pass in the navigation graph where you defined the deep link. You pass in `nav_graph` because it includes all the other graphs

When you build the project, Navigation component will replace this tag with intent filters for every deep link inside the graph. Pretty neat!

> **Note**: If you're still stuck in Android Studio 3.1, you'll have to add the intent filters yourself because it doesn't support `nav-graph`.

Setting Up the Navigation Action

You can now set up the actual navigation action. Go to `OnboardingFragment` in the `onboarding` module. Locate `navigateToAnimalsNearYou()` and delete any code inside, replacing it with:

```
// 1
val deepLink = NavDeepLinkRequest.Builder
    .fromUri("petsave://animalsnearyou".toUri())
    .build()

// 2
val navOptions = NavOptions.Builder()
    .setPopUpTo(R.id.nav_onboarding, true)
    .setEnterAnim(R.anim.nav_default_enter_anim)
    .setExitAnim(R.anim.nav_default_exit_anim)
    .build()

// 3
findNavController().navigate(deepLink, navOptions)
```

Here's what's going on in this code:

1. It creates the deep link through `NavDeepLinkRequest`. You pass in the same `Uri` as the one that the deep link in `nav_animalsnearyou` defines.
2. The navigation action in `nav_onboarding` has some logic to it. It pops up the back stack until it reaches `OnboardingFragment`, popping it along as well. This prevents the app from showing **onboarding** again if the user presses the back button while in **animals near you**. It also adds enter and exit animations. Notice that the code pops up the whole `nav_onboarding` graph. That way, even if you add new screens to **onboarding**, they all get popped out of the back stack.
3. As before, the code calls `navigate()` on the `navController`. But now, instead of passing the ID of the navigation action, it passes the deep link request and the navigation options.

Build the app and do a clean install. You'll see **onboarding**. Type some data and tap **Submit** and the app will navigate to **animals near you**. Just be sure to enter a valid postal code; otherwise, you won't see any animals. The app isn't ready to handle the **invalid postal code** case yet. :]

Well done! You can delete the old navigation action from `nav_onboarding`, as you won't need it anymore.

Additional Improvements

While the current code works, you could improve it further. The first thing to do would be to extract the deep link `Uri` to ensure you use the same one everywhere.

Another possibility, as you add more navigation to the app, is to create a specific module just for navigation actions. Otherwise, you'd start to have deep link resources repeated throughout the modules. This navigation module would also encapsulate all other navigation details, such as different `navOptions` configurations.

You've finished your module, congratulations! You won't create any tests in this chapter because the module is simple enough that testing it wouldn't give you any additional information.

In the next chapters, you'll venture further down the modularization rabbit hole.

Key Points

- There are three types of modules: application modules, library modules and Kotlin modules. Library modules can be core modules or feature modules. Kotlin modules are like library modules, but without Android framework code.
- Every app needs an application module, which bosses the feature modules around. The application module can also depend on core modules. Each one generates an APK.
- Feature modules can depend on core modules, but never on each other. Core modules can depend on each other.
- Modularization brings a lot to the table. Its applicability depends on the app you're working on, so you should carefully evaluate the pros and cons. Instead of diving in blindly and modularizing everything, try to understand if it makes sense for your app.
- Navigation is hard. It gets harder in multi-module apps, but Android provides a possible solution.

Chapter 9: Dynamic Features Theory

By Ricardo Costeira

In real life, you'll probably have many more modules in your app than **PetSave** has at this point. You might also have some kind of analytics logic in the app, which gives you insight into how users interact with it.

Suppose you have a **share animal** feature module. This feature allows the user to share an animal's information on their social networks. Through analytics, you know that this feature is seldom used. However, even users that don't want to use the feature still have to install it, taking up precious disk space.

Android app size has a direct relationship to the number of app installs and user retention, with larger apps tending to have fewer installs and lower user retention.

Say that the **share animal** feature module takes up half the space of the whole app. Wouldn't it be frustrating to see your app being frequently uninstalled due to a large feature module that almost no one uses?

The Android team is aware of this, so they came up with some mechanisms to mitigate the problem. One of these mechanisms is the **app bundle** publishing format. Using this publishing format can already help you reduce your app size.

For the most part, however, this chapter focuses on another mechanism: **Play Feature Delivery**. This mechanism takes advantage of advanced app bundle features to allow you to develop dynamic features.

This chapter is **optional** if you already know what app bundles and dynamic features are. On the other hand, if you don't understand those concepts thoroughly yet, what you read here will help.

The chapter focuses on the theoretical side of dynamic features. You'll learn about:

- The app bundle publishing format.
- What dynamic features are.
- The delivery options for dynamic features.
- Two of the most common challenges with dynamic features: dependency injection and navigation.

Android App Bundle

Before diving into dynamic features, you need to know about **app bundles**. An app bundle is Google's clever app delivery format, which splits the APK into different pieces. It then delivers **only** the pieces the user's device requires.

When you upload an APK to Google Play, all users receive that **universal APK** when they download your app. When you upload an app bundle, however, Google Play uses it to create a few different APKs, called **split APKs**. These split APKs are available from Android API 21 onwards. There are three different types:

- **Base APK**: Google Play generates this APK from the app module of the app. It contains everything you need to configure and launch the app as well as shared code, in most cases. It's the first APK that the user downloads and installs.

- **Configuration APKs**: APKs related to different screen densities, languages, CPU architectures or native libraries. When the user downloads the app, Google Play installs only the configuration APKs related to the user's device.
- **Dynamic feature APKs**: APKs with code and resources for each dynamic feature.

Even if you don't care about dynamic features, it's a good idea to use app bundles. If your app is properly modularized, it'll reduce the final app size. Besides, since August 2021, Google requires that new apps submitted to Google Play use app bundles. Moreover, apps larger than 150 MB will have to use either **Play Feature Delivery** or **Play Asset Delivery**.

Play Feature Delivery delivers dynamic features to the user via app bundle features and APIs. You'll learn more about these later. As for Play Asset Delivery, the logic is the same as Play Feature Delivery, but it applies to game assets.

Dynamic Delivery

Google Play installs the split APKs on the user's device and makes them appear as a single app. This is called an **optimized APK**. This optimized APK is built through a process called **dynamic delivery**. This optimizes the APK because dynamic delivery generates it using only the components that matter for the user's specific device.

For instance, suppose you have a Portuguese-speaking user, like yours truly. My device has a resolution of 560 dpi and runs on an ARM 64 processor. When I download an APK that uses dynamic delivery, I'll get:

1. The base split APK.
2. The split APKs for ARM 64, Portuguese string resources and xxxhdpi resources.
3. Any split APKs for install-time dynamic features. You'll learn more about dynamic delivery types later.

With dynamic delivery, you don't need to manage and optimize multiple APKs for different devices anymore. The process manages them for you!

Another advantage is that creating an optimized APK from split APKs makes it possible for you to decide which APKs to deliver. More specifically, it lets you pick which dynamic feature APKs to deliver.

What Are Dynamic Features?

When you have a multi-module app, each feature usually has its own module. If you do it right, each feature module will — for the most part — be independent. You still need an application module to use the feature and it might depend on a few core modules, but everything that defines the feature will be in its module. This module isolation is essential to creating dynamic features.

A dynamic feature module is similar to a normal feature module. Apart from the details that allow the Android framework to handle it as a dynamic feature, there are two main differences from normal modules: Play Core and module dependencies. Next, you'll learn more about each one.

Play Core

The first main difference is that you can specify how and when the user can access a dynamic feature. You can even define when the feature is installed, or uninstalled. This behavior is possible due to the **Play Core Library**.

The Play Core Library is what your app uses to interface with the Google Play Store. Although only its dynamic feature capabilities are important here, it allows you to do a few interesting things:

1. Download resources
2. Manage feature module delivery
3. Manage asset pack delivery
4. In-app updates
5. In-app review

Using the Play Core API, you can implement your own logic to decide how to handle dynamic features. Google Play Store handles the rest.

Play Core provides four different feature delivery options:

- **On demand delivery**: The app asks to download features under specific conditions, which is useful for features that most users don't need. You can have the app download those features only when the user tries to use them.
- **Install-time delivery**: This option installs dynamic modules with the app, along with all regular modules. You can then request to uninstall them later, which is useful to get rid of one-use features, like onboarding.

- **Conditional delivery**: This installs dynamic features according to certain device conditions. For instance, the app could install specific features for specific API levels. Or, the app could download camera-related features only when the device has a camera. If the conditions hold true, the feature downloads at install time.
- **Instant delivery**: You've probably heard of instant apps by now. Instant delivery lets users try specific features without having to install the whole app. This one's more complex than the others because there are specific — and very strict — size requirements for the base module.

To implement any of these options, you need to properly set up the dependencies between the base and dynamic feature modules.

Module Dependencies

The second main difference between regular feature modules and dynamic feature modules is the way the dependencies between base and feature modules work. In a regular multi-module app, the **app module depends on feature modules**:

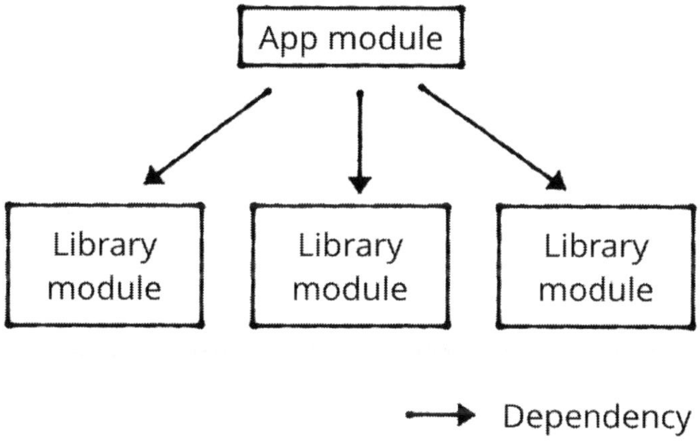

Figure 9.1 — Typical dependency graph between base module and regular feature (library) modules.

Things are a little different when using dynamic feature modules. Because dynamic feature modules can be installed at any point, they might not come with the app when you install it. As a consequence, the base module can't depend on dynamic features. After all, it can't depend on something that might not exist!

On the other hand, the base module contains the app configuration, along with access to all shared code from core modules. For these reasons, **dynamic feature modules depend on the app module**. This translates into an inversion of dependencies:

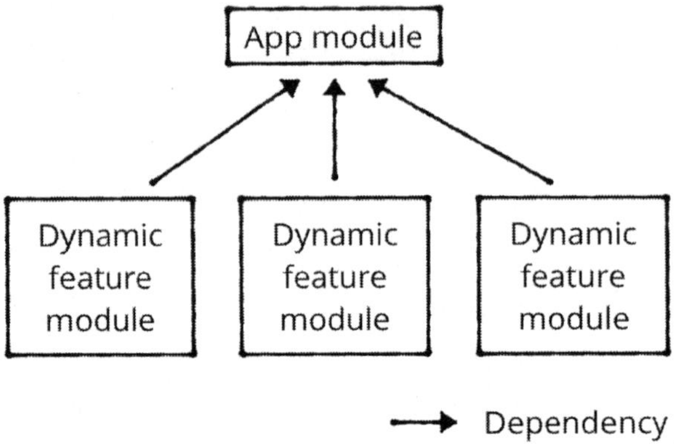

Figure 9.2 — Dependency graph between base module and dynamic feature modules.

Note that this doesn't mean the app module is completely unaware of dynamic feature modules. It can't access code from dynamic feature modules — at compile time, at least. Still, it's somewhat aware of their existence through Play Core.

This inversion of dependencies introduces new challenges in modularization. The most notable ones are with dependency injection and navigation between features.

Injecting Dynamic Dependencies

PetSave uses Hilt for dependency injection. Hilt requires the entire dependency graph to be built at compile time. Hilt builds the dependency graph starting at the `Application` annotated with `@HiltAndroidApp`. This class is in the base module, which works out of the box for a monolithic app. For a multi-module app, it'll work as long as the base module is aware of all the dependencies, like you've seen in Chapter 8, "Multi-Module Apps".

With dynamic features, the base module can't access all the feature modules. This means that the dependency graph is forcefully split into different pieces. In other words, Hilt can't figure out the dynamic modules' dependencies.

The Hilt team expects to fix this at some point, but only time will tell. For now, you can use Dagger to work around this. You'll see how in Chapter 10, "Building a Dynamic Feature".

Navigation With Dynamic Features

You've already learned that navigating between features in multi-module apps is a challenge. In the previous chapter, you solved the problem using the Navigation component with deep links.

The Navigation component has some support for dynamic features, but it has some limitations as well. It lets you dynamically include navigation graphs, for instance. However, it does not support deep links for dynamically included graphs. Gotta love these Android framework caveats. :]

You have a few options here:

1. Using reflection. Ew.

2. Creating a new `com.android.library` module that has interfaces for dynamic features. This module would depend on both feature and base modules. At runtime, you'd load the dynamic features with `ServiceLoader`. However, this option is **no longer viable** because R8 doesn't support using `ServiceLoader` for dynamic features anymore. Using `ServiceLoader` without R8 optimization is a bad idea for performance reasons.

3. Using a Navigation component feature called **DynamicNavHostFragment**. It replaces `NavHostFragment` and lets the navigation controller navigate to dynamic features.

Reflection works, but it's neither the safest option nor the most performant. The second option would also affect performance since you can't use R8. So, in the next chapter, you'll go with option number three.

In fact, this is all the theory you need to start implementing dynamic features. It's time to get your hands dirty!

Key Points

- App bundle is a publishing format that optimizes and tailors APKs for users' devices.
- Play Feature Delivery uses advanced app bundle features that allow you to optimize app installations to the next level.
- The Play Core Library provides the mechanisms for you to decide how and when you want to deliver dynamic features.
- Navigation and dependency injection become more challenging with dynamic features.

Chapter 10: Building a Dynamic Feature

By Ricardo Costeira

The App Bundle publishing format is here to stay. Google Play now requires you to publish new apps with the App Bundle format. Moreover, if your app's size exceeds 150 MB, it must use either Play Feature Delivery or Play Asset Delivery.

This chapter assumes you're aware of the theory behind dynamic features explained in Chapter 9, "Dynamic Features Theory". Now, you'll work on refactoring a normal feature module and turning it into a dynamic feature.

Along the way, you'll learn:

- How to create an app bundle.
- How to refactor a library module to a dynamic feature module.
- How to navigate with dynamic features using the Navigation component.
- How to inject dependencies into dynamic features.
- How to test dynamic feature module installs.

You'll focus on a new feature module that you'll turn into a dynamic feature module, letting users install the feature only if they want to use it.

PetSave's New Features

The **PetSave** team has been hard at work, and the app has two updates. Open the **starter project** to check them out.

Start by expanding **features**. You'll notice there's a new feature module called **sharing**. This feature lets the user share a specific animal on their social networks.

Figure 10.1 — The Sharing Feature

The code is similar to `onboarding`'s, so if you're familiar with that code already, there's not much to gain in exploring the module.

You navigate to this screen through a deep link, thanks to the app's other new feature. Go to the `animalsnearyou` module and expand **presentation**. You'll find two packages inside:

- **main**: Home to the code of the **animals near you** main screen, which you're already familiar with.
- **animaldetails**: Contains the code for a new screen that shows an animal's details.

This screen appears when you click an animal in the list. It shows the animal's name, picture and a few other details.

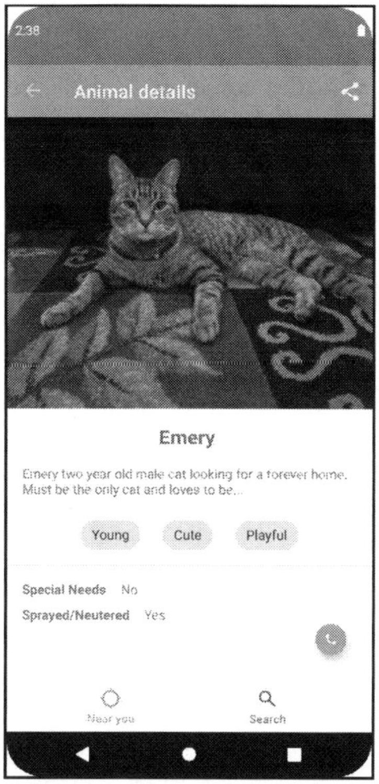

Figure 10.2 — Animal Details Screen

At the top-right corner of the screen is a **share** icon. Clicking it triggers the deep link into the **sharing** feature. The code behind it is similar to what you've seen so far, but there's one difference worth noting: This screen uses sealed classes to handle the view state, making the view state that handles code in the `Fragment` similar to the event handling code in the `ViewModel`.

In the long term, both **animals near you** and **search** will use this screen. For now, however, you'll handle it as if it's part of **animals near you** for simplicity.

With the introductions out of the way, it's time to get to work. You'll refactor the `sharing` module into an **on-demand** dynamic feature module. With this change, only users who want that feature need to download it.

Deciding How to Create Your Dynamic Feature

To create a dynamic feature module, you have two options:

1. Follow Android Studio's dynamic feature module creation wizard.
2. Refactor a normal `com.android.library` module into a dynamic feature module.

In this case, you'll use the second option. Not only is it a lot more interesting, but it'll help you learn more, too.

To use this option, you'll need to make changes in both the `app` and `sharing` modules.

Preparing the App MNodule

When using app bundles, you install the Gradle module defined as a `com.android.application` first, so it makes sense to start from there. Typically, this is the `app` module.

> **Note**: Although PetSave doesn't need it, some apps require that you add some specific configuration to your app module's **AndroidManifest.xml** to support dynamic features. Find out how to do this at https://developer.android.com/guide/app-bundle/configure-base.

Start by opening the `app` module's **build.gradle**. Locate the `sharing` module dependency and remove it:

```
implementation project(":features:animalsnearyou")
implementation project(":features:search")
implementation project(":features:onboarding")
implementation project(":features:sharing") // <- Remove
implementation project(":common")
implementation project(":logging")
```

Remember that dynamic feature modules depend on the base module, not the other way around. That said, add the following line at the bottom of the `android` tag, just below `packagingOptions`:

```
dynamicFeatures = [":features:sharing"]
```

No matter how many dynamic features you have, you only have to set up the app module once. As you add more dynamic features, however, you'll need to let the app module know about them here.

Managing Dependencies

Go back to the `dependencies` tag. Since dynamic features depend on the app module, it's a common practice to serve some of the common dynamic features dependencies through app. To do so, start by changing:

```
implementation project(":common")
implementation project(":logging")
```

to:

```
api project(":common")
api project(":logging")
```

Do the same for these:

```
// Kotlin
implementation "org.jetbrains.kotlin:kotlin-stdlib-
jdk8:$kotlin_version"

// Support Libraries and material
implementation "androidx.appcompat:appcompat:$appcompat_version"
implementation "com.google.android.material:material:
$material_version"

// Navigation
implementation "androidx.navigation:navigation-fragment-ktx:
$nav_version"
implementation "androidx.navigation:navigation-ui-ktx:
$nav_version"
```

Changing them to:

```
// Kotlin
api "org.jetbrains.kotlin:kotlin-stdlib-jdk8:$kotlin_version"

// Support Libraries and material
api "androidx.appcompat:appcompat:$appcompat_version"
api "com.google.android.material:material:$material_version"

// Navigation
api "androidx.navigation:navigation-fragment-ktx:$nav_version"
api "androidx.navigation:navigation-ui-ktx:$nav_version"
```

Finally, below the last Navigation component dependency, add:

```
api "androidx.navigation:navigation-dynamic-features-fragment:
$nav_version"
```

This last dependency gives you two things:

1. The Dynamic Navigator dependency. You'll use this later to navigate to the dynamic feature.
2. The Play Core dependencies the app needs to support dynamic features.

Dynamic Navigator handles dynamic feature installation for you. If you wanted to do it manually without using Dynamic Navigator, you'd include the `com.google.android.play:core$version` dependency, instead.

Sync Gradle to make sure everything is OK.

Defining Module Names

When your app requests a dynamic feature, you usually ask the user to confirm that they want to install it. For that, you need the module's name. Since you might need the module's name before the user downloads it, you should define it in the base module as a string resource of up to 50 characters.

When you have enough dynamic features and/or string resources, it makes sense to have a separate string resource file just for dynamic feature names.

Go to **res** in the app module and open **strings.xml** under **values**. Add the `sharing` module title:

```
<string name="dynamic_feature_sharing_title">Share an animal</
string>
```

Giving the App Access to the Dynamic Features

Your last step is to enable access to dynamic feature code and resources on the app. To do this, enable **SplitCompat**.

You can enable `SplitCompat` in one of three ways:

1. Declaring `SplitCompatApplication` as the `Application` subclass in the manifest, through the `android:name` property of the `application` tag. This won't work, in this case, because PetSave uses a custom `Application`.
2. Having your custom `Application` extend `SplitCompatApplication`.
3. Having your custom `Application` override `attachBaseContext(base: Context)`. That lets you avoid extending `SplitCompatApplication`, which performs the override for you internally.

In the app module, locate and open **PetSaveApplication.kt**. To enable `SplitCompat`, change the class to extend `SplitCompatApplication` instead of `Application`:

```
class PetSaveApplication: SplitCompatApplication()
```

If you don't want to extend `SplitCompatApplication`, override `attachBaseContext()`, as mentioned above:

```
override fun attachBaseContext(base: Context) {
  super.attachBaseContext(base)

  SplitCompat.install(this)
}
```

Whichever one you prefer to use, the result is the same. On a side note, you have to override this method in all dynamic feature `Activity` instances. You do this by replacing `SplitCompat.install(this)` with `SplitCompat.installActivity(this)`. Since PetSave only has one `Activity`, however, you don't need to worry about it here.

Now you can try to build the app. You'll get a compile-time error stating: **Could not resolve project :features:sharing.** because `sharing` isn't a dynamic feature module yet.

```
Could not determine the dependencies of task ':app:checkDebugLibraries'.
> Could not resolve all task dependencies for configuration ':app:debugReverseMetadataValues'.
   > Could not resolve project :features:sharing.
     Required by:
         project :app
      > The consumer was configured to find a usage of 'android-reverse-meta-data' of a component,
  as well as attribute 'com.android.build.api.attributes.BuildTypeAttr' with value 'debug'. However
```

Figure 10.3 — Gradle Sync Error

This is a problem you need to fix.

Preparing the Feature Module

Now, it's time to refactor the `sharing` module. Start by opening its **AndroidManifest.xml**.

First, define the distribution namespace as a property in the `manifest` tag:

```
xmlns:dist="http://schemas.android.com/apk/distribution"
```

Then, inside the `manifest` tag, add the following:

```
<dist:module // 1
  dist:instant="false" // 2
  dist:title="@string/dynamic_feature_sharing_title"> // 3
  <dist:delivery> // 4
```

```
    <dist:on-demand /> // 5
  </dist:delivery>
  <dist:fusing dist:include="true" /> // 6
</dist:module>
```

> **Note**: If you copy the code above, you'll have to remove the inline comments. XML doesn't allow comments inside tags.

There's quite a lot going on here:

1. Open the `dist:module` tag. This is the main tag for dynamic feature configuration.
2. Set the `dist:instant` property of `dist:module` to `false`. This means that the feature module won't be available through Google Play Instant. If you set it to `true`, you'd have to set it in the base module's manifest as well.
3. Set the `dist:title` property of the `dist:module` tag. Here, you use the string resource you declared earlier in the app module.
4. This is where the fun starts. This tag encapsulates all the information about how you deliver the feature module. You can only use one of these tags per feature.
5. You want the app to request the feature when the user tries to access it. This tag makes it so that the feature isn't available at install time, but is available for download later.
6. Setting this to `true` will include the module in multi-APKs targeting devices with Android API 20 or lower. It seems redundant when PetSave's minimal SDK level is 23, but you still need to set this tag.

Build the project now... and you'll get the same error. While the manifest is ready, Gradle isn't aware that this module represents a dynamic feature yet.

Notifying Gradle About the Dynamic Feature

Locate the **features.sharing** module's **build.gradle**. Open it and delete everything inside. Then, add these lines at the top of the file:

```
apply plugin: 'com.android.dynamic-feature'
apply plugin: 'kotlin-android'
apply plugin: 'kotlin-kapt'
apply plugin: 'dagger.hilt.android.plugin'
```

The first plugin tells Gradle to handle the module as a dynamic feature. You should already be familiar with the others.

Below these, add the `android` block:

```
android {
  compileSdkVersion rootProject.ext.compileSdkVersion

  defaultConfig {
    minSdkVersion rootProject.ext.minSdkVersion
    targetSdkVersion rootProject.ext.targetSdkVersion
  }

  compileOptions {
    sourceCompatibility JavaVersion.VERSION_1_8
    targetCompatibility JavaVersion.VERSION_1_8
  }

  buildFeatures {
    viewBinding true
  }
}
```

It has just enough information for the code to compile and run. Things like app signing, code shrinking and app versioning should be handled by the `app` module.

Finally, add the `dependencies` block below:

```
dependencies {
  implementation project(':app')

  // Constraint Layout
  implementation "androidx.constraintlayout:constraintlayout:
$constraint_layout_version"

  // UI
  implementation "com.github.bumptech.glide:glide:
$glide_version"
  kapt "com.github.bumptech.glide:compiler:$glide_version"

  // DI
  implementation "com.google.dagger:hilt-android:$hilt_version"
  kapt "com.google.dagger:hilt-android-compiler:$hilt_version"
}
```

That first `implementation` is the most important one. As you already know, all dynamic features depend on the app module. The remaining dependencies are pretty standard.

Sync Gradle and build the app. It fails, and Logcat tells you there was a manifest merger error. The app module is complaining because it can't find a navigation XML file called `nav_sharing`.

Go to the app module's **res**, expand **navigation** and open **nav_graph.xml**. You'll see there's an include for `nav_sharing`.

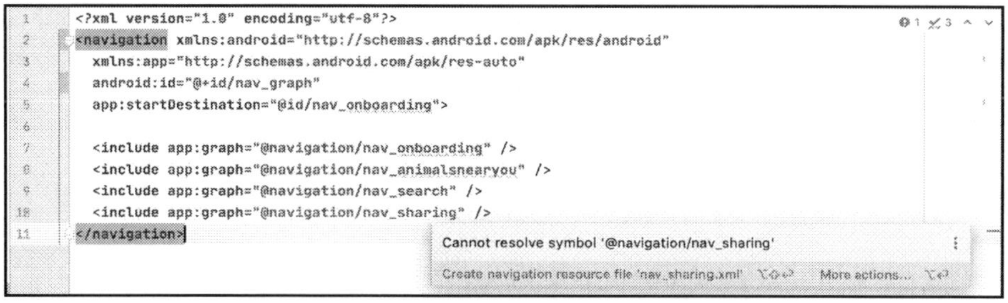

Figure 10.4 — Missing Navigation Definition

`nav_sharing` is the `sharing` module's navigation graph. The include is in red, which tells you there's an error. The app module doesn't depend on the `sharing` module now, so it can't reach its navigation graph.

Delete the line in red. Now, you can build and run without any problems... as long as you don't click the **Share** button in the **animal details** screen.

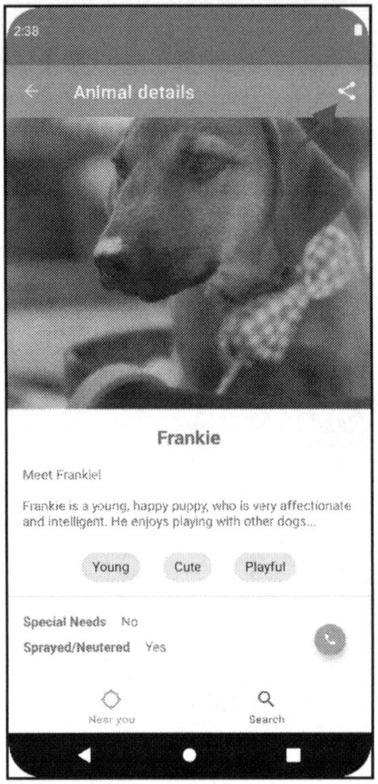

Figure 10.5 — Don't Click the Share Button Yet!

If you do, the app will crash because it has no idea how to navigate to the module! You'll fix that next.

Handling Navigation

The Dynamic Navigator from the Navigation component library is just like the regular navigator. In fact, it's an extension of the regular navigator, letting you navigate to dynamic feature modules just as you would to regular modules.

Before you can use it, the first change you have to make is in the `app` module. You need to replace any `NavHostFragments` in the app with `DynamicNavHostFragments`. You only have one `NavHostFragment`, so go to **res** and open **activity_main.xml** from the **layout** directory. Locate `FragmentContainerView` and change it to this:

```
<androidx.fragment.app.FragmentContainerView
  android:id="@+id/nav_host_fragment"

android:name="androidx.navigation.dynamicfeatures.fragment.Dynam
icNavHostFragment"
  android:layout_width="match_parent"
  android:layout_height="0dp"
  android:layout_weight="1"
  app:defaultNavHost="true" />
```

Then, go to the module's root and open the file **MainActivity.kt** in the **main.presentation** package. Locate the `lazy` delegate for `navController` and update the cast to match the change you just made:

```
private val navController by lazy {

(supportFragmentManager.findFragmentById(R.id.nav_host_fragment)
as DynamicNavHostFragment)
    .navController
}
```

The app will build and run now, and navigation should work as expected... apart from the **Share** button crash, which you still need to fix.

Fixing the Share Button

So far, you nested the `nav_sharing` graph into the `nav_graph` by including it there. Dynamic Navigator lets you do the same thing, but you need to use a different tag. You'll include the `sharing` module to keep the code similar to how it was before. Note that Dynamic Navigator lets you navigate to a `fragment` tag, just as the normal navigator does.

In the app module, open **res.navigation.nav_graph.xml** and add this block of code below the `include` tags, but still inside the `navigation` tag:

```
<include-dynamic
  android:id="@+id/dynamicFeatureSharing"
  app:graphPackage="com.realworld.android.petsave.sharing"
  app:graphResName="nav_sharing"
  app:moduleName="sharing" />
```

The `include-dynamic` tag works like the `include` tag, but for dynamic features. For it to work, you need to set a few important properties:

- **id**: The dynamic navigator uses this ID instead of the ID in the root element of the included graph.
- **graphPackage**: The root package of the dynamic feature.
- **graphResName**: The name of the navigation graph to include.
- **moduleName**: The feature module's name.

If you were navigating to a `fragment` tag, you'd only need to add the `app:moduleName`, like this:

```
<fragment
  android:id="@+id/sharingFragment"

android:name="com.realworld.android.petsave.sharing.presentation
.SharingFragment"
  app:moduleName="sharing" />
```

However, these dynamically included graphs don't support deep links yet. Therefore, you'll need to change things so you can navigate to **sharing** from the **animal details** screen.

Navigating Between the Animal Details and Sharing Screens

First, you need to create the navigation action shown in the graph. Go to the `animalsnearyou` module and open **nav_animalsnearyou.xml** in **res.navigation**. In the `fragment` tag for `AnimalDetailsFragment`, below the `argument` tag already there, add this code:

```
<action
  android:id="@+id/action_details_to_sharing"
  app:destination="@id/dynamicFeatureSharing">

  <argument
    android:name="id"
    app:argType="long" />
</action>
```

This action lets you navigate to the dynamically included destination. The start destination of that graph, `SharingFragment`, needs the ID of the animal. Hence, the `argument` tag inside the action.

You'll see a red squiggly line below the ID. Nevertheless, you can build the app and it will even run. To get rid of that squiggly line, you need to:

1. Create the ID here by changing `@id` to `@+id`.

2. Remove the plus (+) sign from the ID in the `include-dynamic` tag you added earlier.

Since app depends on `animalsnearyou`, this avoids any dependency error. It will work if you have the plus sign in both places, but you don't have to recreate the same ID.

> **Note**: In case the red squiggly line persists, "invalidate caches and restart" should be enough to fix it. One day, I'll have a T-shirt with "Hello IT, have you tried invalidating caches and restarting?" stamped on it. :]

Running the Navigation Action

Now, your last step is to run the navigation action in the code. Open **AnimalDetailsFragment.kt** in the **animalsnearyou.presentation.animaldetails** package of `animalsnearyou`. Build the app to generate the navigation directions. Then, locate `navigateToSharing()` and delete the code inside.

In its place, add:

```
val animalId = requireArguments().getLong(ANIMAL_ID)
val directions =
AnimalDetailsFragmentDirections.actionDetailsToSharing(animalId)

findNavController().navigate(directions)
```

If you're used to the Navigation component, you won't find anything unfamiliar here. It's the same code you'd use to navigate to any other module.

Build and run. Try to access the **sharing** feature by clicking the **Share** button. The app crashes!

The error states that the included navigation ID, `nav_sharing`, is different from the destination ID, `dynamicFeatureSharing`. It also tells you to either remove the navigation ID or make the two IDs match.

Even if you make them match, it'll still complain because they live in different namespaces. So go to the `sharing` module, open **res.navigation.nav_sharing.xml** and remove the ID from the `navigation` tag. While you're at it, remove the deep link from the `fragment` tag as well.

Build and run again. Click the **Share** button in the **animal details** screen. Oops — another crash!

Remember how you can't properly use Hilt with dynamic features? Well, here's the proof. Look at the error and you'll see that it failed when it tried to inject things into `SharingFragment`. You'll have to make some changes to the way you're injecting dependencies to fix this.

Handling Dependency Injection

Hilt doesn't work well with dynamic features because of its **monolithic component architecture**.

Hilt creates a component for each type. For example, all `Activity` instances come from the same component, all `Fragment` instances from another component and so on. To handle this, Hilt needs to know about every binding at compile time. Since dynamic features are loaded dynamically, Hilt can't directly access their bindings.

Hilt creates the dependency graph from the `app` module. That's where the `@HiltAndroidApp` annotation is — it annotates `PetSaveApplication`. For that reason, the solution — at least for now — is to create the dependencies that dynamic features need in the `app` module.

At the root of the `app` module, next to the **main** package, create a new package called **di**. In it, create **SharingModuleDependencies.kt**, then inside, create an interface with the same name.

Annotate the interface:

```
@EntryPoint
@InstallIn(SingletonComponent::class)
interface SharingModuleDependencies
```

Notice that the first annotation is `@EntryPoint` and **not** `@AndroidEntryPoint`. The latter is for Android components. As for the `@InstallIn`, you have to do it in `SingletonComponent`.

You'll access the dependencies through `Application`, so Hilt needs to install the dependencies in `SingletonComponent` for everything to work. Try using a different component and you'll get an error.

Here's a list of the dependencies that the `sharing` module needs:

1. Any `ViewModel` instances and use cases.
2. `DispatchersProvider`.
3. `AnimalRepository` — which, in turn, needs `Cache`, `Preferences`, `PetFinderApi` and `Context`.

The **sharing** feature uses the `GetAnimalDetails` use case. This is why you defined the use case in the `common` module, instead of in `animalsnearyou`.

Use cases are regular classes, so their `@Inject` annotation will do the work for you. `ViewModel` instances are a beast of their own, so you'll handle them with regular Dagger inside the `sharing` module.

Declaring Dependencies

So, which dependencies should you handle here? Declare these operations in the interface:

```
fun petFinderApi(): PetFinderApi
fun cache(): Cache
fun preferences(): Preferences
```

There's another caveat: You can only inject dependencies that you would normally install in the `SingletonComponent` through this interface. This means that you can't inject `AnimalRepository` and `DispatchersProvider` here, since they're installed in `ActivityRetainedComponent`.

Hilt will use these methods to find the right bindings in the dependency graph. For everything else, well... you have to use Dagger. You'll also use it to inject `Context` the old-fashioned way.

Before using it, you need the dependencies. Go to `sharing`'s **build.gradle**, and add them next to the Hilt ones:

```
implementation "com.google.dagger:dagger:$dagger_version"
kapt "com.google.dagger:dagger-compiler:$dagger_version"
```

Also, remove `apply plugin: 'dagger.hilt.android.plugin'` at the top. Sync Gradle.

Bringing In Dagger

At the root of the `sharing` module, next to **presentation**, create a **di** package. Inside, create a file called **SharingComponent.kt**, with a `SharingComponent` interface inside.

Annotate the interface:

```
@Component(dependencies = [SharingModuleDependencies::class])
interface SharingComponent
```

This interface is a regular Dagger `Component`. Passing `SharingModuleDependencies` as its dependency lets you connect it to Hilt's dependency graph.

Inside the interface, add the following code:

```
fun inject(fragment: SharingFragment) // 1

// 2
@Component.Builder
interface Builder {
  fun context(@BindsInstance context: Context): Builder
  fun moduleDependencies(sharingModuleDependencies:
SharingModuleDependencies): Builder
  fun build(): SharingComponent
}
```

Having cold sweats yet? No need! Here's what you're seeing in the code:

1. The method you'll use to inject dependencies into `SharingFragment`.
2. Your trusty old Dagger component builder. You'll inject the application `Context` through the builder, along with the dependencies that Hilt can provide.

After this, expand **presentation** and open **SharingFragmentViewModel.kt**. Change the class definition from:

```
@HiltViewModel
class SharingFragmentViewModel @Inject constructor
```

to:

```
class SharingFragmentViewModel @Inject constructor
```

You removed the Gradle plugin that allowed you to use the annotation, so you'll get a compile-time error if you don't change this.

Build the app. You'll get another error, but this one's in `SharingFragment`. To fix it, open **SharingFragment.kt** and remove the `@AndroidEntryPoint` annotation at the top.

Build the app so Dagger generates `Component`, and it will work this time. Don't run yet, because you still need to set up `SharingFragment` to inject the dependencies.

Preparing SharingFragment

In `SharingFragment`, above `onCreateView()`, override `onCreate()`:

```
override fun onCreate(savedInstanceState: Bundle?) {
  super.onCreate(savedInstanceState)
}
```

Below the `super` call, call the `Component` that Dagger generated and use it to inject the dependencies:

```
DaggerSharingComponent.builder()
  .context(requireActivity())
  .moduleDependencies(
      EntryPointAccessors.fromApplication(
          requireActivity().applicationContext,
          SharingModuleDependencies::class.java
      )
  )
  .build()
  .inject(this)
```

Everything is standard Dagger code except `EntryPointAccessors.fromApplication`. This Hilt method gives you access to the entry point of the app, which gives you access to the dependency graph.

Build and run. It'll still crash if you try to open the **sharing** feature.

Up to this point, you relied on Hilt to build and inject `SharingFragmentViewModel` into `SharingFragment`. Now, however, the app has no idea how to handle the injection.

Using Dagger Multibindings

To fix this, you'll use Dagger multibindings to build a generic solution for `ViewModel` injection. In the **di** package you created just now, create **ViewModelKey.kt**. In it, add the following:

```
@MapKey
@Retention(AnnotationRetention.RUNTIME)
@Target(
    AnnotationTarget.FUNCTION,
    AnnotationTarget.PROPERTY_GETTER,
    AnnotationTarget.PROPERTY_SETTER
)
annotation class ViewModelKey(val value: KClass<out ViewModel>)
```

This annotation allows you to create a Key out of each ViewModel. You'll use it to map the ViewModels themselves.

You also need a generic way to create ViewModel instances, so create **ViewModelFactory.kt** in the same package. In it, define the factory:

```
class ViewModelFactory @Inject constructor(
    private val viewModels: MutableMap<Class<out ViewModel>,
Provider<ViewModel>>
) : ViewModelProvider.Factory {

  override fun <T : ViewModel> create(modelClass: Class<T>): T {
    var creator: Provider<out ViewModel>? =
viewModels[modelClass]

    if (creator == null) {
      for ((key, value) in viewModels) {
        if (modelClass.isAssignableFrom(key)) {
          creator = value
          break
        }
      }
    }

    if (creator == null) {
      throw IllegalArgumentException("Unknown viewModel class
$modelClass")
    }

    try {
      @Suppress("UNCHECKED_CAST")
      return creator.get() as T
    } catch (e: Exception) {
      throw RuntimeException(e)
    }
  }
}
```

This class takes a MutableMap of ViewModel instances and returns the correct instance type you're trying to create. Dagger will inject the Map in this class.

Now, you defined a way to create a Key to the Map, but you haven't specified how to create a Value yet. In other words, you're not binding any ViewModel instances yet.

Binding the ViewModels

To bind the `ViewModel` instances, start by creating **SharingModule.kt**. In it, add `SharingModule` and annotate it with `@Module`:

```
@Module
abstract class SharingModule
```

In the abstract class, add these bindings:

```
// 1
@Binds
@IntoMap
@ViewModelKey(SharingFragmentViewModel::class) // 2
abstract fun bindSharingFragmentViewModel(
    sharingFragmentViewModel: SharingFragmentViewModel
): ViewModel

// 3
@Binds
@Reusable // 4
abstract fun bindViewModelFactory(factory: ViewModelFactory):
ViewModelProvider.Factory
```

Here's what's happening above:

1. The first binding method binds `SharingFragmentViewModel` using `@Binds` and `@IntoMap`. Now, Dagger knows that it should add this binding to the `Map`.
2. You use the `@ViewModelKey` annotation and pass in the `ViewModel`. Dagger will set it as the `Key` for the `Value` of the `Map`, a `SharingFragmentViewModel` instance.
3. You can't create and inject the `ViewModel` instances on your own. For that, you need `ViewModelFactory`. The second binding method allows you to inject it.
4. `@Reusable` is similar to `@Singleton`. It'll make Dagger try to reuse the same `ViewModelFactory` instance, if available. It doesn't ensure that the same instance lives throughout the whole app's lifetime, though.

You now have to let `SharingComponent` know about `SharingModule`.

Notifying SharingComponent of SharingModule

Open **SharingComponent.kt** and refactor the `@Component` annotation to:

```
@Component(
    dependencies = [SharingModuleDependencies::class],
    modules = [SharingModule::class]
)
interface SharingComponent
```

Finally, you need to actually inject the `ViewModel`. Go to **SharingFragment.kt**. Below the `companion object`, inject the factory:

```
@Inject
lateinit var viewModelFactory: ViewModelFactory
```

Then, refactor the `by viewModels` delegate by passing in the factory:

```
private val viewModel by viewModels<SharingFragmentViewModel>
{ viewModelFactory }
```

That's it! Android and Dagger will handle the rest.

Build the app. You'll get an error in the `SharingModule` stating that the module's missing an `@InstallIn` annotation. This happens because you're still depending on Hilt, which checks every `@Module` for the `@InstallIn` annotation.

You could disable this, but it could come in handy if you really forget to add the annotation. Instead, you'll let Hilt know it doesn't have to check this module.

Fixing Errors

To do this, go to **SharingModule.kt** and add this annotation below `@Module`:

```
@DisableInstallInCheck
```

This will tell Hilt to not check this specific `Module`.

Build the app again and it will fail and complain about not being able to find `DispatchersProvider` and `AnimalRepository` bindings. While it's true that you can't inject them through `SharingModuleDependencies` due to the reasons explained above, nothing's stopping you from doing so through `SharingModule`.

Open **SharingModule.kt** and add the missing bindings:

```
@Binds
abstract fun bindDispatchersProvider(
    dispatchersProvider: CoroutineDispatchersProvider
): DispatchersProvider

@Binds
abstract fun bindRepository(
    repository: PetFinderAnimalRepository
): AnimalRepository
```

You now have bindings for these dependencies in two different places in the app. Not ideal, but it's the best you can do with what you have available.

Build and run now. Once again, access the **sharing** feature — it'll work!

Figure 10.6 — A Working Share Button!

However, you set the feature to be downloaded on demand. Why is it available right away? You'll test the module install next.

Testing Module Install

Android Studio installs all your modules by default, including dynamic features. You can edit the run/debug configuration and choose not to install dynamic features right away. Unfortunately, if you use this method, they won't install later, either. For instance, choosing not to install the `sharing` module triggers this screen:

Figure 10.7 — Dynamic Navigator Handles Everything for You, Even the Failure Screen

To test the installation of dynamic feature modules, you have two options:

1. Publish the app on Google Play, then use the internal test track.
2. Use **bundletool**, a command-line tool.

Google Play's internal test track is a great way to test your apps. Not only is it useful for larger-scale tests, but you can also see exactly how the dynamic feature code will behave in a real-life scenario.

However, as you might know, Google Play's app review process takes quite a while — often, days. And you can't test your app until Google Play reviews and accepts it!

So in this case, you'll use bundletool. Download the latest version here: https://github.com/google/bundletool/releases.

Preparing to Use Bundletool

Before using it, you need to create an App Bundle. A debug one will do.

In Android Studio, go to **Build ▸ Build Bundle(s) / APK(s) ▸ Build Bundle(s)**.

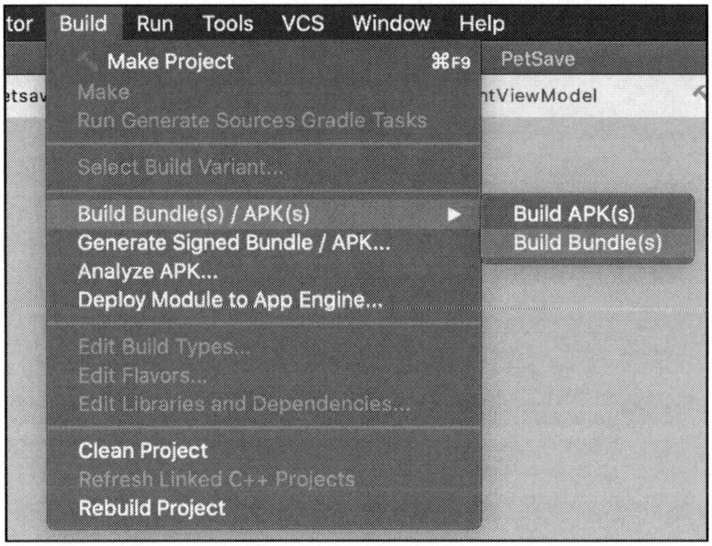

Figure 10.8 — Building a Debug App Bundle

This process outputs **app-debug.aab**. Locate the file and move it to the directory that contains **bundletool.jar**, for convenience. Then, open a command-line window in that same directory and run the command:

```
java -jar bundletool.jar build-apks --local-testing --bundle
app-debug.aab --output app-debug.apks --connected-device
```

Here, bundletool uses the **app-debug.aab** to create **app-debug.apks**, which contains all the split APKs you need to install the app.

`--connected-device` tells bundletool to produce **app-debug.apks** with only the split APKs needed for the connected device, whether that's a real device or an emulator. It's a cool way of testing App Bundles, by seeing which split APKs get installed.

`--local-testing` is what saves you from having to publish the app. It makes it possible for the Play Core library to use the split APKs to install dynamic features without connecting to the Play Store.

Now, to install **app-debug.apks** on a device, run this command:

```
java -jar bundletool.jar install-apks --apks app-debug.apks
```

Check the output to see which APKs bundletool installs. Using a Pixel 4 emulator with API 29, this was my output:

```
Pushed "/sdcard/Android/data/com.realworld.android.petsave/
files/local_testing/base-xxhdpi.apk"
Pushed "/sdcard/Android/data/com.realworld.android.petsave/
files/local_testing/base-master.apk"
Pushed "/sdcard/Android/data/com.realworld.android.petsave/
files/local_testing/base-en.apk"
Pushed "/sdcard/Android/data/com.realworld.android.petsave/
files/local_testing/sharing-xxhdpi.apk"
Pushed "/sdcard/Android/data/com.realworld.android.petsave/
files/local_testing/sharing-master.apk"
```

Note: There's currently a bug in Android 11 (API 30) that won't let you install the APKs through bundletool. If that's your case, you can work around it by using a device with a different API version.

Open the app on the device and try the feature again. You'll see a screen with a progress bar like this one:

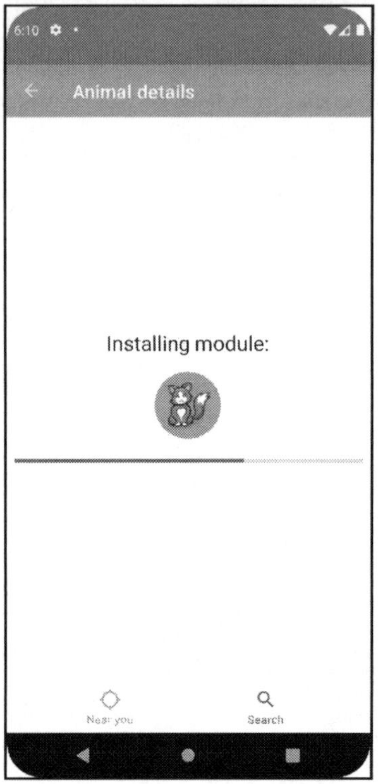

Figure 10.9 — Installing the Dynamic Feature

After a few seconds, you'll see the **sharing** feature's screen! As you can see, Dynamic Navigator handles everything for you. It shows the screen with a progress bar, triggers the feature download and handles any installation errors that occur.

Dynamic Navigator is also open for extension. It lets you have fine-grained control over things like reacting to different installation events yourself or even using your own progress bar screen. Pretty neat!

Key Points

- The `app` module doesn't depend on dynamic feature modules. However, you still have to make it aware of them through the `dynamicFeatures` array in its Gradle configuration.
- Navigation component's Dynamic Navigator does all the heavy lifting of requesting and installing dynamic features for you. It also handles network errors and even provides a basic installation progress `Fragment`. It's also open for customization.
- You can continue to use Hilt in your app when you have dynamic feature modules. Hilt currently provides some basic functionality to inject bindings into dynamic features, but Dagger does most of the work.
- bundletool is a great way of testing dynamic feature installation without having to publish your app on Google Play's internal test track.

This chapter concludes Section 2. In the next section, you'll learn how to create and animate custom UI components. Have fun! :]

Where to Go From Here?

Great job on refactoring the module to a dynamic feature module. It took a lot of work, especially regarding Hilt/Dagger and navigation. Well done!

To learn more about App Bundles and Play Feature Delivery, check the official documentation at https://developer.android.com/guide/app-bundle.

If you're interested in knowing more about the Play Core library, you can find its official documentation at https://developer.android.com/guide/playcore/play-feature-delivery.

For Dynamic Navigation, read the official documentation at https://developer.android.com/guide/navigation/navigation-dynamic and raywenderlich.com's article about it at https://www.raywenderlich.com/7023243-navigation-and-dynamic-features.

Finally, the Android team released a series of videos as part of the MAD Skills series about App Bundles. You should check it out at https://youtu.be/hTC0rKllhIw.

Section III: Enhancing Your UI

The user interface (UI) is one of the most important aspects of any real world app. How your user interacts with the features of your app is what decides if the app is successful or not.

When you build your app, you have three options for creating your UI. Most of the time you'll use what the Android SDK provides. In other cases, you customize the existing components. Your third option is to create your own custom components.

In this section, you'll learn how to enhance the user interface of your app. You'll create and customize animation using the new **Animation Editor**, which comes with recent versions of Android Studio. You'll also learn how to master themes and styles and to create a custom view.

After reading this section, you'll have a more appealing app and happier users.

Chapter 11: Animations

By Subhrajyoti Sen

Can you recall an app that was a pleasure to use? If so, it's most likely because the app had great animations.

Animations are an excellent way to improve your app's user experience. Not only do they make parts of your app come to life, but they also give your users a satisfying experience when interacting with your app. Animations make your app stand out.

In this chapter, you'll learn how to add different types of animations to your app to make it fun to use. You will do so by:

- Using **Lottie** to add complex loading animations without writing a single line of animation code yourself.
- Using **LottieFiles** to find and play suitable frames in the animation.
- Making an animated icon using **Animated Vector Drawables**.
- Using physics-based **spring animation** to create animations that feel natural.
- Using **fling animation** to let the user move a UI element with gestures.

You'll start with an introduction to Lottie.

Lottie

Lottie is an animation library developed by the folks at Airbnb. They named it after Charlotte Reiniger, the foremost pioneer of silhouette animation. Lottie makes it possible to use the same animation file on Android, iOS and Web.

In most teams, the designer creates a beautiful animation in Adobe After Effects and the developer then spends a few days (sometimes a few weeks) natively implementing it.

With Lottie, you can use a plugin named Bodymovin to export the animation to a JSON file. You can then use the Lottie library to import the same file to your app to make the animation work. No extra animation code is needed.

Why use Lottie

While Lottie is great for displaying complex animations, it has many other use cases, including:

- **Walkthroughs**: Apps generally use GIFs or videos to show feature walkthroughs. Lottie can do the same with a fraction of the file size.
- **Animated Icons**: Lottie's great for displaying animated icons based on user interactions. Although you can make animated icons with Animated Vector Drawables, Lottie supports a wider range of After Effect features. It can also control the animation progress based on user interactions, such as gestures.

Lottie has several advantages over other forms of animations as well:

- Lottie animations scale well.
- You can easily download the animation file over the network.
- The same animation file works across all platforms.
- It's easy to loop between different frames of the animation.

Ready to dive in? Find out how to use Lottie next.

Setting up Lottie

Open the **build.gradle** for the **app** module and add the following dependency for Lottie:

```
implementation "com.airbnb.android:lottie:5.0.1"
```

Sync Gradle by clicking the **Sync Now** button.

Open the **raw** directory under the app resources. You'll see two files named **happy_dog.json** and **lazy_cat.json**. These are your Lottie animations.

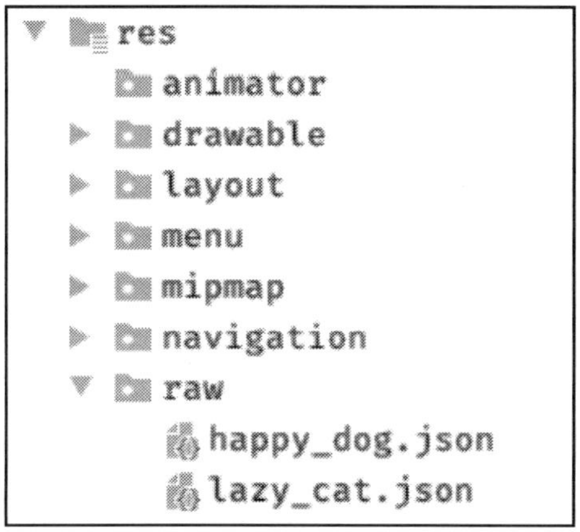

Figure 11.1 — Lottie Animation Files

Now, from the layout directory, open **fragment_details.xml** and replace the `ProgressBar` view with the following code:

```
<com.airbnb.lottie.LottieAnimationView
    android:layout_width="match_parent"
    android:layout_height="match_parent"
    android:id="@+id/loader"
    app:lottie_loop="true"
    />
```

`LottieAnimationView` is responsible for loading the animation and applying various properties. When `lottie_loop` is enabled, it continuously loops the animation.

Now, you need to start playing the animation while the pet's details load. Open **AnimalDetailsFragment.kt** in **details.presentation** and replace `startAnimation` with the following code:

```
private fun startAnimation(@RawRes animationRes: Int) {
    binding.loader.apply {
      isVisible = true
      setAnimation(animationRes) // 1
      playAnimation() // 2
    }
}
```

In this code you use:

1. `setAnimation` to set the JSON file resource that you want Lottie to display
2. `playAnimation()` to start playing the animation.

Next, update `displayLoading` by replacing `displayLoading` with the new `startAnimation`, like this:

```
private fun displayLoading() {
  startAnimation(R.raw.happy_dog) // HERE
  binding.group.isVisible = false
}
```

Also replace `startAnimation()` inside `displayError`, as in the following code:

```
private fun displayError() {
  startAnimation(R.raw.lazy_cat) // HERE
  binding.group.isVisible = false
  Snackbar.make(requireView(),
      R.string.an_error_occurred,
      Snackbar.LENGTH_SHORT).show()
}
```

Don't forget that you need to add functionality to cancel the and hide the animations as well. Replace the current implementation of `stopAnimation` with the following:

```
private fun stopAnimation() {
  binding.loader.apply {
    cancelAnimation() // HERE
    isVisible = false
  }
}
```

`cancelAnimation` stops the Lottie animation.

Build and run. Click on any pet's image to go to its details page. While the data loads, you'll now see a happy dog animation.

Figure 11.2 - Lottie Loading Screen

Customizing the Animation

Lottie allows you to customize various properties of the animation like:

1. Animation speed
2. Fill color
3. Start and end frames
4. Repeat count and repeat mode

Consider a case where you want to use only a certain portion of the animation instead of the entire thing. With Lottie, you don't need to go back to your designer and request changes. Instead, you simply specify the start and end frames of the animation.

For this app, you want to display only the part of the loading animation where the dog's eyes are open.

Open this URL in a browser: https://lottiefiles.com/preview then upload the Lottie file named **happy_dog.json** to it.

Pause the animation and use the SeekBar to find the frame number where the dog's eyes open.

Figure 11.3 — Lottie Animation Preview

In this case, the starting frame is around 50.

By dragging the SeekBar a bit more, you'll find that the dog closes its eyes at frame number 113.

Figure 11.4 — Lottie Animation Preview At a Different Frame

With that information, you know that you want to set the minimum frame to **50** and the maximum frame to **112**. Also, you'll set the animation speed to **1.2x** because the default speed feels a bit slow

To do this, modify `startAnimation`, like this:

```
private fun startAnimation(@RawRes animationRes: Int) {
  binding.loader.apply {
    isVisible = true
    setMinFrame(50) // 1
    setMaxFrame(112) // 2
    speed = 1.5f // 3
    setAnimation(animationRes)
    playAnimation()
  }
}
```

In this code, you:

1. Set the initial frame with `setMinFrame`.
2. Set the final frame with `setMaxFrame`.
3. Change the speed with the `speed` property.

Build and run. You'll notice that only the selected part of the animation plays and that it plays at 1.5x the previous speed.

Customizing Other Animation Properties

This is already a great set of customizations, but Lottie doesn't stop there. It lets you customize a wide range of properties of the animation. For example, you can modify the color of a single path in the animation. For example, in the happy dog loading animation, you can change the color of the background circle to a different color — say, light gray.

Try this out by opening **happy_dog.json** and searching for the **icon_circle** layer. This represents the background circle in the animation. For other animation files, you can ask the designer on your team to help you find the layer you need.

Change `startAnimation` adding the following code:

Add the following code to the end of `startAnimation`:

```
private fun startAnimation(@RawRes animationRes: Int) {
  binding.loader.apply {
    // ...
  }
  binding.loader.addValueCallback( // 1
      KeyPath("icon_circle", "**"), // 2
      LottieProperty.COLOR_FILTER, // 3
      {
```

```
            PorterDuffColorFilter(Color.LTGRAY,
PorterDuff.Mode.SRC_ATOP) // 4
          }
      )
    }
```

Here's what's going on in the code:

1. You use `addValueCallback` to add a callback to the Lottie animation that returns a custom color filter for the layer you want to modify.
2. To do this, you need to pass the layer as the first parameter using a `KeyPath`. You create a `KeyPath`, passing its name as the first parameter and a regular expression that filters layers with the same name. In this case, you use a wildcard, **
3. The second parameter for `addValueCallback` is the property of the layer you want to change. In this case, you want to change its color using `LottieProperty.COLOR_FILTER`.
4. Finally, you set the new value that, in this case, is a `ColorFilter` using a lambda.

Build and run. Go to the details screen and notice that the color of the animation background has changed from light yellow to light gray, as in Figure 11.5.

Figure 11.5 — Change the color of a layer

You've now successfully added a Lottie animation to your app and even customized it without having to go to your designer for help.

Animated Vector Drawables

Android uses **Vector Drawables** to display scalable images in your app. `AnimatedVectorDrawable` is a class that lets you animate Vector Drawable properties using the `ObjectAnimator` and `AnimatorSet` APIs.

Traditionally, `AnimatedVectorDrawable` runs on the UI thread. Starting from API level 25 (Android 7.1), however, it runs on the `RenderThread`. This has the advantage that, even if there's jank in the UI because of long running work taking place in the UI thread, `AnimatedVectorDrawable` will continue to run smoothly.

It's also interesting to note that Lottie animations run on the UI thread. That means that in some cases, it's beneficial to use `AnimatedVectorDrawable` over Lottie animations.

There are two ways to define the animations:

1. Define `VectorDrawable`, `AnimatedVectorDrawable` and `ObjectAnimator` in three separate XML files.

2. Define everything in a single XML file.

The first approach is preferable because it makes it easy to reuse animations and Vector Drawables across multiple views. In this book, you'll use the first approach.

Consider an example of a gesture that lets the user "like" a pet. When the user double-taps the pet's image, an outline of a heart fades in and starts filling up. Once the heart is full, it fades away.

Creating the Vector

You'll start by drawing the heart shape. Create a file named **ic_heart_unfilled.xml** in the **drawable** directory and add:

```
<vector xmlns:android="http://schemas.android.com/apk/res/
android"
    xmlns:tools="http://schemas.android.com/tools"
    android:name="heart"
    android:width="24dp"
    android:height="24dp"
    android:alpha="0"
    tools:alpha="1"
    android:viewportWidth="24"
    android:viewportHeight="24">
  <group
      android:pivotY="12"
      android:pivotX="12">
    <path
        android:fillColor="#ff1744"
        android:pathData="M 16.5 3 C 14.76 3 13.09 3.81 12 5.09
C 10.91 3.81 9.24 3 7.5 3 C 4.42 3 2 5.42 2 8.5 C 2 12.28 5.4
15.36 10.55 20.04 L 12 21.35 L 13.45 20.03 C 18.6 15.36 22 12.28
22 8.5 C 22 5.42 19.58 3 16.5 3 Z M 12.1 18.55 L 12 18.65 L 11.9
18.55 C 7.14 14.24 4 11.39 4 8.5 C 4 6.5 5.5 5 7.5 5 C 9.04 5
10.54 5.99 11.07 7.36 L 12.94 7.36 C 13.46 5.99 14.96 5 16.5 5 C
18.5 5 20 6.5 20 8.5 C 20 11.39 16.86 14.24 12.1 18.55 Z"
        android:strokeWidth="1" />
    <clip-path
        android:name="heart_mask"
        android:pathData="M 12 21.35 L 10.55 20.03 C 5.4 15.36 2
12.28 2 8.5 C 2 5.42 4.42 3 7.5 3 C 9.24 3 10.91 3.81 12 5.09 C
13.09 3.81 14.76 3 16.5 3 C 19.58 3 22 5.42 22 8.5 C 22 12.28
18.6 15.36 13.45 20.04 L 12 21.35 Z" />
    <group
        android:name="circle"
        android:translateY="17">
      <path
          android:fillColor="#ff1744"
          android:pathData="M 12 2 C 9.349 2 6.804 3.054 4.929
4.929 C 3.054 6.804 2 9.349 2 12 C 2 14.651 3.054 17.196 4.929
19.071 C 6.804 20.946 9.349 22 12 22 C 14.651 22 17.196 20.946
19.071 19.071 C 20.946 17.196 22 14.651 22 12 C 22 9.349 20.946
6.804 19.071 4.929 C 17.196 3.054 14.651 2 12 2 Z"
          android:strokeWidth="1" />
    </group>
  </group>
</vector>
```

The above vector draws an unfilled heart, which will be the starting state of the animation. It has an opacity of **0** because the icon will initially be invisible, then fade in. `tools:alpha="1"` lets you see the icon in Android Studio's preview. You can use the Design view in Android Studio for a preview of the image, as Figure 11.6 shows:

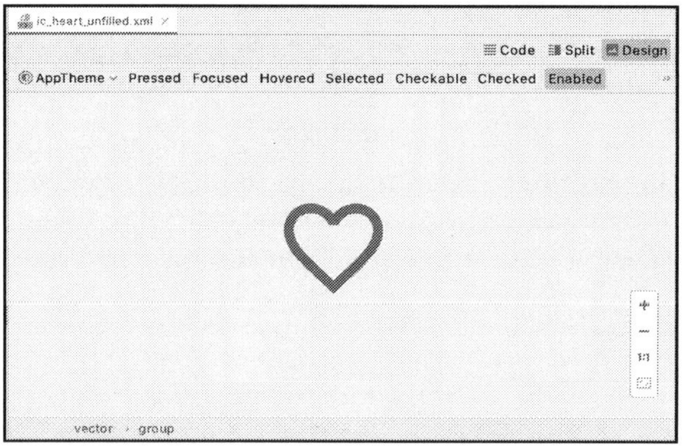

Figure 11.6 — The Heart Vector Drawable

The vector also has a circle that's initially placed below the heart so it's not visible. The aim of the animation is to gradually move this circle up so it gives the illusion of the heart filling up. The part of the circle outside the heart isn't visible to the user because of the `clip-path` defined in the vector.

Creating the Animations

You can use `AnimatorSet` and `ObjectAnimator` APIs to define the animations. For this animation, you'll use both. You'll create the fading animation first.

Create an **animator** resource directory under the **res** folder. Then create a file called **animator_alpha** in the **animator** directory and add:

```
<set xmlns:android="http://schemas.android.com/apk/res/android"
    android:ordering="sequentially">

  <objectAnimator
    android:duration="400"
    android:interpolator="@android:interpolator/linear"
    android:propertyName="alpha"
    android:valueFrom="0"
    android:valueTo="1"
    android:valueType="floatType" />

  <objectAnimator
    android:duration="200"
```

```
        android:interpolator="@android:interpolator/linear"
        android:propertyName="alpha"
        android:startOffset="100"
        android:valueFrom="1"
        android:valueTo="0"
        android:valueType="floatType" />
</set>
```

The above XML defines two animations that run sequentially. The `ordering` attribute specifies whether the animations execute in parallel or in sequence. The first animation animates the value of the `alpha` property from 0 to 1 over a duration of 400 milliseconds. It uses `linear` interpolation, which means the rate at which the property value changes is constant for the entire duration.

The second animation also changes the `alpha` property, but from 1 to 0 and it takes 200 milliseconds. `startOffset` defines the time after which the animation starts. So this animation set will take 400 + 100 + 200 = 700 milliseconds in total to complete.

Now, you have to create the animation for the part where the circle moves up the heart. Create a file called **animator_heart_fillup.xml** in the **animator** directory and add the following XML:

```
<objectAnimator xmlns:android="http://schemas.android.com/apk/
res/android"
    android:duration="250"
    android:interpolator="@android:interpolator/
accelerate_cubic"
    android:propertyName="translateY"
    android:startOffset="100"
    android:valueFrom="17"
    android:valueTo="0"
    android:valueType="floatType" />
```

This animates `translateY` from a value of 17 to 0 over a duration of 250 milliseconds. It uses an `accelerate_cubic` interpolator, which means that it will use a cubic function to accelerate the rate of change of the values.

Defining the Animated Vector

Create a file called **heart_fill_animation.xml** inside the **drawable** directory and add:

```
<animated-vector xmlns:android="http://schemas.android.com/apk/
res/android"
    android:drawable="@drawable/ic_heart_unfilled">
  <target
```

```
        android:name="circle"
        android:animation="@animator/animator_heart_fillup" />

    <target
        android:animation="@animator/animator_alpha"
        android:name="heart"/>
</animated-vector>
```

This file does two important things: First, it specifies the Animated Vector Drawable using the `drawable` attribute. It then specifies that the `animator_alpha` animation has to be applied to the vector constituent named `heart` and the `animator_heart_fillup` animation to the constituent named `circle`. It will throw an exception if it can't find the strings mentioned in the `name` attribute in the specified vector.

Playing the Animation

Open **fragment_details.xml** and add the following attribute to the `ImageView` with the ID `heart_image`:

```
app:srcCompat="@drawable/heart_fill_animation"
```

This is a reference to the `AnimatedVectorDrawable` you just created.

Open **AnimalDetailsFragment.kt** and add the following to the `onDoubleTap` callback inside `doubleTapGestureListener`:

```
(binding.heartImage.drawable as Animatable?)?.start()
```

Here, you're getting a reference to the `Drawable` you just assigned to the `ImageView`. You know it's an `AnimatedVectorDrawable` that implements the `Animatable` interface that abstracts everything that's possible to animate. You then cast the `AnimatedVectorDrawable` to `Animatable` and invoke `start` on it to start the animation.

And that's it. Your `AnimatedVectorDrawable` is good to go. Build and run, then go to any pet's details page and double-tap the image. You'll now see a nice heart animation, showing your love for the cute pet.

Figure 11.7 shows an intermediate state of the animation:

Figure 11.7 — One Frame of the Heart Animation

Physics-based Animations

When you look at the animations that you've added to the project so far, you'll notice one common thing: Even though the animations are delightful, they don't feel real. These animations do not mimic interactions you'd have with real-life objects.

One way to significantly improve the user experience is to add physics-based animations. These animations follow the laws of physics, which makes them seem more natural and relatable to the user. Physics-based animations help you do this without having to worry about a lot of math.

In this chapter, you'll implement two kinds of animations:

1. Fling animation
2. Spring animation

You'll use the Jetpack DynamicAnimation library to create these animations. Open the **build.gradle** for the **app** module and add the following library declaration:

```
implementation
"androidx.dynamicanimation:dynamicanimation:1.0.0"
```

This gives you access to the library to use in the following animations.

Spring Animation

Spring animations give a bouncy feel to objects. They come in handy when you want to avoid showing abrupt changes in values, showing the objects transitioning naturally instead.

Consider a bouncing basketball. With each bounce, the height that the ball reaches reduces until the ball eventually comes to a halt. Springs work in a similar way. You initially stretch them to a certain length, then release them. They repeatedly expand and contract but the expansion keeps reducing until it stops in the contracted state.

When you open any pet's details screen, one of the main actions you want the user to do is to call the organization about the pet. To draw attention to that action, you'll add a bouncy animation to increase the size of the **Call** button, which the arrow in Figure 11.8 points to:

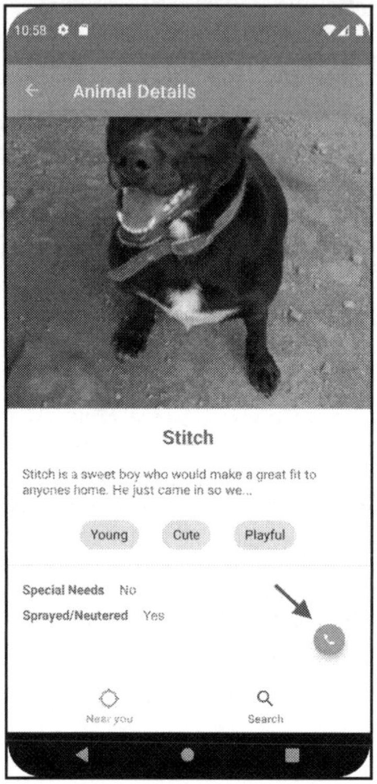

Figure 11.8 — The Call Button

Before you start writing the spring animation, you need to learn about `SpringForce`. Every spring animation uses the concept of a virtual spring. Such a spring has two properties:

1. **Damping Ratio**: Determines how quickly the values change over time.
2. **Stiffness**: Sets the force with which the objects — or views — move.

Now, you're ready to start. Open **AnimalDetailsFragment.kt** in the **details.presentation** package and add the following code before `onCreate`.

```
private val springForce: SpringForce by lazy {
  SpringForce().apply { // 1
    dampingRatio = DAMPING_RATIO_HIGH_BOUNCY // 2
    stiffness = STIFFNESS_VERY_LOW // 3
```

```
    }
  }
```

In this code, you:

1. Create an instance of `SpringForce` that encapsulates the property of the spring animation you want to apply.
2. Set `dampingRatio`, which describes how oscillations in a system decay after a disturbance. In this case, you use `DAMPING_RATIO_HIGH_BOUNCY`, an existing constant for a damping ratio that makes a very bouncy spring.
3. Set the `stiffness`, assigning the existing value `STIFFNESS_VERY_LOW`. The stiffer a spring is, the more force it applies to the attached object when the spring is not at the final position.

To increase the button size, you increase the button's `scaleX` and `scaleY` properties.

In the same **AnimalDetailsFragment.kt** file, add the following code before `onCreate`:

```
private val callScaleXSpringAnimation: SpringAnimation by lazy {
  SpringAnimation(binding.call, DynamicAnimation.SCALE_X).apply
{
    spring = springForce
  }
}

private val callScaleYSpringAnimation: SpringAnimation by lazy {
  SpringAnimation(binding.call, DynamicAnimation.SCALE_Y).apply
{
    spring = springForce
  }
}
```

This creates two `SpringAnimation` instances for the `scaleX` and `scaleY` properties, respectively, and sets `springForce` as their spring.

In **fragment_details.xml**, look at the attributes of the `FloatingActionButton` named `call`. Notice that its `scaleX` and `scaleY` attributes are set to 0.6. The animation will work by increasing the values of these attributes from 0.6 to 1.0.

Go back to **AnimalDetailsFragment.kt** and add the following code at the end of `displayPetDetails`:

```
callScaleXSpringAnimation.animateToFinalPosition(FLING_SCALE)
callScaleYSpringAnimation.animateToFinalPosition(FLING_SCALE)
```

The code calls `animateToFinalPosition` with the `FLING_SCALE` to start both the spring animations. You set the value of `FLING_SCALE` to 1.0 at the beginning of the class.

Build and run. Click on any pet's image to go to the details screen. You'll notice that, right after the details of the pet become visible, the **Call** button bounces and increases in size.

Well done. You've successfully added a realistic animation to your app.

Fling Animation

Consider an example of a user flicking a coin. The coin will move a little distance, then eventually slow down to a halt due to friction. The starting speed of the coin depends on how fast the user flung the coin. Fling animations help mimic this effect.

Wouldn't it be fun if there was an Easter egg somewhere in the app? How about showing a cute doggy picture if the user flings the **Call** button and the button stops on the pet's image?

Similar to the spring animation, you'll need two separate fling animations to accomplish this: one to change the x position of your view and another to change the y position.

Open **AnimalDetailsFragment.kt** in the **details.presentation** package, and add the following code before `onCreate`.

```
private val FLING_FRICTION = 2f

private val callFlingXAnimation: FlingAnimation by lazy {
  FlingAnimation(binding.call, DynamicAnimation.X).apply { // 1
    friction = FLING_FRICTION // 2
    setMinValue(0f) // 3
    setMaxValue(binding.root.width.toFloat() -
binding.call.width.toFloat()) // 4
  }
}

private val callFlingYAnimation: FlingAnimation by lazy {
  FlingAnimation(binding.call, DynamicAnimation.Y).apply { // 1
    friction = FLING_FRICTION // 2
    setMinValue(0f) // 3
    setMaxValue(binding.root.height.toFloat() -
binding.call.width.toFloat()) // 4
  }
}
```

In this code, you:

1. Use the `FlingAnimation` constructor, passing references to which `View` you want to animate and which of its properties to animate.
2. Set the `FlingAnimation`'s `friction`. The greater the friction is, the sooner the animation will slow down. In both cases, you use the existing `FLING_FRICTION`, which has the value `2.0`. That means that it takes a bit of effort to fling the button onto the image.
3. Use `setMinValue` to set the initial value to `0`.
4. Set the end value using `setMaxValue`.

You've defined two `FlingAnimation` — now, you can use them.

Detecting a Fling

Now that you have your animations ready, you need a way to detect the fling gesture so you can start the animations. You'll use a `GestureListener` to detect fling gestures.

In **AnimalDetailsFragment.kt**, in the **details.presentation** package, add the following code inside `displayPetDetails`:

```
val flingGestureListener = object:
GestureDetector.SimpleOnGestureListener() { // 1
  override fun onFling(e1: MotionEvent?, e2: MotionEvent?,
velocityX: Float, // 2
    velocityY: Float): Boolean {
    return true
  }

  override fun onDown(e: MotionEvent) = true // 2
}
val flingGestureDetector = GestureDetector(requireContext(),
flingGestureListener) // 3

binding.call.setOnTouchListener { v, event ->
  flingGestureDetector.onTouchEvent(event)
}
```

In this code, you:

1. Create `GestureDetector.SimpleOnGestureListener`. This is an interface `GestureDetector` provides to listen for specific events like double-taps or, in this case, flings.
2. The `GestureDetector.SimpleOnGestureListener` requires you to implement `onFling` and `onDown`. The former is called when a fling gesture happens, the latter when a tap occurs. The return values tell if the events have been consumed or if they can propagate to other components.
3. To recognize the specific gesture, you need a `GestureDetector`. Here, you create one using `Context` and `flingGestureListener`, which you just created.
4. Finally, you bind the event on the `Call` button to the `GestureDetector`

You call `onFling` whenever the user performs a fling gesture. `velocityX` and `velocityY` represent the x and y velocities of the fling. You'll need this information to start the animations.

Starting the Fling Animation

When a fling gesture happens, you have to start the animations. Add the following code inside `onFling`, which becomes:

```
// ...
val flingGestureListener = object:
GestureDetector.SimpleOnGestureListener() {
  override fun onFling(e1: MotionEvent?, e2: MotionEvent?,
velocityX: Float,
                       velocityY: Float): Boolean {
    callFlingXAnimation.setStartVelocity(velocityX).start() // 1
    callFlingYAnimation.setStartVelocity(velocityY).start() // 2
    return true
  }

  override fun onDown(e: MotionEvent) = true
}
// ...
```

In this code, you:

1. Use `setStartVelocity` to set the velocity that starts the fling animation. You get this value from the `onFling` gesture callback.

2. Start the animation using `start`.

Build and run. Open the details screen for any pet and try flinging the **Call** button. You'll notice that the button moves in the direction of the fling and then starts slowing down.

Listening for the Animation's End

To show the secret image, you need to check if the **Call** button overlaps the image when it stops moving. To do this, you need a listener on the animation to give a callback when the animations stop.

In **AnimalDetailsFragment.kt**, add the following at the end of `displayPetDetails`:

```
callFlingYAnimation.addEndListener { _, _, _, _ ->
  if (areViewsOverlapping(binding.call, binding.image)) {
    val action =
AnimalDetailsFragmentDirections.actionDetailsToSecret()
    findNavController().navigate(action)
  }
}
```

This adds an end listener to the y-fling animation. `areViewsOverlapping` is a helper method that checks if two views overlap. You use it to check if the **Call** button overlaps the image. If it does, start a new fragment to show the secret image.

Build and run the app. On the details page, if you fling the Call button hard enough that it stops on the image, you'll see a cute doggy picture.

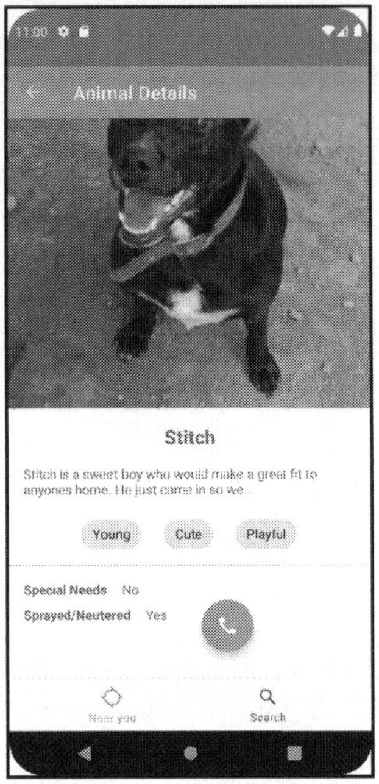

Figure 11.9 — Call Button Fling Animation

Congratulations! You've now seen how easy it is to add next-level animations to your app, giving the user a better overall experience.

Key Points

- Animations make your app stand out and leave an impression on the user.
- Lottie is great for complex animations and can be highly customized.
- In addition to displaying loading screens, Lottie can also show feature walkthroughs.
- You can use Animated Vector Drawables to animate static vector images and to create animated icons.
- Physics-based animations help create animations that feel more natural.
- **Spring animations** can create bouncing animations.
- **Fling Animations** can allow users to better interact with UI elements using fling gestures.

Great! In this chapter, you learned a lot about Lottie and physics-based animations. In the next chapter, you'll learn how to use `MotionLayout` and the new **Motion Layout Editor**.

Chapter 12: MotionLayout & Motion Editor

By Subhrajyoti Sen

Animations and transitions are a great way of improving your app's user experience. Android has a wide set of classes you can use to implement different kinds of animations, but historically, using them to create anything complex has been difficult. Fortunately, Android introduced **MotionLayout** in **ConstraintLayout 2.0** to address these problems.

MotionLayout makes it possible to implement detailed animations entirely in XML, similar to the way you create layouts. In this chapter, you'll learn how to use **MotionLayout** to

- Animate view dimensions.
- Translate views.
- Preview the animation in the IDE.
- Change the shape of images and apply filters.

Getting to Know MotionLayout

Before you start creating beautiful animations with MotionLayout, you need to learn about its three main concepts:

1. **MotionScene**: This is the root element for every animation scene. It contains the different states of the animation and the transitions between them.
2. **ConstraintSet**: A collection of `Constraint` tags. A `Constraint` is a set of `ConstraintLayout` attributes that you apply to a specific view. Typically, you'll have two `ConstraintSets` that define the start and end states of the animation. Although you can have more `ConstraintSets` in theory, XML only lets you use two. If you need to use more than two states in the animation, you have to do that programmatically.
3. **Transition**: Defines the transition between two `ConstraintSets`. You can also set properties, like the animation duration and the interpolator, to change the values of the constraints.

This is in the context of `ConstraintLayout`, where you represent the state of a specific `View`, or a group of `Views`, as the set of the constraints you apply to them. Different constraints produce a different state for the `Views`. You then use a **Transition** to represent how you go from one state to another.

Finally, as Figure 12.1 shows, a **MotionScene** is a way to aggregate different states for a `View` and the way you transition from one to another. This produces an **animation**.

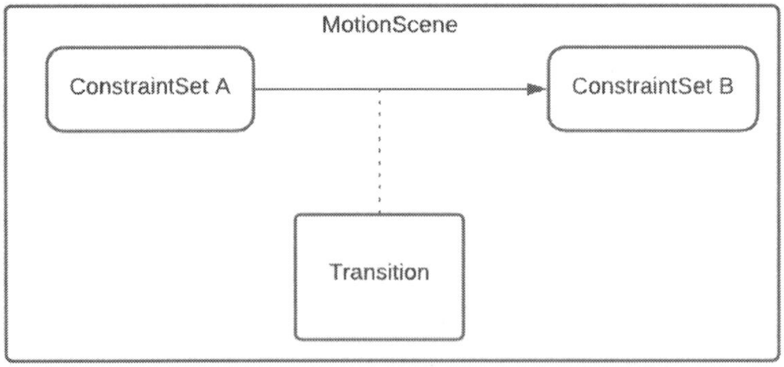

Figure 12.1 — The Concept Behind MotionScene

Getting Started

Open the **starter** project from the downloaded materials and run it, then go to the details page of any pet. You'll notice that the layout of the page is a bit different from what you implemented in the previous chapter. This change adds scrollable content, which lets you create gesture-based animations.

Figure 12.2 — The Starter Project

Open the project **build.gradle** and verify that your `constraint_layout_version` is at least **2.1.4**.

To create your first `MotionScene`, you need to:

1. Create an XML resource with the `MotionScene`.
2. Apply the `MotionScene` to a specific `View`.

> **Note**: A `ViewGroup` is a specific `View` that aggregates other `Views` using the **Composite** design pattern. How you aggregate the other `Views` is what defines a specific **layout**. From now on, anything you read about `Views` also applies to `ViewGroups` or in general layouts.

Defining a MotionLayout

You can define a `MotionLayout` declaratively by using an XML document. Create a file named **fragment_details_scene.xml** in **res/xml** and insert the following code:

```
<MotionScene
  xmlns:android="http://schemas.android.com/apk/res/android"
  xmlns:motion="http://schemas.android.com/apk/res-auto">

  <ConstraintSet android:id="@+id/start">
  </ConstraintSet>

  <ConstraintSet android:id="@+id/end">
  </ConstraintSet>

  <Transition
    motion:constraintSetEnd="@+id/end"
    motion:constraintSetStart="@id/start"
    motion:motionInterpolator="linear"
    motion:duration="1000">
  </Transition>

</MotionScene>
```

In this document, you create a `MotionScene`. In particular:

1. You use `<MotionScene/>` as the root element for the XML document. As described in Figure 12.1, you use the `<MotionScene/>` as the container for the definitions of `ConstraintSet` and `Transition`.
2. Using `<ConstraintSet/>`, you define a specific state. In this case, you're just creating the placeholder for what you consider the starting state by setting its ID to `start`
3. In the same way, you use `<ConstraintSet/>` to define the placeholder for the final state of the transition that you identify with the `end` ID.
4. Using `<Transition/>`, you define how the animation should run.
5. With the `constraintSetStart` and `constraintSetEnd` attributes, you bind the `Transition` to the specific initial and final states. In this case, you're representing how you go from `start` to `end`.

6. With the previous attributes, you said you want to go from `start` to `end` but you didn't specify how this would happen. Using `motionInterpolator`, you now set the `linear` interpolator. This means the rate at which the constraints' values change stays constant over time. For example, by animating the **alpha** of a `View` from 0 to 1 over 200 milliseconds, the alpha will be 0.25 after the initial 50 milliseconds, 0.5 after 100 milliseconds and so on.

7. Finally, you use `duration` to define the duration of the transition in milliseconds.

To get a good feeling of how this works, play around with the previous configuration. Try, for instance, other values for the `motionInterpolator` attribute. You can choose among these values:

- `easeInOut`
- `easeIn`
- `easeOut`
- `linear`
- `bounce`

How do you choose the right interpolator for your animation? Well, there's no definite answer to this. Unless you have specific timing in mind, try out a few interpolators and check which one looks best.

Alternatively, you can also specify your own interpolator with something like:

```
<MotionScene
  xmlns:android="http://schemas.android.com/apk/res/android"
  xmlns:motion="http://schemas.android.com/apk/res-auto">
  <!-- // ... -->
  <Transition
    motion:constraintSetEnd="@+id/end"
    motion:constraintSetStart="@id/start"
    motion:motionInterpolator="cubic(.17,.67,.83,.67)"
    motion:duration="1000">
  </Transition>

</MotionScene>
```

Here, you use `cubic(x1,y1,x2,y2)` to pass coefficients representing the control points of a cubic Bezier from 0,0 to 1,1. Bezier.com has a great interactive tool to get the values for such interpolators. Find it at https://cubic-bezier.com.

Now that you have a `MotionScene`, you can apply it to a specific `View`.

Applying MotionScene to a View

Now, you need to apply the **MotionScene** you just created to a specific View. To do this, first open **fragment_details.xml** and add the following:

```
<androidx.constraintlayout.motion.widget.MotionLayout
  android:id="@+id/motion_layout"
  xmlns:android="http://schemas.android.com/apk/res/android"
  xmlns:app="http://schemas.android.com/apk/res-auto"
  xmlns:tools="http://schemas.android.com/tools"
  android:layout_width="match_parent"
  android:layout_height="match_parent"
  app:layoutDescription="@xml/fragment_details_scene"> <!-- HERE
-->
  <!-- // ... -->
</androidx.constraintlayout.motion.widget.MotionLayout>
```

In this XML document, you:

1. Replaced the root `androidx.constraintlayout.widget.ConstraintLayout` with `androidx.constraintlayout.motion.widget.MotionLayout`.
2. Added `app:layoutDescription="@xml/fragment_details_scene"`, which refers to the `MotionScene` that MotionLayout needs to transition between states.

As you see in Figure 12.3, you'll notice that it doesn't affect the layout preview. That's because `MotionLayout` extends from `ConstraintLayout` and inherits all its features.

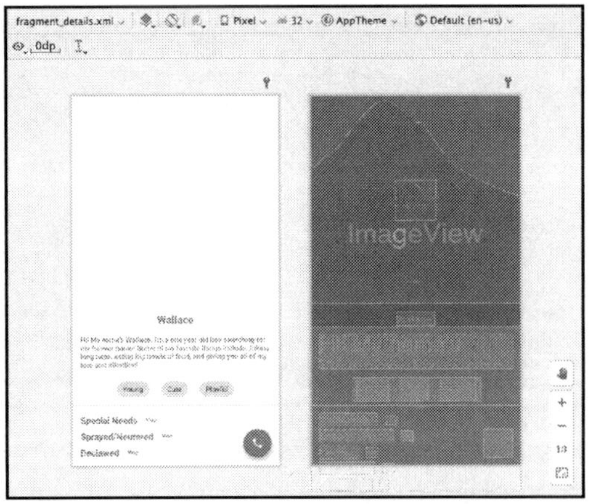

Figure 12.3 — Layout Editor With MotionLayout

Now that you've set up MotionLayout, it's time to explore its various features and see them in action.

Adding Your First Constraint

As mentioned above, MotionLayout works by transitioning between two states, where each state is represented by a `ConstraintSet`. Inside each `ConstraintSet`, you have multiple `Constraints` corresponding to different views. You only need to define a `Constraint` for the views you want to animate, not every view.

You define a `Constraint` using the `id` of the view you want to animate and a set of corresponding attributes that change the position and orientation of the views. For example, you can set the height and width of a `TextView` but not its background.

One important thing to note is that the start and end constraints defined in `MotionScene` both inherit from the layout defined inside `MotionLayout`. That means that if you don't want to change the starting state of a view in the transition, you don't have to add a `Constraint` for it in the start `ConstraintSet`.

For your first animation, you'll create a transition that shrinks the size of the pet's image and places it at the top-left corner. To do this, you only need to add a `Constraint` to the end `ConstraintSet`.

Open **fragment_details_scene.xml** and add the following:

```
<MotionScene xmlns:android="http://schemas.android.com/apk/res/
android"
  xmlns:motion="http://schemas.android.com/apk/res-auto">
  <!-- / ...-->
  <ConstraintSet android:id="@+id/end">
    <Constraint
      android:id="@id/image"
      android:layout_width="100dp"
      android:layout_height="100dp"
      android:layout_marginBottom="@dimen/default_margin"
      android:layout_marginStart="@dimen/default_margin"
      android:layout_marginTop="@dimen/default_margin"
      motion:layout_constraintStart_toStartOf="parent"
      motion:layout_constraintTop_toTopOf="parent">
    </Constraint>
  </ConstraintSet>
  <!-- / ...-->
</MotionScene>
```

In this code, you:

1. Add a <Constraint/> as a child of <ConstraintSet/> with the `end` ID to indicate it's the final state.
2. Add a <Constraint/> for the `View` with the ID `image`.
3. Set the image size to 100dp.
4. Set some margins.
5. Constraintthe image to the `top` and `start` of the parent.

It's time to preview the animation and see how it looks, which you'd usually do by building and running the app. Up to now, this has been the only way of previewing animations on Android. However, now there's a shiny tool that will make the lives of Android developers much easier: **Motion Editor**.

Motion Editor

Motion Editor is a handy tool that comes built-in with **Android Studio 4.0** and later. It lets you preview animations created with MotionLayout without having to leave the IDE. Additionally, it provides a Graphical User Interface to add and edit different `ConstraintSets`, `Constraints`, `Transitions` and much more.

It's similar to how you can create layouts using both XML and Android Studio's **Design View**. For this chapter, you'll mainly use Motion Editor to preview your animations.

To display Motion Editor, open `fragment_details` and choose the **Split** or **Design** tab near the top-right of the screen.

Figure 12.4 — Layout Editor Tabs

Once Motion Editor is open, you'll see a screen like this:

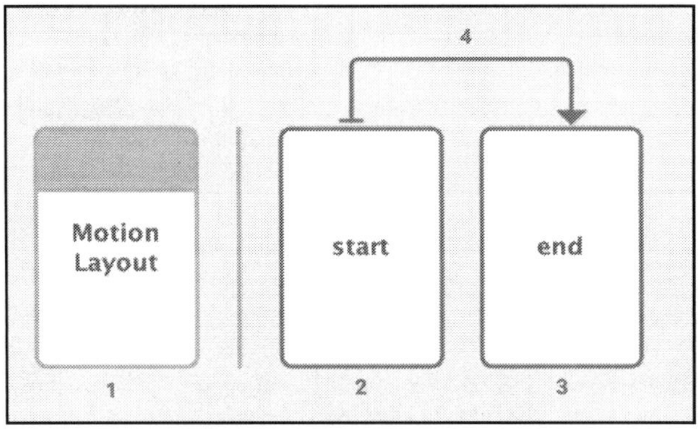

Figure 12.5 — The Motion Editor

The screen shown above has four main components:

1. The base **MotionLayout**
2. The start **ConstraintSet**
3. The end **ConstraintSet**
4. The **Transition**

To preview the animation, select **Transition**. You'll then see a Timeline window, like the one shown below.

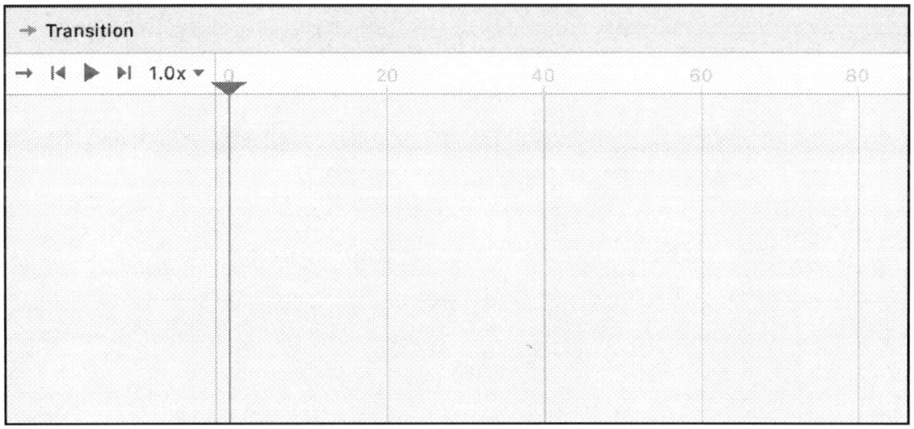

Figure 12.6 — Transition Timeline

With this window, you can play or pause the animation, speed it up or slow it down and even preview the animation running both forward and backward.

Click the **Play** button and you'll see your animation in action. While the animation is playing, you'll notice a dashed line on the preview. This is the **motion path** — it denotes the path the view takes from the start of the transition to the end. Later in the chapter, you'll use this line to improve the transition.

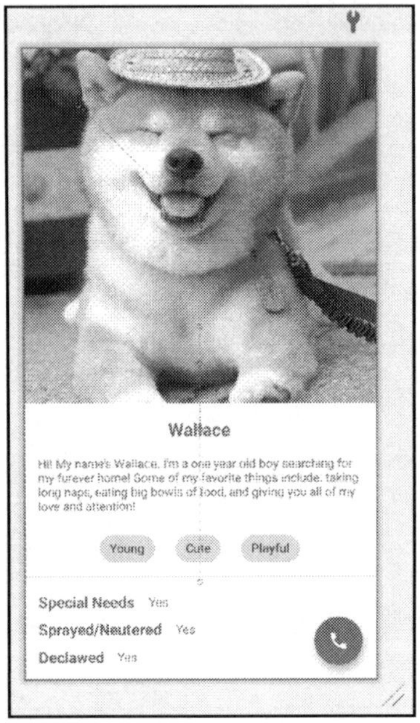

Figure 12.7 — The Motion Path

If you can't view that path, pause the animation midway and it'll appear. You can also view these paths on a device or emulator by adding the `app:showPaths="true"` attribute to the `MotionLayout` tag.

Congratulations, you've successfully created your first animation using MotionLayout. Next, you'll learn how to trigger your animation to start.

Adding a Trigger

Animations seldom start on their own; they're usually associated with an event or user interaction. For example, you click on a button to load something and the button animates to a progress bar. It would be weird for this animation to start on its own.

When you previewed your animation in the Motion Editor, you used a **Play** button. When the app runs on a device, however, you need to give the user a way to trigger the animation. MotionLayout provides two such triggers:

1. **OnClick**: Activates when the user clicks a specific `View`.

2. **OnSwipe**: Activates when the user performs a swipe gesture in a certain direction on a specific `View`.

In this section, you'll use the `OnSwipe` trigger to make the transition start when the user swipes up on the content below the image.

Adding OnSwipe

Open **fragment_details_scene.xml** and add the `<OnSwipe/>` element to `Transition`:

```
<MotionScene xmlns:android="http://schemas.android.com/apk/res/android"
  xmlns:motion="http://schemas.android.com/apk/res-auto">
  <!-- / ...-->
  <Transition
    motion:constraintSetEnd="@+id/end"
    motion:constraintSetStart="@id/start"
    motion:duration="1000"
    motion:motionInterpolator="linear">
    <OnSwipe
      motion:dragDirection="dragUp"
      motion:touchAnchorId="@id/scrollView" />
  </Transition>

</MotionScene>
```

In this code, `dragDirection` specifies the direction of the swipe. The supported drag directions are: up, down, left and right. `touchAnchorId` specifies the `View` the user needs to drag.

Build and run. Slowly drag upwards on the content below the pet's image and you'll see your animation in action. As a bonus, after the animation, swipe downwards on the same part of the content. You'll see your animation run in reverse.

Figure 12.8 — The Scene at the End of the Transition

One of the nice features of **MotionLayout** is that you can make forward and backward animations work without having to create an explicit transition.

Notice that the `Lottie` loading animation is visible even after the page has finished loading and some of the pet details display while the page is still loading. This is due to a special property of `MotionLayout`, which you'll explore in the next section.

Overriding Visibility

`MotionLayout` controls the visibility of all its child views. Even if you tried to control the visibility of child views programmatically, it wouldn't have any effect. Luckily, `MotionLayout` provides functionality to ignore this behavior.

Enter the following code in the **start** `ConstraintSet`:

```
<MotionScene xmlns:android="http://schemas.android.com/apk/res/
android"
  xmlns:motion="http://schemas.android.com/apk/res-auto">

  <ConstraintSet android:id="@+id/start">
    <Constraint android:id="@+id/loader">
      <PropertySet motion:visibilityMode="ignore" />
    </Constraint>

    <Constraint android:id="@+id/call">
      <PropertySet motion:visibilityMode="ignore" />
    </Constraint>

    <Constraint android:id="@+id/scrollView">
      <PropertySet motion:visibilityMode="ignore" />
    </Constraint>
  </ConstraintSet>
  <!-- // ... -->
</MotionScene>
```

`visibilityMode="ignore"` instructs `MotionLayout` to not override the visibility of the view with the ID **loader**.

Build and run the app now and you'll notice that the dog's image is no longer visible during the transition and the pet's details don't display when the loader is shown.

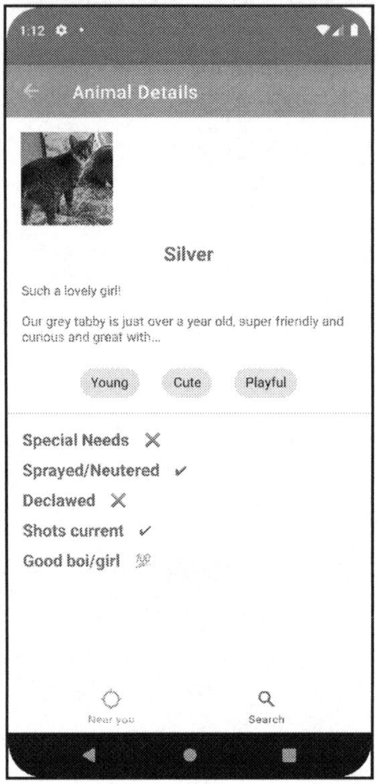

Figure 12.9 — Transaction Without Loader

Animating More Features

The current transition animates only the pet's image. How about animating the pet's name and the **Call** button as well? In this section, you'll add constraints to:

- Change the name's alignment from center- to left-justified while increasing its size.
- Make the **Call** button roll off the screen.

To do this, add the following code to the **end** `ConstraintSet`:

```
<MotionScene xmlns:android="http://schemas.android.com/apk/res/
android"
  xmlns:motion="http://schemas.android.com/apk/res-auto">
  <!-- // ... -->
  <ConstraintSet android:id="@+id/end">
    <!-- // ... -->
    <Constraint
      android:id="@+id/call"
      android:layout_width="wrap_content"
      android:layout_height="wrap_content"
      android:layout_marginBottom="@dimen/default_margin"
      android:rotation="180"
      motion:layout_constraintBottom_toBottomOf="parent"
      motion:layout_constraintStart_toEndOf="parent" />

    <Constraint
      android:id="@+id/name"
      android:layout_width="wrap_content"
      android:layout_height="wrap_content"
      android:layout_marginBottom="@dimen/default_margin"
      android:layout_marginStart="@dimen/default_margin"
      android:layout_marginTop="@dimen/default_margin"
      android:scaleX="1.4"
      android:scaleY="1.4"
      motion:layout_constraintStart_toStartOf="parent"
      motion:layout_constraintTop_toBottomOf="@+id/image" />
  </ConstraintSet>
  <!-- // ... -->
</MotionScene>
```

In the previous code, the first `Constraint` adds a rotation of 180 degrees to the `call` view and also constrains the start of the view to the end of the parent. That places it at the right of the window and hides it from the user. This will make it seem like the view is rotating out of the screen.

The second `Constraint` aligns the `name` view to the start of the parent and scales it to 1.4 times its original size. It also adds a start margin to align the view properly with the rest of the text.

Build and run. You'll observe that, as you slowly drag up, the **Call** button rolls out of the screen and the pet's name moves diagonally to the left while increasing in size.

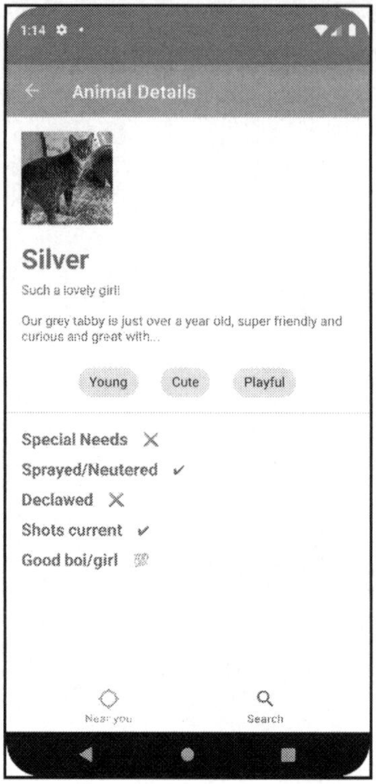

Figure 12.10 — Animation With Multiple Constraints

Adding Non-linear Motion

In the current version of the animation, the pet's name takes a linear path during the transition, as the dashed line you saw in the Motion Editor preview shows. The path line is straight, denoting linear animation. However, the transition would look much better with a curved path.

`MotionScene` uses the concept of frames. Each frame denotes an instant in the transition. The first frame has a position of 0, while 100 denotes the final position.

`MotionScene` provides multiple ways to specify frame properties. The two most important are:

1. **KeyAttribute**: Specifies attributes of a view in the frame.
2. **KeyPosition**: Specifies the position of the view in the frame. You can define the position relative to the parent or the path or define it as a delta of the distance covered by the view over the entire transition.

The supported **KeyAttribute**s are:

- `android:visibility`
- `android:alpha`
- `android:elevation`
- `android:rotation`
- `android:rotationX`
- `android:rotationY`
- `transitionPathRotate`
- `android:scaleX`
- `android:scaleY`
- `android:translationX`
- `android:translationY`
- `android:translationZ`

You define `KeyAttribure` and `KeyPosition` inside a `KeyFrameSet`. To do this, add the following code to the `Transition`:

```
<MotionScene xmlns:android="http://schemas.android.com/apk/res/
android"
  xmlns:motion="http://schemas.android.com/apk/res-auto">
  <!-- // ... -->
  <Transition
    motion:constraintSetEnd="@+id/end"
    motion:constraintSetStart="@id/start"
    motion:duration="1000"
    motion:motionInterpolator="linear">
    <KeyFrameSet>
      <KeyPosition
        motion:framePosition="50"
        motion:keyPositionType="parentRelative"
        motion:motionTarget="@id/name"
        motion:percentX="0.4" />
```

```
    </KeyFrameSet>
    <!-- // ... -->
  </Transition>
</MotionScene>
```

In this code, you use `<KeyPosition/>` to define a frame that applies to the `name` view and is midway in the transition by giving it a `framePosition` of **50**.

You use `percentX` of **0.4** and `keyPositionType` of **parentRelative** to specify that, at frame position 50, the view should cover **40%** of the distance along the X-axis instead of the **50%** it would cover otherwise. This gives a curved path to the motion, which you can verify using the path line in the preview.

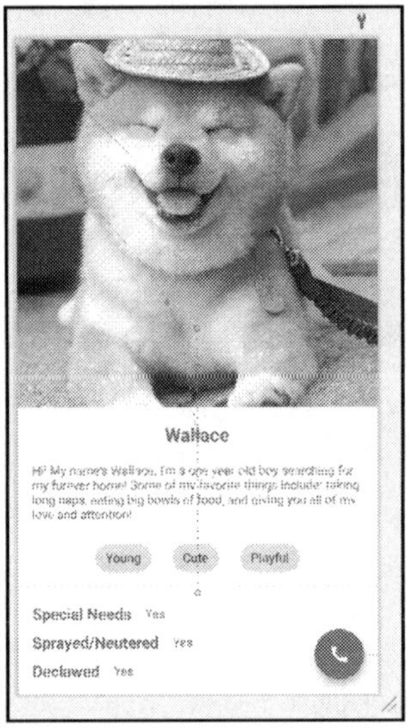

Figure 12.11 — Curved Motion Path

To make it easier to see the changes while the animation is running, use Motion Editor's speed toggle to select an animation speed of **0.25x**.

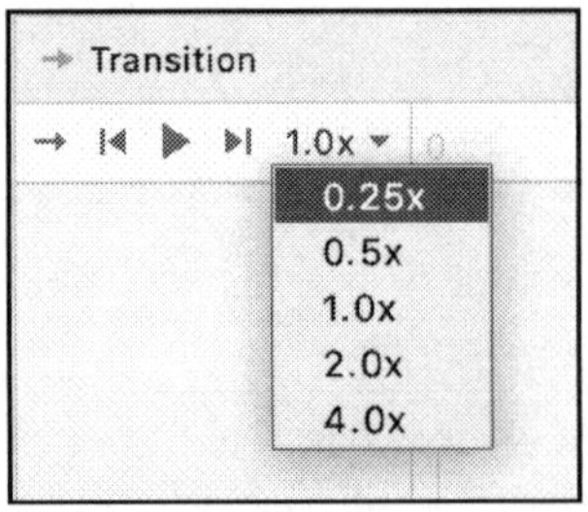

Figure 12.12 — Transition Speed

ImageFilterView

In addition to MotionLayout, ConstraintLayout 2.0 also introduced a utility class named `ImageFilterView`, which extends `AppCompatImageView` and makes it easy to apply filters to images. Now, you no longer need to include a new third-party library to get a circular ImageView. With `ImageFilterView`, you get out-of-the-box support to change the radius of the image, crossfade between two images, change the image saturation and, much more.

In the current transition, the pet's image only shrinks in size and moves to the top-left corner. In this section, you'll modify the transition so the image transforms from a square to a circular image as it moves toward the top.

That might sound complex to implement, but you'll soon see that the combination of `ImageFilterView` and `MotionLayout` makes it quite simple.

CustomAttribute

Look closely at all the view attributes you've animated so far and you'll notice that these are attributes that apply to any `View` or affect the positions of the different views. It's not possible to assign a custom property in any `Constraint`.

That's because `MotionLayout` provides a custom tag named `CustomAttribute` to use with attributes that are either unrelated to the position or are specific to certain views.

For example, you can set the `android:src` attribute of an `ImageView` or the `android:backgroundColor` of a `Button`. You define `CustomAttribute` with the name of the attribute and its value.

To try this out, open **fragment_details.xml** and replace the `id` **image** `ImageView` with the following `ImageFilterView`:

```
<androidx.constraintlayout.motion.widget.MotionLayout
  xmlns:android="http://schemas.android.com/apk/res/android"
  xmlns:app="http://schemas.android.com/apk/res-auto"
  xmlns:tools="http://schemas.android.com/tools"
  android:id="@+id/motion_layout"
  android:layout_width="match_parent"
  android:layout_height="match_parent"
  app:layoutDescription="@xml/fragment_details_scene">
  <!-- // ... -->
  <androidx.constraintlayout.utils.widget.ImageFilterView
    android:id="@+id/image"
    android:layout_width="match_parent"
```

```
        android:layout_height="0dp"
        android:contentDescription="@string/image_of_pet"
        android:scaleType="centerCrop"
        tools:src="@drawable/cute_doggo"
        app:layout_constraintDimensionRatio="H,1:1"
        app:layout_constraintTop_toTopOf="parent"
        app:roundPercent="0" />
    <!-- // ... -->
</androidx.constraintlayout.motion.widget.MotionLayout>
```

Remember to use the fully-qualified name for `ImageFilterView`: `androidx.constraintlayout.utils.widget.ImageFilterView`.

Next, open **fragment_details_scene.xml** and insert the following code inside the `start` ConstraintSet:

```
<MotionScene xmlns:android="http://schemas.android.com/apk/res/
android"
    xmlns:motion="http://schemas.android.com/apk/res-auto">

    <ConstraintSet android:id="@+id/start">
        <!-- / ... -->
        <Constraint
            android:id="@+id/image"
            android:layout_width="match_parent"
            android:layout_height="0dp"
            android:contentDescription="@string/image_of_pet"
            motion:layout_constraintTop_toTopOf="parent"
            motion:layout_constraintDimensionRatio="H,1:1">
            <CustomAttribute
                motion:attributeName="roundPercent"
                motion:customFloatValue="0"/>
            <CustomAttribute
                motion:attributeName="saturation"
                motion:customFloatValue="1"/>
        </Constraint>
    </ConstraintSet>
    <!-- / ... -->
</MotionScene>
```

In this code, `attributeName` specifies the name of the attribute and `customFloatValue` specifies its value. There are separate attributes for different value types, like `customStringValue` when the custom attribute takes a string input or `customBoolean` when the input value must be a Boolean.

`roundPercent` specifies the corner radius of the image. A value of 0 represents a rectangular image while 1 represents a circular image.

Similarly, `saturation` specifies the, well, saturation, of the image with 1 representing the image with its original saturation and 0 representing a monochrome image.

Now, insert the following code inside the `image` constraint in the end `ConstraintSet` in the same file:

```
<MotionScene xmlns:android="http://schemas.android.com/apk/res/
android"
  xmlns:motion="http://schemas.android.com/apk/res-auto">
  <!-- / ... -->
  <ConstraintSet android:id="@+id/end">
    <Constraint android:id="@id/image" ...>
      <CustomAttribute
        motion:attributeName="roundPercent"
        motion:customFloatValue="1"/>
      <CustomAttribute
        motion:attributeName="saturation"
        motion:customFloatValue="0"/>
    </Constraint>
  </ConstraintSet>
  <!-- / ... -->
</MotionScene>
```

Switch over to Motion Editor and play the animation. You'll see it morphs from being rectangular and colorful to circular and monochrome.

That was simple to implement, wasn't it? Without using `MotionLayout`, this would require a lot of complicated Kotlin code and multiple other libraries.

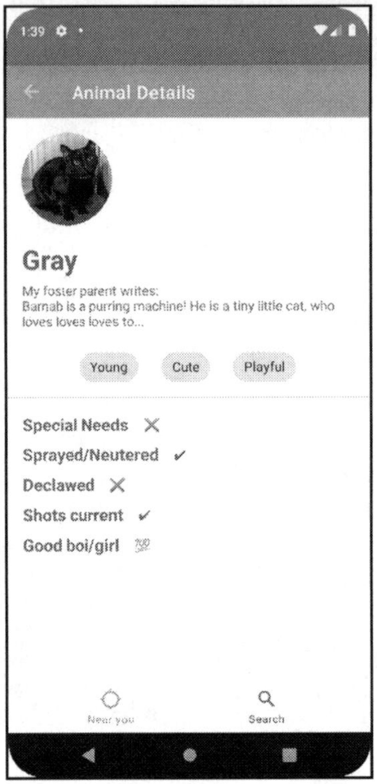

Figure 12.13 — Image Filter and Transformation

Congratulations, you've successfully implemented a set of complex animations, all through XML and without having to deploy your to a device multiple times. This is the true beauty of MotionLayout.

Key Points

- **MotionLayout** is an extension of **ConstraintLayout** that lets you write complex animations in a declarative way through XML.
- You can use **Motion Editor** to preview animations without leaving your IDE.
- A `Transition` defines the start and end state of the motion as well as properties like the motion's duration.
- A `ConstraintSet` defines a state in the transition. It consists of a collection of `Constraints` for each view that you'll animate.
- A `KeyFrameSet` specifies attributes and locations of views at distinct points in the transition.
- `CustomAttribute` sets attribute values that are either `View` properties or are unrelated to the position.
- Use `ImageFilterView` to apply common filters to images and also change properties like the radius.

Chapter 13: Custom Views

By Subhrajyoti Sen

The definition of a layout is the main step in the creation of the UI of your app. Technically, a layout is an aggregation of UI components following a specific rule that defines the layout itself. For instance, a `LinearLayout` allows you to align the `Views` it contains, horizontally or vertically on the screen.

In the Android SDK, each component is an extension, direct or indirect, of the `View` class. Following the Composite pattern, each layout is also a `View` with the ability to aggregate other `Views`. Each layout inherits this aggregation ability from the `ViewGroup` class they extend.

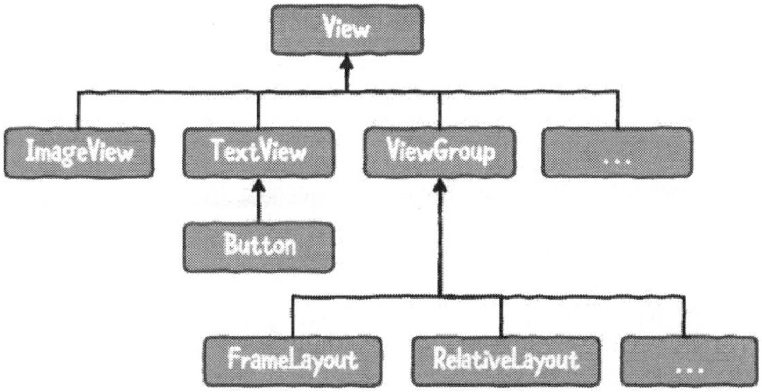

Figure 13.1 — Android SDK View Hierarchy

As you can see in Figure 13.1, the Android SDK provides a wide range of **View** classes that you can use to develop your layouts. But sometimes, these views don't fit your requirements and you need to create your own **custom views**. There are several good reasons to create a custom view:

- Implementing advanced UI designs.
- Creating reusable UI components.
- Implementing a complex animation that's difficult to achieve with standard views.
- Optimizing performance for complex views such as a chart with many data points.

Creating a Custom View can be a challenging task. In this chapter, you'll:

- Learn about Android's View hierarchy.
- Extend `View` and create a custom button.
- Add custom attributes to the custom view.
- Integrate animations inside the custom view.
- Handle state restoration for custom views.
- Learn how to make custom views more performant.

It's time to get started!

Creating Custom Views

You can create a custom view in different ways depending on how much you need to customize the existing Views based on your requirements. You can:

1. **Compose** existing `Views` in a custom way using a custom layout. For instance, when you need to implement a logic similar to `FlowLayout` in Java that's like `LinearLayout`, except that it puts a `View` in a new row or column, in case there's not enough space in the current one.
2. **Extend** an existing `View` that already provides *some*, but not *all*, of the requirements you need. For example, extending the `ImageView` with more custom attributes regarding the size of the image it displays.
3. **Extend** `View` and implement the drawing logic using the **Canvas** API.

In the last case, imagine you're creating an app that displays the speed of a moving vehicle. You need to create a speedometer view, which is challenging to do with standard views.

Instead, you choose to draw the entire view using your own logic. To do so, you need to understand how the Canvas coordinate system works.

Understanding the Canvas Coordinate System

Android's Canvas uses a 2D matrix. The origin is at the top-left of the screen. The x-axis values increase as they move to the right, while the y-axis values increase as they move downwards:

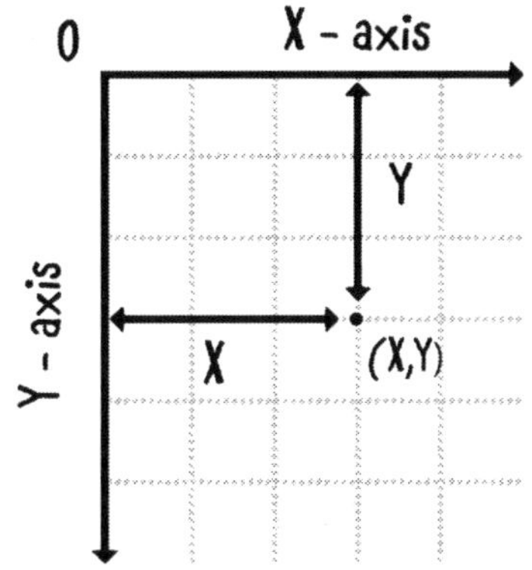

Figure 13.2 — Android Canvas Coordinates System

In Figure 13.2, you can see that an (x,y) pair represents each point, where y is the distance in pixels from the top of the screen and x is the distance from the left edge of the screen.

Implementing a Progress Button

There are cases where it's impossible to develop a certain UI element using the standard Views. In cases like that, you need to manually draw the UI on `Canvas`.

In this chapter, you'll create a button that makes an API call when the user clicks it. After the API call starts, the button transforms into a progress bar. Finally, when the API call completes, the progress bar changes into a Done icon.

To see this in action, open the **final project** in Android Studio, then build and run. Go to the details page for any pet and click the **Adopt** button. You'll see the animation play.

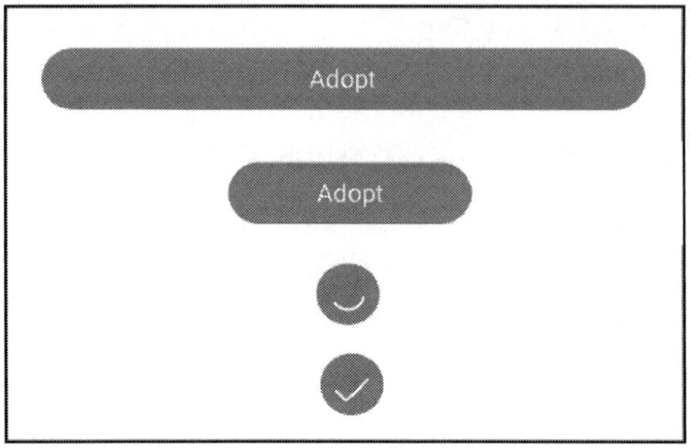

Figure 13.3 — Progress Button Stages

Constructing a view like this is complicated using standard views. Instead, you'll learn how to create that animated view using Canvas.

In this chapter, you'll:

1. Create the `ProgressButton` class, extending directly `View`.
2. Define the custom attributes.
3. Access the custom attribute values from `ProgressButton`.
4. Initialize the `Paint` objects.
5. Design the animation you want to apply.
6. Paint your shape on Canvas.
7. Check your job with a simple preview document.
8. Add the animation.
9. Draw the check icon on the `ProgressButton`'s final state.
10. Enjoy your custom view.

Now, it's time to get to work!

Extending View

For your first step, you need to create the class for your custom view. Create a new file with name **ProgressButton.kt** in **common/presentation** and add the following code to it:

```
class ProgressButton @JvmOverloads constructor( // 1
    context: Context, // 2
    attrs: AttributeSet? = null, // 3
    defStyleAttr: Int = 0 // 4
) : View(context, attrs, defStyleAttr) {

}
```

In the previous code, you:

1. Create `ProgressButton`, which extends `View` and uses `@JvmOverloads` to overload the multiple constructors that all `Views` require. You'll learn about constructors in detail in the next chapter. For now, keep in mind that the constructor has three parameters.
2. Define `context`, which is the only parameter every `View` needs. It allows you to access resources.
3. Every component has some attributes encapsulated into an object of type `AttributeSet`, which you receive as a second primary constructor parameter.
4. As you'll see in Chapter 14, "Style & Theme", you can apply some styles to `Views` that are basically resources. You use this parameter to refer to them.

Right now, the class is nothing more than the `View` it extends. It's time to add some custom attributes.

Creating Custom Attributes

When you create a custom view, you need custom attributes. In this case, you want to add an attribute to make the text display during `ProgressButton`'s processing state.

To see how this works, create an XML file named **attrs.xml** in **res/values** and add the following code:

```
<resources>
  <declare-styleable name="ProgressButton">
    <attr name="progressButton_text" format="string"/>
  </declare-styleable>
</resources>
```

This code does multiple things:

1. Declares a `styleable` resource specific to `ProgressButton`. The custom view uses this to read the attributes.
2. Adds an attribute named **progressButton_text** with the format `string`.

The format of the attributes has two main purposes, letting you:

1. Read values from attributes in a type-safe way.
2. Provide value suggestions when assigning the attributes in XML.

It's a good practice to prefix attribute names with the name of the view. This prevents name clashes if any of the built-in views have an attribute with the same name. It also helps with readability.

It's important to say that here you just defined some resources you can access from any other `View` that knows they exist. There's no strong binding between the name **ProgressButton** and the styleable resources. Of course, you need to access the values you set in the XML layout from the code.

Reading Custom Attribute Values

You can see a custom parameter as a way to configure your component. Of course, you need a way to access the values from the custom view source code.

Open **ProgressButton.kt** and change it, like this:

```
class ProgressButton @JvmOverloads constructor(
    context: Context,
    attrs: AttributeSet? = null,
    defStyleAttr: Int = 0
) : View(context, attrs, defStyleAttr) {

  private var buttonText = ""

  init {
    val typedArray = context.obtainStyledAttributes(attrs,
R.styleable.ProgressButton) // 1
    buttonText =
typedArray.getString(R.styleable.ProgressButton_progressButton_t
ext) ?: "" // 2
    typedArray.recycle() // 3
  }

}
```

Here's what's going on in this code:

1. By invoking `obtainStyledAttributes()` on the `Context`, you access the `TypedArray` that contains the array of attribute values. To do this, you pass the `attrs` you receive in the constructor as the first parameter and `R.styleable.ProgressButton` as the second parameter. Note how the name of the constants is the same as the styleable resource you created earlier.

2. `TypedArray`, which you got above, contains all the custom attributes you've defined. To access each of those, you need to know their type. In this case, you use `getString()` and pass `R.styleable.ProgressButton_progressButton_text` as a parameter. Note how the name for this resource conforms to the template `<ComponentName>_<CustomProperty>`. `TypedArray` provides different methods like `getBoolean()`, `getFont()` and many others to access properties of different types. Note that all attribute references are prefixed with `styleable`.

3. Finally, you invoke `recycle()` on `TypedArray`. This operation lets the Android environment optimize the way resources are used.

Now, you have the values for all the custom attributes for `ProgressButton`. You now have to use them to customize your component.

Initializing the Paint Objects

As you'll see later, you're going to draw your custom component on the `Canvas` using some `Paint` objects. `Paint` is like a paintbrush. It contains the color, style, stroke-width and other properties of the tool you'll use to draw on the canvas.

Open **ProgressButton.kt** and add the following code before the `init` block:

```
class ProgressButton @JvmOverloads constructor(
    context: Context,
    attrs: AttributeSet? = null,
    defStyleAttr: Int = 0
) : View(context, attrs, defStyleAttr) {
  // ...

  private val textPaint = Paint().apply { // 1
    isAntiAlias = true // 2
    style = Paint.Style.FILL // 3
    color = Color.WHITE
    textSize = context.dpToPx(16f)
  }

  private val backgroundPaint = Paint().apply { // 1
    isAntiAlias = true // 2
    style = Paint.Style.FILL // 3
    color = ContextCompat.getColor(context,
R.color.colorPrimary)
  }

  private val progressPaint = Paint().apply { // 1
    isAntiAlias = true // 2
    style = Paint.Style.STROKE // 3
    color = Color.WHITE
    strokeWidth = context.dpToPx(2f) // 4
  }

  private val buttonRect = RectF() // 5
  private val progressRect = RectF() // 5

  private var buttonRadius = context.dpToPx(16f)
  // ...
}
```

In this code, you:

1. Initialize `Paint` objects to use for the text, background and progress state.
2. Set `isAntiAlias` to `true`. **Antialiasing** is a technique that smooths the edges of the shapes you draw on the screen. You'll almost always want to enable it.

3. Use `style` to specify whether `Paint` will draw only the shape outline (`STROKE`) or fill the shape with the current color (`FILL`).

4. Set the width of the paint stroke, which you can think of as the brush size. You set the size using `dpToPx`, which converts values from `dp` to `px`. This is handy because developers are accustomed to providing values in `dp`, but `Canvas` only understands `px`.

5. Initialize the `RectF` that will contain the button and the progress, respectively. `RectF` is a class that allows you to use `Float` to set the position of the `left`, `top`, `right` and `bottom` vertexes.

Now, you have all the tools you need to start drawing on the Canvas. Now, it's time to think about animation.

Designing the Animation Logic

Before you start writing any code to draw your images, break down the animation logic:

Figure 13.4 — The Progress Button Animation

In the image above, consider the dashed box to be the bounds of your view. Your first animation will gradually increase the **offset** value from 0, squishing the button until it becomes circular. The button will be circular when its width equals its height. Therefore, you'll define the final offset as:

```
offset = (initial_width - height) / 2
```

You need to divide the value by 2 because the offset is at both ends of the button. You want half on one side of the button and half on the other.

Now that you have a plan, it's time to start creating your button.

Painting Your Shape

Now, you'll create the **Adopt** button by painting it in Canvas. Add the following code in **ProgressButton.kt**:

```
class ProgressButton @JvmOverloads constructor(
    context: Context,
    attrs: AttributeSet? = null,
    defStyleAttr: Int = 0
) : View(context, attrs, defStyleAttr) {
  // ...
  private var offset: Float = 0f

  override fun onDraw(canvas: Canvas) { // 1
    super.onDraw(canvas)

    buttonRadius = measuredHeight / 2f // 2
    buttonRect.apply { // 3
      top = 0f
      left = 0f + offset
      right = measuredWidth.toFloat() - offset
      bottom = measuredHeight.toFloat()
    }
    canvas.drawRoundRect(buttonRect, buttonRadius, buttonRadius,
backgroundPaint) // 4

    if (offset < (measuredWidth - measuredHeight) / 2f) { // 5
      val textX = measuredWidth / 2.0f -
textPaint.getTextWidth(buttonText) / 2.0f
      val textY = measuredHeight / 2f - (textPaint.descent() +
textPaint.ascent()) / 2f
      canvas.drawText(buttonText, textX, // 6
          textY,
          textPaint)
    }
  }

}
```

In the previous code, you:

1. Define an override for `onDraw`, which is the method where the drawing happens. It has a parameter of type `Canvas`, where all your drawing operations will take place.

2. Initialize `buttonRadius` as half the value of `measuredHeight` so when the button shrinks, it becomes a circle and not an oval. `measuredHeight` represents the height of the component as defined by the `LayoutInflator` while inflating the view from XML.

3. Set the actual edges for the buttonRect using measuredHeight and measuredWidth. Of course, measuredWidth represents the width of the component after the inflation.
4. Draw a rectangle with rounded edges using drawRoundedRect. The first parameter is the RectF instance that defines the edges of the rectangle. The second and third parameters are the radius of the top and bottom buttons. The last parameter is a Paint instance.
5. Draw the button text, as long as the offset is lower than the required value, which leaves enough room on the button for the words. drawText draws a string at the given x and y coordinates using the provided paint. textX and textY use standard calculations that align the text in the center of the view. Note that textX and textY represent the coordinates of the top-left corner of the drawn text.
6. Use drawText on Canvas for the actual drawing of the buttonText using the textPaint object.

You've used Canvas to draw your component. But how can you check if everything is OK? Most of the time, you can use a simple XML layout document for a preview.

Previewing Your Shape

You've drawn your first shape on the canvas. To preview it, open **fragment_details.xml** and add the following code inside the ConstraintLayout tag:

```
<com.realworld.android.petsave.common.presentation.ProgressButto
n
    android:layout_width="match_parent"
    android:layout_height="40dp"
    android:layout_marginTop="16dp"
    android:layout_marginStart="24dp"
    android:layout_marginEnd="24dp"
    android:background="#FFFFFF"
    app:layout_constraintTop_toBottomOf="@id/good_boi_label"
    app:progressButton_text="@string/adopt"
    android:id="@+id/adopt_button" />
```

Build and run, then go to the details screen of any pet and scroll to see the **Adopt** button.

Figure 13.5 — Initial State of the Adopt Button

If you don't want to build and run the app, you can use the Layout Editor Preview using what you have learned in Chapter 12, "MotionLayout & Motion Editor". Follow these steps to see the result in Figure 13.6:

1. Open **fragment_details.xml** in **Preview Editor**.
2. Only display the **Design** view of the layout.
3. Select **Transition** in the **Motion Editor**.
4. Move the animation indicator to the end of the transition.
5. Find the `ProgressButton` at the bottom of the layout.

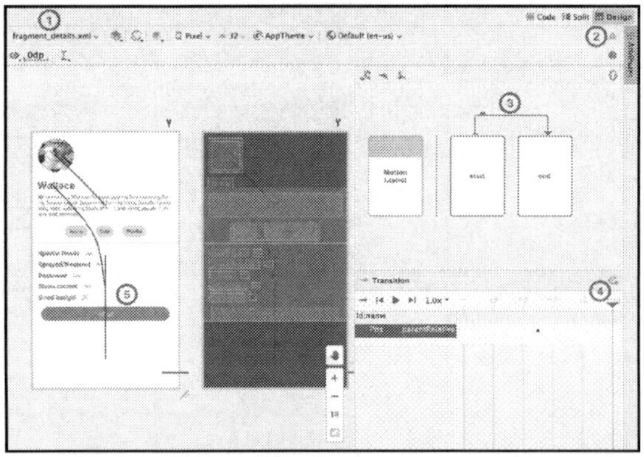

Figure 13.6 — ProgressButton Preview in Layout Editor

However, the `ProgressButton` doesn't animate yet. You'll fix that next.

Adding Animation

Your next step is to add the animation that changes the button from an oval to a circle when the user clicks it. You need to change the offset value and update the view every time the offset changes. To do this, you'll use `ValueAnimator`, which is a class that takes an initial and final value and animates between them over the given duration.

Open **ProgressButton.kt** and add the following member variable declarations:

```
private var widthAnimator: ValueAnimator? = null
private var loading = false
private var startAngle = 0f
```

The code above declares a `ValueAnimator` instance, which you'll use to animate the width of the button. It also declares a flag named `loading` and sets its initial value to `false`. You'll use this flag to indicate whether the view should display the progress bar or not.

Animating the Button

Next, you're ready to begin the animation, so add the following method to `ProgressButton`:

```
fun startLoading() { // 1
  widthAnimator = ValueAnimator.ofFloat(0f, 1f).apply {
    addUpdateListener { // 2
      offset = (measuredWidth - measuredHeight) / 2f *
it.animatedValue as Float
      invalidate() // 3
    }
    addListener(object : AnimatorListenerAdapter() {
      override fun onAnimationEnd(animation: Animator?) {
        super.onAnimationEnd(animation)
        // TODO: call startProgressAnimation()
      }
    })
    duration = 200
  }
  loading = true // 4
  isClickable = false // 5
  widthAnimator?.start()
}
```

In the previous code, you:

1. Define `startLoading`, which animates the button to shrink in width. It uses `ValueAnimator` to animate between 0 and 1 over 200 milliseconds.
2. Use `addUpdateListener` to add a listener that gets a callback every time `ValueAnimator` changes the value. When the value changes, you update the offset to a fraction of the final required value.
3. Call `invalidate`, which tells Canvas that it needs to redraw the view. Canvas will respond by invoking `onDraw`.
4. Set `loading` to `true` to inform `onDraw` that it needs to redraw the progress bar.
5. You also set `isClickable` to `false` so the user can't click the view while a task is in progress.

Note that you don't perform any action inside `onAnimationEnd`. You'll use this callback a bit later.

Drawing the Progress Bar

Now that you've started animating the offset value, you need to write the commands to draw the progress bar. Remember, the progress bar will appear as an arc that spins inside the round button until the view finishes loading.

To do this, add the following code to the end of `ProgressButton`'s `onDraw`:

```
class ProgressButton @JvmOverloads constructor(
    context: Context,
    attrs: AttributeSet? = null,
    defStyleAttr: Int = 0
) : View(context, attrs, defStyleAttr) {
    // ...
  override fun onDraw(canvas: Canvas) {
    super.onDraw(canvas)
    // ...
    if (loading && offset == (measuredWidth - measuredHeight) /
2f) { // 1
      progressRect.left = measuredWidth / 2.0f -
buttonRect.width() / 4 // 2
      progressRect.top = measuredHeight / 2.0f -
buttonRect.width() / 4 // 2
      progressRect.right = measuredWidth / 2.0f +
buttonRect.width() / 4 // 2
      progressRect.bottom = measuredHeight / 2.0f +
buttonRect.width() / 4 // 2
      canvas.drawArc(progressRect, startAngle, 140f, false,
```

```
progressPaint) // 3
      }
    }
    // ...
}
```

In the code above, you :

1. First, check if `loading` is `true` and if the offset has reached its required final value — in other words, if the button is now a circle.
2. If both the conditions are `true`, you set the coordinates of the edges of the `rect` for your progress bar. Take a closer look at the calculations and you'll notice that the `rect` is a bit smaller than the circular shape the button transforms into. That's because the progress bar needs to display inside the shape, not along its edges.
3. Use `drawArc` to draw an arc of a given sweep angle starting from an initial angle. The curve is tangential to the edges of the `rect`. Given a start angle of 30 degrees and a sweep angle of 100 degrees, the canvas will draw an arc from 30 degrees to 130 (30 + 100) degrees. In this case, you start at an angle of 0 degrees and provide a sweep angle of 140 degrees.

The idea here is to gradually increase the start angle so that each time the arc is drawn, it rotates by a few degrees. If this happens fast enough, it will render the illusion of a spinning progress bar. Now you need to start the animation when you click on the `ProgressButton`.

Starting the Animation

Open **AnimalDetailsFragment.kt** and add the following code at the end of `displayPetDetails()`, like this:

```
@AndroidEntryPoint
class AnimalDetailsFragment : Fragment() {
  // ...
  @SuppressLint("ClickableViewAccessibility")
  private fun displayPetDetails(animalDetails: UIAnimalDetailed,
adopted: Boolean) {
      // ...
      binding.adoptButton.setOnClickListener {
        binding.adoptButton.startLoading()
      }
  }
  // ...
}
```

Build and run, then go to the details screen for any pet and click the **Adopt** button. The button will slowly shrink in width until it becomes a circle, then an arc forms a circular shape.

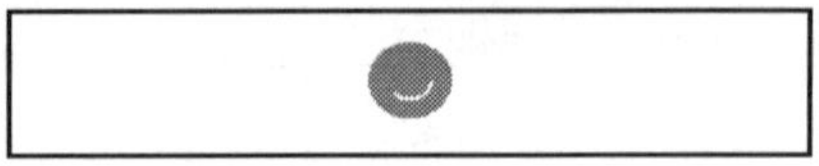

Figure 13.7 — The ProgressButton Animation's Final State

Animating the Progress Bar

The code to animate the value of the starting angle of the arc is similar to the one to animate the button width. Open **ProgressButton.kt** and add the following code:

```
class ProgressButton @JvmOverloads constructor(
    context: Context,
    attrs: AttributeSet? = null,
    defStyleAttr: Int = 0
) : View(context, attrs, defStyleAttr) {
  // ...
  private var rotationAnimator: ValueAnimator? = null

  private fun startProgressAnimation() {
    rotationAnimator = ValueAnimator.ofFloat(0f, 360f).apply
{ // 1
      addUpdateListener {
        startAngle = it.animatedValue as Float // 2
        invalidate() // 2
      }
      duration = 600
      repeatCount = Animation.INFINITE // 3
      interpolator = LinearInterpolator() // 4
      addListener(object : AnimatorListenerAdapter() {
        override fun onAnimationEnd(animation: Animator?) { // 5
          super.onAnimationEnd(animation)
          loading = false
          invalidate()
        }
      })
    }
    rotationAnimator?.start()
  }
}
```

In this code, you:

1. Create an instance of `ValueAnimator` and use it to animate between 0 and 360.
2. Every time the value animates, you assign the new value to `startAngle` and call `invalidate`. This causes the canvas to draw the new starting angle and renders the illusion of rotation.
3. Assign `INFINITE` to `repeatCount`, which specifies the number of times the animation repeats. You do this because you don't know ahead of time how long it will take the view to load, so you don't know how long the animation needs to run.
4. Set `LinearInterpolator` as the `interpolator` since you want to animate the values linearly. This gives the animation a smooth, rather than staggered, look.
5. When the animation ends, you set `loading` to false and invoke `invalidate()` to update the UI.

Starting the Progress Bar Animation

The progress bar animation needs to start when the shrinking animation stops. To do this, invoke `startProgressAnimation` from the `onAnimationEnd` callback inside `startLoading()`, as follows:

```
fun startLoading() {
  //...
  widthAnimator = ValueAnimator.ofFloat(0f, 1f).apply {
    //...
    addListener(object : AnimatorListenerAdapter() {
      override fun onAnimationEnd(animation: Animator?) {
        super.onAnimationEnd(animation)
        startProgressAnimation()
      }
    })
    // ...
  }
}
```

In the above code, as soon as `widthAnimator` stops, the progress bar animation will start.

Build and run, then click the **Adopt** button. You can see the progress bar spinning as soon the button shrinks to a circle.

Drawing the Check Icon

When the progress bar completes, you want to display a check icon as an indication that the action has finished successfully. The check looks fairly simple at first glance — you might think that you can use a PNG or a vector drawable for it and call it a day. But why not make it a bit more interesting? Instead, you'll use Canvas to draw the icon.

The check consists of two straight lines that are perpendicular to one other. To build this, you need to pick three points and connect them using lines. To draw a line in Canvas, use the following method:

```
drawLine(x1, y1, x2, y2)
```

x1 and **y1** represent the coordinates of the starting point and **x2** and **y2** represent the ending point for the line. The ending point of the shorter line is the starting point of the longer line, so you only need to calculate the coordinates for three points.

Looking at the icon, you see that it's tricky to calculate the points because both lines are at an angle. You'd need to do a lot of math to get them right, but, fortunately, there's an easier way. Look what happens when you rotate the check by 45 degrees:

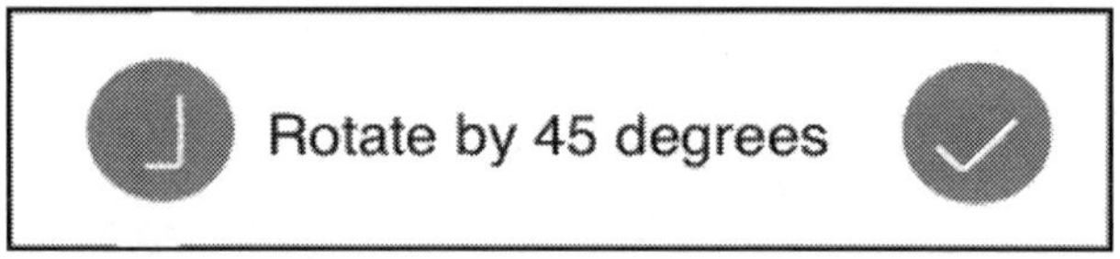

Figure 13.8 — The Rotated Check

That's right, you can eliminate the need for complicated calculations by simply drawing two perpendicular lines and rotating them. So the steps you need to follow are:

1. Rotate Canvas by 45 degrees.
2. Draw the simpler version of the tick.
3. Rotate Canvas back to its original state.

But there's one step you need to take before you do that.

Saving Canvas

Before you can perform that transformation, you need to call `save` on Canvas. `save` creates a **restore point** for Canvas. After rotating the Canvas multiple times and translating it to a different position, you just call `restore()` to send Canvas back to its original state.

That means you don't need to remember the details of every transformation you made and reverse them. Furthermore, calling `restore` retains everything you drew between `save()` and `restore()`.

To do this, add the following code to **ProgressButton.kt**:

```
private var drawCheck = false // 1

fun done() {
  loading = false
  drawCheck = true
  rotationAnimator?.cancel()
  invalidate()
}
```

In this code, you:

1. Declare a flag named `drawCheck` and initialize it to `false`. You'll use this flag to indicate whether Canvas should draw the check icon.
2. Implement the method named `done`, which the developer will call to indicate that the task is complete and that the view can hide the progress bar and display the check icon. The method does this by setting `loading` to `false` and `drawCheck` to `true`. It also cancels the rotation animation on the progress bar. Finally, `done()` calls `invalidate()` to redraw the view.

Now, you need to actually draw the check in Canvas.

Creating the Perpendicular Lines

Now, comes the part where you draw the check — which means it's time for a little math.

The center of the circle is at the coordinates of `measuredWidth / 2f` and `measuredHeight / 2f`. The vertical portion of the tick has to point toward the right of the circle's center.

Therefore, you need the following coordinates:

- **x coordinate of the starting point of the vertical line**: `measuredWidth / 2f + buttonRect.width() / 8`
- **y coordinate**: `measuredHeight / 2f + buttonRect.width() / 4`
- **coordinates of the final point of the vertical line**: `measuredWidth / 2f + buttonRect.width() / 8` and `measuredHeight / 2f - buttonRect.width() / 4`
- **x coordinates of the starting point of the horizontal line**: `measuredWidth / 2f - buttonRect.width() / 8`
- **y coordinates of the starting point of the horizontal line**: `measuredHeight / 2f + buttonRect.width() / 4`

Note that the final point of the horizontal line will be the starting point of the vertical line.

Putting Everything Together

Now, you have all the theory you need to build your icon. To implement it, add the following code at the end of `onDraw` in **ProgressButton.kt**:

```
class ProgressButton @JvmOverloads constructor(
    context: Context,
    attrs: AttributeSet? = null,
    defStyleAttr: Int = 0
) : View(context, attrs, defStyleAttr) {
  // ...
  override fun onDraw(canvas: Canvas) {
    // ...
    if (drawCheck) {
      canvas.save() // 1
      canvas.rotate(45f, measuredWidth / 2f, measuredHeight /
2f) // 2
      // 3
      val x1 = measuredWidth / 2f - buttonRect.width() / 8
      val y1 = measuredHeight / 2f + buttonRect.width() / 4
      val x2 = measuredWidth / 2f + buttonRect.width() / 8
      val y2 = measuredHeight / 2f + buttonRect.width() / 4
      val x3 = measuredWidth / 2f + buttonRect.width() / 8
      val y3 = measuredHeight / 2f - buttonRect.width() / 4
      canvas.drawLine(x1, y1, x2, y2, progressPaint) // 4
      canvas.drawLine(x2, y2, x3, y3, progressPaint) // 4
      canvas.restore() // 5
    }
```

```
  }
  // ...
}
```

There are a few things going on in the code above. You:

1. Save the state of the canvas.
2. Rotate the canvas by 45 degrees, keeping the center of the view as the pivot.
3. Assign the coordinates' values according to the calculations above.
4. Draw the horizontal line first because the final point of the horizontal line is the starting point of the vertical line.
5. Call `restore()` to rotate the canvas back to its original orientation.

Now, you need to bind the animation to the adopt button in the app.

Binding the Animation to the Adopt Button

Start by opening **AnimalDetailsFragment.kt** and adding the following code to the click listener on `adoptButton`:

```
@AndroidEntryPoint
class AnimalDetailsFragment : Fragment() {
  // ...
  @SuppressLint("ClickableViewAccessibility")
  private fun displayPetDetails(animalDetails: UIAnimalDetailed,
adopted: Boolean) {
    // ...
    binding.adoptButton.setOnClickListener {
      binding.adoptButton.startLoading()
      viewModel.handleEvent(AnimalDetailsEvent.AdoptAnimal) // 1
    }
  }
  // ...
  @SuppressLint("ClickableViewAccessibility")
  private fun displayPetDetails(animalDetails: UIAnimalDetailed,
adopted: Boolean) {
    // ...
    if (adopted) { // 2
      binding.adoptButton.done()
      binding.adoptButton.setOnClickListener(null)
    }
  }
}
```

In this code, you:

1. Set the state to `AnimalDetailsViewState.AnimalDetails` with the `adopted` field set to `true`. `AnimalDetailsEvent.AdoptAnimal` is an event that triggers a mock method in `viewmodel` to adopt the pet.
2. Call `done()` on `ProgressButton` when `adopted` is set to `true` and clear the click listener.

Build and run, then click the **Adopt** button — you'll see the full animation in action.

Manually Stopping the Animation

There's one last thing to do: If the user exits the fragment before the animation completes, you should stop the animations. Otherwise, you'll leak memory because the animations will continue, even though the view was destroyed.

To handle this, add the following method to **ProgressButton.kt**.

```
class ProgressButton @JvmOverloads constructor(
    context: Context,
    attrs: AttributeSet? = null,
    defStyleAttr: Int = 0
) : View(context, attrs, defStyleAttr) {
  // ...
  override fun onDetachedFromWindow() {
    super.onDetachedFromWindow()
    widthAnimator?.cancel()
    rotationAnimator?.cancel()
  }
}
```

The code above cancels the animations when the view detaches from the window.

Congratulations! You've successfully built a custom view that draws different shapes and animates them.

Enhancing Performance

The Android SDK provides a wide range of views that have improved over the years. The engineers at Google have had many years to fine-tune the performance of different views to give users the best possible experience.

When you write a custom view, it's up to you to ensure that the view performs well. With increasingly complex user interfaces, it's very easy to focus on getting the visual part right while letting performance take a back seat.

In this section, you'll learn a few common mistakes to avoid when it comes to view performance. In particular, you'll see how to:

1. Avoid creating objects in `onDraw()`
2. Reduce overdraw

Creating Objects Inside onDraw

As a standard practice, you should avoid object creation inside methods that the app calls at a high frequency. Consider `onDraw` — it can be called multiple times in one second! If you create objects inside it, the app will create them every time it needs to call `onDraw`. That's a lot of extra CPU work that you could easily avoid.

Consider the following code:

```
override fun onDraw(canvas: Canvas) {
  super.onDraw(canvas)

  val paint = Paint()
  val rect = Rect(100, 100, 200, 200)
  canvas.drawRect(rect, paint)
}
```

In the code above, you create instances of `Paint` and `Rect` every time you invoke `onDraw`. Memory allocation for objects takes time — and because it happens on the main thread, it will slow down your custom view.

Since `onDraw` is called frequently, the overall time taken by object creation slows down your UI, making the app appear janky to the user.

To avoid performance issues, preallocate objects and reuse them as often as possible. For example, rewrite the code above as follows:

```
val paint = Paint()
val rect = Rect(100, 100, 200, 200)

override fun onDraw(canvas: Canvas) {
  super.onDraw(canvas)

  canvas.drawRect(rect, paint)
}
```

In this version of the code, you allocate the objects only once, then reuse them on every `onDraw` call. Similarly, you should also avoid performing long-running calculations in methods like these.

Understanding Overdraw

Overdraw is the number of times a pixel is redrawn in a single frame. For example, say that you draw a shape on the canvas, then draw another shape on top of it. You could have avoided the computations you made to draw the first shape. In this case, the overdraw is 1 since it was redrawn once.

Your device has a handy tool that helps you debug overdraw on your app. To find it, open **Settings ▸ Developer Tools ▸ Debug GPU Overdraw ▸ Show overdraw areas**. You'll see boxes of multiple colors appear all over your screen. Each color represents the amount of overdraw:

- **True color**: No overdraw.
- **Blue**: Overdrawn one time.
- **Green**: Overdrawn two times.
- **Pink**: Overdrawn three times.
- **Red**: Overdrawn four or more times.

A few commons ways to reduce overdraw are:

- **Remove unneeded background**: Avoid setting a background for a view if its parent view has a similar background. For example, a `TextView` with white background inside a `LinearLayout` with a white background makes no visual difference but will cause overdraw.
- **Flatten view hierarchy**: Avoid nested views. For example, you can convert a `LienarLayout` with a `TextView` and an `ImageView` to a single `TextView`, in most cases.
- **Reduce transparency**: If you draw a transparent view on top of another view, Canvas has to render the lower view first, then apply a transparent mask on top of it. This causes overdraw.

Open the app and go to the details page for any pet. Click the **Adopt** button and wait for the animation to complete. You'll see overdraw around the circular view:

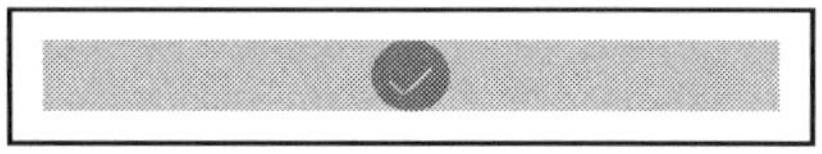

Figure 13.9 — Custom View Overdraw

Now, you'll use the techniques you just learned to address this overdraw.

Reducing Overdraw

Open **ProgressButton.kt** and check for any code that sets a background you don't need. OK, there's no such code here.

Next, check the location where you use the view: in this case, the XML layout. Open **fragment_details.xml** and check if you set a background for `ProgressButton`. You'll notice that you set a white background for the view, which doesn't make any visual difference.

To fix this, remove the following attribute from `ProgressButton`:

```
android:background="#FFFFFF"
```

Build and run. Now, when you click the **Adopt** button, you won't see any overdraw in your custom view.

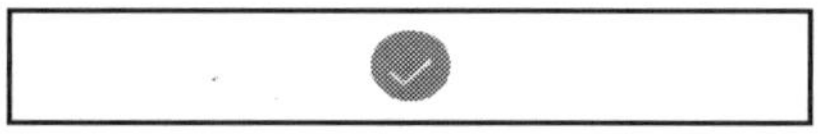

Figure 13.10 — Overdraw Removed

Well done! You've successfully improved the performance of your custom view.

Key Points

- Create custom views when you need to add features to an existing view or draw views that are too complex to implement using standard views.
- You need to extend `View` to create your custom view.
- Draw shapes with Canvas using `drawLine()`, `drawLineRoundedRect()`, etc.
- You can save Canvas' state, move it around and restore it to its original state using `save()` and `restore()`.
- Avoid performing long calculations and creating objects inside `onDraw()`.
- Avoid nested view hierarchy and unnecessary backgrounds to reduce overdraw.

In the next chapter, you'll learn everything you need to know about themes and styles, allowing you to customize the appearance of your custom views.

Chapter 14: Style & Theme

By Subhrajyoti Sen

A polished user interface makes a good first impression. It can even be one of the reasons users like using your app. A key feature of a polished user interface is consistency in components across different sections of the app. These components include color schemes, shapes, typography and more. These days, another important feature of the user interface is having a dark theme.

Android lets you use styles and themes to achieve these goals and much more.

In this chapter, you'll learn about:

- Styles, themes and their differences.
- The order of different modes of styling.
- Using theme overlays to tweak specific attributes.
- Adding styling support to custom views.
- Adding dark theme support to your app.

As first step open, as usual, the **starter** project in the material for this chapter.

Defining Styles and Themes

Usually, you define styles and themes in **res/styles.xml**, which contains a collection of attributes and their values. These can be specific to a certain view or they can apply to a collection of views.

Structure of a Style

A typical style looks like this:

```
<style name="LargeText">
  <item name="android:textSize">@dimen/large_text</item>
</style>
```

This style has the following properties:

- **name**: The name that points to this style.
- **item**: Each item in a style is a pair consisting of a view attribute and its value. In this case, the style sets `textSize` to `@dimen/large_text` which in turn resolves to *18sp*. You can have one or more `<item>`s inside a `<style>`.

Now, what if you want a style to define a **large red text**? You could write something like this:

```
<style name="LargeRedText">
  <item name="android:textSize">@dimen/large_text</item>
  <item name="android:textColor">@android:color/red</item>
</style>
```

Even though the style above is technically correct, you'll notice that you're repeating `textSize` to create a variant of the style. While this might be feasible for a few styles, it can quickly get out of hand. A better approach is to inherit from the style and create a variant.

You can inherit from a style in two ways:

1. Using the **parent** attribute:

```
<style name="LargeRedText" parent="LargeText">
  <item name="android:textColor">@android:color/red</item>
</style>
```

2. Using a prefixed name with a dot separator:

```
<style name="LargeText.Red">
  <item name="android:textColor">@android:color/red</item>
</style>
```

   Note that you can't use this method to extend from styles defined by the Android platform.

Structure of a Theme

The structure of a theme is identical to that of a style:

```
<style name="AppTheme"
parent="Theme.MaterialComponents.DayNight.NoActionBar">
  <item name="colorPrimary">@color/colorPrimary</item>
  <item name="colorPrimaryDark">@color/colorPrimaryDark</item>
  <item name="colorAccent">@color/colorAccent</item>
</style>
```

In this code, you define a theme named `AppTheme`, which inherits from `Theme.MaterialComponents.DayNight.NoActionBar`.

Although styles and themes have identical structures, they function differently. Their key differences are:

1. The item name in a style has to be a view attribute. With themes, the name is a reference to a pre-defined identifier. If you think of an `item` as a pair where the item name is the key, you'd define a style as `Map<View Attribute, Value>` whereas a theme would be `Map<Theme Attribute, Value>`.

2. You can only apply a style to a specific view or a view group, whereas a theme can be applied to any view hierarchy: a `ViewGroup`, `Activity` or even the entire app. When you apply a theme to any view hierarchy, you automatically apply it to all its child views.

3. You apply a style using the `style` attribute, whereas you apply a theme using the `android:theme` attribute.

Style Hierarchy

Android provides a wide variety of ways to set attributes in your app. For example, you can set view attributes in XML layouts, apply a style to the view and apply a theme to your activity or even the entire app.

Given the wide variety of approaches available, it's helpful to know the order of precedence Android follows when applying styles and themes, especially if you repeated the same attributes in multiple places.

The order of precedence, in descending order, is:

1. Styles applied using spans to a `TextView` or any view that extends from `TextView`.
2. Attributes applied programmatically.
3. Attributes applied in XML.
4. Styles applied to a view.
5. The default style of the view.
6. A theme applied to a view hierarchy, activity or the entire app.
7. A `textAppearance` applied to a `TextView`.

For example, if you set the `textColor` of a `TextView` to **blue** in the XML layout and also apply a style that sets the `textColor` to **green**, the text will render in **blue** when you inflate it. That's because attributes applied directly to a view have a higher precedence than styles.

Theme Overlay

Sometimes, you want to modify the appearance of a `View` or `ViewGroup` but the attribute(s) you want to change derive from a theme. Take the example of `MaterialButton`.

Open **fragment_details.xml** and add the following code in the inner `<ConstraintLayout>`, right below `ProgressButton`:

```
<com.google.android.material.button.MaterialButton
  android:id="@+id/red_button"
  android:layout_width="wrap_content"
```

```
    android:layout_height="wrap_content"
    android:background="#DA2222"
    android:layout_marginTop="@dimen/default_margin"
    android:text="Red Button"
    app:layout_constraintBottom_toBottomOf="parent"
    android:layout_marginBottom="@dimen/default_margin"
    app:layout_constraintEnd_toEndOf="parent"
    app:layout_constraintStart_toStartOf="parent"
    app:layout_constraintTop_toBottomOf="@id/adopt_button" />
```

This code adds `MaterialButton` with a red background. Build and run, then open the details page for any pet. You'll notice that the button has a blue background instead of a red one, as shown below:

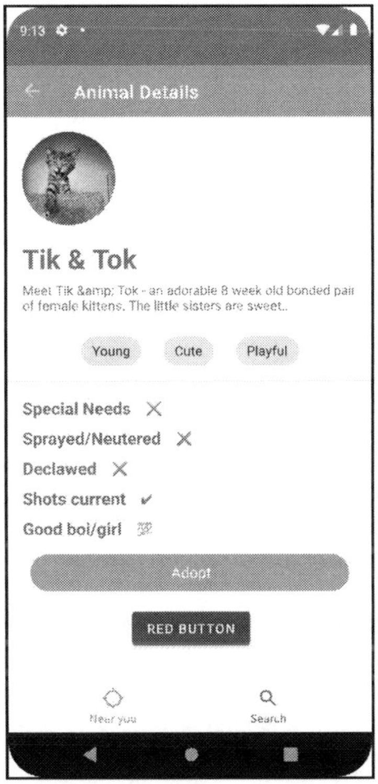

Figure 14.1 — A Blue Button

That's because `MaterialButton`'s background derives from the theme attribute, `colorPrimary`. To change the button's background, you need to modify the theme attribute *only* when it applies to that specific `MaterialButton`. That's where theme overlays are useful.

As the name suggests, theme overlays **overlay** the existing theme rather than replacing it. By applying a theme to the activity and a theme overlay to a specific view in the activity, the attributes defined in the overlay override only the corresponding attributes in the activity's theme and apply them to the view.

To see how this works, open **styles.xml** and add the following style:

```
<style name="ThemeOverlay.PetSave.RedButton" parent="">
  <item name="colorPrimary">#DA2222</item>
</style>
```

This code creates a style named `ThemeOverlay.PetSave.RedButton`. It's a good convention to name theme overlays with the **ThemeOverlay** prefix, followed by the name of your app. This differentiates them from the theme overlays provided by libraries.

The theme overlay above doesn't extend from any other style. This prevents it from accidentally overriding values from the theme of the parent view group, activity or app. The overlay also sets `colorPrimary` to the required red color's HEX code.

Finally, you need to apply this overlay to the view. Open **fragment_details.xml** and replace `background` with `theme`, as shown below:

```
<com.google.android.material.button.MaterialButton
  android:id="@+id/red_button"
  android:layout_width="wrap_content"
  android:layout_height="wrap_content"
  android:theme="@style/ThemeOverlay.PetSave.RedButton"
  android:layout_marginTop="@dimen/default_margin"
  android:text="Red Button"
  app:layout_constraintBottom_toBottomOf="parent"
  android:layout_marginBottom="@dimen/default_margin"
  app:layout_constraintEnd_toEndOf="parent"
  app:layout_constraintStart_toStartOf="parent"
  app:layout_constraintTop_toBottomOf="@id/adopt_button" />
```

Build and run. You'll now see that the button has a red background.

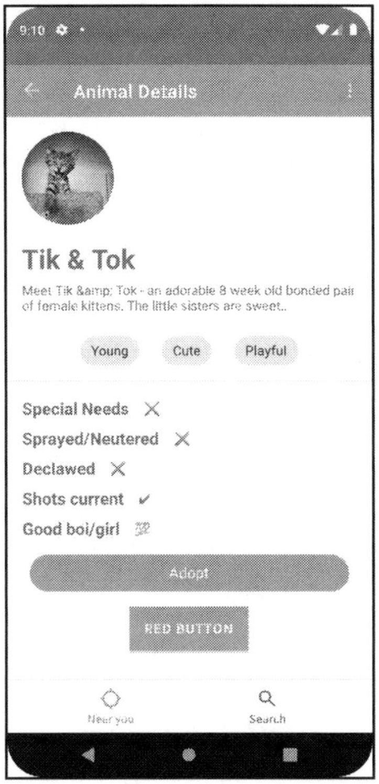

Figure 14.2 — A Red Button

TextAppearance

`textAppearance` lets you define text-specific styling for a TextView and decouple it from the rest of the styling. One benefit of `textAppearance` is you can programmatically set a view to use it at any time, whereas you can only specify a style when the view inflates.

Open **fragment_details.xml**. You'll notice that you've repeated the same set of attributes for `special_needs_label`, `sprayed_neutered_label`, `declawed_label` and so on. Since these are text-specific attributes, you can extract them to `textAppearance`.

Open **styles.xml** and add the following style:

```
<style name="PetLabelTextAppearance"
parent="TextAppearance.MaterialComponents.Headline3" >
  <item name="android:textSize">@dimen/large_text</item>
  <item name="android:textStyle">bold</item>
</style>
```

In the previous code, you set `textSize` and `textStyle` attributes to the values you specified in the layout XML. The style extends from `TextAppearance.MaterialComponents.Headline3` since it's the default text appearance you apply to a TextView.

Next, open **fragment_details** and remove the `android:textSize` and `android:textStyle` attributes. Then, add the `textAppearance` attribute to the TextView with the ID `special_needs_label` as shown below:

```
<TextView
  android:id="@+id/special_needs_label"
  android:layout_width="wrap_content"
  android:layout_height="wrap_content"
  android:layout_marginStart="@dimen/default_margin"
  android:layout_marginTop="@dimen/default_margin"
  android:text="@string/special_needs"
  android:textAppearance="@style/PetLabelTextAppearance"
  app:layout_constraintStart_toStartOf="parent"
  app:layout_constraintTop_toBottomOf="@id/divider" />
```

Check the layout preview inside Android Studio. You'll see that the text looks exactly as it did before, which confirms you set `textAppearance` correctly.

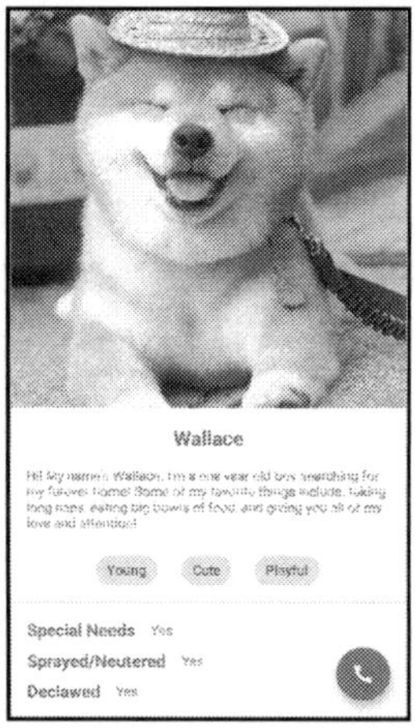

Figure 14.3 — Using TextAppearance

Finally, replace the attributes of the other label headers with `textAppearance`. Now, whenever you want to change the appearance of the header labels, you only need to modify `textAppearance` in **styles.xml** and the change will reflect across all the required TextViews. This is the main benefit of using styling over hard coding attributes in views.

Note: Since `textAppearance` is lower in the style hierarchy, if you specify an attribute in `textAppearance` and also directly in the view, the direct attribute values will display.

Setting Up Dark Themes

Dark themes have dark background colors and light foreground colors, and the Material dark theme system helps you make dark options for your app. Some of the benefits of providing one are:

1. Reduced eye-strain
2. Lower battery consumption on OLED screens
3. Better appearance in low-light environments

Depending on which Android version a device uses, the user can switch to a dark theme in different ways:

- **Android Q and above**: Navigate to **Settings ▸ Display ▸ Dark Theme** or implement the **Dark Theme** tile in the notification tray.
- **Android P:** Use **Settings ▸ System ▸ Developer options ▸ Night mode**.
- **Any other older version**: Use the option provided in the app to switch themes. Note that not all apps provide this option.

When adding dark theme support, the first step is to use the **DayNight** variant of any **AppCompat** or **MaterialComponents** theme.

Open **styles.xml** and verify that the app's theme is a **DayNight** variant. Here is the project's theme:

```
<style name="AppTheme"
parent="Theme.MaterialComponents.DayNight.NoActionBar">
  <!-- Customize your theme here. -->
  <item name="colorPrimary">@color/colorPrimary</item>
  <item name="colorPrimaryDark">@color/colorPrimaryDark</item>
</style>
```

In this code, you see that the parent theme is a DayNight variant of `MaterialComponents`, so the app can support dark themes.

Understanding Material Color Attributes

Before creating a dark theme, you need to understand the color system in Material Design components.

Color attributes consist mainly of primary, secondary, surface, error and background colors. There are also corresponding **on** colors that apply to elements drawn on top of other elements. Some of the most important ones are:

- **colorPrimary**: The primary color that represents your brand. This is one of the dominant colors in your app. The toolbar often uses this colors.
- **colorPrimaryVariant**: A lighter or darker variant of the primary color.
- **colorOnPrimary**: The color of elements that display on top of your primary color. You'll see an example of this in the next section.
- **colorOnSecondary**: The color of elements displayed on top of your secondary colors.
- **colorError**: The color displayed for errors. For example, when the user makes an input error in an input field.
- **colorOnError**: The color of elements that display on top of your error color.
- **colorSurface**: The color used for surfaces like bottom sheets, cards, bottom navigation and more.
- **colorOnSurface**: Use this color for elements that display on top of your surface color, like the text on a card.

Adding a Theme Toggle

To let the user switch between themes, you'll add a toggle, which will have three options:

1. Light
2. Dark
3. System default

It's good practice to follow the system default theme to mail consistency with the user's other apps.

The corresponding constants defined in `AppCompatDelegate` are:

1. **Light**: `MODE_NIGHT_NO`
2. **Dark**: `MODE_NIGHT_YES`
3. **System default**: `MODE_NIGHT_FOLLOW_SYSTEM`

In this section, you'll add an overflow menu to the toolbar that contains options to switch between different modes.

Start by creating a file named **theme_options.xml** inside **res/menu** and adding the following code:

```
<?xml version="1.0" encoding="utf-8"?>
<menu
  xmlns:app="http://schemas.android.com/apk/res-auto"
  xmlns:android="http://schemas.android.com/apk/res/android">
  <item
    android:id="@+id/light_theme"
    android:title="Light theme"
    app:showAsAction="never" />
  <item
    android:id="@+id/dark_theme"
    android:title="Dark Theme"
    app:showAsAction="never" />
  <item
    android:id="@+id/follow_system"
    android:title="Follow System"
    app:showAsAction="never" />
</menu>
```

This code adds three menu items corresponding to the three modes.

Next, you need to display those options as an overflow menu in the toolbar. To do this, add the following method to **MainActivity.kt** in the **common** package:

```
@AndroidEntryPoint
class MainActivity : AppCompatActivity() {
  // ...
  override fun onCreateOptionsMenu(menu: Menu): Boolean {
    val inflater = menuInflater
    inflater.inflate(R.menu.theme_options, menu) // HERE
    return true
  }
}
```

This code inflates the items from **theme_options.xml** and displays them as menu options. When the user selects any one of the menu options, the app switches to the corresponding theme.

Now, add the following method to the same file:

```
@AndroidEntryPoint
class MainActivity : AppCompatActivity() {
  // ...
  override fun onOptionsItemSelected(item: MenuItem): Boolean {
    val themeMode = when (item.itemId) {
      R.id.light_theme -> {
        AppCompatDelegate.MODE_NIGHT_NO
      }
      R.id.dark_theme -> {
        AppCompatDelegate.MODE_NIGHT_YES
      }
      else -> {
        AppCompatDelegate.MODE_NIGHT_FOLLOW_SYSTEM
      }
    }
    AppCompatDelegate.setDefaultNightMode(themeMode)
    return true
  }
}
```

The code above chooses the mode from `AppCompatDelegate` based on the menu item the user selects. `AppCompatDelegate.setDefaultNightMode(themeMode)` sets the night mode using user's selected mode.

Build and run, then click the overflow menu and select the theme of your choice. You'll notice that the app's theme changes whenever you select a new theme.

Figure 14.4 — Theme Options

In the next section, you'll use this toggle to find dark theme issues in the current app.

Resolving Dark Theme Inconsistencies

Use the toggle to switch to the dark theme and explore the app. Observe the same screens in both light and dark themes. Some of the inconsistencies you'll notice are:

1. The toolbar color remains the same in both themes.
2. The background of the search container is white in the dark theme.
3. The floating action button's call icon in the details screen is white in both themes.

You'll fix them one at a time.

Using Theme Attributes

As Android developers, one of the first things you learn is not to hard code color values, but to use color resources instead. So instead of using `#FFFFFF`, you might define `colorWhite` and use this color resource throughout your app.

This approach has a limitation when it comes to theming. For example, when you want to apply a dark theme, it doesn't make sense to change the value of `colorWhite` to a dark color. You'll have to create a new alias for the color and switch between the white and a dark color depending on the theme.

You'll have many such instances across your codebase and this approach will get increasingly complex, both in terms of naming colors and in remembering the names.

That's where theme attributes come in. Instead of thinking of colors based on the widget they apply to, think of them in terms of theme attributes.

To make things clearer, take the example of the floating action button in **fragment_details.xml**:

```
<com.google.android.material.floatingactionbutton.FloatingAction
Button
  android:id="@+id/call"
  android:layout_width="wrap_content"
  android:layout_height="wrap_content"
  android:layout_margin="@dimen/default_margin"
  android:contentDescription="@string/contact"
  android:src="@drawable/ic_call_24dp"
  android:visibility="gone"
  app:backgroundTint="@color/colorPrimary"
  app:layout_constraintBottom_toBottomOf="parent"
  app:layout_constraintEnd_toEndOf="parent"
  app:tint="@android:color/white"
  tools:visibility="visible" />
```

In the code above, you set `tint` to `@android:color/white`. The icon will always render white, regardless of which theme you apply.

Now, go to the details screen and change the theme from light to dark. You'll notice the dialer icon color always remains white.

Instead, think of the icon color in terms of the theme attributes. The background color of the floating action button is the primary color of the theme. What would you call a color that you need to display on top of the primary color? In the previous section, you learned about **colorOnPrimary**, which is exactly what you'll use here.

Set the `tint` attribute to `colorOnPrimary`:

```
<com.google.android.material.floatingactionbutton.FloatingAction
Button
  //...
  app:tint="?attr/colorOnPrimary"
  tools:visibility="visible" />
```

In the code above, `?attr/colorOnPrimary` is a reference to the theme attribute `colorOnPrimary`. **?attr/** refers to theme attributes where **@color** refers to colors in your **res** directory.

Figure 14.5 — Floating Action Button Color

Build and run, then go to the details screen and change themes. Now, the dialer icon is white in light theme and black in dark theme. And with that, you've successfully used theme attribute to support theming in a widget.

Fixing Other Hard-coded Colors

Similarly, open **fragment_search.xml** and look at `AppBarLayout`. You'll notice that background is a static color:

```
<com.google.android.material.appbar.AppBarLayout
  android:id="@+id/collapsible_search_params_container"
  android:layout_width="match_parent"
  android:layout_height="wrap_content"
  android:background="@android:color/white"
  app:layout_constraintEnd_toEndOf="parent"
  app:layout_constraintStart_toStartOf="parent"
  app:layout_constraintTop_toTopOf="parent">
```

This is why the background is white in both light and dark themes. You need to replace this with a theme attribute. Replace `background`'s value with `colorPrimarySurface`:

```
<com.google.android.material.appbar.AppBarLayout
  android:id="@+id/collapsible_search_params_container"
  android:layout_width="match_parent"
  android:layout_height="wrap_content"
  android:background="?attr/colorPrimarySurface"
  app:layout_constraintEnd_toEndOf="parent"
  app:layout_constraintStart_toStartOf="parent"
  app:layout_constraintTop_toTopOf="parent">
```

`colorPrimarySurface` switches between `colorPrimary` in light themes and `colorSurface` in dark themes.

Build and run. Switch to dark theme and go to the search page. You'll see that the search container is no longer white in the dark theme.

Figure 14.6 — Search Bar in Dark Mode

Using Night Colors

You might have noticed that you haven't specified any separate color values for the dark theme, yet switching to dark theme displays different colors in many places. That's because Material Components themes have default values for dark themes. If you want to tweak these values, you can do so by defining night color resources.

Create a new resource directory named **values-night** inside the **res** directory like in Figures 14.7 and 14.8:

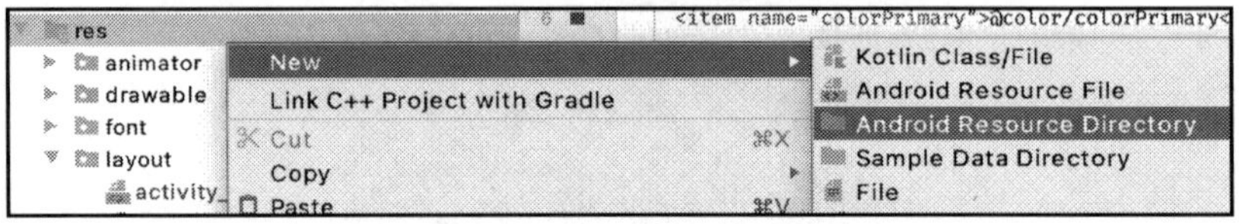

Figure 14.7 — New Resource Directory

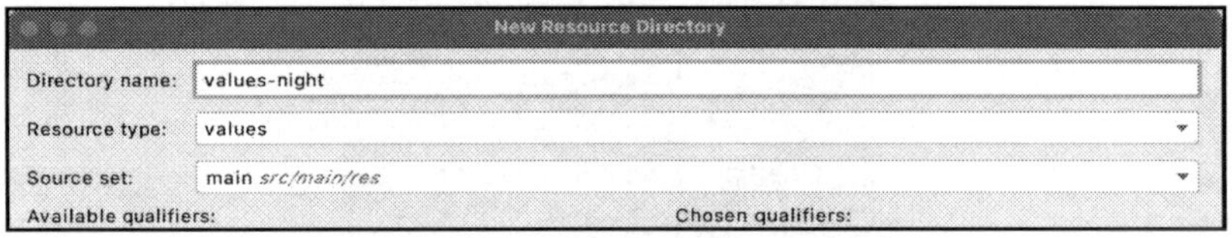

Figure 14.8 — New Resource Directory

This directory will contain the resources you want to override for dark theme. When you apply a dark theme, Android will check **values-night** before it uses a resource. If it finds a defined resource, it will use that value; otherwise, it will pick the resource value from the **values** directory.

To define colors for your dark theme, create a file named **colors.xml** inside **values-night**:

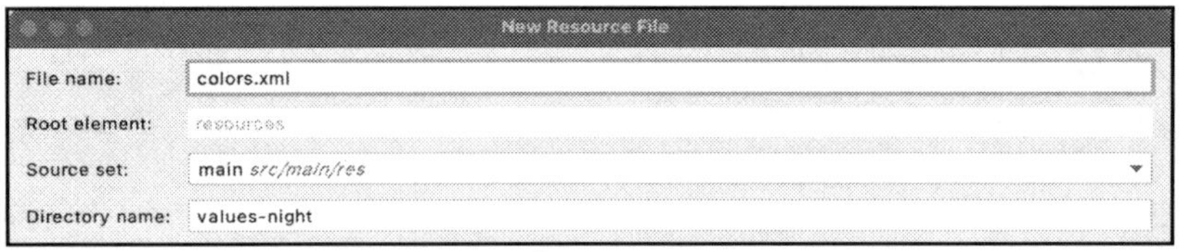

Figure 14.9 — Colors for Night Mode

You now have two **colors.xml** files that differ for the **night** qualifier:

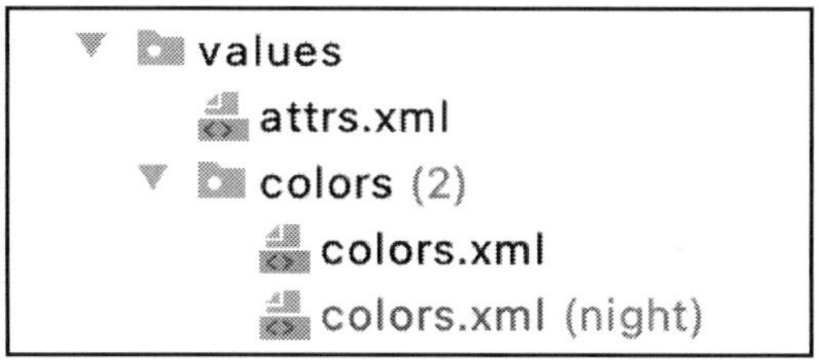

Figure 14.10 — Qualified Color Resources

Now, add the following colors to **colors.xml (night)**:

```
<color name="colorPrimary">#BA86FC</color>
<color name="colorPrimaryDark">#000000</color>
<color name="colorBackground">#000000</color>
```

The code above adds two dark colors to the app's primary colors. It also defines a background color, but you haven't defined `colorBackground` for the light theme yet. To resolve this, add the following to **colors.xml**:

```
<color name="colorBackground">#FFFFFF</color>
```

Now that you've defined `colorBackground` for both themes, you need to point the default background color of the theme to this color resource. Open **styles.xml** and add the following item to `AppTheme`:

```
<item name="android:colorBackground">@color/colorBackground</
item>
```

Build and run. Visit the different screens and switch between light and dark themes. You'll notice that the background is black in dark theme and white in light theme. You'll also notice that the primary color of the app changes to a dark purple in the night theme.

Figure 14.11 — Dark Theme in Action

Great! You've successfully added dark theme support to your app and fixed the inconsistencies using the styling and theming concepts you've learned in this chapter.

Styling Custom Views

Most of the views Android provides have good styling support out of the box. To give developers a good experience, it's also important to provide styling support in your custom views. In this section, you'll make `ProgressButton` styleable.

Adding Styleable Attributes

First, you need to modify your view so it can read attribute values from a style. To do this, you need to remove any hard-coded colors from the view.

Open the **ProgressButton.kt** file in the **common.presentation** package and remove the `color` assignment from `textPaint`, `backgroundPaint` and `progressPaint` so they match the code below:

```
private val textPaint = Paint().apply {
  isAntiAlias = true
  style = Paint.Style.FILL
  textSize = context.dpToPx(16f)
}

private val backgroundPaint = Paint().apply {
  isAntiAlias = true
  style = Paint.Style.FILL
}

private val progressPaint = Paint().apply {
  isAntiAlias = true
  style = Paint.Style.STROKE
  strokeWidth = context.dpToPx(2f)
}
```

Next, define attributes for these colors so you can use them in a style. Open **attrs.xml** and add the following code to `ProgressButton`:

```
<attr name="progressButton_backgroundColor" format="color" />
<attr name="progressButton_textColor" format="color" />
<attr name="progressButton_progressColor" format="color" />
```

In the code above, you define three attributes: background color, text color and progress color. They all have the format `color` since you'll assign color resources to them.

To be consistent with `MaterialTextView`, the default background color of `ProgressButton` will also be `colorPrimary`, as defined in the theme. You can overwrite this by setting the `backgroundColor` attribute in the view XML. Since `colorPrimary` is a theme attribute and not a color resource, you need to use the theme to extract its value.

Open **ProgressButton** and add the following code to `init`, right before the line containing `typedArray.recycle()`:

```
val typedValue = TypedValue()
context.theme.resolveAttribute(android.R.attr.colorPrimary,
typedValue, true)
val defaultBackgroundColor = typedValue.data
```

In the code above, you resolve the value of the `colorPrimary` attribute using the theme from the context. Using the correct context is vital. If you try using an `Activity` context here, it will lead to inconsistencies since the `Activity` and the view can have different themes.

Now that you have the default background color, set the default text and progress color to **white** by adding the following to `init`:

```
val defaultTextColor = Color.WHITE
val defaultProgressColor = Color.WHITE
```

With the default values set, you now need to read the attribute values from the XML, as well as styles. Add the following code to `init`:

```
val backgroundColor =
typedArray.getColor(R.styleable.ProgressButton_progressButton_ba
ckgroundColor, defaultBackgroundColor)
backgroundPaint.color = backgroundColor

val textColor =
typedArray.getColor(R.styleable.ProgressButton_progressButton_te
xtColor, defaultTextColor)
textPaint.color = textColor

val progressColor =
typedArray.getColor(R.styleable.ProgressButton_progressButton_pr
ogressColor, defaultProgressColor)
progressPaint.color = progressColor
```

The code above is similar to the one you wrote to read the button text in the previous chapter. Your custom view can now read values passed using the XML attributes or a style.

Default Styles

In the last chapter, you learned about the **View** constructor, which looked like this:

```
class ProgressButton @JvmOverloads constructor(
    context: Context,
    attrs: AttributeSet? = null,
    defStyleAttr: Int = 0
) : View(context, attrs, defStyleAttr)
```

In addition to the three arguments above, there's another argument that's important to styling. Open **ProgressButton.kt** and replace the constructor with the following with a new `defStyleRes` parameter.

```
class ProgressButton @JvmOverloads constructor(
    context: Context,
    attrs: AttributeSet? = null,
    defStyleAttr: Int = 0,
    defStyleRes: Int = 0
) : View(context, attrs, defStyleAttr, defStyleRes)
```

In this section, you'll work with:

1. **defStyleAttr**: The attribute in the theme that specifies which style this view uses.

2. **defStyleRes**: The style the view uses. This usually ships with the library or SDK.

Remember the precedence order of the styling hierarchy? `context.obtainStyledAttributes` is the method that resolves the precedence and provides the final values to use. To do this, it needs access to `defStyleAttr` and `defStyleRes`.

Change the first line in `init` to:

```
val typedArray = context.obtainStyledAttributes(attrs,
R.styleable.ProgressButton, defStyleAttr, defStyleRes)
```

In addition to passing `attrs` and `R.styleable.ProgressButton`, you also pass `defStyleAttr` and `defStyleRes` as arguments. This helps check the values and resolve the precedence.

To create a theme attribute that can specify the default style, open **attrs.xml** and add the following code outside `ProgressButton`:

```
<attr name="progressButtonStyle" format="reference"/>
```

The code above creates an attribute named `progressButtonStyle` that has a type `reference` since it refers to a style and not a definite value.

Defining Your Custom View's Style

The next step is to define the style for your custom view. Open **styles.xml** and add the following code:

```
<style name="ProgressButtonStyle">
  <item name="progressButton_backgroundColor">?attr/
colorPrimary</item>
  <item name="progressButton_textColor">?attr/colorOnPrimary</
item>
  <item name="progressButton_progressColor">?attr/
colorOnPrimary</item>
</style>
```

This code creates a style and sets values for `ProgressButton`'s attributes by using theme attributes. To set the style above as the default style for `ProgressButton` in your theme, add the following to the style named `AppTheme` at the top of the file:

```
<item name="progressButtonStyle">@style/ProgressButtonStyle</
item>
```

`AppTheme`'s style now looks like this:

```
<style name="AppTheme"
parent="Theme.MaterialComponents.DayNight.NoActionBar">
  <!-- Customize your theme here. -->
  <item name="colorPrimary">@color/colorPrimary</item>
  <item name="colorPrimaryDark">@color/colorPrimaryDark</item>
  <item name="android:colorBackground">@color/colorBackground</
item>
  <item name="progressButtonStyle">@style/ProgressButtonStyle</
item>
</style>
```

Setting defStyleAttr and defStyleRes

Your final step is to set the values of `defStyleAttr` and `defStyleRes`. Open **ProgressButton.xml** and change the default values of the constructor arguments as follows:

```
class ProgressButton @JvmOverloads constructor(
    context: Context,
    attrs: AttributeSet? = null,
    defStyleAttr: Int = R.attr.progressButtonStyle,
    defStyleRes: Int = R.style.ProgressButtonStyle
) : View(context, attrs, defStyleAttr, defStyleRes)
```

Build and run. Go to the details page and you'll see that the **Adopt** button has the correct default style. Toggle the theme and you'll see that the text color changes according to the theme.

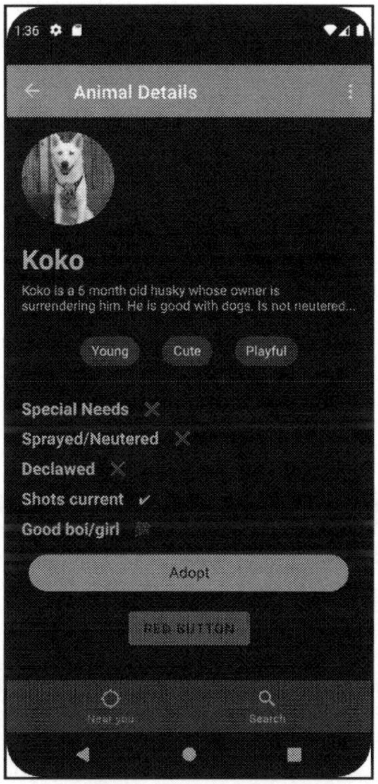

Figure 14.12 — Styled Custom View

Congratulations! You've successfully created a custom view with great support for styles and themes.

Key Points

- Use styles and themes for consistent UI elements throughout the app.
- Styles apply to a specific view but themes apply to a view hierarchy.
- Different styling modes have a different order of precedence.
- Make your custom views styleable and provide a default style.
- Use `textAppearance` to group character level styling attributes.
- Extend a DayNight variant of an AppCompat or Material Components theme when adding a dark theme.
- Use theme attributes as often as possible.

This chapter is the last about UI. In the next chapter you'll start learning everything you need about a very important topic: **security**.

Section IV: Securing Your App

Making your app more secure is an aspect of development that's often ignored, but, at the same time, is absolutely vital. Imagine what would happen if somebody would hack your code, stealing important data or even the usernames and passwords of your users. That would be a disaster.

In this chapter, you'll learn how to handle security from different points of view. You'll learn how to protect user data and how to securely connect to a server. Finally, you'll learn how to make hackers' lives more difficult, by using different methods to protect your code and your data.

Chapter 15: User Privacy

By Kolin Stürt and Antonio Roa-Valverde

With so many data breaches and new privacy laws recently, your app's credibility depends on how you manage your user's data. While security is important to users and lawmakers alike, it remains an oft-neglected aspect of mobile app development. When you build an app, you need to think about security from the ground up.

To assist developers in keeping their user data secure, starting from Android 11 the OS offers new privacy features and device enhancements including scoped storage, hardened permissions, biometric authentication and hardware-backed key storage. Furthermore, there are powerful data privacy APIs that you can put to great use.

In this chapter, you'll learn about:

- Privacy and security basics
- Permissions
- Locking down user data

If you missed the previous chapters, the sample app includes a list of pets and their medical data along with a section that lets you report issues anonymously:

Figure 15.1 — Report Section

In this chapter, you'll focus on keeping that sensitive information secure.

Securing the Foundations

When you first start to build your app, it's important to think about how much user data you need to keep. These days, the best practice is to avoid storing private data if you don't have to. Pets, of course, are always concerned about their privacy rights. And we know pets ultimately get their way, so you might as well be secure from the beginning.

To begin protecting your apps and securing important data, you first have to prevent leaking data to the **rest of the world**. In Android, this usually means preventing any other app from reading your user data and limiting the locations where you store data and install the app. This will be your first step toward securing private information.

Using Permissions

Ever since Android 6.0, you set the files and `SharedPreferences` you save with the `MODE_PRIVATE` constant. That means only your app can access the data. Android 7 doesn't allow any other option, so you'll implement this next.

Open **PetSavePreferences.kt** in the **core.data.preferences** package. You'll notice there are deprecation warnings for `MODE_WORLD_READABLE` and `MODE_WORLD_WRITEABLE`.

```
private val preferences = context.getSharedPreferences(PREFERENCES_NAME,
    Context.MODE_WORLD_READABLE)
private val preferencesWrite = context.getSharedPreferences(PREFERENCES_NAME,
    Context.MODE_WORLD_WRITEABLE)
```

Figure 15.2 — Deprecated Constants

These allow public access to your files for earlier Android versions. If only there was a way to tell those users to update their devices! Well, technically there is, but instead, replace the code in Figure 15.1 with the following:

```
@Singleton
class PetSavePreferences @Inject constructor(
    @ApplicationContext context: Context
) : Preferences {
  // ...
  private val preferences =
context.getSharedPreferences(PREFERENCES_NAME,
      Context.MODE_PRIVATE)
  private val preferencesWrite =
context.getSharedPreferences(PREFERENCES_NAME,
      Context.MODE_PRIVATE)
  // ...
}
```

Great, you've just made your preferences more private. Additionally, when you build and run the app now, those security violations won't cause a crash on Android 7+ versions.

```
Caused by: java.lang.SecurityException: MODE_WORLD_READABLE no longer supported
    at android.app.ContextImpl.checkMode(ContextImpl.java:3218)
    at android.app.ContextImpl.getSharedPreferences(ContextImpl.java:551)
    at android.app.ContextImpl.getSharedPreferences(ContextImpl.java:541)
    at android.content.ContextWrapper.getSharedPreferences(ContextWrapper.java:196)
    at com.realworld.android.petsave.core.data.preferences.PetSavePreferences.<init>(PetSavePreferences.kt:58)
```

Figure 15.3 — MODE_WORLD_WRITEABLE No Longer Supported Error

Another important point regarding private access: You should enforce a secure location for your app's install directory.

Limiting Installation Directories

One of the larger problems Android has faced in the past few years was running out of memory to install the plethora of available apps due to the low storage capacity of many devices. Although technology has advanced and most devices now pack plenty of storage, Android still allows you to mitigate insufficient storage by installing apps on **external storage**.

This works well, but it opens security concerns. Installing apps on external SD cards is convenient, but also a security flaw. Anyone with access to the SD card also has access to the app's data — and that data could hold sensitive information. This is why it's a best practice to restrict your app to internal storage.

To do this, open **AndroidManifest.xml** and find the line that reads `android:installLocation="auto"`, then replace it like this:

```
android:installLocation="internalOnly"
```

With this, you've limited the install location to the device, but you can still back up your app and its data. Users can access the contents of the app's private data folder using **ADB backup**. To disallow backups, find the line that reads `android:allowBackup="true"` and replace the value with `"false"`.

Following these best practices, you've hardened your app data from the outside. On the flip side, you'll want to let the user decide if the app can access other parts of the device's data like the camera or the user's location.

Requesting User Permissions

As mentioned earlier, Android 11 debuted many new privacy features, which you can read about here: https://developer.android.com/about/versions/11/privacy.

For example, users can grant one-time access to location data, the microphone and the camera. The Settings section offers improved control over background access to the user's location. Additionally, there's a consistent place for Google account activity and autofill services and the OS resets permissions if you haven't interacted with an app for a few months.

Because of these privacy features, you must ask for permission before your app can access the user's external data. As such, the first question to consider is how much data your app needs to acquire. A good approach is to avoid gathering any information you don't need.

APIs that access user data require you to declare that access in the manifest file beforehand. In **AndroidManifest.xml**, find the line that reads:

```
<uses-permission
android:name="android.permission.READ_EXTERNAL_STORAGE" />
```

In the past, this was enough. When the user installed the app, they'd see a list of permissions. But Marshmallow changed that with **Runtime Permissions**. Now, your app should request permissions at the moment when it needs them. This approach is more transparent because it shows exactly which features the permission covers. It helps weed out unnecessary permissions. To do this, go to **ReportDetailFragment.kt** and add the following declaration at the top of the file:

```
private val requestPermissionLauncher =
registerForActivityResult(ActivityResultContracts.RequestPermiss
ion()) { granted ->
  if (granted) {
    selectImageFromGallery()
  }
}
```

This code relies on the Activity Result API and registers a `RequestPermission` contract. The method accepts a callback that is executed when the activity gets the result. In this case, the callback receives a boolean indicating if the permission was granted. If that's the case, then you have green light to select the image from the gallery.

> **Note**: The Activity Result API offers other predefined contracts and it also allows you to define your custom ones. For more information about the different possibilities visit https://developer.android.com/training/basics/intents/result.

This code alone doesn't do much. In order to execute it, you need to launch it first. You'll do this next. Replace the contents of `uploadPhotoPressed()` like this:

```
@AndroidEntryPoint
class ReportDetailFragment : Fragment() {
  // ...
  private fun uploadPhotoPressed() {
    context?.let {
      if (ContextCompat.checkSelfPermission(it,
Manifest.permission.READ_EXTERNAL_STORAGE)
          != PackageManager.PERMISSION_GRANTED) { // 1

requestPermissionLauncher.launch(Manifest.permission.READ_EXTERN
AL_STORAGE) // 2
      } else {
        selectImageFromGallery() // 3
      }
    }
  }
  // ...
}
```

Here, you implement runtime permissions by:

1. Checking if the user has already granted permission for `READ_EXTERNAL_STORAGE`.
2. In case the permission is not granted, you request it launching `requestPermissionLauncher` that you declared previously.
3. If already granted you directly invoke the method to select an image.

If the user grants permission, the image selection starts. Build and run the project after you've made the changes. When prompted for permission, tap **Allow**. You can now select an image. :]

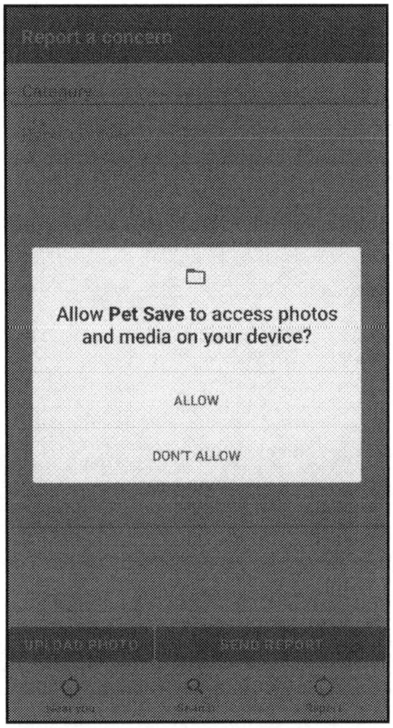

Figure 15.4 — Photo Permission Request

> **Note**: Android 11 enforces scoped access to app files and media. It requires that you use the Storage Access Framework https://developer.android.com/about/versions/11/privacy/storage to access folders on external storage the app doesn't own. It's best practice to access external media using the Media Store: https://developer.android.com/training/data-storage/shared/media. For apps where these APIs cannot be used effectively, it is possible to request the `MANAGE_EXTERNAL_STORAGE` permission. However, you should take into account that Google Play imposes very hard restrictions in the kind of apps that are allowed to use it: https://developer.android.com/training/data-storage/manage-all-files#all-files-access-google-play.

These aren't the only ways you can pass data between apps. In the past, IPC has been a popular choice for developers.

Using IPC

Permissions cover most of what you need to access and pass data outside of the app. But sometimes you pass data via IPC to other apps that you build. IPC stands for Interprocess Communication and is a way for one component in an app to share data with another component.

There have been cases where developers have left shared files on the storage or have implemented sockets to exchange sensitive information. This is not secure. Instead, the best practice is to use **Intents**. You can send data using an `Intent` by providing the package name, like this:

```
val intent = Intent()
val packageName = "com.example.app" //1
val activityClass = "com.example.app.TheActivity" // 2
intent.component = ComponentName(packageName, activityClass)
intent.putExtra("UserInfo", "Example string") //3
startActivityForResult(intent) //4
```

Here you're specifying:

1. The package name of the app where you'll send the intent.
2. The qualified class name in the target app that receives the intent.
3. Data sent with the intent.
4. The intent, by starting the activity with it and then waiting for the result.

To broadcast data to more than one app, enforce that only apps signed with your signing key will get the data. Otherwise, any app that registers to receive the broadcast can read the sent information. Likewise, a malicious app could send a broadcast to your app if you've registered to receive its broadcast.

Securing Data Broadcasts With a Signing Key

In the manifest file, find `protectionLevel` — it's part of the first `permission`. You'll notice it's set to `normal`. Change it to `signature` by replacing that line with the following:

```
android:protectionLevel="signature" />
```

Then replace the `protectionLevel` inside the `<application` tag with:

```
android:protectionLevel="signature"
```

Other apps access the permission by including the following code in the manifest file:

```
<uses-permission
android:name="com.realworld.android.snitcher.permission.REPORT_D
ETAIL_FRAGMENT"/>
```

Apps typically send a broadcast like this:

```
val intent = Intent()
intent.putExtra("UserInfo", "Example string")
intent.action = "com.example.SOME_NOTIFICATION"
sendBroadcast(intent, "com.example.mypermission")
```

Alternatively, you can use `setPackage(String)` when sending a broadcast to restrict it to a set of apps that match the specified package. Also, setting `android:exported` to `false` in the manifest file will exclude broadcasts from outside your app. That setting tells the system whether other apps can invoke or interact with a particular activity or service.

Now, you've set permissions correctly and waited for the user to grant them. But what if the user wants to disallow access later?

Opting Out

Using permissions properly offers another benefit: It grants users the ability to revoke permissions in the system settings and opt out of data sharing if they change their minds later. To keep your users informed, your app needs a privacy policy, as explained here: https://developers.google.com/assistant/console/policies/privacy-policy-guide.

Privacy policies disclose the types of personally identifiable information (PII) apps collect, such as unique device identifiers. If you're collecting such data intentionally, you must provide a place in your UI where the user can opt out. It's also prudent to understand the laws in any jurisdiction where your app is available. EU member countries, for example, require explicit consent for data collection.

To learn more about privacy policies, visit the Android Privacy Section: https://play.google.com/about/privacy-security-deception and Android's best practices for unique identifiers: https://developer.android.com/training/articles/user-data-ids.

When users opt out, you should delete the stored data you have for them. But during this process, be sure not to overlook temporary data files.

Clearing Caches

If users opt out, you must delete any data you've collected. This includes temporary files and caches! Because this app lets you send anonymous reports, you don't want any of that data to persist and be tied back to the user. Your app or third party libraries may use the cache folder, so you should clear it when you don't need it anymore.

To do this, add the following function to **ReportDetailFragment.kt**:

```
@AndroidEntryPoint
class ReportDetailFragment : Fragment() {
  // ...
  override fun onPause() {
    context?.cacheDir?.deleteRecursively()
    context?.externalCacheDir?.deleteRecursively()
    super.onPause()
  }
}
```

Here, you tell the OS to delete the cache directories when you pause the fragment.

> **Note**: You can also delete your shared preferences by removing **/data/data/com.your.package.name/shared_prefs/your_prefs_name.xml** and **your_prefs_name.bak** and clearing the in-memory preferences with the following code: `context.getSharedPreferences("prefs", Context.MODE_PRIVATE).edit().clear().commit()`.

Disabling the Keyboard Cache

Your app also has a keyboard cache for text fields with autocorrect enabled. Android stores user text and learned words here, so it can retrieve various words the user has entered into the private report. To prevent leaking this information, you need to disable this cache.

To disable the keyboard cache, you need to turn off the autocorrect option. Open **fragment_report_detail.xml** and switch to the **Code Editing Mode** tab. Find the first `EditText` and replace the `android:inputType="textMultiLine"` line with the following:

```
android:inputType="textNoSuggestions|textVisiblePassword|
textFilter|textMultiLine"
```

For the second `EditText` that doesn't need the the multiline setting, replace it with this:

```
android:inputType="textNoSuggestions|textVisiblePassword|
textFilter"
```

Various devices and OS versions have some bugs where some of these flags do nothing on their own. That means it's a good idea to implement all these flags.

> **Note**: You should also mark password fields as `secureTextEntry`. Secure text fields don't display the password or use the keyboard cache.

Disabling Other Caches

There are a few other caches to consider. For example, Android caches data sent over the network to memory and on-device storage. You don't want to leave that data behind, either. In `provideOkHttpClient()` inside **APIModule.kt**, replace `//TODO: Disable cache here` with:

```
.cache(null)
```

That disables the cache for OkHttp, but you might use a different implementation in your app. For example, this disables the cache for the native `HttpsURLConnection` session:

```
connection.setRequestProperty("Cache-Control", "no-cache")
connection.defaultUseCaches = false
connection.useCaches = false
```

For `WebView`, you can remove the cache at any time with this code:

```
webview.clearCache(true)
```

Check other third-party libraries you use for a way to disable or remove the cache. In this app, you've used the popular Glide image loading library. It allows you to cache photos in memory instead of in storage. Navigate to **Extentions.kt** and replace `// TODO: Disable disk cache here` with the following:

```
.diskCacheStrategy(DiskCacheStrategy.NONE)
```

Libraries may also leak other kinds of data. For example, check if there's an option to disable logging. That's what you'll look at next.

Disabling Logging

Android saves debug logs to a file that you can retrieve for the production builds of your app. Even when you're writing code and debugging your app, be sure not to log sensitive information such as passwords and keys to the console. You wouldn't want to forget to remove the logs before releasing your app!

There's a class called `BuildConfig` that contains a flag called `DEBUG`. It's set to `true` when you're debugging and automatically set to `false` when you export a release build. Here's an example:

```
if (BuildConfig.DEBUG) {
  Log.v(TAG, "Some log stuff...")
}
```

In theory, that's good for non-sensitive logging; in practice, it's dangerous to rely on. There have been bugs in the build system that set the flag to `true` for release builds. You can define your own constant, but then you're back to the problem of developers remembering to change it before release.

The solution is to not log sensitive variables. Instead, use a breakpoint to view them.

For example, in **AuthenticationInterceptor.kt**, notice `Log.d("Pet Save", "The auth token is: $token")` outputs the real PetFinder authentication token to the console. Looks like someone was debugging and forgot to remove it! Select the line and delete it.

The anonymous report section is getting much safer to use. However, there are a couple more things you can do to be diligent about not leaking data.

Disabling Screenshots

You've ensured no traces of the report are left behind, but it's still possible for the app to take a screenshot of the entire reporting screen. The OS takes screenshots of your app, too. It uses them for the animation it plays when it puts an app into the background or for the list of open apps in the task switcher. Those screenshots are stored on the device.

You should disable this feature for views revealing sensitive data. Back in **MainActivity.kt**, find `onCreate()`. Replace `//TODO: Disable screenshots` with:

```
window.setFlags(WindowManager.LayoutParams.FLAG_SECURE,
```

```
WindowManager.LayoutParams.FLAG_SECURE)
```

Here, you've told the window to have FLAG_SECURE, which prevents explicit and implicit capturing of the screen. This is especially important for private messaging or video streaming apps, deterring someone from taking a snapshot.

Keep in mind that it's not foolproof. A user can still take a picture from another device, for example.

Build and run, then make a report:

Figure 15.5 — Filled Report

Try to take a screenshot. You'll notice that you can't!

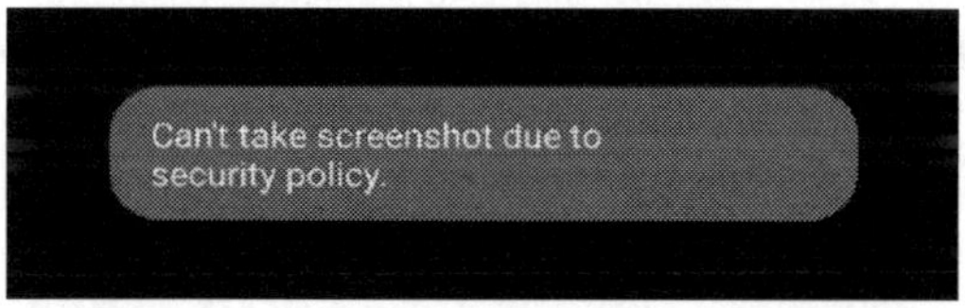

Figure 15.6 — Screenshot Security Alert

Now, users can make anonymous reports without accidentally leaving a screen-grabbed copy of their report behind.

You've taken care of most of the privacy-related points by either preventing or removing data. When it comes to removing data there's a way to make sure it's done securely.

Wiping Memory Securely

When an OS deletes a file, it only removes the reference, not the data. To completely remove that data, you must overwrite the file with random data:

```
fun wipeFile(file: File) {
  if (file.exists()) {
    val length = file.length()
    val random = SecureRandom()
    val randomAccessFile = RandomAccessFile(file, "rws")
    randomAccessFile.seek(0)
    randomAccessFile.filePointer
    val data = ByteArray(64)
    var position = 0
    while (position < length) {
      random.nextBytes(data)
      randomAccessFile.write(data)
      position += data.size
    }
    randomAccessFile.close()
    file.delete()
  }
}
```

The code above iterates over a `File`, replacing the bytes with random data generated from `SecureRandom`.

You'll also notice most security functions work with `ByteArray` or `CharArray` instead of objects such as `String`. That's because `String` is immutable and there's no control over how the system copies or garbage collects it.

If you're working with sensitive strings or data, it's better — though not foolproof — to store the information in a mutable array, then overwrite the sensitive arrays when you're done with them. For `ByteArray` that would be:

```
Arrays.fill(byteArray, 0.toByte())
```

and for `CharArray`, it's:

```
Arrays.fill(charArray, '\u0000')
```

Depending on the platform, some types of solid-state storage devices, such as solid-state drives (SSD) in modern laptops, won't write to the same area of memory each time. This preserves the longevity of the SSD. Depending on the platforms you port your code to, a secure erase method may not work.

A better solution for this type of scenario is to encrypt the stored data in the first place. As long as you discard the encryption key, you don't need to securely erase the data. And that's what the next chapter is about!

Key Points

In this chapter, you've discovered a lot about data privacy, and your users can now trust you to follow best practices to protect their data. Feel free to download the completed final project.

Here are a few points to remember:

- Only collect sensitive information when it's necessary for your app.
- You can restrict access to internal app data with permissions.
- Request user consent to let the app access data outside the app.
- Clearing caches and wiping sensitive files helps protect the user's data.

Where to Go From Here?

So you tightened access to the data at a high level. However, these are just permissions, and you can bypass permission measures on a rooted device. The solution? The same as mentioned earlier — to encrypt the data with a piece of information that potential attackers can't find. So to learn the finer details of encryption, head on to the next chapter.

In the meantime, to learn more about some of the more recent privacy laws, check out these resources:

- CCPA: https://oag.ca.gov/privacy/ccpa
- PIPEDA: https://www.priv.gc.ca/en/privacy-topics/privacy-laws-in-canada/the-personal-information-protection-and-electronic-documents-act-pipeda/
- GDPR: https://en.wikipedia.org/wiki/General_Data_Protection_Regulation

Chapter 16: Securing Data at Rest

By Kolin Stürt and Antonio Roa-Valverde

This chapter starts with a simple approach to protect your stored data and builds up to more fine-tuned and advanced implementations. You can stop at any time if you have what you need. If you only want to implement a simple login for your app, great, you'll find that near the beginning. If your project requires customized protocols, carry on to the end of the chapter.

In this chapter, you'll learn how to:

- Store a password securely.
- Protect saved data.
- Use encryption.

If you missed the previous chapters, the sample app includes a list of pets, their medical data and a section that lets you report safety issues while remaining anonymous.

Launch the starter app for this chapter and you'll see a simple sign-up screen. Once you enter an email and select **Sign Up**, the list of pets will populate. Tap the **Report** tab to report a concern:

Figure 16.1 — Report Section

This is quite easy but, is your app also secure? As first step you'll now implement a login for the user.

Implementing the Login

The app saves data about you, such as your pet's home address and medical history, your login passwords and the safety reports you've submitted. If someone were to take your device, they'd have access to all that personal information.

To ensure only you can access that app data, it's standard to require a password. Many modern devices have biometric readers like face, retina and fingerprint scanners.

In this first section, you'll implement a biometric prompt to log in so only you can access the app on your device. You'll also implement a password fallback, giving the user an alternative log-in option.

First, you need to have the app check that the device is able to use biometrics. In **MainActivity.kt**, replace the contents of `loginPressed()` like in the following code:

```
@AndroidEntryPoint
class MainActivity : AppCompatActivity() {
  // ...
  fun loginPressed(view: View) {
    val biometricManager = BiometricManager.from(this)
    when (biometricManager.canAuthenticate(BIOMETRIC_STRONG)) {
      BiometricManager.BIOMETRIC_SUCCESS ->
          displayLogin(view, false) // 1
      BiometricManager.BIOMETRIC_ERROR_NO_HARDWARE ->
          displayLogin(view, true) // 2
      BiometricManager.BIOMETRIC_ERROR_HW_UNAVAILABLE ->
          toast("Biometric features are currently unavailable.")
      BiometricManager.BIOMETRIC_ERROR_NONE_ENROLLED ->
          toast("Please associate a biometric credential with
your account.")
      else ->
          toast("An unknown error occurred. Please check your
Biometric settings")
      }
  }
  // ...
}
```

In this code you see that:

1. You call `displayLogin()` if the device can perform biometric authentication with `BIOMETRIC_SUCCESS`.
2. Otherwise, the `fallback` flag is set to `true`, allowing for password or PIN authentication.

> **Note**: Android 11 divides the biometric features in strong and week. Fingerprint is considered strong, while face recognition is considered weak.

Next, add the following variables to the same `MainActivity` class:

```
private lateinit var biometricPrompt: BiometricPrompt
private lateinit var promptInfo: BiometricPrompt.PromptInfo
```

`BiometricPrompt` is a class from AndroidX.

Next, replace the contents of `displayLogin()` with the following:

```
@AndroidEntryPoint
class MainActivity : AppCompatActivity() {
  // ...
  private fun displayLogin(view: View, fallback: Boolean) {
    val executor = Executors.newSingleThreadExecutor()
    biometricPrompt = BiometricPrompt(this, executor, // 1
        object : BiometricPrompt.AuthenticationCallback() {
          override fun onAuthenticationError(errorCode: Int,
                                             errString:
CharSequence) {
            super.onAuthenticationError(errorCode, errString)
            runOnUiThread {
              toast("Authentication error: $errString")
            }
          }

          override fun onAuthenticationFailed() {
            super.onAuthenticationFailed()
            runOnUiThread {
              toast("Authentication failed")
            }
          }

          override fun onAuthenticationSucceeded(result:
BiometricPrompt.AuthenticationResult) {// 2
            super.onAuthenticationSucceeded(result)

            runOnUiThread {
              toast("Authentication succeeded!")
              if (!isSignedUp) {
                generateSecretKey() // 3
              }
              performLoginOperation(view)
            }
          }
        })

    if (fallback) {
      promptInfo = BiometricPrompt.PromptInfo.Builder()
          .setTitle("Biometric login for my app")
          .setSubtitle("Log in using your biometric credential")
          // Cannot call setNegativeButtonText() and
          // setDeviceCredentialAllowed() at the same time.
          // .setNegativeButtonText("Use account password")
          .setAllowedAuthenticators(DEVICE_CREDENTIAL) // 4
          .build()
    } else {
      promptInfo = BiometricPrompt.PromptInfo.Builder()
          .setTitle("Biometric login for my app")
          .setSubtitle("Log in using your biometric credential")
          .setNegativeButtonText("Use account password")
```

```
            .build()
      }
      biometricPrompt.authenticate(promptInfo)
    }

    // ...
  }
```

Here's what's happening:

1. You create a `BiometricPrompt` object for authentication.
2. You override `onAuthenticationSucceeded` to determine a successful authentication.
3. You create a secret key that's tied to the authentication for first-time users.
4. You create a fallback to password authentication by calling `.setAllowedAuthenticators(DEVICE_CREDENTIAL)`.

Be sure you have a face, fingerprint or similar biometric scanner on your device to test the biometric part. Build and run. You'll now be able to log in with your credentials:

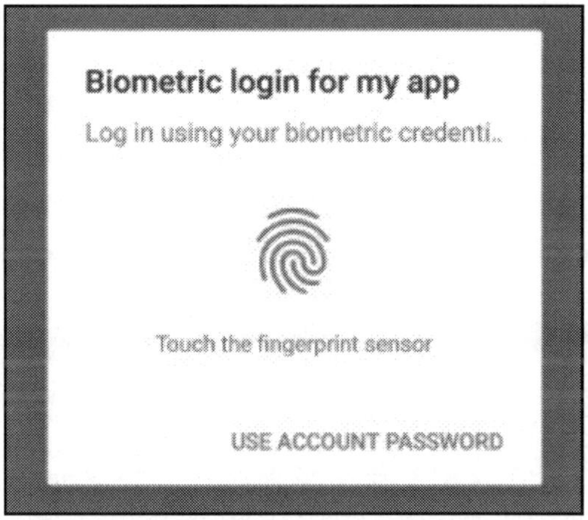

Figure 16.2 — Biometric Prompt

Once the authentication is successful, you'll see the pet list:

Figure 16.3 — Animals Near You

With that, you've secured access to the app with biometric security! That was easy.

Deciding What Security Options To Use

Is biometrics always the safest type of security for your app? To answer that question, it helps to use a **threat model**, a risk-based approach to making decisions. In other words, you need to consider what the biggest risks your user will face are.

People can use biometrics maliciously. For example, someone could steal your phone and hold it up to your face while you're unconscious, or law enforcement could hold your device to your finger after they handcuff you.

In cases like these, a password is always better.

On the other hand, biometrics are better if your users are in the spotlight with people streaming to social media. There's no chance a live streamer will capture their password.

Another thing to consider is: Even though access is limited, your data, such as reports and passwords, are not encrypted. Encryption uses a key to scramble the data. But if it's all done in the app, you're still vulnerable.

You'll address all that next, but first, a little theory.

Exploring Hardware Security Modules

A **Trusted Execution Environment** (TEE) is software separate from the OS. It safely sandboxes security operations, and though it's inside the main processor, it's cordoned off from the main operating system. Security keys that are isolated this way are *hardware-backed*. You can find out if a key is hardware-backed by using `KeyInfo.isInsideSecureHardware()`.

An example of a TEE is the ARM processor that has the TrustZone secure enclave, available in modern Samsung phones.

A **Secure Element** (SE) takes this a step further by putting the environment on a segregated chip. It has its own CPU and storage, as well as encryption and random-number generator methods. Security chips that exist outside of the main processor are harder to attack. Google's devices contain the Titan M security chip, which is an SE.

In both cases, security operations happen at the hardware level in a separate environment that's less susceptible to software exploits.

Android 9 and above provides the StrongBox Keymaster API for these features: https://developer.android.com/training/articles/keystore#HardwareSecurityModule. To ensure the key exists inside a segregated secure element, you can call `KeyGenParameterSpec.Builder.setIsStrongBoxBacked(true)`.

Now, it's time to put this information to use!

Hardening Data in the KeyStore

To protect your data, you'll use `MasterKey` to generate a key in the KeyStore. This will encrypt your reports that you wish to send.

As you learned above, the benefit of storing a key in the KeyStore is that it allows the OS to operate on it without exposing the secret contents of that key. Key data does not enter the app space.

For devices that don't have a security chip, permissions for private keys only allow your app to access the keys — and only after user authorization. This means you have to set up a lock screen on the device before you can use the credential storage. This makes it more difficult to extract keys from a device, called extraction prevention.

The security library contains two new classes: `EncryptedFile` and `EncryptedSharedPreferences`. In **Encryption.kt**, there are a few empty boilerplate methods set up for you. Replace `encryptFile()` with this:

```
class Encryption {
  companion object {
    // ...
    fun encryptFile(context: Context, file: File): EncryptedFile
{
      val masterKey = MasterKey.Builder(context)
        .setKeyScheme(MasterKey.KeyScheme.AES256_GCM)
        .build() // 1
      return EncryptedFile.Builder(
          context,
          file,
          masterKey,
          EncryptedFile.FileEncryptionScheme.AES256_GCM_HKDF_4KB
// 2
      ).build()
    }
  }
  // ...
}
```

Here's what you did:

1. Created a new master key.
2. Encrypted the file using the popular secure AES encryption algorithm. (Visit https://en.wikipedia.org/wiki/Advanced_Encryption_Standard if you're interested in the finer details).

In **ReportDetailFragment.kt**, find `sendReportPressed()`. Replace the two lines right after `//TODO: Replace below for encrypting the file` with the code block below:

```
val file = File(theContext.filesDir?.absolutePath,
"$reportID.txt") // 1
val encryptedFile = encryptFile(theContext, file) // 2
encryptedFile.openFileOutput().bufferedWriter().use {
    it.write(reportString) // 3
}
```

Here's what you changed:

1. You created a file named `"$reportID.txt"`.
2. You created an `EncryptedFile` instance using the file object created in the last step.
3. You used the `EncryptedFile` instance to write to file all the report data.

You've hardened the data stored on the device by using a secure key in the KeyStore. While this is an excellent first step, you can make the data even more secure by tying it to your biometric or password credentials. That way, even if someone accessed that cordoned-off key, it would be useless without your credentials.

Securing Data with Biometrics

For additional security, you can auto-generate a key in KeyStore that's also protected by your biometric credential. If the device becomes compromised, the key is still encrypted.

This time, you'll get a bit more advanced. Instead of using a high-level `EncryptedFile`, you'll use an encryption class that lets you customize what you want to encrypt later. This is powerful because you can encrypt items in a database or information to send over a network, for example.

In **Encryption.kt**, add the following to `generateSecretKey()`:

```
class Encryption {
  companion object {
    // ...
    @TargetApi(Build.VERSION_CODES.R)
    fun generateSecretKey() {
      val keyGenParameterSpec = KeyGenParameterSpec.Builder(
          KEYSTORE_ALIAS,
          KeyProperties.PURPOSE_ENCRYPT or
KeyProperties.PURPOSE_DECRYPT)
          .setBlockModes(KeyProperties.BLOCK_MODE_GCM) // 1
          .setEncryptionPaddings(KeyProperties.ENCRYPTION_PADDIN
G_NONE)
          .setUserAuthenticationRequired(true) // 2
          .setUserAuthenticationParameters(120,
KeyProperties.AUTH_BIOMETRIC_STRONG) // 3
          .build()
      val keyGenerator = KeyGenerator.getInstance(
          KeyProperties.KEY_ALGORITHM_AES, PROVIDER) // 4
      keyGenerator.init(keyGenParameterSpec)
```

```
        keyGenerator.generateKey()
      }
      // ...
    }
  }
```

Here are the changes you made:

1. You chose GCM, a popular and safe block mode that the encryption uses. More on this later.
2. By passing in `.setUserAuthenticationRequired(true)`, you require a lock screen to be set up and the key to be locked until the user authenticates. Enabling the authentication requirement also revokes the key when the user removes or changes the lock screen.
3. You made the key available for 120 seconds from authentication. After this time, the user will need to authenticate again using the fingerprint.
4. You create a `KeyGenerator` with the above settings and set it to the `AndroidKeyStore` `PROVIDER`.

There are a few more options worth mentioning here:

- `setRandomizedEncryptionRequired(true)` requires you to have sufficient randomization. Using this ensures that if you encrypt the same data a second time, that encrypted output will be different. This prevents an attacker from getting clues about the ciphertext based on feeding in the same data.
- Another option is `.setUserAuthenticationValidWhileOnBody(boolean remainsValid)`. It locks the key once the device has detected it's no longer on the person.

Because you use the same key and cipher in different parts of the app, add the following helper functions to **Encryption.kt**, inside the companion object code block:

```
class Encryption {
  companion object {
    // ...
    private fun getSecretKey(): SecretKey {
      val keyStore = KeyStore.getInstance(PROVIDER)

      // Before the keystore can be accessed, it must be loaded.
      keyStore.load(null)
      return keyStore.getKey(KEYSTORE_ALIAS, null) as SecretKey
    }
```

```
    private fun getCipher(): Cipher {
      return Cipher.getInstance(KeyProperties.KEY_ALGORITHM_AES
+ "/"
          + KeyProperties.BLOCK_MODE_GCM + "/"
          + KeyProperties.ENCRYPTION_PADDING_NONE)
    }
  }
}
```

The first function returns the secret key from the KeyStore. The second returns a pre-configured `Cipher`.

Next, you'll use that `Cipher` to do the actual encryption.

Encrypting Data

At this point, you've stored the key in the KeyStore, protected by your credentials. But so far, you've stored the user's generated password in the clear. For your next step, you'll update the login method to encrypt it using the `Cipher` object, given the `SecretKey`.

Start by going to **Encryption.kt** and replacing the contents of `createLoginPassword()` with the following:

```
class Encryption {
  companion object {
    // ...
    fun createLoginPassword(context: Context): ByteArray {
      val cipher = getCipher()
      val secretKey = getSecretKey()
      val random = SecureRandom()
      val passwordBytes = ByteArray(256)
      random.nextBytes(passwordBytes) // 1
      cipher.init(Cipher.ENCRYPT_MODE, secretKey)
      val ivParameters =
cipher.parameters.getParameterSpec(GCMParameterSpec::class.java)
      val iv = ivParameters.iv
      PreferencesHelper.saveIV(context, iv) // 2
      return cipher.doFinal(passwordBytes) // 3
    }
    // ...
  }
}
```

Here's what's happening in that code:

1. You create a random password using `SecureRandom`.
2. You gather a randomized initialization vector (IV), which you need to decrypt the data, and save it into the shared preferences. An IV is some initial random data, discussed in more detail during the Customizing encryption section later.
3. You return a `ByteArray` containing the encrypted data.

Decrypting Data

You've encrypted the password, so now you need to decrypt it when the user authenticates.

Open **Encryption.kt** and replace the contents of `decryptPassword()` with the code below:

```
class Encryption {
  companion object {
    // ...
    fun decryptPassword(context: Context, password: ByteArray):
ByteArray {
      val cipher = getCipher()
      val secretKey = getSecretKey()
      val iv = PreferencesHelper.iv(context) // 1
      val ivParameters = GCMParameterSpec(128, iv)
      cipher.init(Cipher.DECRYPT_MODE, secretKey,
ivParameters) // 2
      return cipher.doFinal(password) // 3
    }
    // ...
  }
}
```

Here's what's happening:

1. You retrieve the IV required to decrypt the data.
2. You initialize `Cipher` using `DECRYPT_MODE`.
3. You return a decrypted `ByteArray`.

Back in **MainActivity.kt**, find `performLoginOperation()`. Replace the line that calls `createDataSource`, where it says `//TODO: Replace with encrypted data source below`, with:

```
val encryptedInfo = createLoginPassword(this)
UserRepository.createDataSource(applicationContext, it,
encryptedInfo)
```

On sign-up, you create a password for the account. Right after the `//TODO: Replace below with the implementation that decrypts the password`, in `performLoginOperation()`, replace `success = true` with the following:

```
val password = decryptPassword(this,
    Base64.decode(firstUser.password, Base64.NO_WRAP))
if (password.isNotEmpty()) {
  //Send password to authenticate with server etc
  success = true
}
```

On log-in, you retrieve the password to decrypt the data. The app shouldn't work without the key.

Build and run, then try to log in. You'll encounter the following exception:

```
kotlin.TypeCastException: null cannot be cast to non-null type
javax.crypto.SecretKey
```

That's because you didn't create a key during the previous sign-up.

Delete the app to remove the old saved state, then rebuild and run. You'll be able to log in now. :]

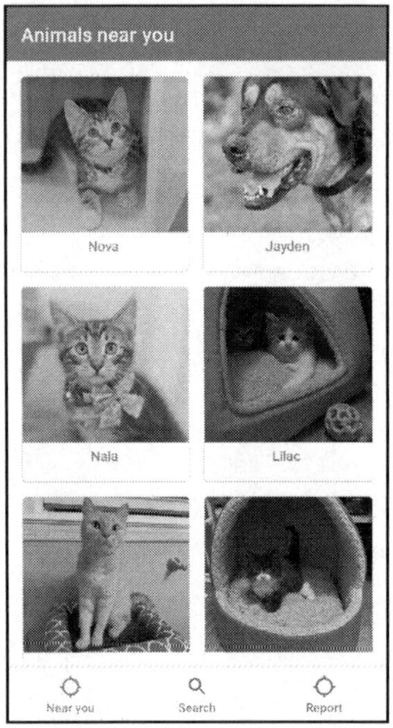

Figure 16.4 — Animals Near You

You've now created an encrypted password that will only be available once you've authenticated with your credentials. Your data is protected.

Using `Cipher` opens the door to powerful customization. You can stop here, but if you want to learn about advanced encryption or if your company requires you to use certain protocols, carry on.

Customizing Encryption

In this part, you'll focus on the recommended standard for encryption, Advanced Encryption Standard (AES). AES uses a substitution–permutation network to encrypt your data with a key. Using this approach, it replaces bytes from one table with the bytes from another, and so creates permutations of data. Just like before, AES requires an encryption key. You'll customize how that key is created.

Creating a Key

As mentioned above, AES uses a key for encryption. You also use that same key to decrypt the data. This property is called **symmetric encryption**.

You can use different specific lengths for the key, but 256 bits is standard.

Directly using the user's password for encryption is dangerous because it likely won't be random or large enough. A function called **Password-Based Key Derivation Function (PBKDF2)** comes to the rescue. It takes a password and, by hashing it with random data many times over, creates a key. That random data is called a **salt**. PBKDF2 creates a strong and unique key, even if someone else uses the same or a very simple password.

Because each key is unique, if an attacker steals and publishes the key online, it doesn't expose all the users with the same password.

To use PBKDF2, start by generating the salt. Open **Encryption.kt** and add the following code to `encrypt()`, where it reads `//TODO: Add custom encrypt code here`:

```
class Encryption {
  companion object {
    // ...
    fun encrypt(dataToEncrypt: ByteArray,
                password: CharArray): HashMap<String, ByteArray>
{
      val map = HashMap<String, ByteArray>()
      val random = SecureRandom() // HERE
      val salt = ByteArray(256)
      random.nextBytes(salt)

      return map
    }
    // ...
  }
}
```

Here, you use `SecureRandom`, a **cryptographically strong random number generator**, which makes sure the output is difficult to predict. You should always use a secure class like this, instead of using `java.util.Random`, for example.

Next, you'll generate a key with the user's password and the salt. Add the following right under the code you just added in `encrypt()` in **Encryption.kt**:

```
class Encryption {
  companion object {
    // ...
    fun encrypt(dataToEncrypt: ByteArray,
                password: CharArray): HashMap<String, ByteArray>
{
      val map = HashMap<String, ByteArray>()
      val random = SecureRandom()
      val salt = ByteArray(256)
      random.nextBytes(salt)

      val pbKeySpec = PBEKeySpec(password, salt, 1324, 256) // 1
      val secretKeyFactory =
SecretKeyFactory.getInstance("PBKDF2WithHmacSHA1") // 2
      val keyBytes =
secretKeyFactory.generateSecret(pbKeySpec).encoded // 3
      val keySpec = SecretKeySpec(keyBytes, "AES") // 4
      return map
    }
    // ...
  }
}
```

Here's what is going on inside that code. You:

1. Put the salt and password into `PBEKeySpec`, a password-based encryption object. The constructor takes an iteration count (1324). The higher the number, the longer it would take to operate on a set of keys during a brute force attack.
2. Passed `PBEKeySpec` into the `SecretKeyFactory`.
3. Generated the key as a `ByteArray`.
4. Wrapped the raw `ByteArray` into a `SecretKeySpec` object.

Now you have a secure key. The next part of customization involves the mode of operation.

Choosing an Encryption Mode

The mode defines how the data is processed. One example is **Electronic Code Book (ECB)**. It's simplistic in that it splits up the data and repeats the encryption process for every chunk with the same key. Because each block uses the same key, this mode is highly insecure. **Don't use this mode**.

On the other hand, **Counter Mode (CTR)** uses a counter so each block encrypts differently. CTR is efficient and safe to use.

There are a few other modes that are useful: **GCM** offers authentication in addition to encryption, whereas **XTS** is optimized for full disk encryption. You'll use **Cipher Block Chaining (CBC)** when you XOR each block of plaintext with the previous block.

> **Note:** To learn more about the various modes of operation, go here: https://en.wikipedia.org/wiki/Block_cipher_mode_of_operation. To understand more about XOR, check this out: https://whatis.techtarget.com/definition/logic-gate-AND-OR-XOR-NOT-NAND-NOR-and-XNOR.

You're almost ready to encrypt, but there's one more thing you need to consider when it comes to modes.

Adding an Initialization Vector

As mentioned above, you're going to use the standard mode, **cipher block chaining** (CBC), to encrypt your data one chunk at a time. You'll XOR each block of data in the pipeline with the previous block that it encrypted. That dependency on previous blocks makes the encryption strong.

But can you see a problem? What about the first block? It has no previous block to help with its encryption.

If you encrypt a message that starts off the same as another message, the first encrypted block would be the same! That provides a clue for an attacker, and you don't want that. In fact, you're striving for a concept known as **Perfect Secrecy**, where the ciphertext conveys zero information about the plaintext.

To remedy the first block problem, you'll use an **initialization vector (IV)**.

An IV is a fancy term for a block of random data that you XOR with the first block. Remember that each block relies on all blocks processed up until that point. This means that identical sets of data encrypted with the same key will not produce identical outputs.

Create an IV now by adding the following code to the **Encryption.kt** file in `encrypt()` like this

```
class Encryption {
  companion object {
    // ...
    fun encrypt(dataToEncrypt: ByteArray,
                password: CharArray): HashMap<String, ByteArray>
{
      val map = HashMap<String, ByteArray>()
      val random = SecureRandom()
      val salt = ByteArray(256)
      random.nextBytes(salt)
      val pbKeySpec = PBEKeySpec(password, salt, 1324, 256)
      val secretKeyFactory =
SecretKeyFactory.getInstance("PBKDF2WithHmacSHA1")
      val keyBytes =
secretKeyFactory.generateSecret(pbKeySpec).encoded
      val keySpec = SecretKeySpec(keyBytes, "AES")

      val ivRandom = SecureRandom() //not caching previous
seeded instance of SecureRandom
      val iv = ByteArray(16)
      ivRandom.nextBytes(iv) // 1
      val ivSpec = IvParameterSpec(iv) // 2
      return map
    }
    // ...
  }
}
```

Here, you:

1. Create 16 bytes of random data.
2. Package it into `IvParameterSpec`.

This ensures the first block of data is random, strengthening your security.

Finalizing the Encryption

Now that you have all the necessary pieces, you can finally get to the encryption! Add the following code to `encrypt()` in the **Encryption.kt** file to perform the customized encryption:

```
class Encryption {
  companion object {
    // ...
    fun encrypt(dataToEncrypt: ByteArray,
```

```
                password: CharArray): HashMap<String, ByteArray>
{
      val map = HashMap<String, ByteArray>()
      val random = SecureRandom()
      val salt = ByteArray(256)
      random.nextBytes(salt)
      val pbKeySpec = PBEKeySpec(password, salt, 1324, 256)
      val secretKeyFactory =
SecretKeyFactory.getInstance("PBKDF2WithHmacSHA1")
      val keyBytes =
secretKeyFactory.generateSecret(pbKeySpec).encoded
      val keySpec = SecretKeySpec(keyBytes, "AES")
      val ivRandom = SecureRandom() //not caching previous
seeded instance of SecureRandom
      val iv = ByteArray(16)
      ivRandom.nextBytes(iv)
      val ivSpec = IvParameterSpec(iv)

      val cipher = Cipher.getInstance("AES/CBC/PKCS7Padding") //
1
      cipher.init(Cipher.ENCRYPT_MODE, keySpec, ivSpec)
      val encrypted = cipher.doFinal(dataToEncrypt) // 2
      return map
    }
    // ...
  }
}
```

Here:

1. You passed in the specification string, "`AES/CBC/PKCS7Padding`". It chooses AES with cipher block chaining mode. **PKCS7Padding** is a well-known standard for padding. Since you're working with blocks, not all data will fit perfectly into the block size, so you need to pad the remaining space. By the way, blocks are 128 bits long and AES adds padding before encryption.
2. `doFinal` does the actual encryption.

Next, complete `encrypt()` in **Encryption.kt** adding the following code:

```
class Encryption {
  companion object {
    // ...
    fun encrypt(dataToEncrypt: ByteArray,
                password: CharArray): HashMap<String, ByteArray>
{
      val map = HashMap<String, ByteArray>()
      val random = SecureRandom()
      val salt = ByteArray(256)
      random.nextBytes(salt)
```

```
        val pbKeySpec = PBEKeySpec(password, salt, 1324, 256)
        val secretKeyFactory =
SecretKeyFactory.getInstance("PBKDF2WithHmacSHA1")
        val keyBytes =
secretKeyFactory.generateSecret(pbKeySpec).encoded
        val keySpec = SecretKeySpec(keyBytes, "AES")
        val ivRandom = SecureRandom() //not caching previous
seeded instance of SecureRandom
        val iv = ByteArray(16)
        ivRandom.nextBytes(iv)
        val ivSpec = IvParameterSpec(iv)
        val cipher = Cipher.getInstance("AES/CBC/PKCS7Padding")
        cipher.init(Cipher.ENCRYPT_MODE, keySpec, ivSpec)
        val encrypted = cipher.doFinal(dataToEncrypt)


        map["salt"] = salt // HERE
        map["iv"] = iv // HERE
        map["encrypted"] = encrypted // HERE
        return map
      }
      // ...
    }
}
```

Here, you packaged the encrypted data into a `HashMap`. You also added the salt and the IV to the map because you need all those pieces to decrypt the data.

This isn't the only way to go about this. It's common to prefix the ciphertext with the IV and then strip it off and use it for the decryption. For the purposes of learning, you use a map here so you' won't be distracted with sub-arrays and off-by-one counts. :]

If you followed the steps correctly, you shouldn't have any errors and `encrypt` is ready to secure some data!

It's okay to store salts and IVs, but reusing or sequentially incrementing them weakens the security.

You should never store the key!

Now, you've built the means of encrypting this data, but you still need to decrypt it. You'll see how to do that next.

Decrypting with Salts and IVs

You have some encrypted data. To decrypt it, you'll have to change the mode of `Cipher` in the `init` method from `ENCRYPT_MODE` to `DECRYPT_MODE`.

Start by adding the following to `decrypt` in **Encryption.kt**, where the line reads `// TODO: Add custom decrypt code here`:

```
class Encryption {
  companion object {
    // ...
    fun decrypt(map: HashMap<String, ByteArray>, password:
CharArray): ByteArray? {
      var decrypted: ByteArray? = null
      try {
        // 1
        val salt = map["salt"]
        val iv = map["iv"]
        val encrypted = map["encrypted"]

        // 2
        //regenerate key from password
        val pbKeySpec = PBEKeySpec(password, salt, 1324, 256)
        val secretKeyFactory =
SecretKeyFactory.getInstance("PBKDF2WithHmacSHA1")
        val keyBytes =
secretKeyFactory.generateSecret(pbKeySpec).encoded
        val keySpec = SecretKeySpec(keyBytes, "AES")

        // 3
        //Decrypt
        val cipher = Cipher.getInstance("AES/CBC/PKCS7Padding")
        val ivSpec = IvParameterSpec(iv)
        cipher.init(Cipher.DECRYPT_MODE, keySpec, ivSpec)
        decrypted = cipher.doFinal(encrypted)
      } catch (e: Exception) {
        Log.e("MYAPP", "decryption exception", e)
      }
      return decrypted
    }
    // ...
  }
}
```

In this code, you did the following:

1. Used the `HashMap` that contains the encrypted data, salt and IV necessary for decryption.
2. Regenerated the key given that information plus the user's password.
3. Decrypted the data and returned it as a `ByteArray`.

Notice how you used the same configuration for the decryption, but you've traced your steps back. That's because you're using a symmetric encryption algorithm. You can now encrypt data as well as decrypt it!

Oh, and did I mention? Never store the key! :]

Updating the Saving Method

Now that the encryption process is complete, you need to test it. The app is already writing data to storage.

In **ReportDetailFragment.kt**, uncomment the line below `//TODO: Test your custom encryption here`. Then add the following to `testCustomEncryption()`:

```
@AndroidEntryPoint
class ReportDetailFragment : Fragment() {
  // ...
  private fun testCustomEncryption(reportString: String) {
    val password = REPORT_SESSION_KEY.toCharArray()
    val bytes = reportString.toByteArray(Charsets.UTF_8)
    val map = Encryption.encrypt(bytes, password) // 1
    val reportID = UUID.randomUUID().toString()
    val outFile = File(activity?.filesDir?.absolutePath,
"$reportID.txt")
    ObjectOutputStream(FileOutputStream(outFile)).use { // 2
      it.writeObject(map)
    }

    //TEST decrypt
    val decryptedBytes = Encryption.decrypt(map, password) // 3
    decryptedBytes?.let {
      val decryptedString = String(it, Charsets.UTF_8)
      Log.e("Encryption Test", "The decrypted string is:
$decryptedString") // 4
    }
  }
  // ...
}
```

In the updated code, you:

1. Fed the data into the encryption method.
2. Saved the encrypted data.
3. Called `decrypt` using the encrypted data, IV and salt.
4. Tested that it worked.

Build and run now. Then go to the report section and enter a message you want to test, for example: "Very lovely cat is looking for help!" After you send the report, you'll see the decrypted string in the logs:

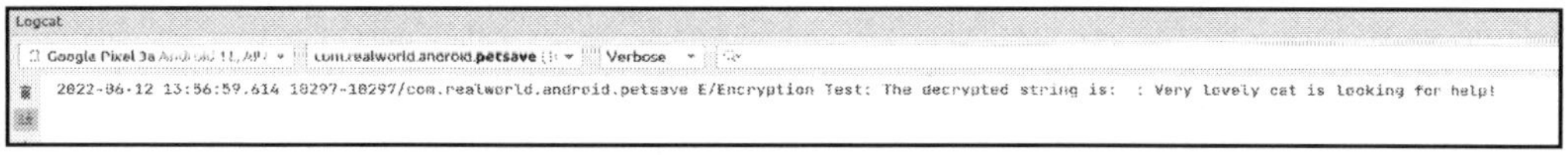

Figure 16.5 — Encryption Test

Congratulations!

Key Points

In this chapter, you learned the following:

- How to add a simple login with a password or biometrics.
- How to tie that to protect your data and keys in the KeyStore.
- That `EncryptedFile` is a high-level encryption helper that you can use with those keys.
- You can customize the encryption using `Cipher`.

It's great to know how to properly implement security. Armed with this knowledge, you'll be able to confirm if third-party security libraries are up to the best practices.

On the other hand, implementing it all yourself, especially if you're in a rush, can lead to mistakes. If you're in that situation, consider using an industry-approved or time-tested third party.

One drawback to using a third-party solution comes when hackers expose a vulnerability in a popular library. This affects all the apps that rely on that library at the same time. Apps with custom implementations are immune to wide-spread, scripted attacks.

You've secured your data at rest. With that knowledge, you'll secure data in transit in the next chapter.

Chapter 17: Securing Data in Transit

By Kolin Stürt and Antonio Roa-Valverde

Network security is an integral part of development. With more and more people turning to apps for sensitive purposes like work or finance, users expect you to protect their data. Almost every app communicates over a network. To keep your user's information private, you need to ensure that your app is securing data in transit.

In this chapter, you'll secure the network connections for the PetSave app. During the process, you'll learn the following best practices:

- Using HTTPS for network calls.
- Trusting a connection with certificate pinning.
- Verifying the integrity of transmitted data.

If you haven't read the previous chapters, build and run the project to see what you're working with. Browse through the selection of pets and try tapping the report tab, which lets you send anonymous concerns:

Figure 17.1 — Report Session

In the previous chapter, you secured that data at rest. Now, your job is to ensure the data is secure when it leaves the app.

Understanding HTTPS

URLs that start with **http://** transmit unprotected data that anyone can view — and many popular tools are available to monitor that data. Some examples are:

- **Wireshark**: https://www.wireshark.org
- **mitmproxy**: https://mitmproxy.org
- **Charles**: https://www.charlesproxy.com

Because pets tend to be fussy about their privacy, the requests in this app use HTTPS. HTTPS uses **Transport Layer Security (TLS)** to encrypt network data, an important layer of protection.

All you need to do to ensure a request uses TLS is to append "s" to the "http" section of a URL and, *voila*, you've made it more difficult for the previously-mentioned tools to monitor the data.

However, this doesn't provide perfect protection.

Using Perfect Forward Secrecy

While encrypted traffic is unreadable, IT companies can still store it. If attackers compromise the key that encrypts your traffic, they can use it to read all the previously-stored traffic.

To prevent this vulnerability, **Perfect Forward Secrecy (PFS)** generates a unique session key for each communication session. If an attacker compromises the key for a specific session, it won't affect data from other sessions.

Android 5.0+ implements PFS by default and prohibits TLS ciphers that don't support it. As of Android N, you enforce this by using Network Security Configuration: https://developer.android.com/training/articles/security-config. You'll add this to your app now.

Enforcing TLS with Network Security Configuration

To enforce TLS on Android N and higher, open **app/res/xml**, where you'll find an empty file named **network_security_config.xml**. In this file, add the following code:

```
<?xml version="1.0" encoding="utf-8"?>
<network-security-config>
  <domain-config cleartextTrafficPermitted="false">
    <domain includeSubdomains="true">petfinder.com</domain>
  </domain-config>
</network-security-config>
```

Here, you set `cleartextTrafficPermitted` to `false`. It blocks network requests that don't use TLS for specified domains. You then add `petfinder.com` as a domain and set its `includeSubdomains` attribute to `true`. This enforces TLS for subdomains like `api.petfinder.com`.

Next, you need to tell the Android system to use that file. In **AndroidManifest.xml**,add the `android:networkSecurityConfig` attribute to `<application/>` like in the following code:

```
<?xml version="1.0" encoding="utf-8"?>
<manifest package="com.raywenderlich.android.petsave"
    xmlns:android="http://schemas.android.com/apk/res/android"
    xmlns:tools="http://schemas.android.com/tools">
  <!-- // ... -->
  <application
      android:networkSecurityConfig="@xml/
network_security_config"
  >
    <!-- // ... -->
  </application>
</manifest>
```

To test that it works, replace the `BASE_ENDPOINT` value in **ApiConstants.kt** with this:

```
const val BASE_ENDPOINT = "http://api.petfinder.com/v2/"
```

Here, you changed the URL to use **HTTP** to test what happens when you send data without encryption.

Build and debug the project in an emulator or device running Android N or newer. You'll see an error message in **Debug** that says **CLEARTEXT communication to api.petfinder.com not permitted**, as shown below:

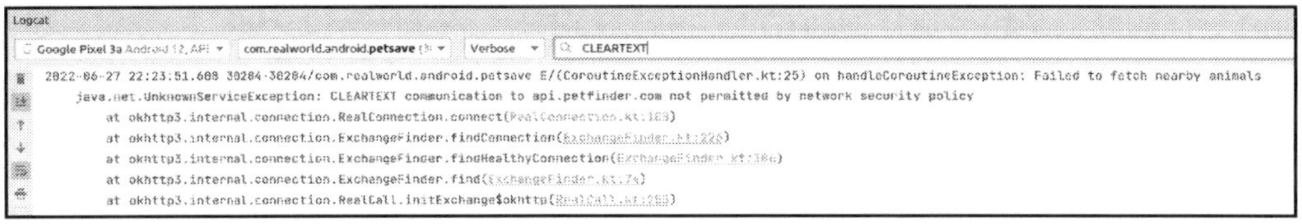

Figure 17.2 — CLEARTEXT Error Messages

That's because Android blocked the calls so it won't retrieve unencrypted data. Because you've previously launched the app, you might still get some pre-cached pet data.

Undo that change so the code is back to this:

```
const val BASE_ENDPOINT = "https://api.petfinder.com/v2/"
```

Build and debug the app. The app displays the data again, but this time without the error — so you know it enforced TLS.

Don't stop now! There are a few more simple changes that will make your app more secure.

Updating Security Providers

Often, when security researchers find vulnerabilities in software, the software company releases a patch. It's a good idea to make sure you've patched the security provider for TLS. If you see an error such as, **SSL23_GET_SERVER_HELLO:sslv3 alert handshake failure** during your debugging, this usually means you need to update the provider.

For more information about this procedure, see Android's Update Your Security Provider page: https://developer.android.com/training/articles/security-gms-provider#patching.

Understanding Certificate and Public Key Pinning

Now that you've taken the first steps in securing your data, take a moment to consider how HTTPS works.

When you start an HTTPS connection, the server presents a **certificate** that verifies it's the real entity. This is possible because a trusted **certificate authority (CA)** signed the certificate.

An intermediate authority might also have signed an intermediate certificate — there can be more than one signature. The connection is secure as long as a root certificate authority that Android trusts signed the first certificate. The Android system evaluates that certificate chain and, if a certificate isn't valid, it closes the connection.

That sounds good, but it's far from foolproof. There are many weaknesses that can make Android trust an attacker's certificate instead of one that's legitimately signed. For example, a company might have a work device configured to accept its own certificate. Or hackers can manually instruct Android to accept their installed certificate.

This is called a **man-in-the-middle attack** — it allows the entity in possession of the certificate to decrypt, read and modify the traffic.

Certificate pinning comes to the rescue by preventing connections when these scenarios occur. It works by checking the server's certificate against a copy of the expected certificate.

Implementing Certificate Pinning

Certificate pinning is easy to implement on Android N+. Instead of comparing the entire certificate, it compares the **hash** (more on this later) of the public key, often called a **pin**:

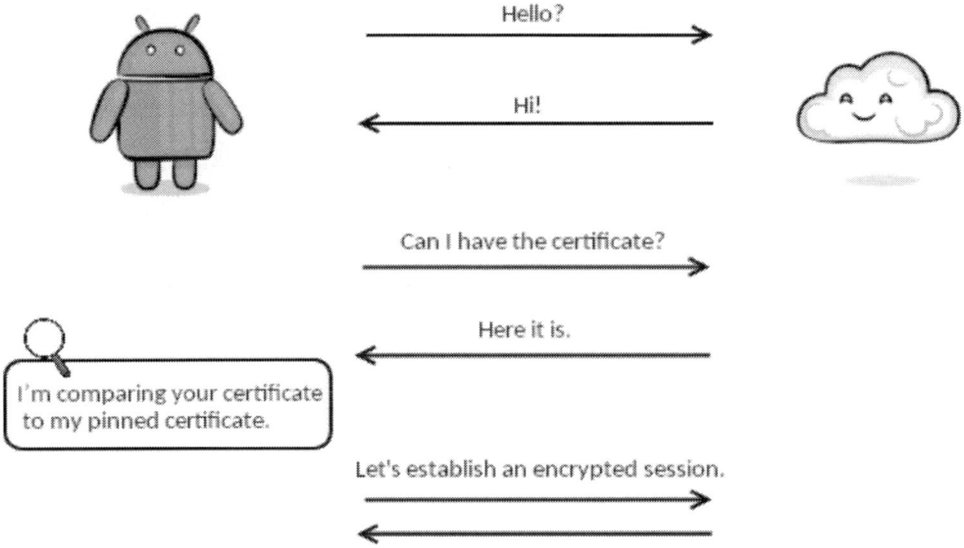

Figure 17.3 — Certificate Pinning

To get the pin for the host you're talking to, head to SSL Lab's website: https://www.ssllabs.com/ssltest/analyze.html. Type **api.petfinder.com** for the **Hostname** field and click **Submit**:

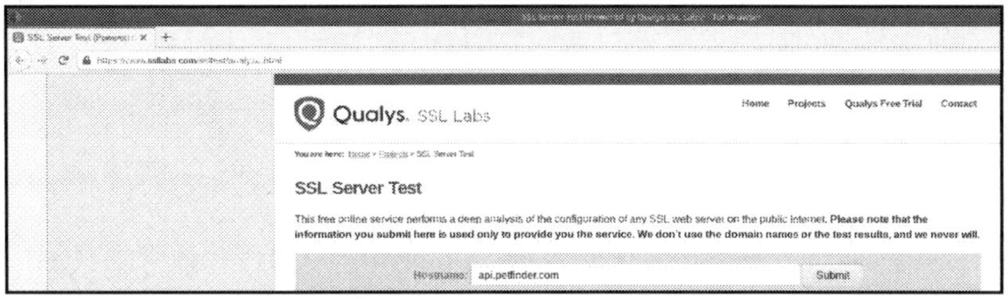

Figure 17.4 — Insert Your Domain into the SSL Lab Website

On the next page, select one of the servers from the list:

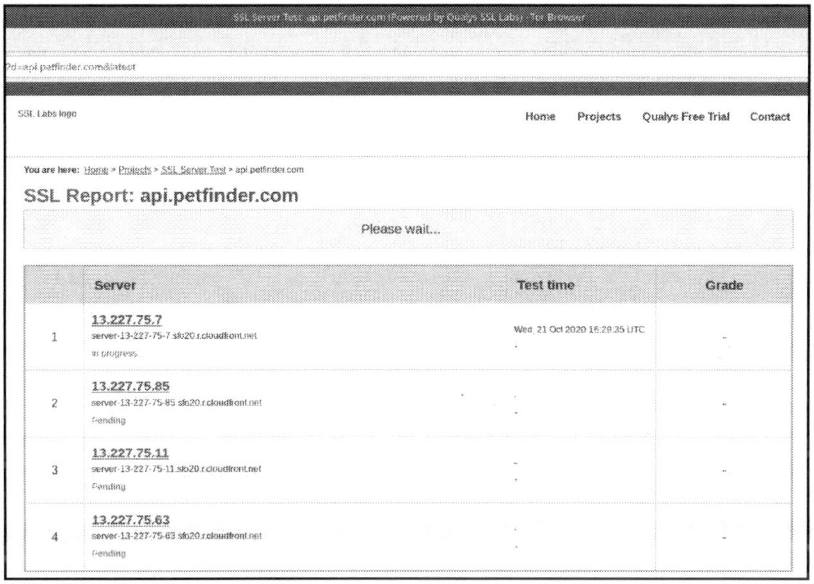

Figure 17.5 — Select the Server

You'll see there are two certificates listed; the second one is a backup. Each entry has a **Pin SHA256** value:

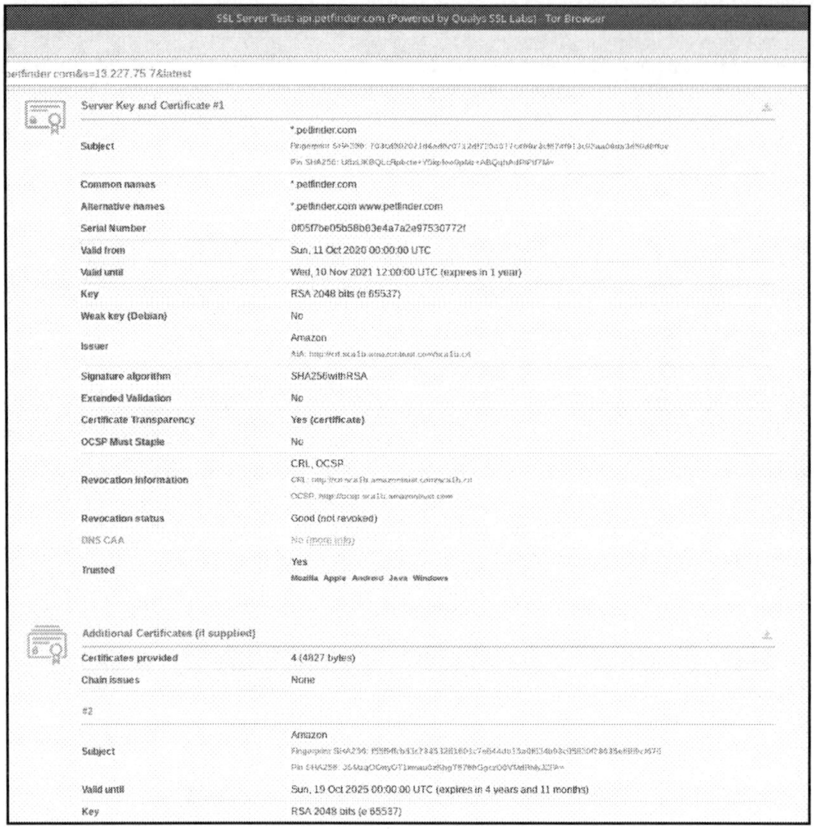

Figure 17.6 — Select the Server From

These values may change over time, so be sure to look them up before using them. They're the hashes of the public keys that you'll add to the app.

Return to **network_security_config.xml** and add them right after the **domain** tag for **petfinder.com** like this:

```
<?xml version="1.0" encoding="utf-8"?>
<network-security-config>
  <domain-config cleartextTrafficPermitted="false">
    <domain includeSubdomains="true">petfinder.com</domain>
    <!-- FROM HERE -->
    <pin-set>
      <pin
digest="SHA-256">U8zLlKBQLcRpbcte+Y0kpfoe0pMz+ABQqhAdPlPtf7M=</
pin>
```

```
        <pin
digest="SHA-256">JSMzqOOrtyOT1kmau6zKhgT676hGgczD5VMdRMyJZFA=</
pin>
      </pin-set>
      <!-- TO HERE -->
    </domain-config>
</network-security-config>
```

> **Note**: There are many ways to get the public key hash. One alternative is to download the certificate directly from the website and run OpenSSL commands on it. Or, if you're developing an app for a company, you can bug IT for one. :]

Build and run, and you won't see any changes. To test that everything works, change any character other than = for each of the pin digest entries. Here's an example:

```
<pin
digest="SHA-256">U8zLlT56PmiT3SR0WdFOR3dghwJrQ8yXx6JLSqTIRpk=</
pin>
<pin
digest="SHA-256">JSMzq7xBsOVe1PQRwOsHsw3bsGT2VzIqz5K+59sNQws=</
pin>
```

Build and run now and you'll see an error that says something like **javax.net.ssl.SSLHandshakeException: Pin verification failed**:

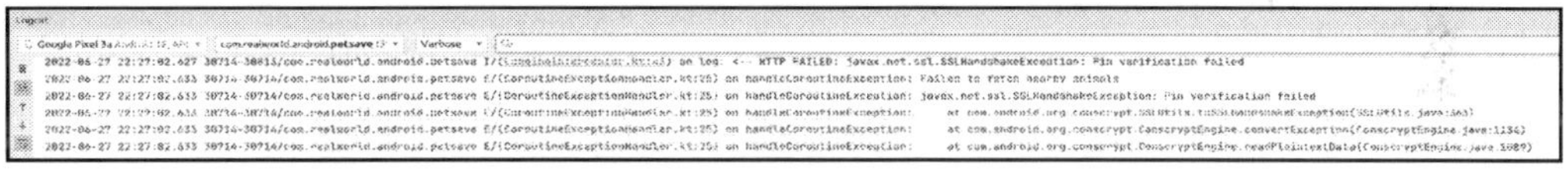

Figure 17.7 — Pin Verified Failed

Don't forget to undo those changes! With that, you've added certificate pinning support for Android N and higher… but what if your app needs to support versions under N? You'll handle this case next.

Implementing Pinning for Early Android Versions

In this app, you're using **OKHttp** as the network library. Fortunately, this library lets you add pinning manually.

Head to **APIModule.kt** and add this to `provideOkHttpClient`, where it reads `TODO: Add pinning for versions lower than M`:

```
val hostname = "**.petfinder.com" //Double-asterisk matches any
number of subdomains.
val certificatePinner = CertificatePinner.Builder()
    .add(hostname, "sha256/
U8zLlKBQLcRpbcte+Y0kpfoe0pMz+ABQqhAdPlPtf7M=")
    .add(hostname, "sha256/
JSMzqOOrtyOT1kmau6zKhgT676hGgczD5VMdRMyJZFA=")
    .build()
```

This tells OKHttp to enable certificate pinning with the pins for **petfinder.com**. For the hostname, one asterisk before the domain enables it for a single subdomain only. A double asterisk enables it for any number of subdomains.

Next, add this right after the line that reads **return OkHttpClient.Builder()**:

```
.certificatePinner(certificatePinner)
```

This tells the `OkHttpClient` builder to involve the interceptor when making a connection. That will make sure the certificates match before completing the connection.

There are some other solutions for different network libraries:

- TrustKit is a third party library that uses the same format in **network_security_config.xml** to add support for versions under Android N. You can find it here: https://github.com/datatheorem/TrustKit-Android.
- For implementations for other libraries or more information about certificate pinning in general, see the OWASP documentation: https://www.owasp.org/index.php/Certificate_and_Public_Key_Pinning.

While pinning is popular, some companies don't like having to update their apps from time to time with new pins as the old certificates expire. That's a problem that **Certificate Transparency** solves.

Using Certificate Transparency

Certificate Transparency is a new standard that audits the presented certificates when you set up an HTTPS connection without requiring hard-coded values in the app.

When a CA issues a certificate, it must submit it to a number of append-only certificate logs. Certificate Transparency has nearly real-time monitoring to determine if someone has compromised the CA or if the CA issued the certificate maliciously. The owner of the domain can scrutinize the entries, and your app cross-checks the logs. The certificate is only valid if it exists in at least two logs.

When an entity revokes a certificate, you want to know about it immediately. You can use Certificate Transparency on top of pinning for greater security, so you'll add it to your app next.

Implementing Certificate Transparency

In the app module **build.gradle**, add the following to the list of dependencies and sync Gradle:

```
implementation
"com.appmattus.certificatetransparency:certificatetransparency-
android:1.1.1"
```

Go back to `provideOkHttpClient` in **APIModule.kt** and add this to the top of the imports:

```
import
com.appmattus.certificatetransparency.certificateTransparencyInt
erceptor
```

Find the line that reads `TODO: Add certificate transparency here` and add the following right under that line:

```
val ctInterceptor = certificateTransparencyInterceptor {
  // Enable for the provided hosts
  +"*.petfinder.com" //1 For subdomains
  +"petfinder.com" //2 asterisk does not cover base domain
  //+"*.*" - this will add all hosts
  //-"legacy.petfinder.com" //3 Exclude specific hosts
}
```

Here, you:

1. Enabled Certificate Transparency for the subdomains of **petfinder.com**.
2. Since an asterisk doesn't cover the base domain in this case, you added it explicitly.
3. Added a comment to exclude specific domains using –. That example would allow all **petfinder.com** domains except the one starting with **legacy**.

Then, add this to the `OkHttpClient` builder, after the line you previously added that reads `.certificatePinner(certificatePinner)`:

```
.addNetworkInterceptor(ctInterceptor)
```

Now the `OkHttpClient` builder will invoke both certificate pinning and certificate transparency. You'll be able to build and run the app without any issue.

Next, you'll learn about a few more options that affect certificate checking.

Preventing Information Leaks with OCSP Stapling

The traditional way to determine if an entity revoked a certificate is to check a **Certificate Revocation List (CRL)**. To do this, your app must contact a third party to confirm the validity of the certificate, which adds network overhead. It also leaks private information about the sites you want to connect with to the third party.

Online Certificate Status Protocol (OCSP) stapling comes to the rescue. When you start an HTTPS request to the server using this method, the validity of the server's certificate is already **stapled** to the response.

OCSP stapling is enabled by default, but you can disable it or customize the behavior of certificate revocation using `PKIXRevocationChecker.Option`. You can look at the commented code inside **ReportManager.kt**'s `init` block for sample code, or visit the documentation for `PKIXRevocationChecker` here: https://developer.android.com/reference/kotlin/java/security/cert/PKIXRevocationChecker.Option.

With OCSP stapling, the server you're connecting to can't forge this info. That's because the CA **signs** that info ahead of time, and it's why it doesn't know which site you want to access.

So what is signing? It's a way to verify the data's integrity. Even though your data is encrypted, how do you know was authentic in the first place? Signing and authentication help ensure the integrity of the information you send and receive over the network.

Understanding Authentication

During World War II, German bombers used Lorenz radio beams to navigate and to find targets in Britain. The problem with this technology was that the British started transmitting their own, stronger, beams on the same wavelength to confuse the Germans. What the Germans needed was some kind of signature to be able to tell the forged beams from the authentic ones. Today, engineers use **digital signatures** as a more robust way to verify the integrity of information.

Digital signatures ensure that *you're* the one accessing your health data, starting a chat or logging into a bank. They also ensure no one has altered the data.

At the heart of a digital signature is a **hash function**. A hash function takes a variable amount of data and outputs a signature of a fixed length. It's a one-way function, also known in math as a trap-door function. Given the resulting output, there's no computationally-feasible way to reverse it to reveal what the original input was.

The output of a hash function is always the same if the input is the same. The output is drastically different if you change even one byte or character. That makes it the perfect way to verify that a large amount of data isn't corrupted — you simply hash the data and compare that hash with the expected one.

To authenticate that data is untampered, you'll use **Secure Hash Algorithm (SHA)**, which is a well-known standard that refers to a group of hash functions.

> **Note**: SHA1 hash functions are unsafe and should never be used, but anything from the SHA-2 family, such as SHA-512, is recommended. For more information about SHA, go here: https://en.wikipedia.org/wiki/Secure_Hash_Algorithms.

Authenticating With Public-Key Cryptography

In many cases, when an API sends data over a network, the data also contains a hash. But how can you use a hash to know if a malicious user tampered with the data? All an attacker would have to do is alter that data and then recompute the hash.

What you need is to add some secret information to the mix when you hash the data. Developers call this kind of hash a **signature**. The attacker cannot recompute the signature without knowing the secret. But how do both parties let each other know what the secret is without someone intercepting it? That's where **Public-Key Cryptography** comes into the picture.

Public-Key Cryptography works by creating a set of keys, one public and one private. The private key creates the signature, while the public key verifies it.

Given a public key, it's not computationally feasible to derive the private key. Even if malicious users know the public key, all they can do is to verify the integrity of the original message. Attackers can't alter a message because they don't have the private key to reconstruct the signature. The most modern way to do this is through **Elliptic-Curve Cryptography (ECC)**:

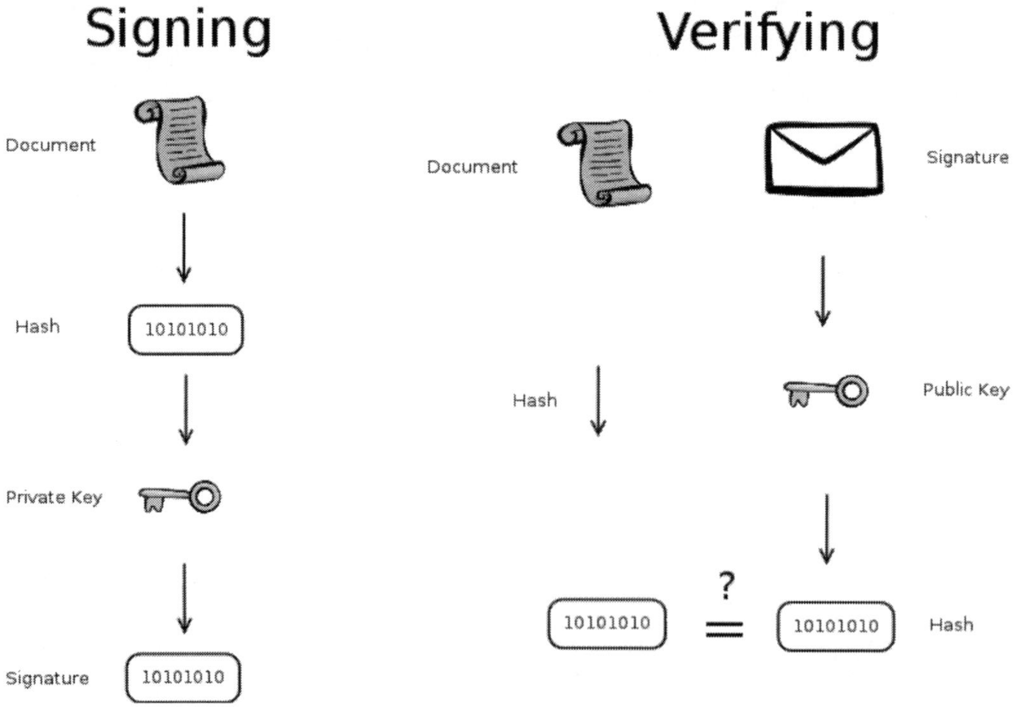

Figure 17.8 — Elliptic Curve Digital Signature Algorithm

Verifying Integrity With Elliptic-Curve Cryptography

ECC is a new set of algorithms based on elliptic curves over finite fields. While the math is out of scope for this chapter, you can read more about it here: https://en.wikipedia.org/wiki/Elliptic-curve_cryptography.

You can use ECC for encryption, but in this chapter, you'll use it for authentication, known as **Elliptic Curve Digital Signature Algorithm (ECDSA)**.

To start using ECDSA, open **Authenticator.kt**. This is a template that imports the necessary key and factory classes that you can use to create your public and private key pair.

Adding Public and Private Keys

Add a public key and private key just after the `Authenticator` class definition:

```
class Authenticator {

  private val publicKey: PublicKey
  private val privateKey: PrivateKey
  // ...
}
```

You need to initialize these keys, so right after the variables, add the `init` block:

```
class Authenticator {
  // ...
  init {
    val keyPairGenerator = KeyPairGenerator.getInstance("EC") //
1
    keyPairGenerator.initialize(256) // 2
    val keyPair = keyPairGenerator.genKeyPair() // 3

    // 4
    publicKey = keyPair.public
    privateKey = keyPair.private
  }
  // ...
}
```

Here's what you did in this code:

1. Created a `KeyPairGenerator` instance for the Elliptic Curve (EC) type.
2. Initialized the object with the recommended key size of 256 bits.
3. Generated a key pair, which contains both the public and private key.
4. Set the `publicKey` and `privateKey` variables of your class to those newly-generated keys.

Adding the Sign and Verify Methods

To complete this class, update the sign and verify methods. Replace the contents of `sign()` with this:

```
class Authenticator {
  // ...
  fun sign(data: ByteArray): ByteArray {
    val signature = Signature.getInstance("SHA512withECDSA") //
1
    signature.initSign(privateKey) // 2
    signature.update(data) // 3
    return signature.sign() // 4
  }
  // ...
}
```

This method takes in a `ByteArray` and:

1. Gets an ECDSA instance using the recommended hash type of SHA-512.
2. Initializes `Signature` with the private key for signing.
3. Adds the `ByteArray` data.
4. Returns a `ByteArray` signature.

Next, you'll need a way to verify data given a public key you receive. Replace the last `verify()` in the class with the following:

```
class Authenticator {
  // ...
  fun verify(signature: ByteArray, data: ByteArray,
publicKeyString: String): Boolean {
    val verifySignature =
Signature.getInstance("SHA512withECDSA")
// 1
    val bytes = android.util.Base64.decode(publicKeyString,
```

```
        android.util.Base64.NO_WRAP)
    val publicKey =

KeyFactory.getInstance("EC").generatePublic(X509EncodedKeySpec(b
ytes))
    verifySignature.initVerify(publicKey) // 2
    verifySignature.update(data) // 3
    return verifySignature.verify(signature) // 4
  }
  // ...
}
```

This code:

1. Converts a Base64 public key string into a `PublicKey` object.
2. Initializes the `Signature` with the public key for verification.
3. Updates the `Signature` with your data.
4. Performs the verification. The method returns `true` if the verification succeeds.

Base64 is a format that allows you to pass raw data bytes over the network as a string. You can read more about it here: https://en.wikipedia.org/wiki/Base64.

Update the helper function to convert the key object into a `String` by replacing `publicKey()` with the following:

```
class Authenticator {
  // ...
  fun publicKey(): String {
    return android.util.Base64.encodeToString(publicKey.encoded,
android.util.Base64.NO_WRAP)
  }
}
```

Now that you have an `Authenticator`, you'll use it to sign requests to the report server.

Why You Sign a Request

The PetSave app uses test code to simulate connecting to the pet report server via a back-end API. Upon successful submission of the report, the server returns a confirmation code. For your privacy, the test code doesn't really send your data anywhere. It's just a simulation. :]

In the previous chapter, you created an app login session that authenticates your credentials by using a fingerprint or a device passcode. This ensured that only you could access the app's data stored on the device. It created a unique token, protected by the device's keystore, that's only accessible upon authenticating on your device.

Now, you'll use that token to log in to the Pet Reporter server. The app will send your token and public key to the server before you can access the report endpoints.

Once the server knows who you are, the app needs to sign its requests to the Send Report endpoints to use them successfully. That way, the server authenticates that only you are accessing the endpoints.

How to Build the Signature

Open **MainActivity.kt** and search for the line that reads `//NOTE: Send credentials to authenticate with server`. Here, you've logged in to the server with your token and public key. Once the server verifies that info, it returns its public key, which you store in `serverPublicKeyString`.

When signing a request, it's common to take selected parts of the request — such as HTTP Headers, GET or POST parameters — and the URL and join them into a string. You use that string to create the signature. On the back end, the server repeats the process of joining the strings and creating a signature. If the signatures match, it proves that the user must have possession of the private key. No one can impersonate the user because they don't have that private key.

Since specific parameters of the request are part of the string, it also guarantees the integrity of the request by preventing attackers from altering the request parameters. For example, a bank wouldn't be happy if attackers could alter the destination account number for a money transfer or alter the mailing address to receive the victim's credit card statements in the mail.

For your next step, you'll create a signature for the request to send the report.

Creating the Signature

Back in **ReportDetailFragment.kt**, add the following code to `sendReportPressed()`, just under the line that reads `//TODO: Add Signature here`:

```
val stringToSign = "$REPORT_APP_ID+$reportID+$reportString" // 1
val bytesToSign = stringToSign.toByteArray(Charsets.UTF_8) // 2
val signedData =
mainActivity.clientAuthenticator.sign(bytesToSign) // 3
requestSignature = Base64.encodeToString(signedData,
Base64.NO_WRAP) // 4
```

Here's what this code does:

1. Concatenates the parameters for the request string.
2. Converts the string into a `ByteArray`.
3. Signs the bytes using your private key and returns the signature bytes.
4. Turns the signature bytes into a Base64 string that you can easily send over the network.

Now that you've created a signature, you'll verify that it worked.

Verifying the Signature

To verify that your signature is correct, head to **ReportManager.kt** and look at `sendReport()`. You'll find simulated server code that calls `serverAuthenticator.verify`.

Debug and run to check that it worked. Set a breakpoint on the `if (success) {` line to check that `success` is `true`:

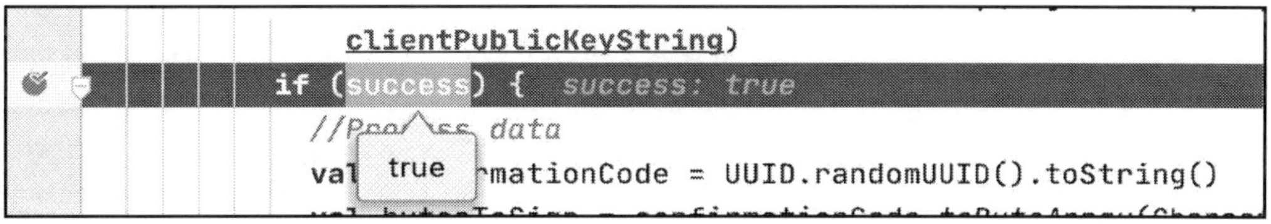

Figure 17.9 — Server Authentication Success

To test what happens when there are problems, alter the data the server receives. Add the following right after `val bytesToVerify = stringToVerify.toByteArray(Charsets.UTF_8)`:

```
bytesToVerify[bytesToVerify.size - 1] = 0
```

The above line of code replaces the last byte of the data with `0`.

Debug and run again. This time `success` is `false`:

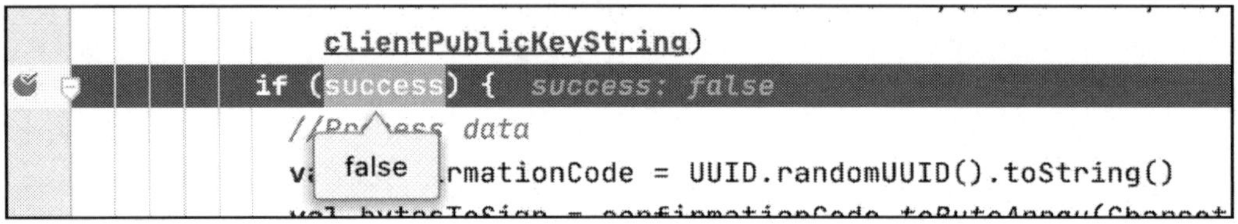

Figure 17.10 — Server Authentication Failed

You just secured your data with a signature. Don't forget to remove that test line you just added!

Authenticating the Response

Now that the server has authenticated the report, you also want to authenticate the response so you know the confirmation code, or any other communication from the server, is legitimate. Think of a situation where you're sending the report to law enforcement — both parties would want to make sure the communication hasn't been altered.

Just as you provided your public key when you registered with the reporting service, the reporting service passed its public key back. A chat app might use the same setup, for example, where each user might exchange public keys upon initiating a chat session.

In this case, however, you'll use the server's public key to verify the report data that the server returned. Back in **ReportDetailFragment.kt**, replace `success = true` right after the line that reads `TODO: Verify signature here` in `sendReportPressed()`:

```
// 1
val serverSignature = it["signature"] as String
val signatureBytes = Base64.decode(serverSignature,
Base64.NO_WRAP)

// 2
val confirmationCode = it["confirmation_code"] as String
```

```
val confirmationBytes =
confirmationCode.toByteArray(Charsets.UTF_8)

// 3
success =
mainActivity.clientAuthenticator.verify(signatureBytes,
    confirmationBytes, mainActivity.serverPublicKeyString)
```

Here's what you did:

1. Retrieved the signature string and converted it to bytes.
2. Obtained the result data — the confirmation code.
3. Verified the result data with the signature from the server.

Testing Your Authentication

To test that it worked, set a breakpoint on the `if (success) {` line inside `onReportReceived()`. Build and debug to see the result in the **Debug** tab.

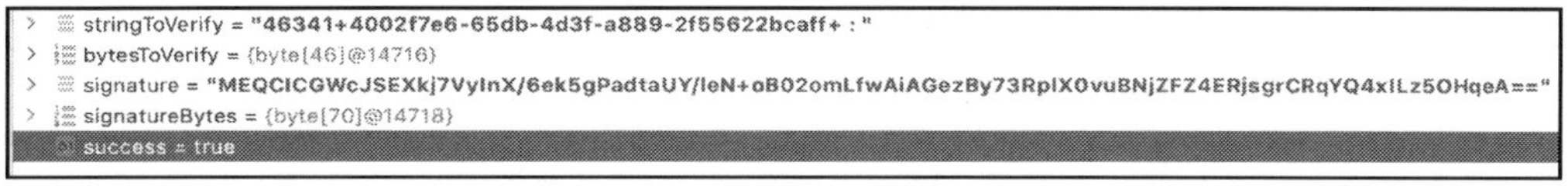

Figure 17.11 — Authentication Success

Alter the request data to see what happens. Add the following code right before calling `clientAuthenticator.verify()` in `sendReport()` in the **ReportManager.kt** file:

```
confirmationBytes[confirmationBytes.size - 1] = 0
```

Build and run. This time, `success` is `false` in the **Debug** tab:

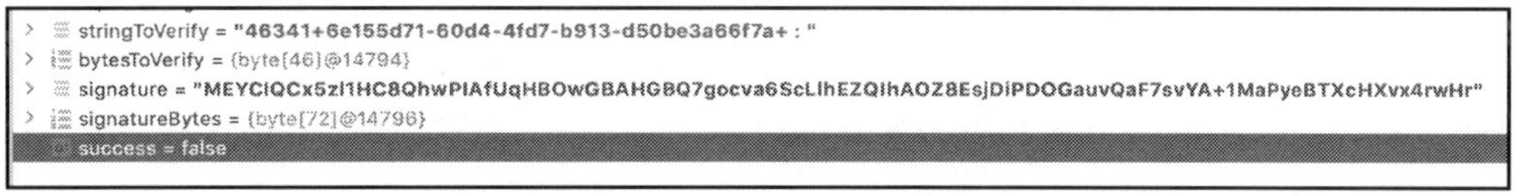

Figure 17.12 — Authentication Failed

Congratulations! You've secured both sides of the communication. Don't forget to remove the test code that makes it fail. You should also be aware of a few other standards when it comes to authentication:

- RSA is a popular and accepted standard. Its key sizes must be much larger, such as 4096 bits, and key generation is slower. You might use it if the rest of your team is already familiar with or using this standard.
- HMAC is another popular solution that, instead of using public-key cryptography, relies on a single shared key. You must exchange the secret key securely. Developers use HMAC when speed considerations are very important.
- OAuth is a standard to delegate access so users can grant a service access to their information without revealing their password. You used it in previous chapters to perform basic authentication with the petfinder.com API. PetFinder uses this to control its API use by weeding out botting and abuse by spammers. Read more about it here: https://developer.android.com/training/id-auth/authenticate.html.
- The Account Manager is a centralized helper for user account credentials so your app doesn't have to deal with user passwords directly. Read more about it here: https://developer.android.com/reference/android/accounts/AccountManager.html.

End-to-end Encryption

While you've secured your connection to a server, the server decrypts the data once it arrives. Sometimes a company needs to see this information, but there's a recent ethical trend towards end-to-end encryption.

An example of end-to-end encryption is a chat app where each user begins by exchanging their public key. Then when a user, Alice, wants to send a message to Bob, she encrypts the message using Bob's public key, which she received. Bob then decrypts the message using his private key. Only the sender and receiver have the private keys to decrypt each others' messages.

The chat service never receives the private keys; it has no way of knowing what the content is. This is a proactive way to avoid liability during a server-side data breach or compromise.

To learn more about implementing this approach, a good place to start is the open-source Signal App GitHub repo: https://github.com/signalapp.

Key Points

In this chapter, you discovered that you should:

- Always use HTTPS instead of HTTP.
- Enable certificate transparency, certificate pinning or both for maximum security.
- Authenticate your network requests.

Where to Go From Here?

Here are some other points about network safety:

- Google has a network security testing tool to help you spot cleartext traffic or other connection vulnerabilities in your app. Visit **nogotofail** for more info: https://github.com/google/nogotofail.
- For more security tools, check out the SafetyNet API, which includes safe browsing, integrity and reCAPTCHA to protect your app from spammers, phishing URLs and other malicious traffic. Find it here: https://developer.android.com/training/safetynet/attestation.

You've been securing and verifying the integrity of the data, but that's not a replacement for regular data validation checks like type and bounds checking.

For example, if you expect a string of 256 characters or less in the network response, you should still check for that. If the server expects a parameter with only numbers, you'd want to sanitize that output.

This is called **app hardening**, and it's what the next chapter is all about!

Chapter 18: App Hardening

By Kolin Stürt and Antonio Roa-Valverde

As network communications and OSs become more secure, hackers have shifted their focus from basic eavesdropping to attacking devices and apps. In the previous chapters, you've secured your data in transit and at rest. Now, to protect your app from these additional kinds of attacks, you need to understand and use app hardening effectively.

From minimizing pointer use to null safety and type checks, Kotlin is a great language for secure development. So much so that it's tempting to forget about secure coding altogether. However, even Kotlin has vulnerabilities that you need to protect your app against.

In this chapter, you'll learn how to:

- Avoid code vulnerabilities.
- Validate input and sanitize output.
- Perform integrity checking.

Right now, the app has an overflow of code vulnerabilities which you'll eventually fix!

Introducing Overflows

In a language like C, hackers exploit security vulnerabilities by causing an app to write data to an area it's not supposed to, such as beyond an expected boundary and into adjacent memory locations. That's called an **overflow**, and it can overwrite important data.

In certain environments, this can be an area that contains code the device executes, giving attackers a way to maliciously change a program. Bug bounty hunters refer to it as "gaining arbitrary code execution". It's a very important preoccupation for them.

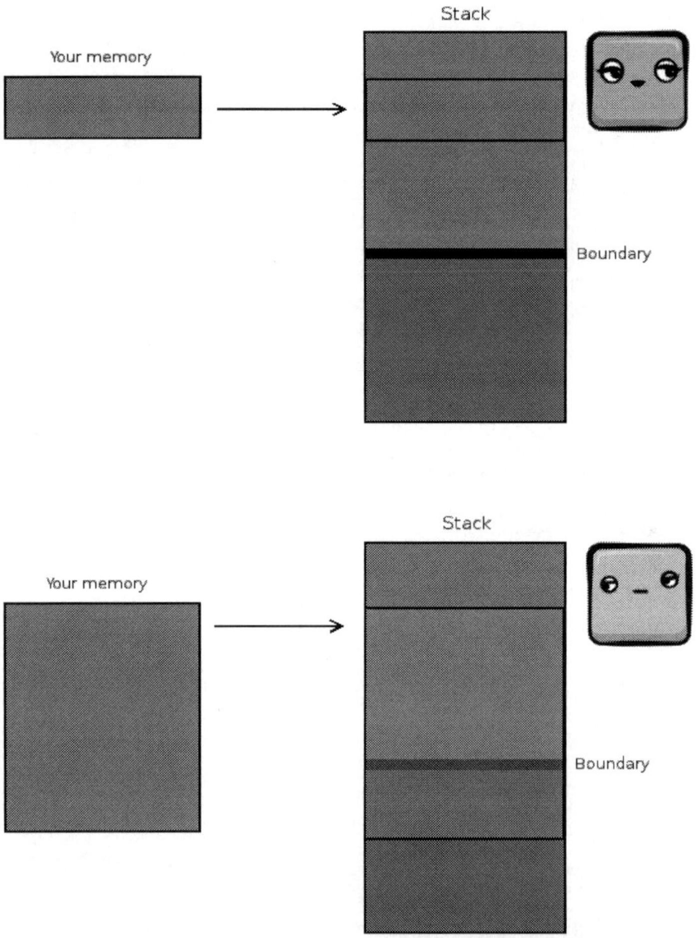

Figure 18.1 — Overflow Explained

One example of an overflow in Kotlin is when a recursive function ends up in an infinite loop. Because the size of the stack runs out, you'll get a `StackOverflow` exception.

> **Note**: You can read more about stacks at https://www.programmerinterview.com/data-structures/difference-between-stack-and-heap/.

Kotlin provides safety modifiers, such as `tailrec`, which help avoid the chances of a stack overflow by adding rules and throwing an error if you break them. The rules are:

- The last operation of the function can only call itself.
- There cannot be more code after a recursive call.
- Use within `try/catch/finally` blocks is prohibited.

These rules are especially helpful when your implementation changes later and you forget to check that it's still safe.

To implement this, open **Timing.kt** and add `tailrec`, right after the private modifier in the method definition of `factorial`. Your modified method definition should look like this:

```
private tailrec fun factorial(number: Int, accumulator: Int = 1)
: Int {
```

You've just added a safety modifier, but Android Studio also provides important security warnings for potential overflows.

Paying Attention to Warnings

Exceptions and crashes are obvious indicators that something is wrong, but a worse problem is an incorrect value that goes undetected for some time. This is what happens with an integer overflow. Kotlin doesn't throw an exception for a signed integer overflow. Instead, the app continues with the wrong values!

The good news is that Android Studio detects most integer overflows at compile time. To see how this looks, open **ReportDetailFragment.kt** and look at the warning by hovering over `REPORT_APP_ID * REPORT_PROVIDER_ID` on the line right under the `//Add Signature` comment.

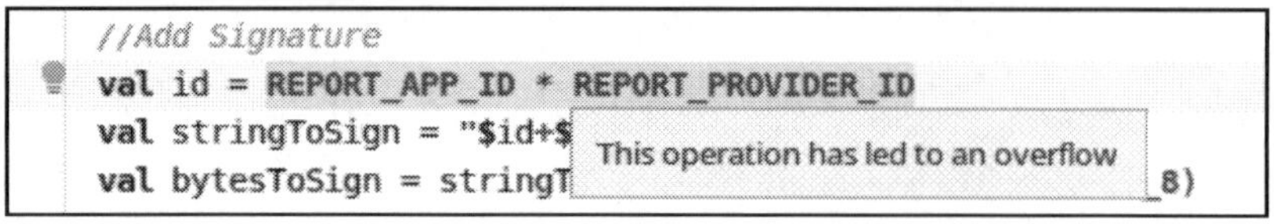

Figure 18.2 — Warnings Are Important

Regular numbers defined like this are integers, but multiplying them exceeded the maximum size of the container. That's why it's a best security practice to treat warnings as errors.

At the top of the file, replace `REPORT_APP_ID` and `REPORT_PROVIDER_ID` with the following:

```
private const val REPORT_APP_ID = 46341L
private const val REPORT_PROVIDER_ID = 46341L
```

You've now added `L` to the end of the numbers, which defines them as `Long` and fixes the warning. That's because `Long` is a number that can hold a much larger value.

> **Note**: You can read more about `Long` here: https://kotlinlang.org/api/latest/jvm/stdlib/kotlin/-long/index.html.

Another vulnerable area is when your app interacts with languages that use pointers. Pointers allow you to access raw memory locations, making it easier to read and write to the wrong area.

Kotlin is much safer than many languages because it mostly does away with pointers, but it still allows you to interface with C using `CPointer` and `COpaquePointer`.

> **Note**: You can read more about interoperating with C in Kotlin on the official website: https://kotlinlang.org/docs/reference/native/c_interop.html.

If you'll be working with NDK, it's extremely important to do bounds checking on the input to make sure it's within range. Avoid unsafe casts using `.reinterpret()` or `.toLong()` and `.toCPointer()`.

Because attackers can manipulate data in your app, another possible place for vulnerabilities is when your app passes data to a server for further processing. To make sure this is secure, you should sanitize all data that leaves your app.

Sanitizing Data

You should always sanitize your pet's output, especially when it happens indoors. If your app sends the data in text fields to a server, then sanitizing it reduces the potential for an attack. The most basic technique is to limit the amount of input that you can enter into your fields. This reduces the likelihood that a specific code snippet or payload can get through.

To do this, open **activity_main.xml** and make sure you're in the XML editing view. Add the following to the first `EditText` element, which has the ID `login_email`:

```
android:maxLength="254"
```

This states that mail addresses can have a maximum of 254 characters. Now, open **fragment_report_detail.xml** and add the following to the `EditText` field, which has the ID `details_edtxtview`:

```
android:maxLength="512"
```

You now made the maximum character limit 512 for the report. Finally, add this to the next `EditText`, with the ID `category_edtxtview`:

```
android:maxLength="32"
```

This sets the maximum category length to 32 characters.

Try out your changes by building and running the app and entering a large amount of text into the category field.

Next, you'll want to remove characters that are dangerous for the language that your server uses. This prevents **command injection attacks** — when you pass data to an environment that should store it, but instead executes the data as commands. The app's underlying datastore uses an SQLite database, while the report server is SQL.

Avoiding SQL Injection

The SQL language uses quotes to terminate strings, slashes to escape strings and semicolons to end a line of code. Attackers use this to terminate the string early and then add commands.

For example, you could bypass a login by entering `') OR 1=1 OR (password LIKE '*` into the text field. That code translates to "where password is like anything", which bypasses the authentication altogether!

One solution is to escape, encode or add your double quotes in code. That way, the server sees quotes from the user as part of the input string instead of a terminating character. Another way is to strip out those characters — which is what you're going to do next.

Stripping Out Dangerous Characters

Find `sendReportPressed()` in **ReportDetailFragment.kt**, then add the following below the line that reads `//TODO: Sanitize string here:`

```
reportString = reportString.replace("\\", "")
    .replace(";", "").replace("%", "")
    .replace("\"", "").replace("\'", "")
```

This strips the vulnerable characters from the string.

Test that it works by building and debugging the app, then entering some illegal characters in the report field. Set a breakpoint after the line you just added and send the report. Notice `reportString` removes those characters.

> **Note**: If you're also developing the server-side code, clauses such as `LIKE` and `CONTAINS` allow wild cards that you should avoid. Doing this prevents attackers from getting a list of accounts when they enter `a*` for the account name, for example. If you change the `LIKE` clause to ==, the string has to literally match `a*`.

More Sanitization Tips

Only you will know what the expected input and output should be, given the design requirements, but here are a few more points about sanitization:

- Dots and slashes may be harmful if they're passed to file management code. A directory traversal attack is when a user enters `../`, for example. This lets them view the parent directory of the path instead of the intended sub-directory.
- If you're interfacing with C, one special character is the `NULL` terminating byte, which pointers to C strings require. This lets attackers manipulate the string by introducing a `NULL` byte. The attacker might want to terminate the string early if there was a flag such as **needs_auth=1** removing it and allowing access without authorisation.
- HTML, XML and JSON strings have their own special characters. Make sure to encode special characters from the user input so attackers can't instruct the interpreter:< must become **&lt.**> should be **&gt.**& should become **&amp**.Inside attribute values, any " or ' need to become **&quot** and **&apos**, respectively.
- You can find more information about URL encoding at https://developer.android.com/reference/kotlin/java/net/URLEncoder and more about escaping at https://developer.android.com/guide/topics/resources/string-resource#FormattingAndStyling.

Just as it's important to sanitize data before sending it out, you shouldn't blindly trust the input your app receives, either. The best practice is to validate all input to your app.

Validating Input

Subconsciously, pets are constantly validating their environment for danger, sometimes in better ways than humans. While we may not be as equipped to validate danger in the wild, at least we can add validation to our apps.

As well as removing special characters for the platform you're connecting with, you should only allow the correct format for the type of input required. Right now, users can enter anything into the email field.

Validating Emails

To fix this, navigate to **DataValidator** and add a regular expression definition just after the `companion object {` line:

```
private const val EMAIL_REGEX = "^[A-Za-z0-9._%+\\-]+@[A-Za-z0-9.\\-]+\\.[A-Za-z]{2,4}$"
```

That makes sure emails have a format of **test@example.com**. Now, add the following right after that line:

```
fun isValidEmailString(emailString: String): Boolean {
  return emailString.isNotEmpty() &&
Pattern.compile(EMAIL_REGEX).matcher(emailString).matches()
}
```

This method verifies an email address via that regular expression. Finally, go back to **MainActivity** and import your new method:

```
import
com.realworld.android.petsave.core.utils.DataValidator.Companion
.isValidEmailString
```

Then find `// TODO: Replace this with email check` inside `loginPressed()`. Replace the line below it with the following:

```
var success = false
val email = login_email.text.toString()
if (isSignedUp || isValidEmailString(email)) {
  success = true
} else {
  toast("Please enter a valid email.")
}
```

Here, you perform email validation before the user can sign up. Test it by deleting the app to remove the previous login, then building and running it again. Enter an invalid email such as **my.invalid.email** and press **SIGN UP**. You'll see that the email address fails:

Figure 18.3 — Invalid Email

Designing by Contract

If you're expecting specific kinds of characters, such as numbers, you should check for this. Some methods that are helpful include:

- `Char.isLetterOrDigit(): Boolean`
- `Char.isLetter(): Boolean`
- `Char.isDigit(): Boolean`
- `String`'s `length` method

For example, if your server expects a string of 32 characters or less, make sure that the interface will only return up to and including 32 characters.

This is a good programming practice called **design by contract**, where the inputs and outputs of your methods satisfy a contract that defines specific interface expectations.

You've hardened the text inputs of your app, but it's a good idea to make an inventory of *all* input to your app. The app allows the user to upload a photo. Right now, you could attach a photo containing malware! You'll fix that now.

Validating Photos

Add the following to the end of the companion object in **DataValidator**:

```
fun isValidJPEGAtPath(pathString: String?): Boolean {
  var randomAccessFile: RandomAccessFile? = null
  try {
    randomAccessFile = RandomAccessFile(pathString, "r")
    val length = randomAccessFile.length()
    if (length < 10L) {
      return false
    }
    val start = ByteArray(2)
    randomAccessFile.readFully(start)
    randomAccessFile.seek(length - 2)
    val end = ByteArray(2)
    randomAccessFile.readFully(end)
    return start[0].toInt() == -1 && start[1].toInt() == -40 &&
        end[0].toInt() == -1 && end[1].toInt() == -39
  } finally {
    randomAccessFile?.close()
  }
}
```

For the JPEG format, the first two bytes and the last two bytes of a valid image are always **FF D8** and **FF D9**. This method checks for that.

To implement it, navigate to **ReportDetailFragment** and import the method you just added:

```
import
com.realworld.android.petsave.core.utils.DataValidator.Companion
.isValidJPEGAtPath
```

Then find `showFilename()` and replace its complete implementation with the following:

```
val isValid = isValidJPEGAtPath(decodableImageString)
if (isValid) {
  //get filename
  val fileNameColumn =
arrayOf(MediaStore.Images.Media.DISPLAY_NAME)
  val nameCursor =
activity?.contentResolver?.query(selectedImage, fileNameColumn,
      null, null, null)
  nameCursor?.moveToFirst()
  val nameIndex = nameCursor?.getColumnIndex(fileNameColumn[0])
  var filename = ""
  nameIndex?.let {
    filename = nameCursor.getString(it)
  }
  nameCursor?.close()

  //update UI with filename
  upload_status_textview?.text = filename
} else {
  val toast = Toast.makeText(context, "Please choose a JPEG
image", Toast
      .LENGTH_LONG)
  toast.show()
}
```

The first line calls the photo check when the user imports a photo, validating if it's a valid JPEG image file.

More About Validating Input

Here are a few more tips for validating input:

- Be careful when displaying an error alert that shows a message directly from the server. Error messages could disclose private debugging or security-related information. The solution is to have the server send an error code that the app looks up to show a predefined message.
- An overlooked area for input is inside deep link or URL handlers. Make sure input data fits expectations and that it's not used directly. You shouldn't allow a user to enter info that manipulates your logic. For example, instead of letting the user choose which screen in a stack to navigate to by index, allow only specific screens using an opaque identifier, such as **t=qs91jz5urq**.
- Check out Android's input validation tips: https://developer.android.com/training/articles/security-tips#InputValidation.

Another vulnerability that developers often overlook is serialized and archived data from storage. You'll address that next with null and type checks.

Nullability and Safety Checks

Does nothing exist? Or does it exist only in reference to something tangible? How can you divide several things among no things? These are the concepts that our pets surely contemplate while we're away working. Okay, well, maybe not since nothing is a concept tied to language, and in the Kotlin language, the closest relative is null. To write solid code, it's important to understand the concept of null.

Understanding Null

In Java, all variables except primitive variables actually store references to memory addresses. Because they're references, you can set the variables to `null`.

When the system expects a valid reference but receives `null` instead, it throws a **NullPointerException**, or NPE for short. If you haven't implemented exception handling, the app questions the nature of reality, and then crashes.

Kotlin aims to be a safer language. As you know, variables are non-null references — you can't set them to `null`. However, you can make variables nullable by adding ? to the end of the variable. So Kotlin attempts to eliminate NPEs but not do away with them entirely.

The best practice is to start with non-null variables at the narrowest possible scope. You should only change the variable to nullable or move it to a broader scope if absolutely necessary.

NPEs can cause security vulnerabilities, especially when they happen in security-related code or processes. If attackers can trigger an NPE, they might be able to use the resulting exception to bypass security logic or cause the app to reveal debugging information that's valuable in planning attacks. NPEs are also security vulnerabilities if sensitive files aren't cleaned up before the process terminates.

Checking Stored Data

Open **UserRepository.kt** and look at `createDataSource`. Notice the code assumes that the stored data exists and is uncorrupted. You'll change that now.

Replace the declaration of `users` inside `createDataSource` with the following:

```
val users = try { serializer.read(Users::class.java,
inputStream) } catch (e: Exception) {null}
```

The code above catches exceptions when the data is read into `User`. To prevent overuse, Kotlin discourages exceptions in favor of better flow control. For the most part, a better approach is to use safety checks because they make methods resilient to errors. The method contains the failure instead of propagating it outside the method, which can become an app-wide failure.

Replace everything after the `try/catch` you just added with this:

```
users?.list?.let { // 1
  val userList = ArrayList(it) as? ArrayList // 2
  if (userList is ArrayList<User>) { // 3
    val firstUser = userList.first() as? User
    if (firstUser is User) { // 4
      firstUser.password = Base64.encodeToString(password,
Base64.NO_WRAP)
      val fileOutputStream = FileOutputStream(outFile)
      val objectOutputStream =
ObjectOutputStream(fileOutputStream)
      objectOutputStream.writeObject(userList)
      // 5
      objectOutputStream.close()
```

```
        fileOutputStream.close()
      }
    }
  }
  inputStream.close()
```

Here, you:

1. Added null checks for the user list.
2. Used a safe cast to make sure the instance type is what you expected.
3. Made sure the `ArrayList` contains `User` objects.
4. Added an extra check to ensure `firstUser` is really a `User` object.
5. Made sure to clean up resources after use.

Adding sanity checks around your code is called **Defensive Programming** — the process of making sure your app still functions under unexpected conditions.

Note that in step two you removed `!!`. That's Kotlin's non-null assertion operator that force-casts a nullable variable to a non-null one. But if the variable is null, you'll get an NPE! That's why in most cases, `!!` is dangerous to use. As the complexity of a program increases, the edge cases that you originally thought would never happen, start to happen. In a way, the double exclamation mark is Kotlin yelling at you not to use it often!! :]

If you use `!!`, declare and initialize the `!!` variable right before you use it to reduce its scope. Use each variable for exactly one purpose. That way there's less chance that other parts of the code will set that variable to null.

More Tips for Using Nullability and Safety Checks

Here are a few other best practices to keep in mind:

- Avoid unclear optionals. Write clear and consistent class interfaces as opposed to ones that require a magic combination of parameters.
- Don't make assumptions about how other developers will use a function. If you have to pass null into the class constructor to initialize some internal state, it's a good indicator that the class is too specific and aware of its current use.

- Don't depend on knowledge of private implementation like not calling `a.initialize()` because you know `a.execute()` will lazy-initialize if it needs to. Maybe it won't in the future, and then you'll get an NPE.
- Isolate nullable operations into a single method or class. That way, you don't have to strew `?` in many places throughout your code.

You've now gotten through all the best practices for nullability in Kotlin. Although Kotlin is safer than Java, you won't always work with a pure Kotlin app. An example is legacy code that's too expensive to change — plus, some teams simply prefer Java.

Nullability in Java

There are no null safety checks for types you declare in Java. Types coming from Java subvert the checking system!

The best practice is to treat all variables coming from Java as nullable in your Kotlin code. To avoid unnecessary refactoring, another solution is to update Java methods to include **nullability annotations**.

Annotations don't alter any existing logic but, instead, tell the Kotlin compiler about nullability. The two important annotations are `@Nullable` and `@NotNull`.

While it's sometimes acceptable to return null on an error, using null to represent a state is problematic. Variables shouldn't have hidden or double meanings. A worse example is an `Int?` that stores the number of logged-in users unless it's null, which then means the app is in maintenance mode.

Say you have a method that returns `ByteArray`. Another solution is to have it return an empty `ByteArray` on failure instead of null. This is **Failsafe Programming** — where you return a default or safe value that causes minimal harm if something goes wrong.

Depending on your design requirements you'll want to consider whether your app should be **robust** or **correct**. For example, if your app shows the temperature outside and the value is null during one of the iterations, you'd use a safe value or skip that iteration and show the previous reading.

On the other hand, if your app controls factory equipment, you'd want to immediately abort whenever your app finds an incorrect value!

Nullability in C++

For code that's performance-sensitive or portable, it's common to use C++ as the preferred language. C++ is powerful because it allows you to work with memory pointers. Here are a few points about pointers:

- As with references, you can set a pointer to null.
- C++ doesn't offer nullability annotations like Java does. Instead, document your functions well by stating whether the parameters and return values can be null or not.
- In normal cases, you set a pointer to null when you're finished with it, and don't store or return pointers for later use. That allows you to work with the pointer only while it's valid.
- The true native meaning of null is actually a zero. Zero was late to the party in computational systems, arriving only after 5,000BC. It was null before that. :]

You've done a lot to harden the app where the logic and flow is obvious. But there are cases where intermittent and unexpected states can appear, and that's usually due to concurrent code.

Concurrency

As soon as you have more than one thread that needs to write data to the same memory location at the same time, a **race condition** can occur. Race conditions cause data corruption.

For instance, an attacker might be able to alter a shared resource to change the flow of security code on another thread. In the case of authentication status, an attacker could take advantage of a time gap between when a flag is checked and when it's used. Wikipedia has a good explanation of the issue: https://en.wikipedia.org/wiki/Time_of_check_to_time_of_use.

Open **ReportDetailFragment** and find `sendReportPressed()`, then search for the code that tracks `ReportTracker.reportNumber`. Notice it's set before the network call and read after the network fires a callback. Because network calls are asynchronous, if users repeatedly press the **SEND REPORT** button, they'll cause the report number to fall out of sync.

Add an `if (!isSendingReport) {` check right at the beginning of the method so that the entire body is inside that check. This follows the best practice of designing your classes so that you don't need to implement special concurrency-related code.

Other best practices are to use high-level frameworks like Kotlin coroutines or use **thread confinement** — where the logic exists only in one thread.

Using Mutual Exclusion

But say this callback happens on a separate thread. The way to avoid those race conditions is to synchronize the data. Synchronizing data means locking it so only one thread can access that part of the code at a time, called **mutual exclusion**.

Add the following right above the definition for the `isSendingReport` variable:

```
@Volatile
```

In Kotlin, `@Volatile` is an annotation for atomic. Keep in mind it only secures linear read/writes, not actions with a larger scope. Making a variable atomic doesn't make it thread-safe. You'll do that now for the `reportNumber` variable.

Making Variables Thread-safe

Find the `reportNumber` definition and replace it with the following:

```
var reportNumber = AtomicInteger()
```

An atomic variable is one where the load or store executes with a single instruction. It prevents an attacker from slipping steps in between the save and load of a security flag.

Navigate to `sendReportPressed()` and find the line that reads `ReportTracker.reportNumber++`, then replace it with the following:

```
synchronized(this) {
  ReportTracker.reportNumber.incrementAndGet()
}
```

Now, inside `onReportReceived`, replace the line that sets the `report` variable:

```
synchronized(this) { //Locked.
  report = "Report: ${ReportTracker.reportNumber.get()}"
}
```

You've now synchronized `reportNumber` between two threads. Build and run the app. Try pressing the **SEND REPORT** button multiple times and notice you can only send one report at a time.

More About Synchronization

Here are a few more tips about synchronization:

- Keep synchronization code in one place. It's hard to remember which places you've synchronized if you've scattered those locations all around your code.
- A good way to do this is by using accessor methods. By using only getter and setter methods and only using them to access synchronized data, you can do everything in one place. This avoids having to update many parts of your code when you're changing or refactoring it.
- Good interface design and data encapsulation are important when designing concurrent programs. They ensure you protect your shared data. It's pointless to have synchronization inside a class when its interface exposes a mutable object to the shared data. Instead, mark synchronized variables as private and return immutable variables or copies to the data.
- It's good for code readability to write your methods with only one entry and one exit point, especially if you add locks later. It's easy to miss a `return` hidden in the middle of a method that was supposed to lock your data later. Instead of `return true`, for example, you can declare a `Boolean`, update it along the way and then return it at the end of the method.

You've taken all these steps to harden your app against malicious attackers. But it's also good to know when your app is under attack.

Checking App Integrity

Users that try to crack your app need to use debuggers and emulators. You can often detect these states and monitor or reject those users, which is known as **integrity checking**. Since spammers use these tools, it helps keep them out of your app too!

Open up **WatchDog.kt** and check out the various methods; each looks for tell-tale signs someone has altered the environment. They check if popular emulators are running, or if the device is rooted by the existence of super-user features and privileges.

It's not fool-proof and sometimes you can get false positives. If keeping up to date with the latest changes is tiring, there are also third-party solutions that you can add to the mix:

- Find an open-source solution called Rootbeer here: https://github.com/scottyab/rootbeer.
- If you're already using Fabric or Firebase Crashlytics, call `CommonUtils.isRooted(context)`.
- GuardSquare, the makers of ProGuard, have a commercial solution called DexGuard that provides app and device integrity checking. It also encrypts classes, strings, assets and resources to thwart reverse-engineering. Check it out here: https://www.guardsquare.com/en/products/dexguard.
- You can also use Google's SafetyNet Attestation API. It includes device integrity checking, a Safe Browsing API to check for malicious URLs and a reCAPTCHA API to protect your app from spammers and other malicious traffic. Find it here: https://developer.android.com/training/safetynet/attestation.

Key Points

In this chapter, you covered all the major areas for hardening your app. Here's a summary of the most important points:

- Make sure to sanitize all input and output for the app.
- Adding native code increases the app's attack surface in regards to pointer and buffer vulnerabilities.
- If you're not using high-level concurrency APIs, you need to synchronize or use locks around the shared data.
- Use integrity checking if your app is susceptible to spammers or malicious users.

There's no such thing as a perfectly secure app. There are always changes and you'll find new bugs along the way. That's why a big part of designing a robust app comes from the feedback after your release regarding user experience, bugs and crashes.

In the following chapters, you'll switch gears to look at your release, including how to analyze it and handle debugging and lifecycle considerations.

Section V: Maintaining Your App

When you're developing your real world app, you might think that publishing is your end goal. But really, your work isn't over just because you've released your app. You still need to understand if your app is working properly and what problems your users are experiencing.

In this section, you'll learn everything you need to know about maintaining and controlling your app after it's published and available to users. In particular, you'll learn how to use Firebase for logging crashes, how to enable or disable certain features and how to use A/B tests to understand what solution is the best for your users.

Finally, you'll see how to optimize your app's size and how to use Android Studio as a profiling tool.

After reading this section, you'll be ready to use all the available tools for improving your app's quality.

Chapter 19: Firebase Integration

By Subhrajyoti Sen

Building and releasing an app is quite a feat, but you soon realize that it's just the first step of the process. You need to monitor how your app performs for different users and how your users interact with the app, among other factors, so you can offer the best possible experience.

Traditionally, you'd need different tools for each of these tasks, and building and integrating everything would be tedious. Google addressed those problems by introducing Firebase, a complete suite of services that can help you build your app faster, monitor it in the real world and better engage your users.

In this section, you'll learn how to use:

1. The Firebase Console to set up Firebase for your project.
2. Crashlytics to detect and understand app crashes.
3. Remote Config to add dynamic content to your app.
4. Test Lab to perform different tests across a wide range of devices.

You'll start at the beginning: getting Firebase ready to use.

Setting up Firebase

To set up Firebase, you first need to create a new project at https://console.firebase.google.com. Log in using a Google Account and you'll see the Firebase Console. Firebase will prompt you to create a new project, as shown below:

Figure 19.1 — Creating a Firebase Project

Creating a Firebase Project

Clicking **Create a project** will bring you to the **Create a project** page. You'll see a prompt to provide a project name, as shown below. Enter **PetSave**.

Figure 19.2 — Insert Firebase Project Name

Click **Continue**. Next, you'll get an option to enable Google Analytics for your project. Disable Google Analytics, since you won't use it in this project.

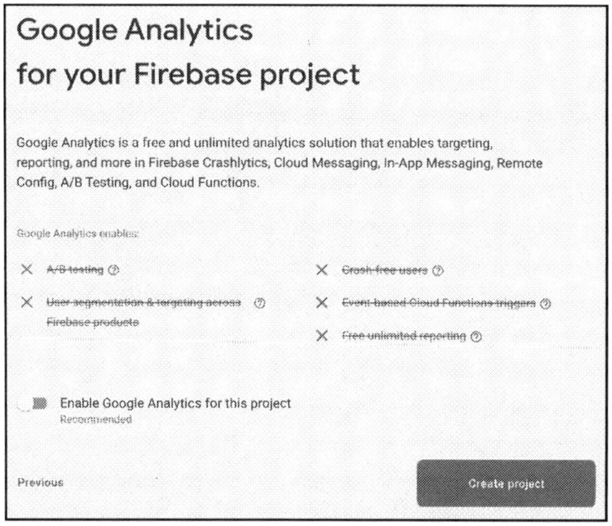

Figure 19.3 — Google Analytics Configuration

Once done, click **Create Project** and Firebase will get to work. When it finishes creating your project, click **Continue**.

Registering an App

Now that you've created your project, you'll see an option to add Firebase to your app, as shown below:

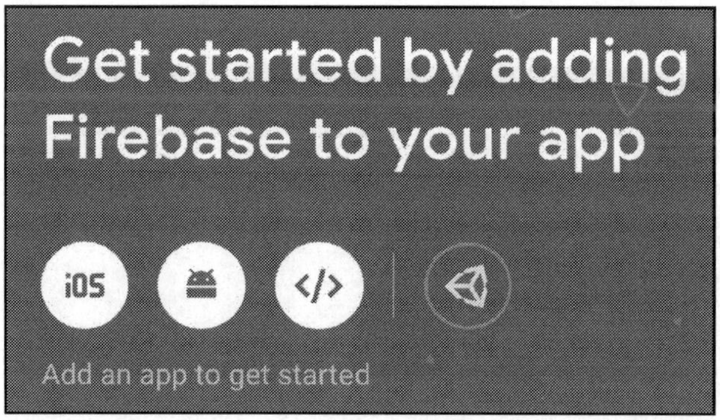

Figure 19.4 — Adding Firebase to Your App

Click the Android icon and the **Add Firebase to your Android app** page will appear. First, you need to add the package name of your app. For this project, the package name is **com.realworld.android.petsave**.

> **Note**: You can find the package name in the app **build.gradle**, as the `applicationId` value.

Skip the next two input fields; you won't need them for this chapter.

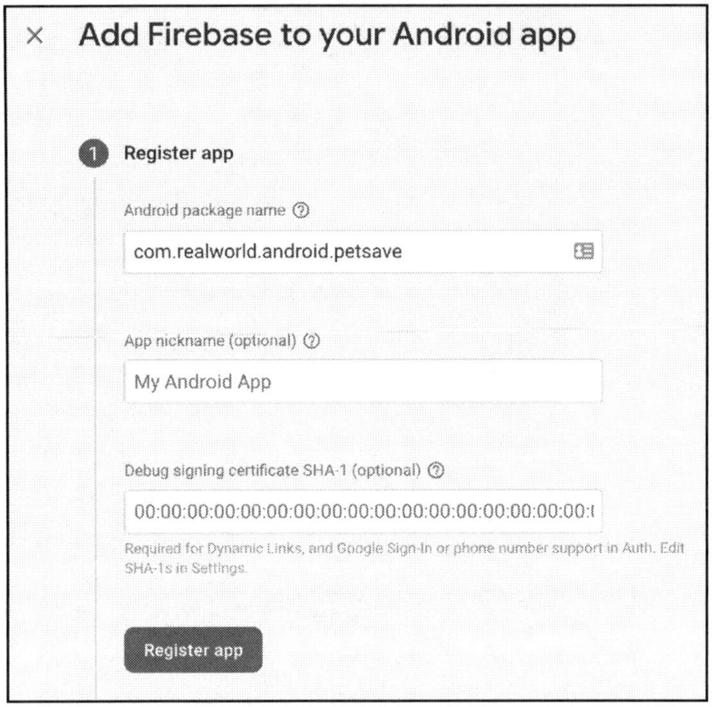

Figure 19.5 — Register Your App

Click **Register app**. Next, click **Download google-services.json** and move the downloaded file to the **app** module directory.

Finally, you need to add the Firebase plugin and dependency. Open the project **build.gradle** and add the following line to the **dependencies** block:

```
classpath 'com.google.gms:google-services:4.3.13'
```

The code above adds the Google Services plugin.

Now, add the following line to the app **build.gradle**, right above the **android** block:

```
apply plugin: 'com.google.gms.google-services'
```

This enables the plugin.

Finally, you need to add the following dependency inside the **dependencies** block in the same file:

```
implementation platform('com.google.firebase:firebase-
bom:30.2.0')
```

Click **Sync now** to download the dependencies, then build the project to make sure the dependencies haven't caused any issues.

Back in the Firebase Console, click **Next**, then **Continue to console**. And that's it. You've successfully added Firebase to your project.

Crashlytics

App crashes are among the things developers dread the most. Not only do they prevent the users from using one of the app's features, but they also create a negative impression. Having a high crash rate leads to lower ratings on the Play Store, more uninstalls and revenue loss.

It's crucial to be able to detect and fix crashes on user devices. Crashlytics is one of the most popular services when it comes to crash reporting. Best of all, it's simple to configure.

Setting up Crashlytics

Setting up Crashlytics is straightforward. Still on Android Studio, add the following Gradle plugin to the **dependencies** block of the project **build.gradle**:

```
classpath 'com.google.firebase:firebase-crashlytics-
gradle:2.9.1'
```

Next, apply the Crashlytics Gradle plugin by adding the following line to the app **build.gradle**:

```
apply plugin: 'com.google.firebase.crashlytics'
```

Finally, add the following dependencies in the app **build.gradle**:

```
implementation 'com.google.firebase:firebase-crashlytics-ktx'
implementation 'com.google.firebase:firebase-analytics-ktx'
```

Click **Sync now** to download the dependencies and... that's it! The setup for Crashlytics is complete. Crashlytics' SDK uses content providers to auto-initialize on app startup. Therefore, you don't need to add any initialization code.

Testing and Debugging

To test your Crashlytics setup, you need to cause an intentional crash. Do this by opening **AnimalsNearYouFragment.kt** and adding the following code to **onViewCreated**:

```
throw NullPointerException()
```

The code above adds an unhandled exception that makes the app crash.

Build and run the project, and you'll see the app crash soon after launching. Try opening the app again to verify the crash.

Next, head over to the Firebase Console and select Crashlytics from the Release & Monitor section on the left navigation bar. You'll now be able to view the crashes and the stack trace for each crash, like this:

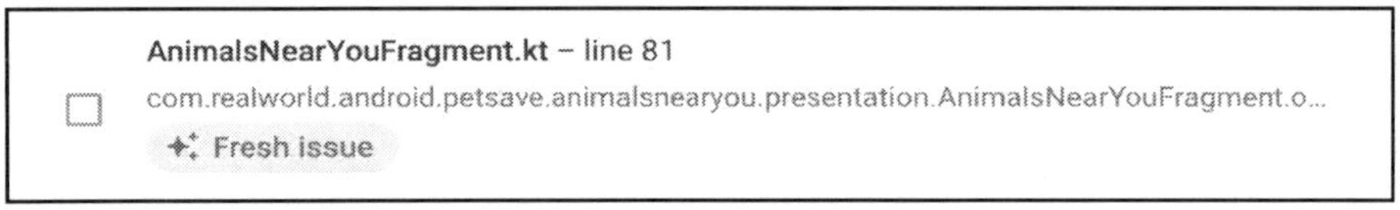

Figure 19.6 — Simulating a Crash

From now on, whenever your app crashes, Crashlytics will upload a report to Firebase along with the stack traces. If you don't see any logged crashes, revisit the page after a few minutes; Crashlytics sometimes takes a while to upload the data.

Non-fatal Exceptions

You can also use Firebase to log non-fatal exceptions. In most cases, you log such exceptions locally. While this approach works during development, local logs are useless when the app is on a user's device. Instead, you'll log them in Crashlytics.

In `onViewCreated` of **AnimalsNearYouFragment.kt**, wrap the unhandled exception in a try-catch block, as shown below:

```
try {
  throw NullPointerException()
} catch (exception: Exception) {
  FirebaseCrashlytics.getInstance().recordException(exception)
}
```

In the code above, you use `FirebaseCrashlytics.getInstance().recordException` to log the exception to Crashlytics.

Build and run. The app will no longer crash, but it will log the exception. To view the exception on Firebase, go to the Crashlytics page on Firebase Console and click **Filter ▸ Event type ▸ Non-fatals**, as shown below:

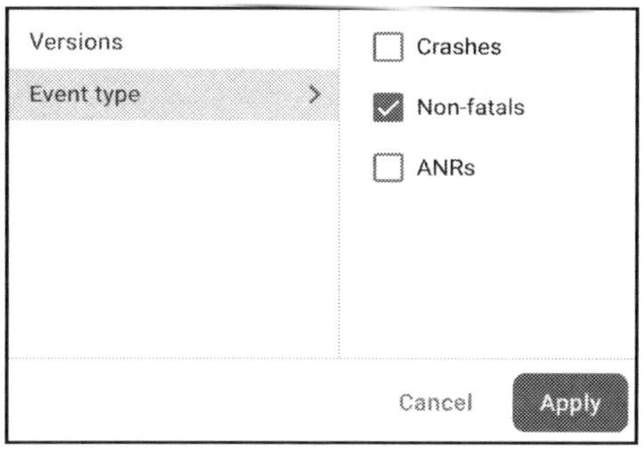

Figure 19.7 — Filtering a Non-Fatal Exception With Crashlytics

You can view the exception now. If the exception doesn't appear on the page, check back after some time; to optimize CPU and battery usage, Firebase uploads non-fatal data in batches.

Using Crashlytics With Proguard

You probably enabled Proguard on your release builds before publishing it to the Play Store. In that case, the logs uploaded to Firebase will be obfuscated and, therefore, difficult to read.

You can enable Proguard on your debug builds to ensure that Proguard itself didn't introduce any crashes. Open the app **build.gradle** and add the following code to the **buildTypes** block:

```
debug {
  minifyEnabled true
  proguardFiles getDefaultProguardFile('proguard-android.txt'),
'proguard-rules.pro'
}
```

The code above enables Proguard on the debug variant and also uses **proguard-rules.pro** to get the Proguard rules defined by the developer.

Open **AnimalsNearYouFragment.kt** and remove the try-catch block around `NullPointerException` so it becomes a fatal exception.

To make sure that Firebase can provide correct line numbers and source files in the crash report, you need to add the following line to **proguard-rules.pro**:

```
-keepattributes SourceFile,LineNumberTable
```

The Proguard rule above prevents the line number and source file from getting obfuscated.

Build and run. As expected, the app will crash. Head to the Crashlytics dashboard and verify that the stack trace isn't obfuscated.

Uploading the Mapping File

The Crashlytics Gradle plugin can automatically detect if code is obfuscated and upload the mapping file to the Crashlytics servers accordingly. Though this process is handy, it slows down build times.

When developing locally, you can use **Logcat** instead of Crashlytics to debug crashes. Therefore, you'll disable uploading the mapping file on **debug** builds.

Open the app **build.gradle** and add the following code to the debug build variant:

```
firebaseCrashlytics {
  mappingFileUploadEnabled false
}
```

The debug variant will be similar to the one shown below:

```
debug {
  minifyEnabled true
  proguardFiles getDefaultProguardFile('proguard-android.txt'),
'proguard-rules.pro'
  firebaseCrashlytics {
    mappingFileUploadEnabled false
  }
}
```

To verify that the mapping file isn't getting uploaded, build and run the app. A few minutes after the build crashes, go to the Crashlytics dashboard and look at the stack trace for the crash. You'll notice that it's obfuscated.

Finally, remember to remove the unhandled exception from **AnimalsNearYouFragment.kt** so the app doesn't keep crashing.

Remote Config

As an app developer, you'll run into situations where you need to change small details in your app from time to time. Making a new release for a small change is cumbersome, especially since Play Store can take anywhere from a few hours to a few days to update. For these cases, Firebase provides **Remote Config**.

Remote Config is a set of key-value pairs stored on the cloud. Your app can fetch them and cache them locally on the device after a fixed duration.

Consider the secret pet image you show the user when they drag the **Call** button onto the pet's image. At the moment, you don't have a way of changing this image without releasing a new update. Next, you'll use Remote Config to dynamically change the image URL for the secret pet.

Setting up Remote Config

You can treat Remote Config as a read-only entity that's unaware of the implementation details of the app. You can also treat it as a source of key-value pairs.

Create a new Android module by clicking **File ▸ New module ▸ Android library**. Give it the name **remoteconfig** and choose a **Bytecode Level** of 7.

Once you have the module, add the following dependencies to **build.gradle** in the **remoteconfig** module:

```
implementation platform('com.google.firebase:firebase-
bom:30.2.0')
implementation 'com.google.firebase:firebase-config-ktx'
```

The dependencies above add the Firebase Remote Config SDK. Click **Sync now** and wait for the dependencies to sync.

Next, create a new file named **RemoteConfigUtil.kt** in the **remoteconfig** module and add the following code:

```
object RemoteConfigUtil {

  private val DEFAULTS: HashMap<String, Any> = hashMapOf()

  private lateinit var remoteConfig: FirebaseRemoteConfig

  fun init(debug: Boolean = false) {
    remoteConfig = getFirebaseRemoteConfig(debug)
  }

  private fun getFirebaseRemoteConfig(debug: Boolean):
FirebaseRemoteConfig {

    val remoteConfig = Firebase.remoteConfig

    val configSettings = remoteConfigSettings {
      if (debug) {
        minimumFetchIntervalInSeconds = 0
      } else {
        minimumFetchIntervalInSeconds = 60 * 60
      }
    }

    remoteConfig.setConfigSettingsAsync(configSettings)
    remoteConfig.setDefaultsAsync(DEFAULTS)
    remoteConfig.fetchAndActivate()

    return remoteConfig
  }
}
```

The code above does the following:

1. Serves as a utility singleton class to set the Remote Config configuration.
2. `minimumFetchIntervalInSeconds` specifies the cache interval. If the elapsed time since the last fetch is less than the cache interval, the SDK will use the cached values. Else, it will fetch the latest values. During debugging, it's useful to set the duration to **0 seconds** to always get the latest values.
3. `DEFAULTS` is a HashMap that specifies the default values for the different Remote Config keys. You'll use the default values until you set new values in the Firebase Remote Config dashboard.
4. `fetchAndActivate` fetches the latest values and activates them. If you only call `fetch()`, the values will only be available to your app in the next user session.

Remote Config values are fetched asynchronously, so you should be careful about how you handle updated values. You don't want scenarios where the app's behavior changes while the user is in the app.

Consider a case where a user is on an order confirmation page and there are two buttons named **Cancel** and **Order**. The user decides to cancel the order, but just as they are about to tap **Cancel**, a Remote Config value swaps the positions of the button. The user will understandably be very annoyed. In some cases, it's acceptable for the Remote Config changes to appear in the app in a later session.

To initialize Remote Config using this helper class, first add the **remoteconfig** module as a dependency to the **app** module. Open the app **build.gradle** and add the following line of code to the **dependencies** block:

```
implementation project(":remoteconfig")
```

Next, open **PetSaveApplication.kt** and add the following code inside **onCreate**:

```
RemoteConfigUtil.init(BuildConfig.DEBUG)
```

The code above calls the `init` of the helper class and passes a parameter indicating whether the current build is a debug build.

Adding a Config

Open **fragment_secret.xml**. You'll notice an `android:src` attribute specifying the image to display. Remove the attribute and add an `id` to the **ImageView**, as follows:

```
<ImageView
  android:id="@+id/secret_image"
  android:layout_width="match_parent"
  android:layout_height="match_parent" />
```

Now, you'll use Remote Config to get the URL of the image to display. Open **RemoteConfigUtil.kt** and add the following member variable to it:

```
private const val SECRET_IMAGE_URL = "secret_image_url"
```

`secret_image_url` will serve as the key for the image URL config.

Since you've added a new key, you also have to provide a new default value for it. Modify `DEFAULTS`, as shown below:

```
private val DEFAULTS: HashMap<String, Any> =
```

```
  hashMapOf(
      SECRET_IMAGE_URL to "https://images.pexels.com/photos/
1108099/pexels-photo-1108099.jpeg"
  )
```

In the code value, you set a default value for the `secret_image_url` key.

You also need to provide a getter method so the Pet Details page can access the value. Add the following method to the same file:

```
fun getSecretImageUrl() =
remoteConfig.getString(SECRET_IMAGE_URL)
```

In the code above, you use `getString()` to get the value from Remote Config using the key. There are similar methods for other types, like `getBoolean()`, `getLong()`, etc. You store the values as strings on Remote Config. It's your responsibility to call the appropriate function to cast the value properly.

Using a Dynamic Value to Update the UI

The only thing left to do on the app side is updating **SecretFragment.kt** to use the updated value and setting the image in the ImageView.

Open **SecretFragment.kt** and add the following method:

```
override fun onViewCreated(view: View, savedInstanceState:
Bundle?) {
  super.onViewCreated(view, savedInstanceState)


binding.secretImage.setImage(RemoteConfigUtil.getSecretImageUrl(
))
}
```

In this code, you call the extension function `setImage()` and pass the value from Remote Config as a parameter.

Build and run. Go to the details screen for any pet and flick the **Call** button onto the pet's image. The secret screen will appear — and it will now have the image you set as the default Remote Config value!

Figure 19.8 — Testing Remote Config

Updating the Remote Config Value

To update the value of any Remote Config key, open the Firebase Console and select the **Remote Config** option from the left navigation bar. It's in the **Engage** section.

On the Remote Config dashboard, click **Create configuration**.

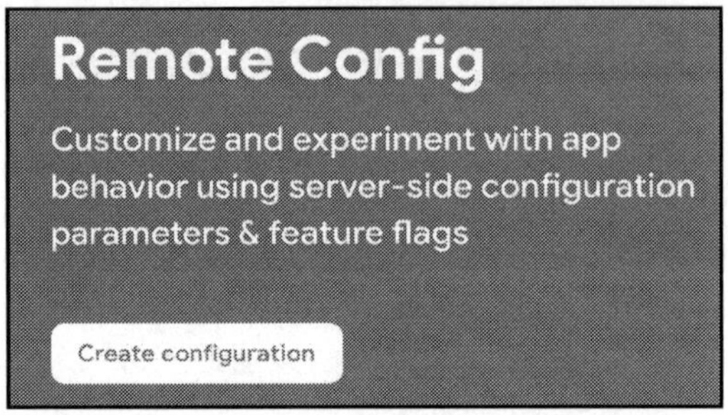

Figure 19.9 — Create Configuration Button

You'll get a dialog like the one below:

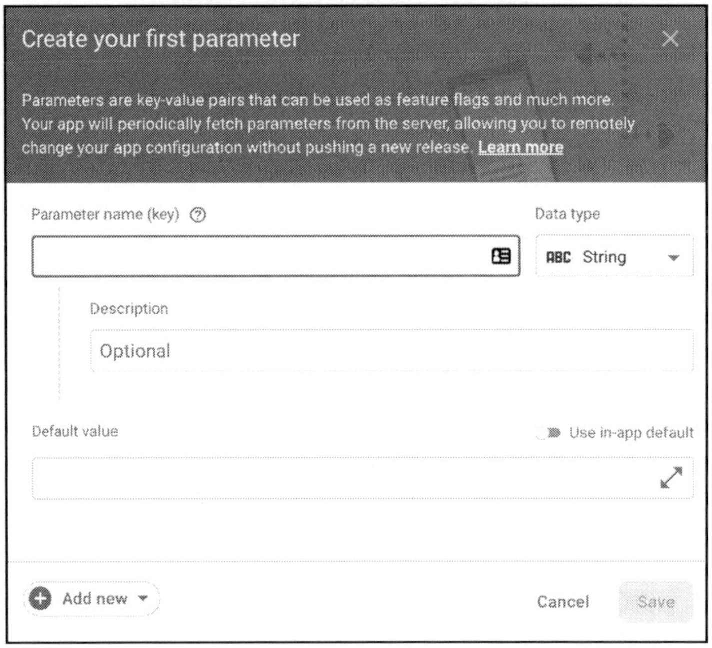

Figure 19.10 — Add a New Parameter to Remote Config

For the **Parameter key**, use the same key you used in the codebase. In this case, it's `secret_image_url`. For the **Default value**, add the URL of the image you want to change to. For this project, use `https://images.pexels.com/photos/2253275/pexels-photo-2253275.jpeg`, which contains a picture of a cute dog. Click **Save**.

You'll see a banner at the top that tells you that changes have been made, but they're not published yet.

Figure 19.11 — Unpublish Changes

Click **Publish changes**, then click **Publish changes** again on the confirmation pop-up. The updated values will be available immediately.

Close and open the app, then use it for about 10 to 20 seconds so the Remote Config SDK has enough time to fetch the new value. Now, go to the details screen and unlock the secret screen. The screen will now have the updated image from Remote Config.

Figure 19.12 — Testing Configuration Changes With Remote Config

Congratulations, you've successfully used Remote Config to set up a feature that you can control without having to push any new updates!

Firebase Test Lab

Android is a highly fragmented operating system. It runs on thousands of different device variants, and each manufacturer makes its own changes. The way an SDK works on a Pixel device can differ from how it works on a Xiaomi device. Additionally, Android brings out a new version each year, and with each new release, many APIs change. Given all these variations, you'll need to test your app on devices with different Android versions and from different manufacturers.

Unless you have access to a wide collection of mobile test devices, such a testing approach is quite difficult, for three reasons:

1. **Cost**: It's expensive to buy so many devices.
2. **Availability**: Many devices disappear from the market after just one or two years. Trying to procure a used device might be your only option.
3. **Management**: It's quite a task to test your app on each device.

Fortunately, Firebase introduced Test Lab , which automates this entire process at a lower cost. It lets you choose a set of devices from different manufacturers, upload your app, then test it on all the selected devices.

Running Your First Test

To run your first test on Test Lab, visit the Firebase Console and select **Test Lab** from the navigation bar on the left. It's in the **Release & Monitor** section.

You'll get a set of options, as shown below:

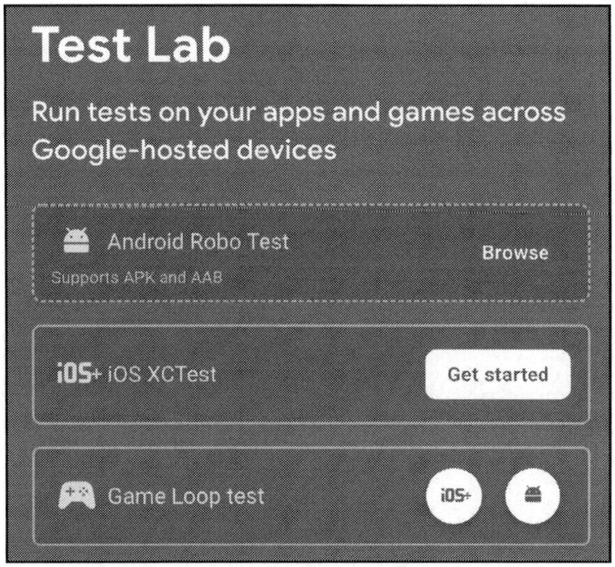

Figure 19.13 — Getting Started With Test Lab

You can use both debug and release APKs (or AABs) on Test Lab. Generate a debug APK and upload it to the **Android Robo Test** option. In a Robo test, a crawler goes through different screens on your app and interacts with different UI elements. The crawler records all the interactions and takes screenshots along the way.

Once you've uploaded the APK, Test Lab will start running a Robo test on a **Pixel** device at **API Level 30** using **English (United States)** locale and **Portrait** orientation.

Figure 19.14 — Test Lab Default Test Matrix

This is the default configuration that Test Lab uses. A combination of test devices, API levels, locales and orientations is called a **test matrix**. You can create a new matrix to suit your requirements.

The test will take a few minutes to complete. Once it's done, you'll receive an email with the test report. A Robo test fails if the app crashes during the test. When you open the test results, you'll get details of the test, like:

- The time the test took.
- The number of actions the crawler performed.
- A crawl graph along with screenshots to demonstrate the different paths the crawler took.
- A video of all the interactions.
- Logs produced on the device during the test.
- CPU, memory and network performance statistics.
- Accessibility issues, warnings and suggestions.

Creating a Robo Test Preset

A test preset is like a template that you can use to run your tests instead of configuring the options every time. A preset consists of the following:

1. Name
2. Description
3. Test type: Robo test, instrumentation test or game loop
4. The set of devices to use
5. Additional options, depending on the test type

To create a new preset, select **Presets** on the Test Lab page. Since this is your first preset, you'll see a page like the one below:

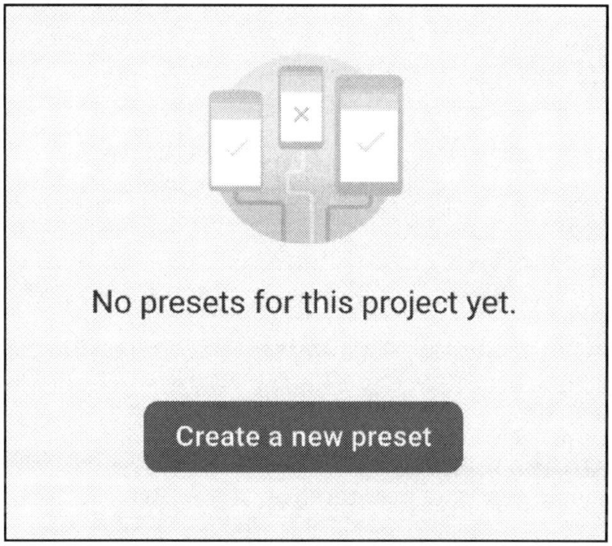

Figure 19.15 — Test Lab New Preset

Click **Create a new preset** and you'll come to the **New Preset** page. Give the preset any name and description you want.

In the test type, select **Robo test**. You'll create an Instrumentation test later.

Since you haven't created a test matrix before, you'll see a section like the one below:

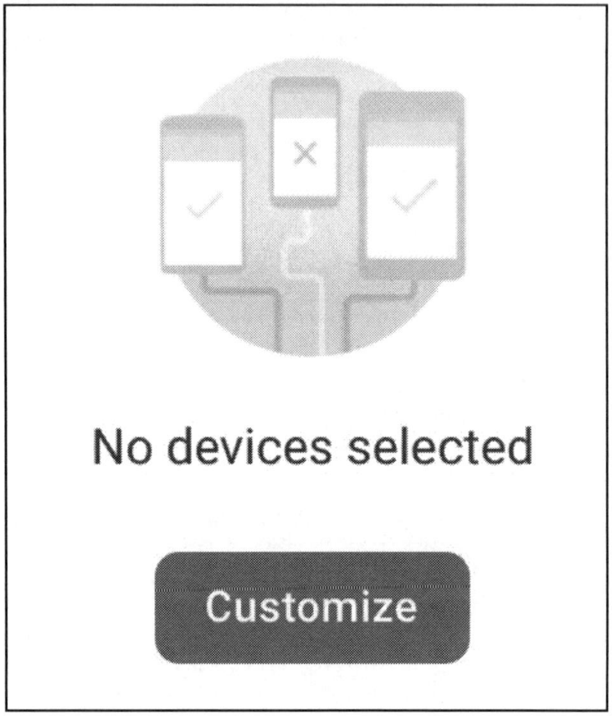

Figure 19.16 — Customize Your Test Matrix

Click **Customize** to proceed to the **Customize device selection** screen, where you can choose from a huge list of devices. Test Lab has two types of devices:

1. **Virtual**: Emulators that run on Google Cloud Platform.
2. **Physical**: Actual devices that are stored at Google data centers.

The number and types of devices you can run on your tests depends on your Firebase plan. Physical devices are much more expensive than virtual ones.

Once you select a device, you can choose from the available API levels, locales and orientations. You can add the same device multiple times with different configurations. For now, add a **Pixel 2** and a **Redmi 6A** with **English (United States)** locale and **Portrait** orientation. Once you're done, click **Confirm**.

Next, expand the **Additional option** section. You'll get the following options:

- **Test timeout**: How long you want the test to run before stopping it. This comes in handy if you're paying for Test Lab by the minute.
- **Test account credentials**: If your app implements a custom login screen, you can add the login credentials along with the ID of the EditTexts to input them during the test.
- **Robo directives**: You can specify the behavior of the crawler when it encounters a resource with a specific name.
- **Deep links**: You can specify up to three deep links. The crawler will open the app using these links and crawl them for 30 seconds each.

Once you've entered your desired values, click **Save preset**.

Creating an Instrumentation Test Preset

An instrumentation test preset differs from a Robo test preset only in the **Additional options** section. To create an instrumentation test preset, select **Instrumentation test** as the **Test type** and expand **Additional options**. There are three options in this category:

1. **Test timeout**: This option is the same as the one for the Robo test.
2. **Android Test Orchestrator**: Using Orchestrator insulates your tests so crashes and state changes in one test don't affect others.
3. **Sharding**: This allows you to run your tests in parallel by grouping them into different sets, thus speeding up the test suite. Each shard counts as a new device, so depending on your Firebase plan, you might need to use this option cautiously.

Running a New Test

To run a new test, visit the Test Lab dashboard and click **Run a test**. Select the type of test you want from the drop-down menu.

When you select a **Robo test**, you have to upload an APK — either a debug APK or a release APK. You can also upload a Robo script to direct the crawler.

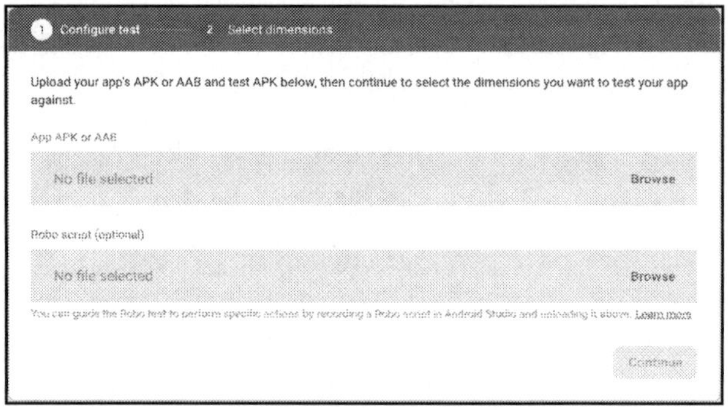

Figure 19.17 — Robo Script Configuration

To create a new Robo script, open Android Studio and go to **Tools ▸ Firebase**. If the Firebase option is missing, make sure you've enabled **Firebase Services** and **Firebase Testing** in **Preferences ▸ Plugins ▸ Installed**.

Once the Firebase panel loads, select **Test Lab ▸ Record Robo Script and use it to Guide Robo Test**, then follow the steps displayed on the screen.

When you select an **Instrumentation test**, you have to upload a regular APK and a test APK. To generate a test APK, run the following command in the **Terminal** tab in Android Studio:

```
./gradlew assembleAndroidTest
```

This generates an APK that includes your instrumentation tests. You can find it in **app/build/outputs/apk/androidTest/debug**.

Once you've uploaded the APKs, click **Continue**, then choose between creating a new device set or using a preset. Once you've chosen a set, click **Run 2 tests**. Here, **2** signifies that you're running tests on two devices with a sharding of **1**. You'll receive an email when the testing completes.

That's all there is to it! You now have thousands of devices at your disposal for testing, and you didn't even have to visit the store. :]

Key Points

- Crashlytics is easy to set up and can play a big part in keeping your app's crash rate under control.
- Use **Crashlytics** to log non-fatal exceptions.
- Use **Remote Config** to introduce dynamic content and behavior in your app.
- Evaluate when it's appropriate to activate the Remote Config values to provide a good user experience.
- **Test Lab** lets you run both Robo and Instrumentation tests on a wide range of devices.
- Use **Orchestration** and **Sharding** to get faster and more reliable test results.

Chapter 20: Release Optimizations

By Kolin Stürt and Antonio Roa-Valverde

App development today favors small apps rather than large ones. This supports popular trends, like entry-level devices and the "internet of things". Furthermore, smaller apps download, install and run faster, which is important for your business. This chapter will help you keep your apps as small as possible.

In this chapter, you'll learn how to prepare a build for release. You'll learn about the optimizations that ProGuard performs and how to translate to a certain level of obfuscation. This adds a minimal layer of security to help prevent reverse engineering or tampering with your app.

In the process, you'll learn:

- How to use APK Analyzer.
- How to leverage optimization rules.
- How to fix compile and runtime errors.

Using APK Analyzer

APK Analyzer is a tool that inspects your finalized app and determines what contributes to its size. It presents a breakdown of your app's files. You can see what takes up the most space, along with the total method and reference counts.

Launch the analyzer by selecting **Build ▸ Analyze APK**, which opens a dialog for your file system. If it isn't already selected, navigate to your debug folder and select **app-debug.apk**. Click **OK** to open APK Analyzer.

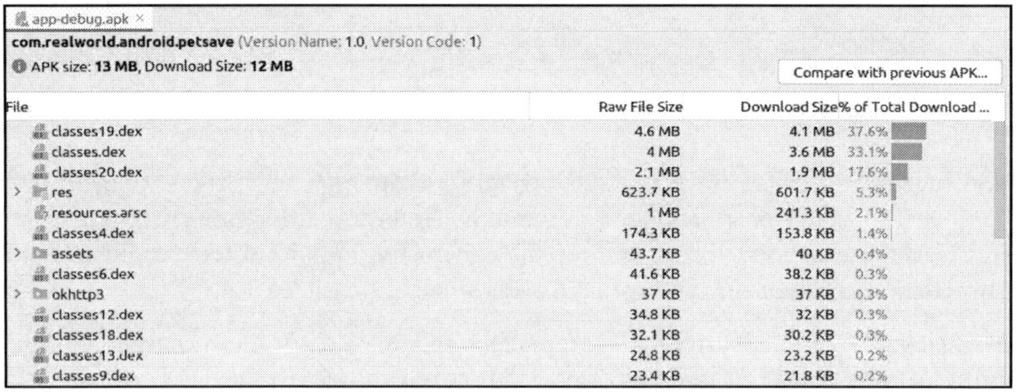

Figure 20.1 — Using APK Analyzer

Note the file size of the current APK. You'll use this tool again later in the chapter to see the result of your changes.

Enabling an Optimizer

Next, you'll use an optimizer to evaluate your app size.

Enabling an optimizer is simple. In your app **build.gradle**, replace `buildTypes` with the following:

```
buildTypes {
  release {
    minifyEnabled true
    proguardFiles getDefaultProguardFile('proguard-
android.txt'), 'proguard-rules.pro'
  }
  debug {
    minifyEnabled true
    proguardFiles getDefaultProguardFile('proguard-
android.txt'), 'proguard-rules.pro'
```

```
    }
}
```

Setting `minifyEnabled` to `true` enables an optimizer — in this case, R8.

ProGuard Versus R8

Android Studio comes with an optimizer by default: **R8**. **ProGuard** was the de facto tool for Android for a long time, while R8 is the newer Google alternative. They're compatible with each other and perform similar operations to optimize Java bytecode. Both remove unused code, such as methods, fields and classes, and attempt to optimize code for performance.

The optimizer looks at the entry points of your app and maps out the code that the app can reach. It removes the rest, and replaces the names of classes and methods with shorter ones, making for a much smaller APK size!

The trade-off is that using any optimizer results in slower build times. The most common problem you'll face when enabling Proguard starts with compile errors.

> **Note**: R8 is Google's recommendation when using a code optimizer. It is also the default option in Android Gradle Plugin 7.*. Through the rest of the chapter notice that when mentioning ProGuard, you'll be in fact using R8. The main reason for this naming is that R8 works with the ProGuard rule format. If you are interested in a sound comparison between both tools, check out this blog post from the authors of Proguard: https://www.guardsquare.com/blog/comparison-proguard-vs-r8-october-2019-edition.

Even though R8 is now the default tool, you can still use ProGuard in your project if you want to. You'll find all the needed Gradle configuration in this guide: https://www.guardsquare.com/manual/setup/gradleplugin.

Fixing Compilation Errors

As optimizers do their work, they often mistakenly obfuscate and remove code that they think you're not using — even when you are. Therefore, as you go along, you'll need to test that everything still works with ProGuard enabled. The earlier you find problems in the build, the easier it will be to fix them. :]

Sync Gradle, then build and run. Notice that there are already compiler errors:

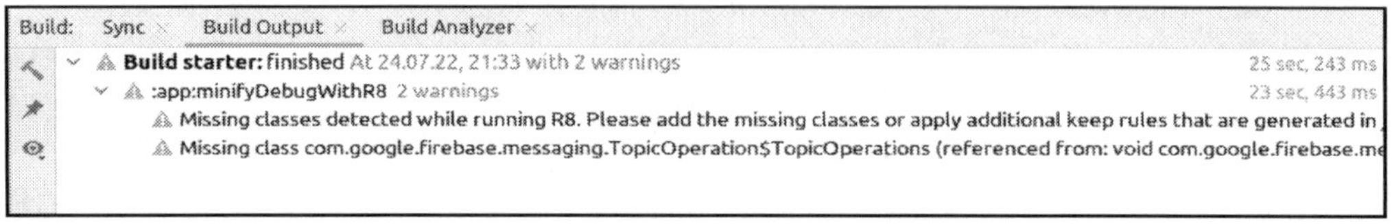

Figure 20.2 — Compilation Errors

The compiler problems include two warnings. Click on the header to reveal more information in Android Studio:

```
> Task :app:minifyDebugWithR8
AGPBI: {"kind":"warning","text":"Missing classes detected while
running R8. Please add the missing classes or apply additional
keep rules that are generated in /home/user/adva-materials/20-
release-optimizations/projects/starter/app/build/outputs/
mapping/debug/missing_rules.txt.\n",

...

Missing class
com.google.firebase.messaging.TopicOperation$TopicOperations
(referenced from: void
com.google.firebase.messaging.TopicOperation.<init>(java.lang.St
ring, java.lang.String))
Missing class javax.xml.stream.Location (referenced from:
javax.xml.stream.Location
org.simpleframework.xml.stream.StreamReader$Start.location and 2
other contexts)
Missing class javax.xml.stream.XMLEventReader (referenced from:
javax.xml.stream.XMLEventReader
org.simpleframework.xml.stream.StreamReader.reader and 4 other
contexts)
Missing class javax.xml.stream.XMLInputFactory (referenced from:
javax.xml.stream.XMLInputFactory
org.simpleframework.xml.stream.StreamProvider.factory and 2
other contexts)
Missing class javax.xml.stream.events.Attribute (referenced
from: javax.xml.stream.events.Attribute
org.simpleframework.xml.stream.StreamReader$Entry.entry and 7
other contexts)
```

```
Missing class javax.xml.stream.events.Characters (referenced
from: javax.xml.stream.events.Characters
org.simpleframework.xml.stream.StreamReader$Text.text and 2
other contexts)
Missing class javax.xml.stream.events.StartElement (referenced
from: javax.xml.stream.events.StartElement
org.simpleframework.xml.stream.StreamReader$Start.element and 3
other contexts)
Missing class javax.xml.stream.events.XMLEvent (referenced from:
void
org.simpleframework.xml.stream.StreamReader$Start.<init>(javax.x
ml.stream.events.XMLEvent) and 4 other contexts)
```

There seems to be issues with Firebase and `javax.xml.stream`.

Adding "don't warn" Rules

Don't warn rules tell Android Studio to ignore warnings. This is dangerous, but if you know for sure that you're not using part of the code, it can come in handy.

Don't warn rules work by specifying the package name. * is a wildcard – it doesn't include sub-packages, whereas ** includes sub-packages. The rules for ProGuard go in **proguard-rules.pro**.

Sometimes, R8 is giving you some hints about the missing rules that you need to apply, like in this case. Open the following generated file in your app build path: **app/build/outputs/mapping/debug/missing_rules.txt**. You'll find the following there:

```
# Please add these rules to your existing keep rules in order to
suppress warnings.
# This is generated automatically by the Android Gradle plugin.
-dontwarn
com.google.firebase.messaging.TopicOperation$TopicOperations
-dontwarn javax.xml.stream.Location
-dontwarn javax.xml.stream.XMLEventReader
-dontwarn javax.xml.stream.XMLInputFactory
-dontwarn javax.xml.stream.events.Attribute
-dontwarn javax.xml.stream.events.Characters
-dontwarn javax.xml.stream.events.StartElement
-dontwarn javax.xml.stream.events.XMLEvent
```

You just need to copy the lines starting with `-dontwarn` to your **proguard-rules.pro** file.

Build and run the project. Great, now those warnings are gone!

Adding Keep Rules

Keep rules tell ProGuard not to obfuscate certain parts of your code. Some options are:

- **keep**: Preserves entire classes and class members.
- **keepclassmembers**: Preserves just the class members.
- **keepclasseswithmembers**: Preserves all classes that have a specified member.

Some other options you can use include `keepnames`, `keepattributes`, `keep class` and `keep interface`.

The rules are written in a specific template format, which you can find at https://www.guardsquare.com/en/products/proguard/manual/usage#classspecification.

When you first opened **proguard-rules.pro**, there was some boilerplate code at the top, which consisted mostly of commented-out lines that Android Studio provides, as well as a few enabled lines:

```
-keep class kotlin.reflect.jvm.internal.** { *; }
-keep class kotlin.Metadata { *; }
-dontwarn com.google.crypto.tink.**
```

This code allows you to use reflection with cryptography.

> **Note**: If you're sharing your code, write keep rules as you write your code. Then, be sure to publish them on your site, GitHub or GitLab **README** page so other developers can easily use your code without any problems.

If you use an AAR that includes some predefined ProGuard rules, R8 will apply them when compiling your project. You can learn more about this mechanism in the official Google documentation: https://developer.android.com/studio/build/shrink-code#configuration-files.

Run your APK Analyzer again. You'll notice the APK size is much smaller now. That's because ProGuard has removed all the code you're not using.

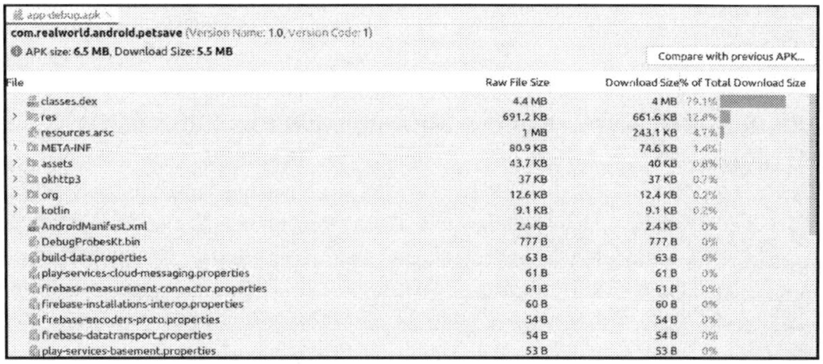

Figure 20.3 — The APK Is Smaller Now

Enabling More Optimizations

At this point, you've successfully applied optimizations for your app. However, there are a few more steps you can take for your release version.

ProGuard provides an advanced optimization profile. By default, it isn't used because it can cause build and runtime errors. You enable advanced optimizations by swapping the default **proguard-android.txt** with **proguard-android-optimize.txt**.

To experiment with this in your app, navigate to the app **build.gradle**. Replace the `proguardFiles` line in the debug section with the following:

```
proguardFiles getDefaultProguardFile('proguard-android-
optimize.txt'),
        'proguard-rules.pro'
```

The build time will be much longer because ProGuard will perform more analysis and optimizations inside and across methods. You'll also need to spend more time making sure your app still works as expected after the change.

Sync Gradle, then build the app. Everything still works! You should continue to remove assets and resources that your project doesn't need.

Shrinking Resources

As long as you've set `minifyEnabled` in the optimizer, you can enable the resource shrinker, which removes unused resources after the code shrinker does its job. It will also remove resources in libraries that you include. To make sure it knows which resources your app uses, remove unused library code to make the resources in the library unreferenced.

You can compress resources that your app does use with the help of a PNG crusher. The PNG crusher should be on by default, but because build types don't always define this correctly, it's best to add it explicitly.

To enable both resource shrinking and PNG crushing, add the following to your **build.gradle**:

```
buildTypes {
    release {
        ...
        shrinkResources true
        crunchPngs true
        ...
```

Other options for resources are to use vector-drawable XML files or to convert your images to a format that allows smaller compression, such as WebP. You can find instructions at https://developer.android.com/studio/write/convert-webp#convert_images_to_webp.

NDK Optimizations

If you've been working with NDK, you'll have an **Android.mk** file under the project's **jni** directory. This file tells the compiler how it should optimize native code. Changing the option is as simple as appending a line in the file, as follows:

```
LOCAL_CFLAGS  := -O3
```

The number after the `-O` refers to the level of optimization. There are four basic levels:

- **O0**: The default option for debug builds, this performs no optimizations. This setting reduces compile time and makes debugging easier because it produces expected results.
- **O1**: The default level for release builds. This is the first level of optimization that attempts to reduce code size.
- **O2**: This enables all supported compiler optimizations that don't involve a space-to-speed trade-off. It improves the performance of the generated code, but takes longer to compile.
- **O3**: The most aggressive optimization level. It enables the following options: `-finline-functions`, `-funswitch-loops`, `-ftree-vectorize`, `-fpredictive-commoning`, `-fgcse-after-reload`, `-ftree-partial-pre`, `-fvect-cost-model` and `-fipa-cp-clone`.

Optimizers like ProGuard may have issues when you call a method from **JNI (Java Native Interface)**. You can often find solutions in the JNI training article, here: https://developer.android.com/training/articles/perf-jni#faq-why-didnt-findclass-find-my-class.

Congratulations, you now know all about the main release optimizations you can do for your app.

A Few Things To Keep in Mind...

The makers of ProGuard, GuardSquare, also have a commercial solution called DexGuard. It minimizes code, but offers more protection regarding its side effect of obfuscation. DexGuard encrypts the classes and strings as well as assets and resource files. It also provides app and device integrity checking, which is important to keep spammers out of your app.

If you want to use ProGuard's obfuscation to protect proprietary code, this is a good choice. You can find more information at https://www.guardsquare.com/en/products/dexguard.

This chapter focused on release optimizations. You should not use them in place of the code profiling and code tuning stages of your lifecycle. During development, you shouldn't forget about concepts like putting the nominal case first in a flow control case or breaking out of loops early. You should always use good coding practices when it comes to memory management and performance.

The optimizations you've applied in this chapter change your code. You should perform them as part of the end of a development phase, before your app goes to quality assurance. If QA finds problems and you make changes to the optimization configuration, the change needs to be thoroughly tested.

When it comes to developer testing and debugging, it helps to compare the before and after states of your app, and actually look at what the optimizer did to your compiled code. This ensures that the optimizations did what you expected.

For example, if you're looking for a way to obfuscate or protect the code, just adding optimization might not work. In fact, it makes the logic even more visible in some cases — by unrolling loops, for instance. That's why it's always good to check the result of your changes and check how your compiled app looks in the App Store. You'll learn more about that in Chapter 22, "App Analysis".

Key Points

- R8 is the default code shrinker and minification tool in Android.
- **Don't warn** rules ignore warnings and errors.
- **Keep** rules allow you to keep the optimizer from touching specific code.
- Instead of keeping entire classes or large parts of code, keep only the minimum code you need, giving you better optimizations.

Chapter 21: Advanced Debugging

By Subhrajyoti Sen

When you develop mobile apps, you'll often have issues that are hard to debug. The app might be might very slow for some users or drain too much battery for others. Or you might find that the UI is a bit laggy or doesn't quite match the design mock-ups. Debugging these issues can be tedious. Fortunately, there are tools that make the process easier.

In this chapter, you'll learn about:

- Finding and fixing memory leaks using **LeakCanary**.
- Using the **Memory Profiler** to find Fragment and Activity leaks.
- Examining network calls using the **Network Inspector**.
- Finding Wake Locks using the **Energy Profiler**.
- Using **Layout Inspector** to improve your layouts.

You'll start by looking at memory leaks.

Memory Leaks

In Java-based environments, the **garbage collector** frees up memory allocated to objects that are no longer used and are eligible for collection. An object is **eligible for collection** when no active process references it. Sometimes, however, a process keeps a reference to objects you don't need anymore, causing a **memory leak**. Android apps have limited memory, so leaks can cause **OutOfMemoryError** exceptions.

Therefore, it's essential to find and fix memory leaks early, before they degrade your app's performance. **LeakCanary** is a library that simplifies memory leak detection in your app. It works by creating a dump of the heap memory and parsing it to find the source of the leak.

Installing LeakCanary

To install LeakCanary, add the following dependency to your app **build.gradle**:

```
debugImplementation "com.squareup.leakcanary:leakcanary-
android:2.8.1"
```

Click **Sync now** and wait for Gradle to download the dependency.

Adding Obfuscation Support

Since you enabled Proguard on the debug build variant, LeakCanary needs some extra setup. You can skip this setup if you disable Proguard for debugging.

Add the following `classpath` to the main project **build.gradle**:

```
classpath 'com.squareup.leakcanary:leakcanary-deobfuscation-
gradle-plugin:2.9.1'
```

The Gradle plugin above finds the mapping file during the build process and pushes it into the APK. The mapping file enables LeakCanary to deobfuscate the heap dump when it finds a leak.

Now, open the app **build.gradle** and add the following line above the **android** block:

```
apply plugin: 'com.squareup.leakcanary.deobfuscation'
```

This enables the plugin.

Finally, you need to tell the plugin which build variants could be obfuscated. Do this by adding the following code before the **dependencies** block:

```
leakCanary {
  filterObfuscatedVariants { variant ->
    variant.name == "debug"
  }
}
```

The code above checks if the name of the build variant is **debug**. It uses the result to inform the plugin that you've enabled obfuscation on the debug variant.

With the setup complete, you're ready to start hunting for leaks.

Detecting Memory Leaks

There's no secret map that can help you find memory leaks. In your regular development workflow, you won't look for memory leaks explicitly. Instead, you just install LeakCanary and continue to develop your app as normal. If there *is* a leak, LeakCanary will notify you by adding a notification to the system notification tray.

Run the app, go through the various user flows and check if LeakCanary notifies you. Remember to check the **secret** flows too.

You'll notice that when you visit the **Secret Doggo** screen and come back to the Details screen, LeakCanary notifies you of a leak.

> **Note**: Remember that you can reach the **Secret Doggo** screen from the Detail screen by dragging the phone icon to the top.

Repeat the flow to confirm the leak. The notification will be similar to the one below:

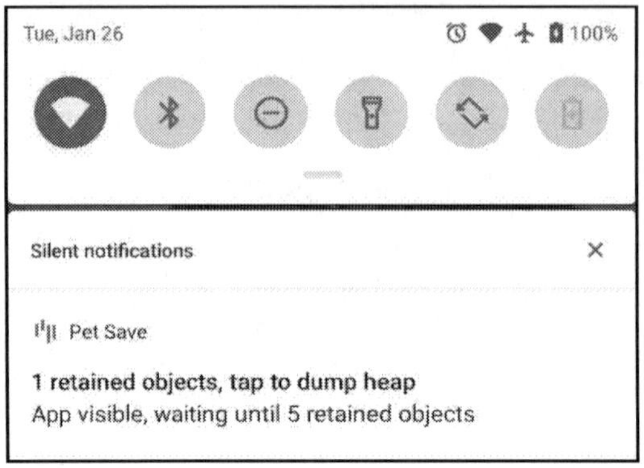

Figure 21.1 — LeakCanary Memory Leak Notification

Finding the Leak Source

In this section, you'll use the heap dump to find the source of the leak.

Since a heap dump is a long operation, LeakCanary prefers to batch them. LeakCanary, by default, waits for five leaks before dumping the heap. However, you can tap the leak notification to force a heap dump even with one leak.

Tap the leak notification and wait for the heap dump to complete. It will take a few seconds. Once complete, open your device's app drawer and search for an app named **Leaks**. LeakCanary installs this app to help you view the leak logs. Open the app.

Figure 21.2 — The Leaks App

The app lists all the memory leaks LeakCanary detected in your app. At the moment, there's only one leak, as shown below:

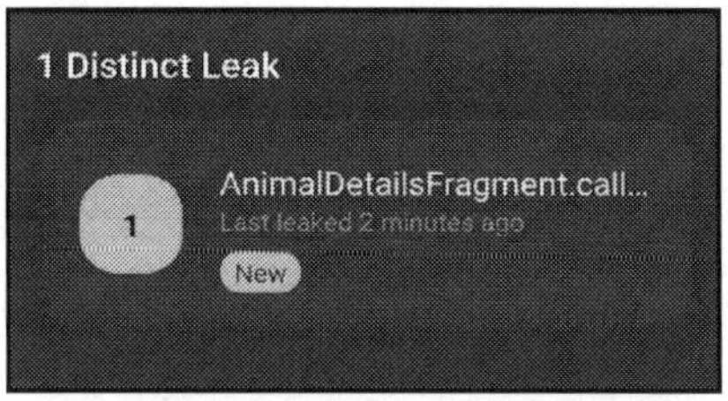

Figure 21.3 — LeakCanary Leak List

Tap the list item and open the **leak details** screen. You'll get a screen that displays all the details of the leak:

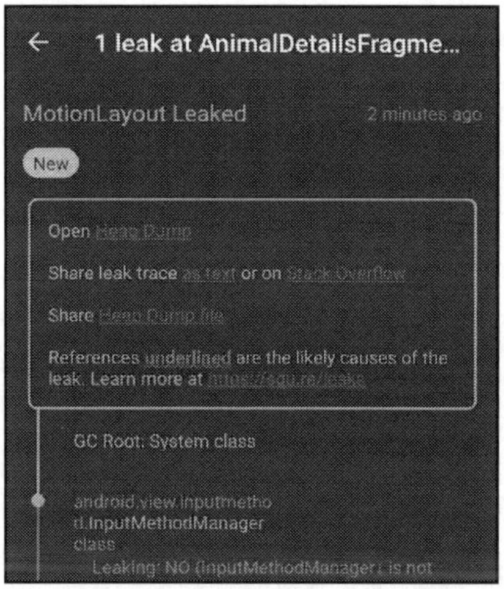

Figure 21.4 — Leak Information Details

The image above shows that:

1. `Fragment` is leaking **MotionLayout.** This is your first clue.
2. References underlined in red are the likely causes of the leak.

Scroll through the leak details until you find something underlined in red. You'll come across the following section:

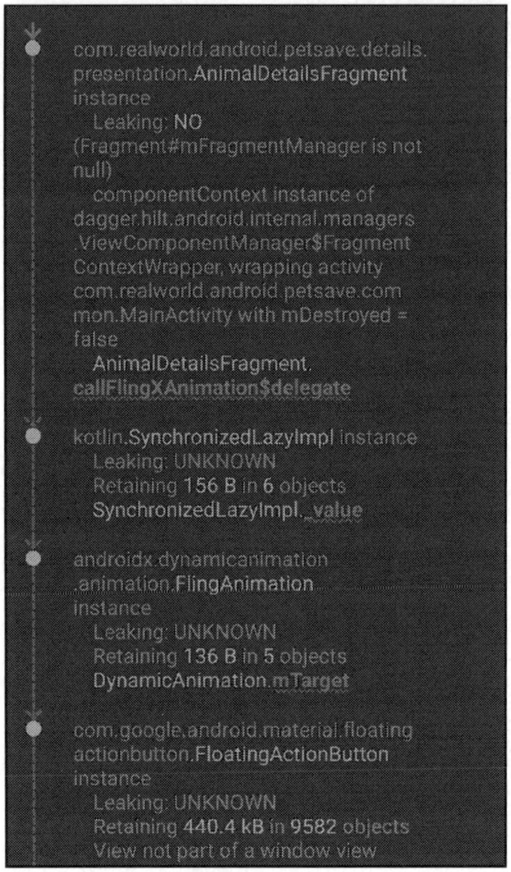

Figure 21.5 — Leak Sources

In the image above, you can see that **callFlingXAnimation** is underlined in red. It's leaking its target. Right below that, you can also see that its target points to a **FloatingActionButton** with the ID **call**. You've found the source of your bug.

The `FlingAnimation` instance leaks an instance of the **Call** button, which ultimately leaks the `MotionLayout` instance.

Understanding the Leak Cause

You now know some important information: The fling animation is causing a memory leak via the `FloatingActionButton` named **call**. It's time to figure out why.

In most cases involving a leaked view, the problem is that an object that holds a reference to the view outlives the lifecycle of that view.

It's time to take a step back and revisit lifecycles. One significant difference between **Activity**s and **Fragment**s is their lifecycle. An `Activity` has a single lifecycle, whereas a `Fragment` has two lifecycles: one for the `Fragment` as a whole and another for the `Fragment`'s view. Because of this, `Fragment` has different `onDestroyView` and `onDestroy` callbacks, whereas `Activity` has only the `onDestory` callback.

With this knowledge, you can figure out why the fling animation is leaking the view. `callFlingXAnimation` has a reference to the **call** view but you declared it as a global variable. When the user navigates back to the Pet Details screen from the Secret screen, only the view contained inside `AnimalDetailsFragment` is recreated, not the entire `Fragment`. Therefore, the app retains the memory allocated to `callFlingXAnimation` — and it contains a reference to the old view that was destroyed. This is your memory leak.

Plugging the Leak

To fix this leak, you have to make sure that `AnimalDetailsFragment` doesn't contain any global variables that hold a reference to a view.

Open **AnimalDetailsFragment.kt** and look at the following initializations:

```
private val callScaleXSpringAnimation =
SpringAnimation(binding.call, DynamicAnimation.SCALE_X).apply {
  spring = springForce
}

private val callScaleYSpringAnimation =
SpringAnimation(binding.call, DynamicAnimation.SCALE_Y).apply {
  spring = springForce
}

private val callFlingXAnimation = FlingAnimation(binding.call,
DynamicAnimation.X).apply {
  friction = FLING_FRICTION
  setMinValue(0f)
  setMaxValue(binding.root.width.toFloat() -
binding.call.width.toFloat())
}

private val callFlingYAnimation = FlingAnimation(binding.call,
DynamicAnimation.Y).apply {
  friction = FLING_FRICTION
  setMinValue(0f)
  setMaxValue(binding.root.height.toFloat() -
```

```
binding.call.width.toFloat())
}
```

You don't want to keep their references in the `View`, but you do want to limit their scope so the garbage collector can remove them when that scope completes. In this case, the new scope is `displayPetDetails()`, so just move the initializations to the beginning of `displayPetDetails()`. This removes the `private` visibility modifier, which you don't need for local variables.

`displayPetDetails()` will now be as follows:

```
private fun displayPetDetails(animalDetails: UIAnimalDetailed,
adopted: Boolean) {
  val callScaleXSpringAnimation = SpringAnimation(binding.call,
DynamicAnimation.SCALE_X).apply {
    spring = springForce
  }

  val callScaleYSpringAnimation = SpringAnimation(binding.call,
DynamicAnimation.SCALE_Y).apply {
    spring = springForce
  }

  val callFlingXAnimation = FlingAnimation(binding.call,
DynamicAnimation.X).apply {
    friction = FLING_FRICTION
    setMinValue(0f)
    setMaxValue(binding.root.width.toFloat() -
binding.call.width.toFloat())
  }

  val callFlingYAnimation = FlingAnimation(binding.call,
DynamicAnimation.Y).apply {
    friction = FLING_FRICTION
    setMinValue(0f)
    setMaxValue(binding.root.height.toFloat() -
binding.call.width.toFloat())
  }

  binding.call.scaleX = 0.6f
  binding.call.scaleY = 0.6f
  //... rest of the method
}
```

Build and run. Repeat the same workflow as before and verify that there's no longer a memory leak. Congratulations, you've resolved your first memory leak!

Android Studio Profiler

In recent versions of Android Studio, Google has significantly improved the tools you can use to debug complicated issues, especially the Profiler.

The Profiler consists of four main components:

1. CPU Profiler
2. Memory Profiler
3. Network Profiler (now moved to Network Inspector in recent versions of Android Studio)
4. Energy Profiler

In this section, you'll learn how to use the Memory, Network and Energy Profilers.

Start by opening the Profiler by selecting **View ▸ Tools Windows ▸ Profiler**.

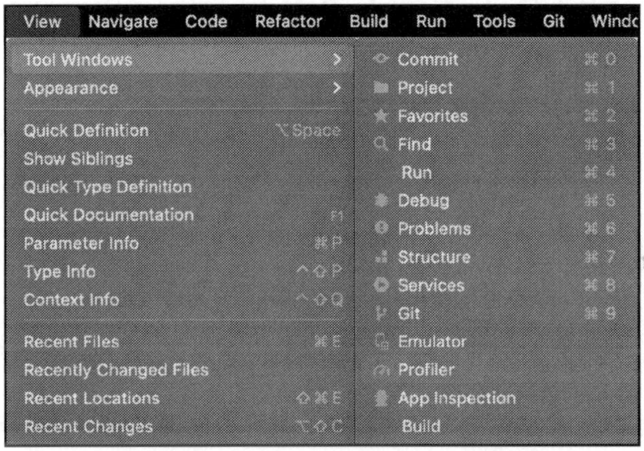

Figure 21.6 — Android Studio Profiler

Finding Memory Leaks With the Memory Profiler

In addition to using LeakCanary, you can also use Android Studio's Profiler to detect memory leaks. Android Studio 3.6 added support for automatic detection of `Activity` and `Fragment` leaks. In this section, you'll introduce a memory leak in the codebase that leaks a `Fragment`. You'll then use the Memory Profiler to find and trace the leak.

Introducing a Fragment Leak

Open **MainActivity.kt** and add the following global variable before `onCreate()`:

```
lateinit var currentFragment: Fragment
```

The code above adds a public variable that holds an instance of a `Fragment`.

Next, open **AnimalDetailsFragment.kt** and add the following code inside `onViewCreated()`:

```
(requireActivity() as MainActivity).currentFragment = this
```

The code above does the following:

1. It gets a reference to `MainActivity` since `AnimalDetailsFragment` is attached to `MainActivity`.
2. It then initializes `currentFragment` with the current instance of `AnimalDetailsFragment`.

This is a common source of memory leaks. Exiting `AnimalDetailsFragment` invokes its `onDestroy()`, so you'd expect its memory to be garbage collected. But since `MainActivity` has a reference to the `AnimalDetailsFragment` instance, the garbage collector can't collect that instance, which results in a leak.

Detecting and Tracing the Leak

Build and run. Once the app is running on a device, open the **Profiler** tab and start a session as shown below:

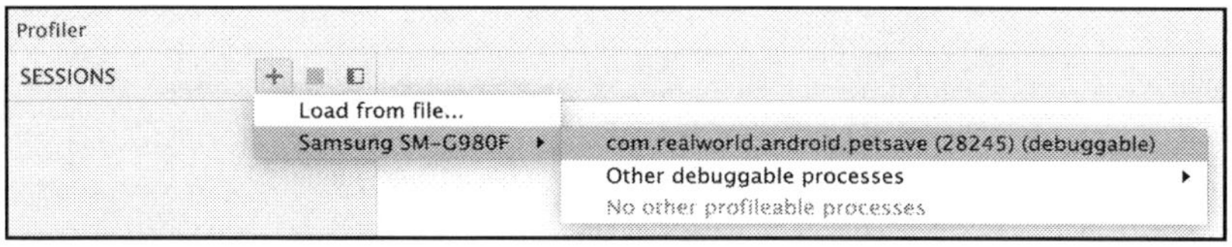

Figure 21.7 — Starting a Profiler Session

Select the **MEMORY** row. You will see a screen like the one below:

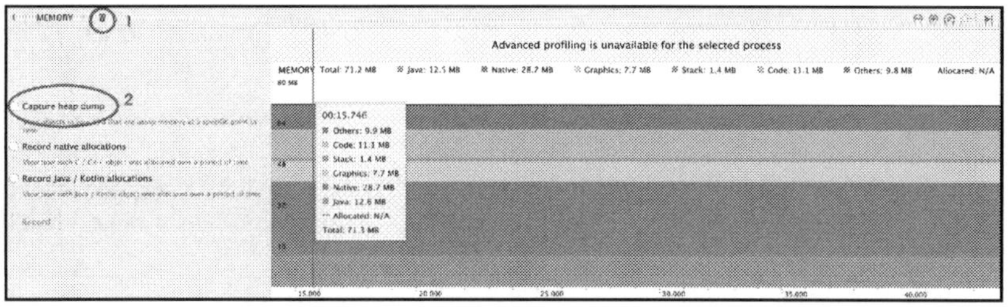

Figure 21.8 — Memory Profiler

In the image above, you see the two tools that you'll use to find the leak:

1. **Force garbage collection**: This tool can force garbage collection at any point in time. You need this because you can't determine when garbage collection will occur, so it would be difficult to figure out when to look for a memory leak.

2. **Capture heap dump**: This tool will create a dump of the current Java heap, allowing you to analyze the heap's memory allocation in greater detail.

On the app, open the details page for any pet, interact with the UI, then press **Back** to return to the previous page.

Back in the Android Studio Memory Profiler, click **Force garbage collection**, select **Capture heap dump** and click **Record**. Recording the heap dump will take a few seconds. Once it's done, you'll get a screen like the one below:

Figure 21.9 — Memory Profiler Heap Dump

In the heap dump, you can view the different types of objects in the heap and the memory each of them takes up. You'll also notice that the dump alerts you of a memory leak. Click the alert about the leak.

Android Studio will apply a filter that shows the `Activity/Fragment` leaks in the dump. In this case, it will tell you that **AnimalDetailsFragment** is leaking, as shown below:

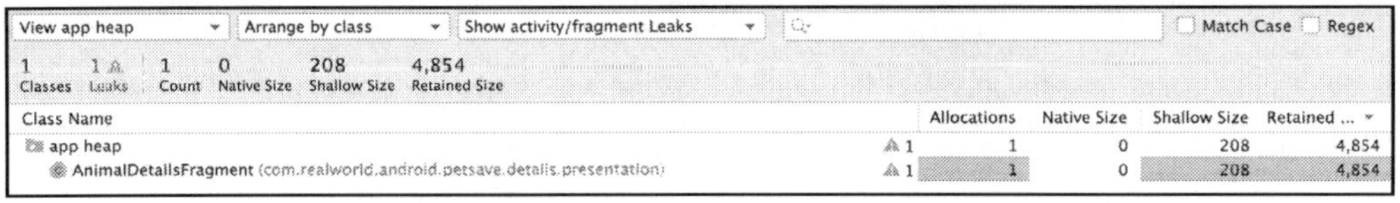

Figure 21.10 — Example of Memory Leak in the Memory Profiler

Click the **AnimalDetailsFragment** row to open the **Instance List**. This will help you figure out which instances of **AnimalDetailsFragment** are leaking. Since only one instance is leaking, you'll have one row in the instance list, as shown below:

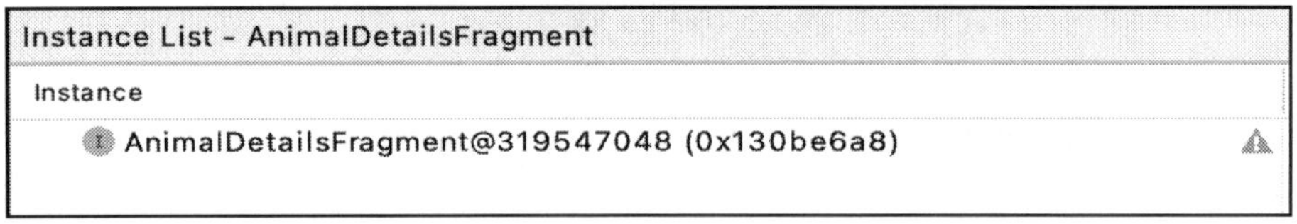

Figure 21.11 — Memory Profile Leak Instance List

Click the instance to open the **Instance Details** panel. The panel has two tabs: **Fields** and **References**. Choose the **References** tab. You'll get a window like the one shown below:

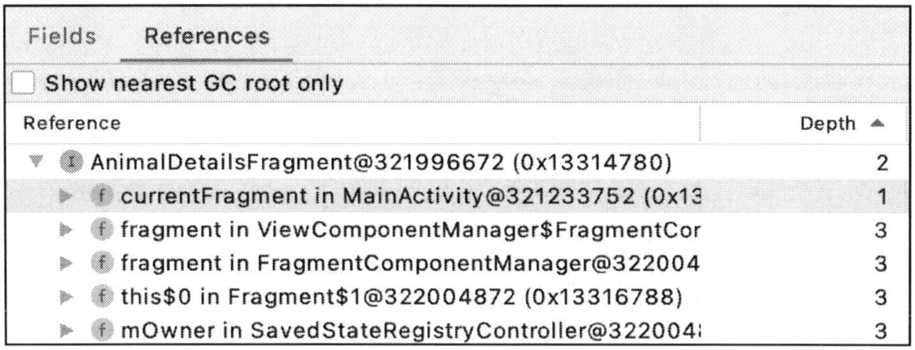

Figure 21.12 — Memory Profile Leaks References

In the window, you can see that `currentFragment` inside `MainActivity` has a reference to the leaked `Fragment`. You've successfully found the source of the leak using the Memory Profiler!

As an exercise, try using the lessons from the Memory Leak section above to resolve this `Fragment` leak. If you get stuck, you can always refer to the final project for the chapter.

Network Inspector

Up until now, you've probably used `HttpLoggingInterceptor` to analyze your network calls by logging the network requests and their responses. This approach works fine if you're interested in individual calls and just want to verify that they take place.

Now, however, you have a new option. Android Studio introduced the Network Inspector to help you visualize all the network calls taking place in your app, as well as the details of each call.

> **Note**: Network Inspector only supports **HttpURLConnection** and **OkHttp** networking libraries.

Why Network Profiling Matters

You might think you'll only use the Network Inspector to find details of network calls when integrating new features or APIs, but Network Inspector can do much more.

Network Inspector lets you visualize the frequency of the network calls happening in your app. This is very important when it comes to **radio battery consumption**. If the user is on mobile data, a network call awakens the mobile chip to find a radio signal and make your request go through. After making the request, the chip stays awake for a few more seconds to wait for the response. Every time this happens, the network call wakes up the chip, making it consume more power. And users don't like apps that consume too much battery, especially when they are on the go.

A good way to save battery is to use the Network Inspector to discover which calls happen frequently. You can then determine if you can defer any of them. For example, an API call to make a purchase has to be instant, whereas you can defer a call to sync profile images of different contacts on a messaging app. You can batch the deferrable calls and perform them in one go. This keeps the chip awake for a single duration instead of waking it up repeatedly.

Another good use of the Network Inspector is finding unexpected network calls that arise from bugs in the code or from third-party libraries. If a library you integrate is making network calls, you want to know about them.

Navigating the Network Inspector

Before inspecting your network activity, you need to disable proguard on the debug build. Remove the `leakCanary` block from the app **build.gradle**. Also, set `minifyEnabled` to `false` for the `debug` build type.

Build and run. Open the App Inspection window by going to **View ▸ Tools Windows ▸ App Inspection**. Next, switch select the **Network Inspector** tab.

In the app, navigate to the **Search** tab and search for a pet. In the Network Inspector, you'll get a screen like this:

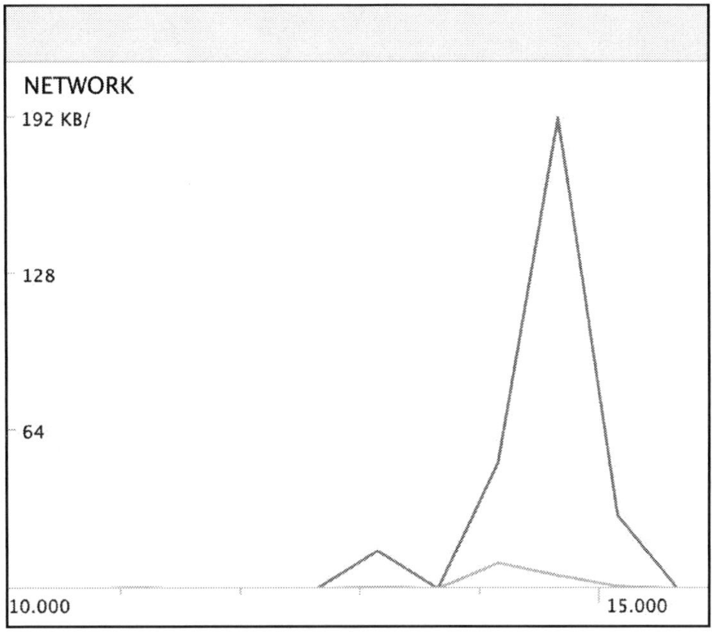

Figure 21.13 — Android Studio Network Inspector

In the image above, you can see a few things:

- The **y-axis** represents the network speed.
- The **x-axis** represents time.
- A **yellow spike** represents the network request. The width of the spike represents the time taken by the request, while its height indicates the amount of data transferred.
- A **blue spike** represents the server response. The width and height of the spike represent statistics similar to the yellow spike's.

To dig deeper into how the network works, select a section of the timeline and view the details. Drag your cursor across a part of the timeline to select it, as shown below:

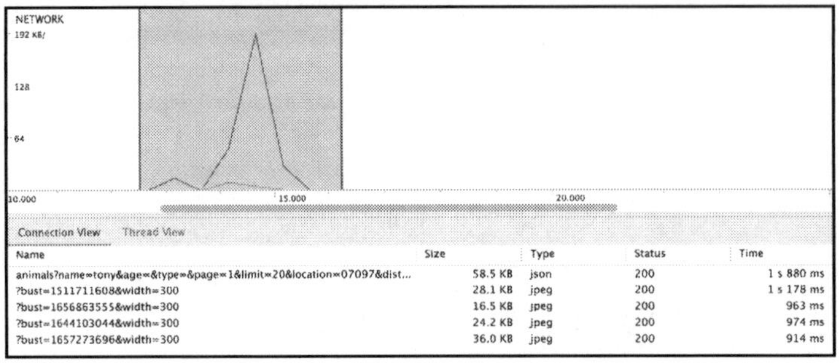

Figure 21.14 — Network Inspector Details

In the image above, you can see that the app has made five network calls and all of them have a status code of **200**. You can also see that four requests have the type **jpeg**, while one has the type **json**.

The calls with the **jpeg** types are mostly from **Glide**. You can confirm this by switching to the **Thread View**. You'll notice that the Glide threads have made many calls, whereas the OkHttp thread has made one call.

Figure 21.15 — Network Inspector Thread View

Switch back to the **Connection View** tab and note how hovering over any request will display the URL for that request. Clicking any of the Glide requests will show the image that was downloaded, assuming the download is complete. Clicking the call with the **json** type will open the details windows for the request, as shown below:

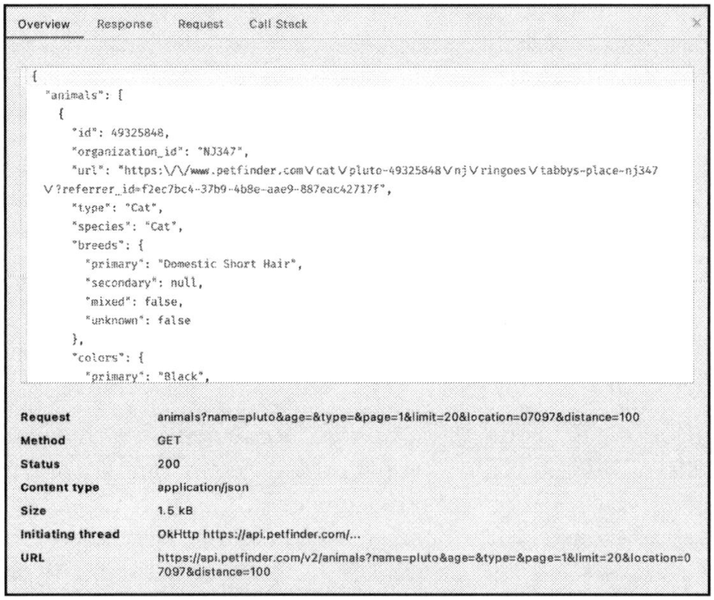

Figure 21.16 — Network Inspector Request Detail

Use this window to find the details of the network request as well as the response. As a bonus, it also auto-formats the response JSON.

Now, you'll move on to learn more about another tool that can help you reduce your app's battery drain.

Energy Profiler

The battery usage of an app is a vital metric to track. Users care a lot about their phone's battery.

There are many reasons an app might be consuming a lot of battery, including:

1. Frequent GPS location requests
2. Unbatched network calls
3. Wake locks
4. Frequent alarms to schedule tasks

and many more. Android Studio added Energy Profiler to help monitor the energy consumption of components, like CPU, radio and GPS sensors, as well as events that cause battery drain, like alarms and wake locks.

Run the app. Go to the **Profiler** tab in Android Studio and click anywhere in the **ENERGY** timeline. This opens the Energy Profiler. Hover your cursor over the Energy Profiler timeline to see a screen like the one below:

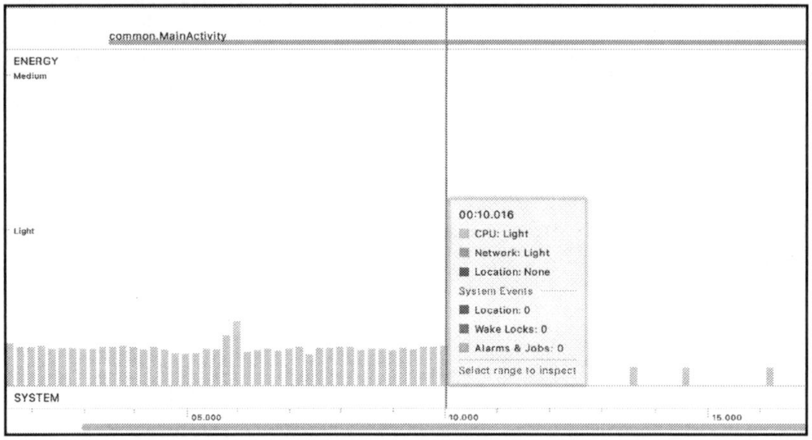

Figure 21.17 — Android Studio Energy Profiler

From the tooltip in the image above, you can see that the **CPU** and **Network** energy usage for the app is **Light**. It also indicates there are no system events that affect the app's energy consumption.

Finding a System Event

Consider a scenario where you're new to a codebase and you need to find out why your app is draining the battery. The Energy Profiler is one of the best places to start.

Keeping the Battery Profiler open, explore and interact with the different screens of the app. You'll notice that, when you enter the Animal Details screen, a red bar appears at the bottom of the Energy Profiler, as shown below:

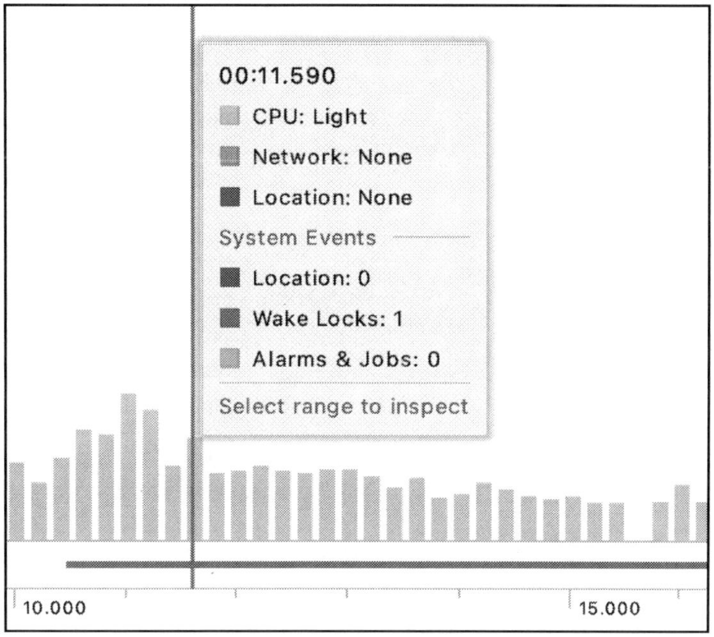

Figure 21.18 — Energy Profiler Tooltip

From the tooltip in the image above, you can infer that the red line represents a **wake lock** in the app. Now, this wake lock should ideally go away once you exit the Details screen, but the Energy Profiler will tell you a different story. The red line continues to show, even after you've left the screen. This is a possible source of energy drain.

Clicking anywhere on the red line will display the following message on newer versions of Android Studio:

Figure 21.19 — System Events Has Moved Message

Open App Inspection and go the **Background Task Inspector** tab.

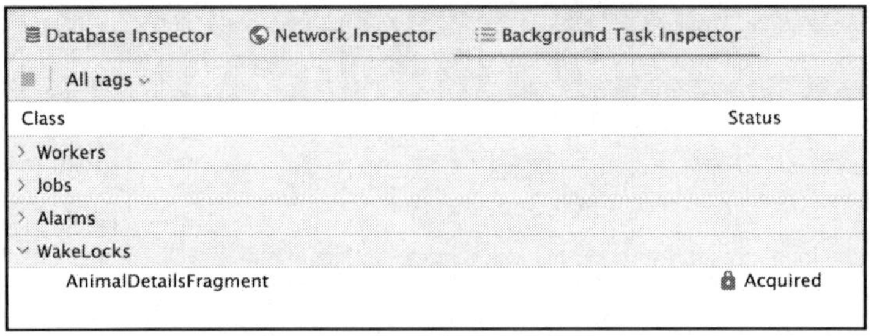

Figure 21.20 — Energy Profiler Wake Lock

Repeat the same set of steps to trigger a wake lock so that App Inspection can record it. You'll see that a wake lock has been recorded as shown below:

In the previous image, `onCreate` in `AnimalDetailsFragment` is calling a **partial wake lock**. To know more about the leak, click on the entry to open the **Task Details** window, as shown below:

Figure 21.21 — Energy Profiler Wake Lock Details

In the image above, a callstack points to **line 104** in `AnimalDetailsFragment`. Open **AnimalDetailsFragment.kt** and go to line 102. You'll notice the following code, which acquires a wake lock:

```
wakeLock =
(requireContext().getSystemService(Context.POWER_SERVICE) as
PowerManager).run {
        newWakeLock(PowerManager.PARTIAL_WAKE_LOCK,
"MyApp::MyWakelockTag").apply {
          acquire()
        }
      }
```

According to the Energy Profiler, this wake lock is never released. Checking for `wakelock` usages confirms that.

To release the wake lock when the user leaves the screen, add the following code at the end of `AnimalDetailsFragment`:

```
override fun onDestroy() {
  super.onDestroy()
  wakeLock.release()
}
```

The code above releases the wake lock when the `Fragment` is destroyed.

Build and run. Start the Energy Profiler and verify that the `Fragment` releases the wake lock after you exit the details screen.

Now, you're ready to learn to use a tool that helps you solve problems in your user interface.

Layout Inspector

When you implement your app's UI, you have to keep many things in mind, like:

- Making sure there's no unnecessary nesting in the layouts.
- Ensuring the layout closely matches the design mocks.

The steps to verify your app's layout are tedious and time-consuming. To ensure flat layouts, you have to go through all the XML, view by view, and figure out if you can flatten anything. Matching your UI with the design mocks involves comparing them visually and going through each detail of the UI. Even then, you might miss that a `TextView` is off by 8dp or your button has an extra margin of 4dp on one side.

To simplify the process of finding visual bugs, Android Studio provides a tool named **Layout Inspector**. It lets you inspect your view attributes after the layout has rendered them on the device and also lets you visualize each layout in 3D. In this section, you'll use the Layout Inspector to flatten the view hierarchy and make sure your UI matches the design mock.

Starting the Layout Inspector

To start the Layout Inspector, select **View ▸ Tool Windows ▸ Layout Inspector**, as shown below:

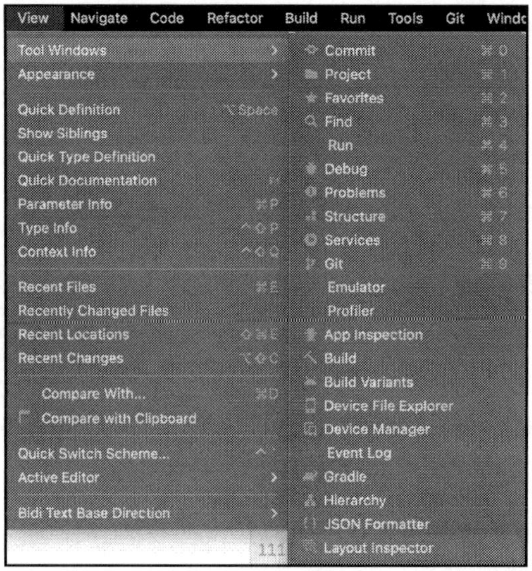

Figure 21.22 — Android Studio Layout Inspector

This will open the Layout Inspector tab. First, you need to choose the process Layout Inspector will use to extract the layout information. Click **Select Process** and choose the process named **com.realworld.android.petsave** from your device:

Figure 21.23 — Layout Inspector Process Selection

The Layout Inspector will now show the layout that your device displays. Click any of the views in the layout and the Layout Inspector will display the components present in the layout on the **Component Tree** panel on the left. It will also display all the attributes of the selected view on a panel to the right, as shown below:

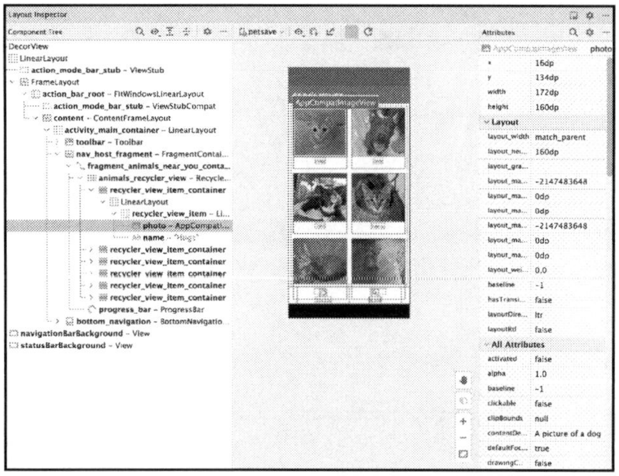

Figure 21.24 — Layout Inspector Components Tree

Finding Unnecessary Nesting

With the Layout Inspector open, visit the **Near You** tab in the app. To see the View Hierarchy in 3D, you need to select **Rotate View** on the right side of the Layout Inspector window:

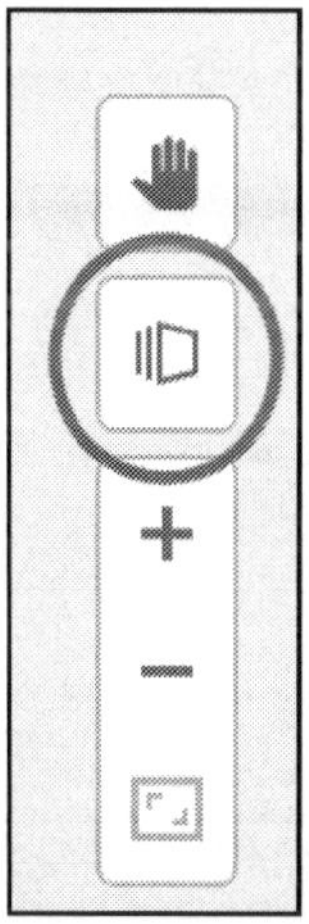

Figure 21.25 — Layout Inspector's Rotate View

Selecting Rotate View displays the different levels of views in the layout. You can drag your cursor around to view the hierarchy from different angles. Keep doing it till you see a view like the one shown below:

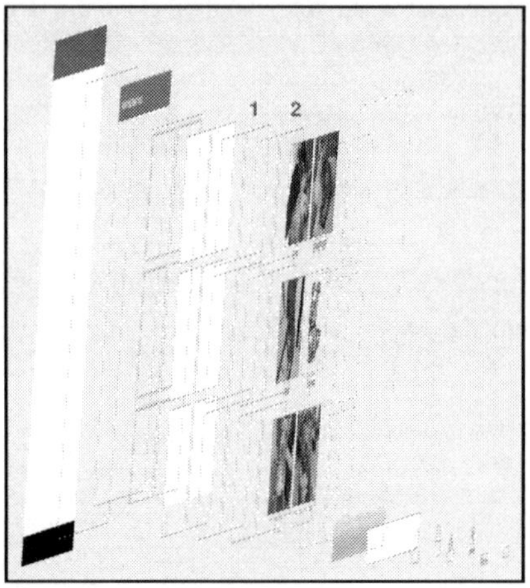

Figure 21.26 — Layout Inspector View Hierarchy

In the image above, look at the views marked **1** and **2**. Do you see any differences between them? By the looks of it, view **2** doesn't add anything new to view **1**, which indicates unnecessary nesting.

Click on the view tagged as **2**. In the Component Tree window, you'll notice that you have a `LinearLayout` inside another `LinearLayout`, as shown below:

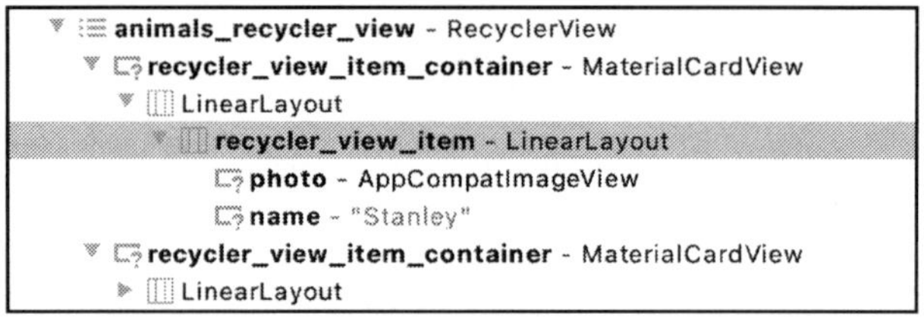

Figure 21.27 - Layout Inspector Nested LinearLayout Example

Open **recycler_view_animal_item.xml** and look for the `LinearLayout` with `recycler_view_item`. You'll notice that it's nested inside another `LinearLayout` with the same set of attributes.

```
<LinearLayout
  android:layout_width="match_parent"
  android:ayout_height="match_parent">

  <LinearLayout
    android:id="@+id/recycler_view_item"
```

```
    android:layout_width="match_parent"
    android:layout_height="match_parent"
    android:orientation="vertical">

    <ImageView...>

    <TextView...>

  </LinearLayout>

</LinearLayout>
```

Remove the outer `LinearLayout` so the structure becomes:

```
<com.google.android.material.card.MaterialCardView>

  <LinearLayout>

    <ImageView/>

    <TextView/>

  </LinearLayout>
</com.google.android.material.card.MaterialCardView>
```

Build and run, then verify the RecyclerView items on the **Near Me** screen look the same as before. Congratulations, you've successfully used Layout Inspector to reduce an extra level of nesting!

Comparing the Layout With a Design Mock

Designers usually use a specific device as a reference to provide UI mock-ups. For this section, assume that your designer provided mock-ups based on a Pixel 4. You'll create a new **Android Virtual Device** based on Pixel 4.

Build and run on the Pixel 4 emulator. Navigate to the Details screen of any pet. Next, open Layout Inspector and click the **Load Overlay** icon, as shown below:

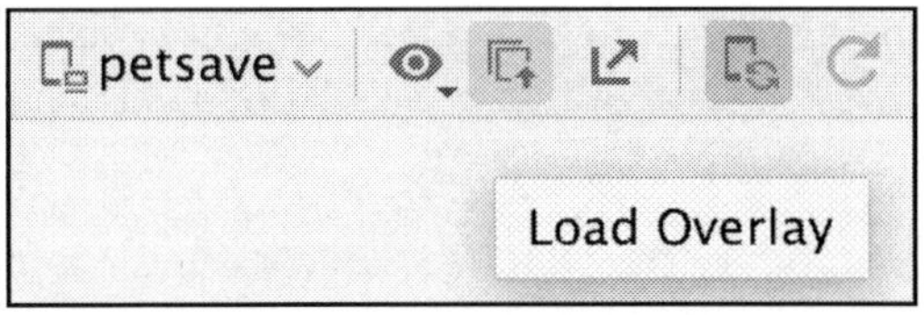

Figure 21.28 — Layout Inspector Overlays

Click **Load Overlay** to open a file chooser, then select **design_mockup.png** inside the starter project. Doing this will lay the mock-up over your layout. Use the slider labeled **Overlay Alpha** to change the transparency of the overlay.

Change the transparency a few times and try to find differences between the mock-up and your layout. You might notice a few differences in the text below the pet's description. However, this is expected since the text length varies from pet to pet. Another difference you'll find is in the position of the **Call** button, as you can see below. Change the **Overlay Alpha** to around **50%** make it clear.

Figure 21.29 — Layout Inspector Overlay Example

Open **fragment_details.xml** and check the margin you used for the `FloatingActionButton`. It's set to `@dimen/half_default_margin`. Change the margin to `@dimen/default_margin`, instead.

Build and run the app. Compare the Details screen using Layout Inspector. You'll find that the **Call** button is in the correct position, and both you and your designer are happy now.

Key Points

- Use LeakCanary to find and rectify memory leaks in your app.
- Avoid holding view references in global variables. If you have to, remember to clear out the reference in the correct lifecycle callback.
- Find `Activity` and `Fragment` leaks using the Memory Profiler.
- Use the Network Inspector to examine your network calls.
- Use batching to avoid making frequent network calls.
- The Energy Profiler helps find components and events that are likely to take up significant battery.
- Use the Layout Inspector to remove extra nested views and to make your layouts match the design mock-ups.

In the next chapter, you'll learn about analyzing databases and the different ways you can reverse engineer code.

Chapter 22: App Analysis

By Kolin Stürt and Antonio Roa-Valverde

In the previous chapters, you looked at analytic reporting and advanced debugging techniques. Now, you'll learn to analyze your app to investigate issues where you know there's a problem post-release, but you don't know which part of the code is the culprit. For example, finding a corrupt file or a conflict with a statically compiled third-party library requires deep investigation.

In this chapter, you'll learn how to:

- Look at data artifacts that aren't obvious from your code.
- Analyze databases.
- Reverse-engineer code you didn't write.

For this chapter, you'll use the **Pixel XL API 30 (R) Emulator**.

Debugging Versus Investigating

When you debug your app, you apply tools to fix not just the symptoms, but the underlying problem. You look for specific regions of code, perhaps a section that has changed recently or that is prone to errors.

There are two types of tests you can run to find problems:

- **Dynamic testing**: Testing while executing the code.
- **Static testing**: Auditing the source code for issues.

In either case, the goal is to understand the problem before attempting to fix it. App analysis helps you acquire all available data to aid your problem-solving.

Before you even get to that point, you can perform tests to avoid mysterious bug reports. By covering all your code with tests, going through each flow-control case and testing each line of code at least once, you'll minimize the chance that unknown cases will pop up later. Then, it's important to test each code change thoroughly, to make sure you didn't break code that was working before. This is called **regression testing**.

Because you wrote the code, you know how to use your app. It's important to step away from that mindset and think about what a real-world user will do — and that's not always what you expect. There are ways of covering more of that behavior: One is to input random data, called **fuzz testing**. Another is to choose extreme values in hopes of finding an edge case. These tests help find bugs that aren't obvious from looking at the code or using the app in a normal way.

Even with all this testing, you'll find unexpected bugs. One example is memory corruption due to race conditions. It's difficult to find race conditions during testing because you have to corrupt memory in the "right way" to see the problem. Sometimes the problems appear a long time later in the app's lifecycle. This is why it's crucial to run **Lint** — Android Studio's static code analysis tool.

Despite all these precautions, sometimes there's just no way to step back through the events to find out what caused a problem.

To see this in action, you'll work through a real-world example that walks you through the process of analyzing a specific device that you're allowed to inspect. This will give you a sense of the process and the complications you'll encounter along the way.

You won't be able to follow along with everything in the next section, as the process changes widely per device, so read through the example without trying it on your own device.

Extracting Data

Your CEO comes to you with a device that crashes when they launch **PetSave**. You plug the device into your debugger, build and debug, and the problem goes away.

However, a week later, the same story happens again. The C-level employees only get the final release version, where you've disabled logs, and Logcat is no help. The fact that it's a release build might be a coincidence. The third time the CEO brings you the device with the issue, you know you have to preserve the state of the defect. You can't just debug this app, you need a way to extract data from the device.

You'll start your investigation by using **Android Debug Bridge (ADB)**, an Android tool that lets you communicate with an Android device via the command line. To follow the remainder of this tutorial, enable ADB debugging on a physical device or an emulator.

One of the simplest things to do with ADB is to list the apps installed on a device:

```
adb shell  # 1
pm list packages -f | grep petsave  # 2
exit
```

Here's what the code above does:

1. Starts the ADB shell so you can run commands on the device.
2. Lists the packages installed on the device and filters them using the **grep** command.

After running this command, if the CEO has correctly installed PetSave, you'll see a line like this in your output:

```
package:/data/app/com.realworld.android.petsave-
ei0L3AJk3xo5M3Gs9SVuTQ==/base.apk=com.realworld.android.petsave
```

Here, **com.realworld.android.petsave** is PetSave's package name.

Extracting Data From a Package

Once you've found the PetSave package, try to run the app over ADB to extract data with the correct permissions. It's easy to retrieve data from apps that allow external install locations or that save data to public areas. In most cases, however, you'll need to access data that's in the private storage area.

On some versions of the Android platform, you can access the private storage of debuggable versions of the app:

```
adb exec-out run-as com.realworld.android.petsave cat databases/
petsave.db > petsave.db
```

Here, you're using `run-as` to execute commands with the same permissions as the app.

If that doesn't work, you can also try to change file permissions and use the `adb pull` command:

```
adb shell
run-as com.realworld.android.petsave  #1
chmod 666 databases/petsave.db  #2
exit
cp /data/data/com.realworld.android.petsave/databases/petsave.db
/sdcard/  #3
run-as com.realworld.android.petsave
chmod 600 databases/petsave.db  #4
adb pull /sdcard/petsave.db .  #5
```

This code:

1. Tells ADB to execute commands with the same app permissions.
2. Executes `chmod`, which lets you change file permissions. Permission **666** means all users can read and write to the file.
3. Copies **petsave.db** to **sdcard**, which is a public area of the device.
4. Executes `chmod` again to reset the file permissions. Permission **600** means only the owner — the app — can read and write to the file.
5. Now that you've put the file in a public area, you copy the file from the device to the working directory of your computer.

You now have a copy of an app's local database on your computer. However, many devices disable these features for security reasons. If that's the case, the next thing you'd try is a device backup. Device backups can include the APKs as well as the private data for each app:

```
adb backup -apk -shared com.realworld.android.petsave
```

Here, you use `backup` to write an archive of the app and its data to the working directory of your computer. The default filename is **backup.adb**.

Feel free to experiment, if you're comfortable doing so, on a test device. But for the sake of time and safety, this chapter will use the Android Emulator to skip to the next step.

Extracting Data From The Emulator

Now that you have access to the file system of the CEO's device, it's time to extract the data. Build and run in the emulator, then make a report.

In the Report screen, fill in the details and tap the **SEND REPORT** button. In Android Studio, select **View ▸ Tool Windows ▸ Device File Explorer**, then choose **Emulator Pixel_XL_API_30** from the drop-down:

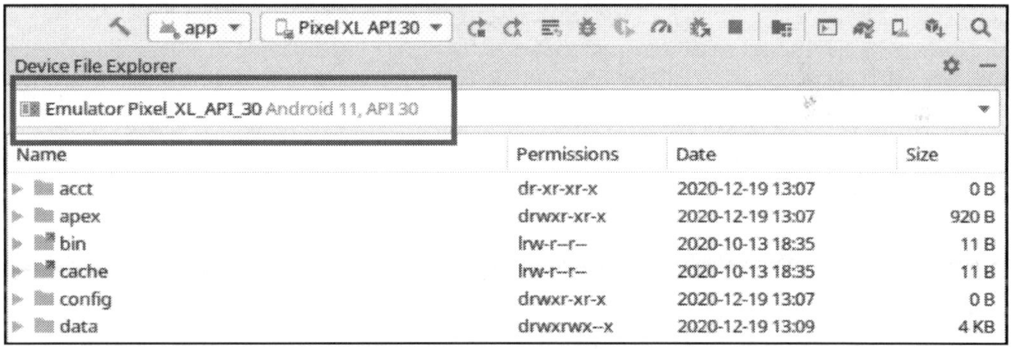

Figure 22.1 — File Explorer

Knowing where apps store information makes it easy to look for artifacts or to recover deleted data. Here are some locations where Android keeps important data:

- All apps store user data in **/data/data**.
- You can find a list of apps on the device at **/data/system/packages.list**.

- You can see when you last used an app at **/data/system/package-usage.list**.
- The operating system stores Wi-Fi connection information, such as a list of access points, at **/data/misc/wifi/wpa_supplicant.conf**.

To try your hand at saving PetSave's data to your device, navigate to **/data/data**. You'll see a list of all the packages:

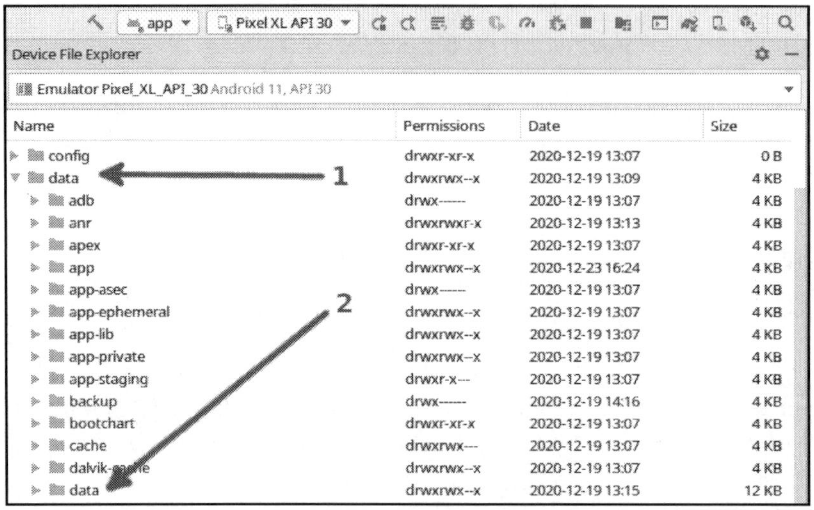

Figure 22.2 — Locate the Data Folders

Find the **com.realworld.android.petsave** entry. Right-click on it and choose **Save As...**. Save the file to a location on your computer and open it to view its contents. You'll see important directories such as:

- **shared_prefs**
- **files**
- **databases**

Now, you'll look at each of these in more detail.

Examining SharedPreferences

Open **MyPrefs.xml** inside **shared_prefs**. You'll notice at least one entry with a timestamp.

Timestamps are very important to any debugging investigation because they give you evidence of what happened at a specific time.

Examining Other Files

Now, select **users.dat** in the **files** directory.

Android serializes objects in a specific record format, but you can still search for strings using the **strings** utility, which both Mac and Linux already include.

If you're using Windows, download the strings utility here: https://docs.microsoft.com/en-us/sysinternals/downloads/strings.

In the terminal, type **strings** and a space followed by the path to **users.dat**. After you press **Space**, drag **users.dat** into the terminal window to populate the path. Press **Enter** and you'll get an output of items.

Upon looking at the output, you'll see **extrat** followed by **nameq** and **passwordq**. You can use that order to deduce that you're looking at the extra info about each account, followed by a login name and an encrypted password. In Chapter 16, "Securing Data at Rest", you encrypted this data. But wait, it looks like this now:

```
"::basic_string(void*,void(*),void(*)_char_\0\0cd.Nico Sell -
CEO"
```

There's a name in there that doesn't look like a password, nor is it encrypted. Also, there seems to be some extra garbage data.

Doing a Google search for ::basic_string leads you to **typedef std::basic_string string**, a class template type for `std::string`. But this is C++.

Choose **Edit ▸ Find ▸ Find in Path** to search for **std::string**. Oh right, when working on your app with the iOS team, you shared some portable code for productivity's sake.

user_processing_jni.cpp shows up in the search. Open it and check out **line 40**. It looks like that could be what's getting in the password field by mistake. Without going into C++ too much, you've found a possible location of a bug that you can report to the other team to fix.

> **Note**: Interested in a bit of C++ and what the bug is? On line 50, the constructor attempts to set this variable to zero, but there's a mistake. In C++, you must explicitly initialize all pointers; otherwise, they point to garbage values. The line attempts to set the variable to all zeros, but `sizeof` only sets the first character.

> In debug mode, that was enough for the app to keep going. In release mode, the optimizer sees that you're setting the variable to zero and not doing anything with it, so it removes that line. Now, when you go to access it, it points to a random part of memory — in this case, a section of the previous `_userNameString` — and crashes! Worse, the memory layout will vary each time, making this crash random.

Now, the other team sent you the fix. Replace **line 50** with the following:

```
_passwordChar = "";
```

Now, you have happy C++ code. :]

> **Note**: If you want to prevent the compiler from optimizing out the secure-wiping of memory contents, check out the proper implementation in the destructor on line 54, which uses `volatile`.

You used the **strings** utility here, but there are a few other tools to extract data, as well:

- A **hex and text viewer** comes in handy to search for strings and patterns.
- A live data imaging tool that may be helpful is **dd**. You'll find it at **/system/bin**.
- To extract the current memory state of the device, check out **LiME**.

Next, you'll learn how to check the data stored in databases.

Analyzing Databases

Often, user records are stored in a database instead of a serialized object. Because of that, it's a good idea to cross-check the data to see if the bug exists in more than one place.

Navigate to the **databases** folder and you'll see some files. Next, you'll see some different ways to examine them.

In Android Studio navigate to **View ▸ Tool Windows ▸ App Inspection**. Then you'll see the following tab:

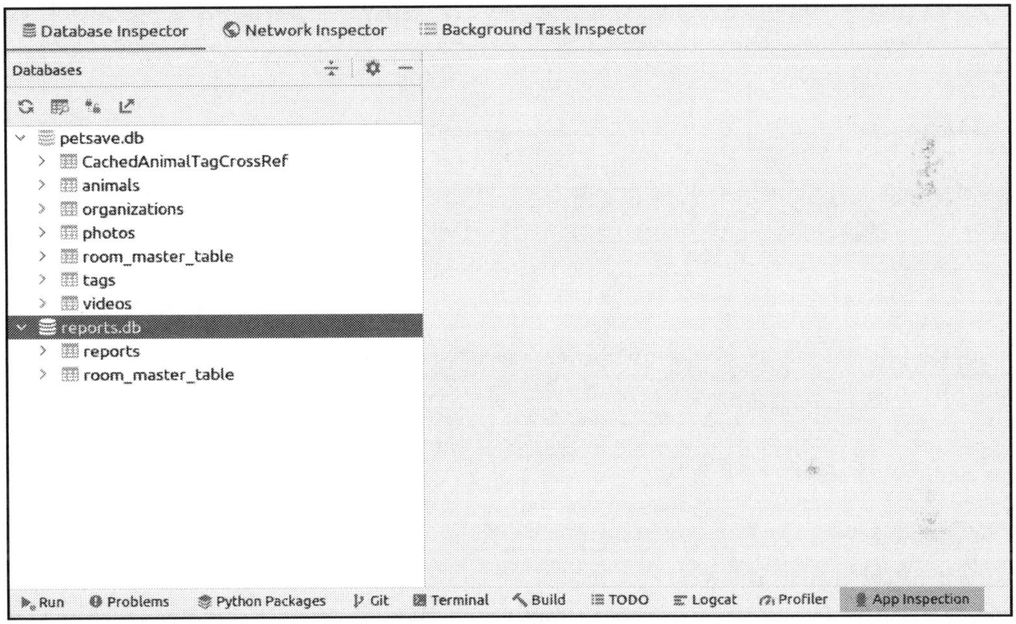

Figure 22.3 — App Inspection

Now, double-click on **reports**:

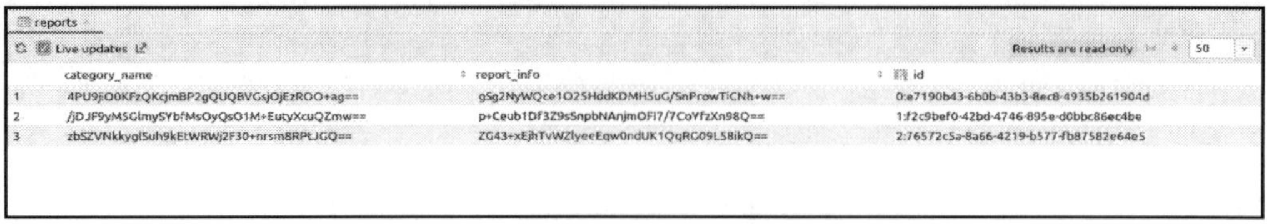

Figure 22.4 — Browser the Data of Your DB

You'll see all the reports. In Chapter 16, "Securing Data at Rest", you encrypted this data and stored it as base 64, so your first step will be to check that it really contains base 64 characters. In this case, these characters include: A–Z, a–z, 0–9 and the + and / symbols.

So far, everything's going well — but analyzing your app doesn't always go this smoothly. For example, users often continue using the app after a bug occurs. They're not developers. They don't understand that the more they use the app, the farther away they put the state of the app at the time of the bug. For example, say that when the CEO experienced the bug, they logged out of the app and submitted the device to QA — not understanding that the logout functionality deleted the user record and reports.

To address this, you need to know how to recover that data.

Recovering Deleted Data

The data you've analyzed so far exists inside a saved SQLite block. SQLite has **unallocated blocks** and **free blocks**. When you delete something from the database, SQLite doesn't overwrite the block immediately. Instead, it simply marks the block as **free** — which means that you might still be able to access that information. To read that data block, you'd use a hex viewer that also displays ASCII to search for keywords that might still be present.

The process of finding and extracting data when you don't have access to the file structure is called **file carving**. Sometimes, searching for a particular string of content helps. Other times, you'd look for the header of a known file format.

For example, say you're searching deleted data for images. In the JPEG format, the first two bytes and the last two bytes are always **FF D8** and **FF D9**. Searching for those headers can help you identify the images.

Here are a few more details about recovering deleted data:

- Find valuable information about SQLite file carving here: https://forensicsfromthesausagefactory.blogspot.com/2011/04/carving-sqlite-databases-from.html.
- **Scalpel** is an open-source data-carving tool, available at https://github.com/sleuthkit/scalpel.
- **DiskDigger** is an automated undelete tool for Android. It scans the device for photos, documents, music and videos: https://diskdigger.org/android.
- A commercial tool for viewing and undeleting SQLite records is **SQLite Viewer**, available here: https://www.oxygen-forensic.com/en/products/oxygen-forensic-detective.

Next, you'll learn how to handle problems in code you don't own.

Black Box Testing And Reverse-engineering

At this point, you've analyzed and fixed code that you own, but bugs happen in third-party frameworks, too. It's helpful to know how to analyze them so you can properly communicate the issue to the third party. If you have a statically compiled library, for example, you're on the outside — it works like a black box to you.

You can get a lot of information by analyzing a binary or app module. This includes the code and files that Android Studio bundles with the APK. First, you'll look at what happens when you compile an app.

When you build your app, Android Studio produces an APK file. This is like a ZIP file that contains a structure of Java's JAR archives. Inside the archive are resources, along with a DEX file. DEX stands for Dalvik Executable.

When Android Studio compiles your app, it puts the code into that DEX file and names it **classes.dex**. That file contains bytecode, an intermediary set of instructions that a Java Virtual Machine (JVM) runs or that ART (the Android Runtime) later converts to native code. So what are JVM, ART and native code?

Apps run on a **Java Virtual Machine (JVM)**. Android traditionally used Dalvik for its JVM, but in recent years, Android replaced Dalvik with **ART** for performance reasons. ART converts DEX into native code by running the **dex2oat** tool to create a native ELF binary. **Native code** refers to the C/C++ code that the operating system understands and the assembly and machine code that the CPU can read.

So now you're thinking, because PetSave is a Kotlin app, reverse-engineering it must be different than for Java apps. The good news is, like Java, Kotlin is a JVM language. While Kotlin has its own syntax, the **kotlinc** compiler transforms the code into a DEX file that contains Java bytecode. Because **kotlinc** compiles Kotlin to the same bytecode as Java, most of its reverse-engineering tools are the same as for apps built in Java!

> **Note**: Sometimes, attackers also reverse-engineer apps in hopes of patching or hooking security checks out of the code. A good example of a target is a feature that's only available with a paid subscription or after a user achieves a level in a game. Keep in mind that these tools and techniques are not only useful for debugging, but for performing a security audit of your app.

So now you're thinking — enough theory already. Show me an example!

Understanding Bytecode

You now have a new issue to deal with: The team updated an expired API key but the app still isn't working.

Your first step is to check that the team used the correct key. Open **ReportDetailFragment** in Android Studio and find `sendReportPressed()`. It adds the report to the local database and prepares a network request to send the report. That network request requires the API key so only authorized apps can make the call.

Open **ApiConstants.kt** and note the `const val SECRET` used to make API requests. It looks like the correct key:

```
object ApiConstants {
  const val BASE_ENDPOINT = "https://api.petfinder.com/v2/"
  const val AUTH_ENDPOINT = "oauth2/token/"
  const val ANIMALS_ENDPOINT = "animals"

  const val KEY = "FQuzd5lGR4guPOnjMvJbxvogIIllwZPGmniegB7Zj5MTCuodWx"
  const val SECRET = "g3kD7XO3eAWCb6ySL1LaQeZZkETOAJK6t5lkhXDs"
  fun aK(): String { //API KEY
    return SECRET.substring( startIndex: 35).reversed() + GO.f1 + "5687" + GO.f2 + "3657"+
        GO.f2 + SECRET.substring(7,10) + GO.f1 + " 4fj6" + GO.f3 +
        SECRET.substring( range: 1..4) + GO.f3
  }
}
```

Figure 22.5 — Access SECRET in ApiConstants

When you set a breakpoint in the debug version, things look fine. Based on your previous experience, it looks like something is happening to the code for the release version.

The release build variant disables debugging in many places. Commenting out those security checks results in a false test. But Android Studio includes a tool called **APK Analyzer**, which lets you view the bytecode of your finalized app.

Using APK Analyzer

APK Analyzer is a tool for inspecting your finalized app. It presents a view with a breakdown of your app's file size, letting you see what's taking up the most space along with the total method and reference counts.

For this example, you'll look at the debug version. Launch the analyzer by selecting **Build ▸ Analyze APK**. This will open a dialog for your file system. Then, navigate to the debug folder, **PetSave-Starter/app/build/outputs/apk/debug**, select **app-debug.apk** and click **OK** to open APK Analyzer:

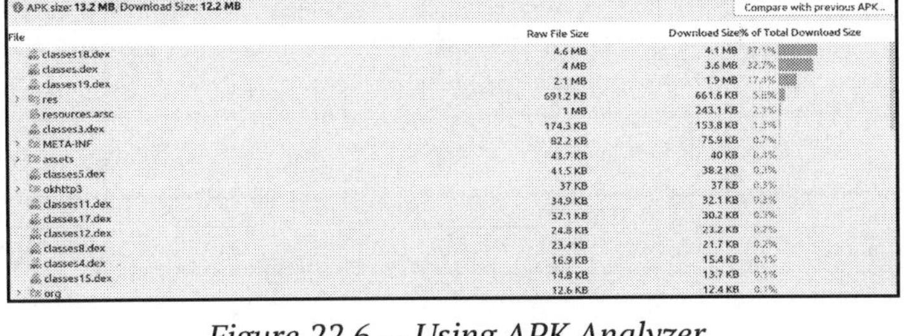

Figure 22.6 — Using APK Analyzer

> **Note:** If the APK file is missing, choose **Build ▸ Build Bundle(s) / APK(s) ▸ Build APK(s)** to generate it.

In APK Analyzer, select **classes5.dex**, then navigate to **com/realworld/android/petsave/core/data/api**:

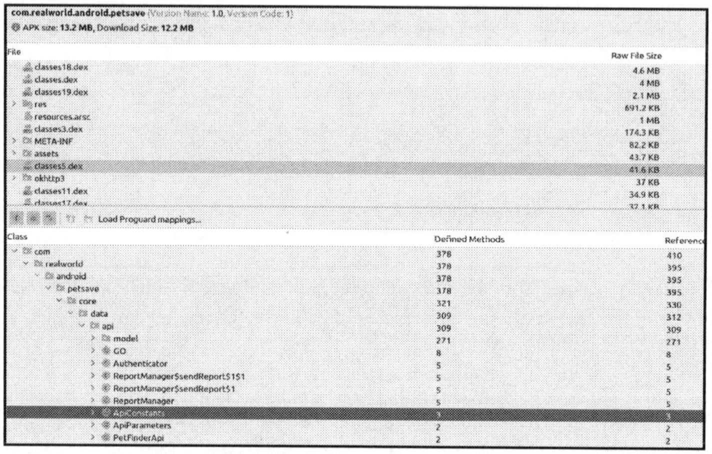

Figure 22.7 — Analyze the Classes in the APK for Your App

Right-click **ApiConstants** and choose **Show Bytecode**. Notice the line that starts with **.field public static final SECRET**:

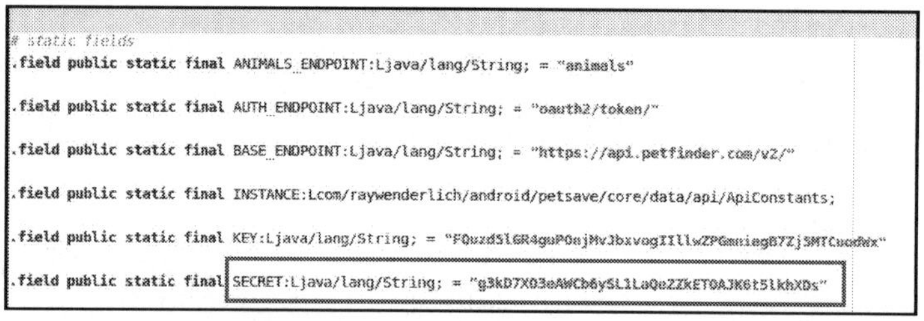

Figure 22.8 — Access the SECRET Constants in the Classes in the APK for Your App

At first glance, it seems that the secret token is correct. But is it? In the previous chapters of this book, you looked at how spammers search for tokens to abuse private APIs. Attackers also reverse-engineer apps, to steal intellectual property, for example, or to clone the app.

Since this API key is sensitive, it's likely protected using obfuscation techniques such as reflection. As a consequence, however, it's harder to debug when something goes wrong.

Introspection and Reflection

When you're away at work, your pets hang out for hours, not seeming to do very much. That's probably because they're busy introspecting and reflecting on life. In Kotlin, introspection and reflection are features of the language that inspect objects and call methods dynamically at runtime.

Open **ApiConstants.kt** and find `aK()`. Notice there's some obfuscation. The previous developer abbreviated the name and created a string from bits and pieces of other strings, as well as from an object called `GO`. You can find the variables in `SN.kt`, in the `object GO` definition. For your next step, you'll check that those values are in the final APK.

In APK Analyzer, select **classes5.dex**. Navigate to **com/raywenderlich/android/petsave/core/data/api**. Right-click **GO** and choose **Show Bytecode**. Integers **f1**, **f2** and **f3** are the variables of **3**, **1** and **5** that create part of the key. Things look OK for those values at first glance:

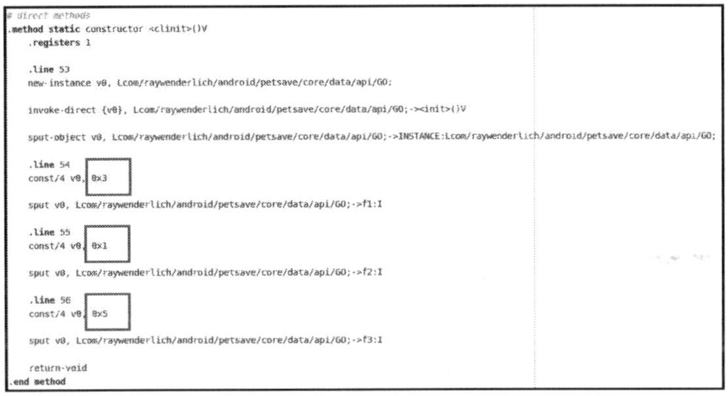

Figure 22.9 — Obfuscation in Practice

However, if you follow those methods to the `GO` companion object, the numbers it returns are not the real ones. As you look through **SN.kt**, you notice this code:

```
val kClass = Class.forName(ownerClassName).kotlin // 1
val instance = kClass.objectInstance ?:
kClass.java.newInstance() // 2
val member =
kClass.memberProperties.filterIsInstance<KMutableProperty<*>>()
    .firstOrNull { it.name == fieldName } // 3
member?.setter?.call(instance, value) // 4
```

Wait, what? What is this magic? This code does the following:

1. Gets the Kotlin class for `ownerClassName`.
2. Instantiates that class at runtime, if it isn't already instantiated.
3. Dynamically gets the property that `fieldName` references for the instantiated class.
4. Calls a setter on that property, passing in `value`.

The real magic happens when the app invokes `sn()` (setupNumbers), which looks for `com.raywenderlich.android.petsave.core.data.api.GO`. It finds the fields named `f1` through `f3` and swaps the values out for something else at runtime.

You've now figured out why the API key change didn't go as planned and where you need to update the real values.

> **Note**: This is also good motivation to document tricky code for future developers.

Using Reverse-engineering Tools

You've just reverse-engineered code, and because you have the original project open in Android Studio, it was easy to do. But this is not the only way to view the bytecode. Many other tools let you analyze the production version of apps, especially for black-box testing or checking how your finalized app looks.

As long as you're able to access the release APK, either by using the methods you learned above or by downloading an APK from a site like https://www.apkmirror.com/, you can reverse-engineer the code without having access to the Android Studio project.

For example, **Apktool** will reverse-engineer the entire Android package back to a workable form, including all resources and original source code. It's available here: https://ibotpeaches.github.io/Apktool/. There are even online versions, such as the one at http://www.javadecompilers.com/apk.

There are also many other tools you can use:

- **smali/baksmali** (https://github.com/JesusFreke/smali) is a set of tools to transform bytecode into another intermediate, but more readable, language. From there, you can convert the code back into Java.
- **Android Asset Packaging Tool** dumps the Android Manifest file.
- **AXMLPrinter2** (https://code.google.com/archive/p/android4me/downloads) parses Android binary XML formats.
- **dex2Jar** (https://github.com/pxb1988/dex2jar) lets you convert a DEX file to a standard Java CLASS file.
- Get all the class names and most source code by opening a **jar** folder in **JD-GUI** (https://github.com/java-decompiler/jd-gui).
- **Dextra** (http://newandroidbook.com/tools/dextra.html) supports ART and OAT.
- **Jadx** (https://github.com/skylot/jadx) lets you browse decompiled DEX code. It also decompiles almost the entire project.
- **JAD** (http://varaneckas.com/jad/) will convert Java class files back to source files.

As you can see, it's easy for anyone to do this. That's the main reason developers use obfuscation to hide or obscure proprietary logic or secret keys, as you saw above. They can do this with string splitting, dummy code, disguising the names of methods or using reflection, as you saw above. But more often, they use optimizers such as **R8** or **ProGuard**. While the tools optimize code, they have the side effect of obfuscating it. That further complicates things when it comes to debugging.

Debugging With ProGuard Output Files

In the app **build.gradle**, replace `buildTypes`'s code with the following:

```
buildTypes {
  release {
    minifyEnabled true
    proguardFiles getDefaultProguardFile('proguard-
android.txt'), 'proguard-rules.pro'
  }
  debug {
    minifyEnabled true
    proguardFiles getDefaultProguardFile('proguard-
android.txt'), 'proguard-rules.pro'
```

```
    }
}
```

Sync Gradle, then build and run. When ProGuard finishes running, it produces four output files. They are:

- **usage.txt**: Lists code that ProGuard removed.
- **dump.txt**: Describes the structure of the class files in your APK.
- **seeds.txt**: Lists the classes and members that were not obfuscated. This helps you verify that you obfuscated your important files.
- **mapping.txt**: Maps the obfuscated names back to the original.

You can use the mapping file to see the original code.

Build and run APK Analyzer again, then select **classes.dex**. Drill down to **com/realworld/android/petsave** and you'll see classes and methods along the lines of **i.n0.r.a**. The single characters you see will vary from this example, but you can follow the directory path of the characters to various methods:

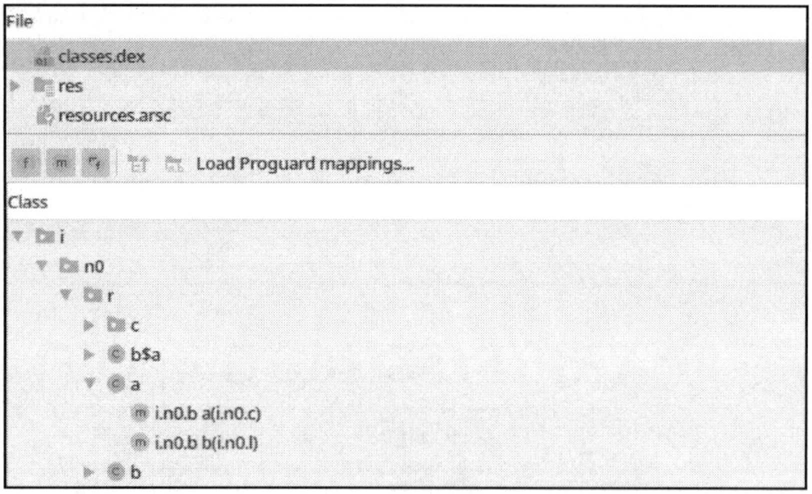

Figure 22.10 — The Code After Proguard Obfuscation

For debugging, it's not clear what the directories are. Click the **Load Proguard mappings...** button to map the obfuscated names back to the original:

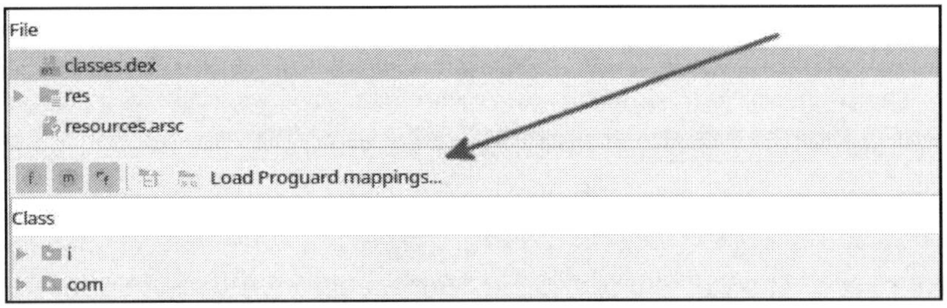

Figure 22.11 — Loading the Proguard Mapping File

Select **mapping.txt** in the debug folder and click **OK**.

Toggle the **Deobfuscate names** button to the left of the **Change ProGuard mappings...** button to switch between obfuscated and deobfuscated code. Now, you can trace the problem down to the specific code again.

There are a few more things you should know about the mappings file:

- Every time you make a release build, you rewrite **mapping.txt**. That means you must save each copy with each release of your app. That way, when you receive an obfuscated stack trace for a particular app release, you'll be able to use it.
- Upload your **mapping.txt** to Google Play to deobfuscate your crash stack traces. Instructions are here: https://support.google.com/googleplay/android-developer/answer/6295281.
- If you're using Firebase, you can find instructions about **mapping.txt** here: https://firebase.google.com/docs/crashlytics/get-deobfuscated-reports?platform=android.

Congratulations, you've now learned how to overcome the most common hurdles when analyzing a compiled app.

Some Final Notes

Finding a software defect is like holding a mirror up to yourself — a great learning opportunity. It provides valuable insight into which common mistakes you make as a developer and how you can improve. App analysis is self-analysis. And, like every other phase of the lifecycle, it's iterative.

Once you find the bug, thinking of how to solve it is iterative as well. It might mean going back to good variables names, high-quality methods and class interfaces, or even further back — maybe you coded the solution before the problem was clearly defined.

Security researchers look at past bug fixes to profile a developer's style. This speeds up the process of finding vulnerabilities by guessing where others might be. Taking the time to check the rest of your code for the same mistake when you encounter a bug is an efficient way of preventing the same issues from appearing again in future releases. It's also good motivation for code reuse; when you fix a problem in one place, you don't have to find all the same occurrences of the problem in the areas of the code you copy-pasted.

App analysis is a complex process. As you progress through the development lifecycle, iterations become more expensive. Code-tuning and refactoring are less expensive than debugging, while working out the initial requirements of the problem domain is even more affordable. In other words, measure twice and cut once to avoid defects in the first place.

This brings you back to the beginning of the cycle. And like any process, you can come back to this book at any time. Just return to Chapter 2, "Starting from the Beginning".

Key Points

- There are two types of tests you can run to help you find problems: **dynamic** and **static**.
- Dynamic testing is testing while executing the code.
- Static testing is auditing the source code for issues.
- Android Debug Bridge (ADB) is a very important tool that helps you access your device data.
- Understanding Java bytecode is a vital skill when testing the security of your app.
- Several tools allow you to reverse-engineer your app. APK Analyzer is one of those.

23 Conclusion

Congratulations! After a long journey, you've learned many important things about how to implement a real-world Android app. Now, you can apply what you've learned to your own apps by using the right architecture and adding animations and custom views. You also learned many important concepts about security and debugging.

Remember, if you want to further your understanding of Kotlin and Android app development after working through *Real-World Android by Tutorials*, we suggest you read *Android Apprentice* and *Kotlin Apprentice*. Both are available in our online store:

- https://www.raywenderlich.com/books/android-apprentice
- https://www.raywenderlich.com/books/kotlin-apprentice

If you have any questions or comments as you work through this book, please visit our forums at https://forums.raywenderlich.com and look for the forum category for this book.

Thank you again for purchasing this book. Your continued support is what makes the tutorials, books, videos, conferences and other things we do at raywenderlich.com possible, and we truly appreciate it!

Wishing you all the best in your continued Android app development!

–The *Real-World Android by Tutorials* book team

Made in United States
Orlando, FL
04 November 2026

90201113R00295